NEW PACIFIC LITERATURES

GARLAND REFERENCE LIBRARY
OF THE HUMANITIES
(VOL. 1054)

NEW PACIFIC LITERATURES

Culture and Environment in the European Pacific

John McLaren

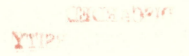

GARLAND PUBLISHING, INC. • NEW YORK & LONDON
1993

Library of Congress Cataloging-in-Publication Data

McLaren, John D.
New Pacific Literatures : culture and environment in the
European Pacific / by John McLaren.
p. cm. — (Garland reference library of the humanities ;
vol. 1054)
ISBN 0-8153-0496-X
1. Literature, Modern—20th century—History and criticism. 2.
Literature, Modern—20th century—Social aspects. 3. English
literature—20th century—History and criticism. 4. Pacific Area—
Literatures—History and criticism. 5. Literature and society. I.
Title. II. Series.
PN771.M44 1993
809'04—dc20   92-1672
                                                                CIP

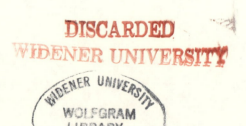
Printed on acid-free, 250-year-life paper
Manufactured in the United States of America

To Shirley, with love.

Contents

Preface   ix
Acknowledgments   xi
Introduction   xiii

PART ONE: INTO THE WILDERNESS

  1. Ideas of the New Worlds   3
  2. Lands of Desire: Patterns of Literature
       in the New World of the United States   33
  3. Myth and Countermyth in Australian Literature   51
  4. Canadian Voyagers and Garrisons   73
  5. Lands Outside Eden: The Case of Africa   93
  6. Islands of Freedom: The Pacific Dream   115

PART TWO: WILDERNESS IN ENCLOSURE

  7. Regenerative Violence:
       Natural Man Against Society   139
  8. Taming the Wilderness   151
  9. Networks of Time   163
  10. Withdrawal from Violence: Writing by and
       About Native Americans   181
  11. The Canadian Pacific: Sense of Time and
       Place in Writing from British Columbia   209
  12. Reclaiming the Land: New Zealand   235
  13. Australia: The Violated Continent   253

PART THREE: LOST EDENS

  14. Living with Darkness: Native Peoples of the Pacific   283
  15. Asia in the Pacific   319

Bibliography   357
Index   373

PREFACE

This work is based on several assumptions about language. These are supported in the text largely on empirical grounds, but they can also be supported theoretically.

In the first place, I reject the dialectical model implicit in most structuralist analyses of literature. Dialecticians propose a conflict in some form between thesis and antithesis. This conflict produces a synthesis which becomes the new thesis, thus instituting a progressive process leading eventually to truth, sanity, meaning or utopia. In its Hegelian form, the dialectic is one of ideas. In its Freudian and Lacanian forms, it is an internal dialectic producing the superego from the conflict between the id, or unconscious desire, and the repressions of rational thought, language or society. In Nietzschean terms, this is the conflict between Apollo and Dionysus which produces art and can be resolved only by the Ubermenschen. In its Marxist form, the underlying dialectic is between forces of production, labour and capital, which provide the material basis of society. Literature, and the culture of which it is part, is seen merely as ideological superstructure. Even those forms of structuralism which insist on the material reality of literature and culture still see it as a response to or product of social structures. Linguistic models remove language from direct contact with reality and explain it instead as one of the symbolic systems of society produced by the interaction between arbitrary lexical paradigms and the fixed syntagmatic structures of syntax.

Rather than the duality of these models, I propose a three-part productive structure which is constantly seeking balance or equilibrium between its parts.

In this structure, the three factors of production are land, individuals, and culture. These correspond to the productive factors of classical economics: land, labour, and capital. By land I mean the whole environment, which later economics reduces to a part of capital. Capital is, however, by definition the product of labour. Although the land can be changed by labour it remains as both a necessary condition of labor and a fundamental limit on the possibilities of human production, and therefore cannot be reduced itself to an artifact or product. By individuals I mean people driven by desire to the labour and love which produce and reproduce their being, and in so doing change the land and produce a culture. By culture I mean the whole of the language, laws, arts, skills, institutions and physical artifacts which pattern, direct, and sustain our lives. These can be grouped under the two aspects of technology and symbolic systems.

This model challenges the progressive implications of the dialectic. Rather, it accepts the proposition that, like languages, there are no simple cultures or unformed individuals. There is no point of origin, societies form us as individuals, and the languages that form us and that we use to produce our further being carry traces from an unmeasurable past which constantly direct us to an unattainable future. Living is a process which constantly produces change, unsettling all the factors of production and therefore requiring us to produce a new balance. Each work of culture, including works of art, artifacts, and social systems, represents a moment of such balance, but at the same time its production changes the situation, upsetting the balance and requiring continuing work of production and interpretation to find a new equilibrium.

This theory of language and production acknowledges an external reality in which we are involved and which produces our selves and our meanings. Language is both a part of this reality and the means by which we enter it and change it. This proposition can be defended by Occam's Razor, which forbids the unnecessary multiplication of categories. Language proposes reality; there is no need to suppose a further reality beyond the language's signification of reality. But neither are we forced to propose that language is the only knowable reality, rather than the only medium we have of reaching into and knowing reality. This proposition leads to total subjectivity or solipsism, and cannot account for the changes forced on language, and on us, by factors outside both, such as a tyrannical society which destroys individuals and their language, or a system of production which destroys the land on which it depends.

ACKNOWLEDGMENTS

A book like this has benefitted from the assistance of more colleagues and students than it is possible either to name or even to remember. In particular, however, I would like to express my gratitude to the Australian-American Education Foundation for the award of a Fulbright Senior Scholarship to the University of Oregon in 1990, so giving me the time and the conditions to start this work. At Oregon, I have particular debts of gratitude to Glen Love, and to Jack Bennett, to John Stuhr and the staff and fellows of the Humanities Research Centre, and to Richard Heinzkill and his colleagues in the university library. For advice, assistance and hospitality I owe profound thanks to Laurie Ricou and Bill New at the University of British Columbia, and to Robert Ross at the Australian Studies Centre at the University of Texas at Austin. I have also been greatly helped over the years by conversations at conferences of ASAL, WLA and SPACLALS, with people including Bruce Bennett, Bernard Hickey, Anna Rutherford, Helen and Chris Tiffin, Elizabeth Webby, Edwin Thumboo, Paul Sharrad, Anne Brewster, John Hanrahan, Laurie Clancy, Brian Matthews, and the late Barry Andrews. I am indebted to Chris Wallace-Crabbe for the suggestions about autobiography that are developed in Chapter 4. Without the support of my colleagues at the Footscray Institute of Technology, now assimilated in the Victoria University of Technology, and particularly of Barbara Shields and Lee-anne Trewatha, the book would not have been possible.

INTRODUCTION

Writers in the new worlds are forced to make a conscious choice between the forms of language and literature brought by the imperialists and those that have developed in the new world itself. These may be the forms recovered from a precolonial past or forms developed during the colonial period itself. But in either case they will now be marked by the experience of imperialism. This experience itself was first shaped by the interplay of language and physical otherness. The discoverers, explorers and settlers took with them concepts of the new world as a new Eden, a land of opportunity, or as a place of fear. The intractable nature of the worlds they encountered, the alien lands and peoples, changed these perceptions, reshaping the patterns of narrative and the connotations of language. These changed perceptions in turn have shaped the further development of imperialism and the literature which records it. Our access to this experience is through language, but this language represents a mental and physical experience which goes beyond it. Although we cannot make this experience fully ours, neither is it entirely other. In reading it, we are caught up by the words into a history which is important because it is different. If its only reality were linguistic, we could account neither for the changes forced on perception and the language in which it is coded, nor for the determination of successive generations and their writers to resist the patterns and perceptions forced on them by the language of imperialism and to reshape language to define the reality they desire. This reshaping gives us the history of the new literatures.

These literatures cannot be understood merely as the product of social forces. They result from deliberate choices made by writers, just as the development of the colonies and new societies was the product of the chosen efforts of rulers, voyagers and venturers. In both cases, however, the choices behind the actions are produced by wider social forces and have consequences which go beyond the intentions of their authors. These consequences are in part produced by those who read the literature and history, and the uses to which they put them.

The new literatures need to be understood as social products sharing in the nature of all human production. All human actions are the expression of individual desire: for security, for harmony, or for fulfilment. Desire is exercised, in the form of work, on the environment, which is in the first place constituted by the physical properties of the land and its denizens, human and animal. This environment is both the object of the work which transforms it by using it to meet the needs of the worker, and the inescapable other, the external reality which frustrates all human intention. The result of the work is the satisfaction of human need, the reproduction of the workers, and the production of culture in the form of social structures, skills, and human capital. This is the language we use to define and use the environment. It embodies the frustration as well as the fulfillment of desire and becomes a part of the environment in which future work is performed. As capital, it enhances the future performance of work, but as environment, it continues to both arouse and frustrate desire. Culture, particularly through language, its most explicit and comprehensible component, provides the meanings of the world around us, and so distinguishes and constitutes the individual as a meaningful part of this environment. It provides no point of origin, but only a continually deferred destiny, which it also obstructs by tying us to the past from which it is constituted.

Literature forms a part of the culture produced through history and defines reality as it has been understood by its writers and readers. While each individual piece of literature is the product of a particular writer or speaker, a national literature is a body of work which produces a particular national identity. This identity provides a part of the culture which further work both continues and contests. This work must be done with the forms and language at hand, while recognizing that these themselves are social products expressing the organisation of the ideas and values of a particular society at a particular time. The writer takes this available language and shapes it to express her sense of reality, internal and external, but at the same time the language shapes both what she can perceive of reality and how it can be expressed. The balance between individual and social shaping will vary from time to time and culture to culture. In traditional and classical cultures from stable societies, ideas and values are taken for granted, and the writer's task becomes one of celebration and consolidation. Nevertheless, when Homer organized the scattered heroic tales that had accrued around the Trojan war into two coherent poems, he brought into existence a consciousness of nationality and of tragic fate which was later adopted as the foundation for the polities of the Hellenic states. By contrast, when Virgil adopted the same forms for his literary epic of Rome, he provided an incentive and justification for imperial power. The Renaissance further adapted Virgilian epic and the concept of manifest destiny to celebrate the quite different imperialism of modern Europe and its eventual product, the imperial presidencies of the United States.

Modern empires have, however, proven much less stable than their predecessor. The Roman empire represented the final political consolidation of classical systems of production, which depended on slaves to provide the agricultural surplus needed to support cities. Unlike eastern empires, it was forced by the geography of Europe to allow wealth and power to accumulate in provincial capitals. When its slaves and soldiers brought it to an end, taking advantage of barbarian invasions to seize control of their own production, these capitals became the centres of new polities erected on the basis of feudal agricultural production. This polity started to crumble when the Black Death broke the economy of mutual obligations based on direct exchange of goods and services and introduced one based on the exchange of labour and commodities for money. The opening of the new worlds of America and Asia accelerated this process by fuelling inflation with fresh supplies of silver and gold, as well as the slaves necessary to provide a corresponding surplus of production. The new wealth completed the destruction of the old order, and the new world provided opportunities for individuals to escape their origins and profit through mercantilism. The empires they built were thus the result not of consolidation but of collapse and new beginnings. Their effect was to unify the world biologically and economically, but not politically. Political events came to have global rather than local effects, and particular powers were able for periods to achieve global hegemony, but no world polity emerged. Instead, continents and oceans became the battlefields of nations, and nations themselves became theatres of political, economic, and cultural contention between classes no longer confined within traditional orders.

New world literatures are the product of these conflicts. As new wealth and opportunities destroyed the traditional societies of the old world, their peoples sought opportunity in the new. At first, they brought home the wealth they generated, enriching the old capitals and building new and self-sustaining metropolitan cultures in Europe. The religious, political, and cultural upheavals of the seventeenth and eighteenth centuries were a consequence of the tensions produced by this new wealth as different groups attempted to keep or seize the power it brought. But as wealth accumulated in the provinces, new cultures emerged there too. These cultures were necessarily derivative, drawing their forms and ideas from the metropolitan capitals, but as they expressed local experience they came to challenge the cultures of the older centres. From Jane Austen's novels onwards, the wealth derived from empire, and its investment in industry, is at the heart of the moral problem of English fiction. In France, while Voltaire and Rousseau wrestled with the concepts of government and authority that had been thrown into question by the new worlds and their native inhabitants, the encyclopaedists tried to bring the whole of knowledge under the imperial edict of a single form of rationality. In the provinces themselves, however, the production rather than the investment and control of wealth was the problem. Walter Scott's romances express the desires of imperialism and capitalism, but when imported into America they become tragic tales of the destruction of desire and of the environment which fulfils it. The search for the new world of fulfilment becomes a search for the old world of innocence. As the United States emerges as the first self-sustaining or metropolitan culture in the new world, the theme of innocence and its betrayal becomes central in its literature.

The history of the new literatures is the story of the emergence of provincial centres of awareness, its interaction with the self-sustaining metropolitan centres, and its own development towards independent metropolitan centres within a global culture and economy. This history is also the story of the destruction of native values by the imperial powers, and the frustration and perversion of imperial hopes by the environment of the new worlds. The new literatures emerge from this record of mutual destruction as they attempt to build cultural structures which will establish new continuities. This purely literary history is in turn affected by such matters as the copyright and publishing agreements which construct markets and determine writers' access to them. At the same time, the established values of the metropolitan centres are themselves under challenge. The concentration of wealth and power in the

United States has simultaneously constructed it as the new metropolitan culture against which all others react, and generated within it pressures from excluded groups, such as women and minorities, who contest its assumptions of cultural integration. In Europe, resistance to the centres comes from older cultures like the Celtic and regional ones like those of the Basques or the Catalonians. In Central Europe, writers led the revolution against Russian power and authority. These movements come together with the literatures of new worlds to suggest the basis for a new global culture based on diversity rather than centrality. Ironically, this may renew the medieval ideal of commonwealth while avoiding the hierarchical organisation which stultified it. We may yet hope to join Miranda in saluting a brave new world that has such people, heirs at once to new and old.

PART ONE

INTO THE WILDERNESS

CHAPTER 1

IDEAS OF THE NEW WORLDS

I

The new worlds of the Americas, Asia, and the Pacific are a product of the European imagination. When the Crusades failed to achieve their goal and the Moors brought the Christian armies to a halt at Ceuta, the Portuguese began a search for ways around Africa that would outflank their enemies, link up with the fabled Christian emperor of Africa, Prester John, and establish an alliance that would finally drive the infidels from the Holy City. Instead, their voyages opened a seaway to the riches of India and founded a Portuguese Empire in the East. In his Virgilian epic *The Lusiads*, Camoens furnished this empire with its imperial ideology. Just as the Roman Empire had brought peace to the old world and provided a seat for the vicars of Christ, so Portugal would become the new Rome uniting the countries of the east under the banner of Christ. This ideology justified the subjugation of the trading posts of Asia and the enslavement of the people of Africa. The labor of these slaves would in turn build the Spanish and English empires of America.

Like the Portuguese Empire, the Spanish Empire was founded on a mistake and on the dream of finding a direct route to the east. The immediate result of the voyages of Columbus and the exploits of the conquistadores was the destruction of the Aztec and Inca empires, the extermination of the people of the Caribbean, and an influx of gold and silver into Europe. This new wealth financed the dreams of the newly-united monarchies of Spain, and so froze their state in the rigid structures of hierarchy. The money to pay for Spanish glory went to bankers and contractors from Italy and the countries of northern Europe, where the bonds of feudalism had already been loosened by the Black Death. This money supported the rise of new mercantile classes in a society based on the exchange

3

of money rather than of goods and services. At the cost of loosening the old ties to land and kin, and so destroying the links which had bound society and nature together, the new economy destroyed for ever the idea that the course of our life is determined by the circumstances of our birth. The tragic paradox is that the surplus value that financed this great emancipation came from the plunder of the Americas and the labour of African slaves. Like Odysseus, sacker of cities, Cortes and Drake and their followers manipulated their destiny by destroying what others had built. Yet in so doing, they laid the foundations of an economic structure which would eventually both offer the promise of freedom to all people and threaten the extermination of all life as a result of its subjugation of nature to human desire.

Imperialism reduces both culture and nature to agents of individual desire. It thus destroys local cultures, breaking their link with particular places, and fragments society, defining people not by their relationships to each other but as independent actors pursuing individual purposes. These changes are reflected in European literature, which moves from narratives of social order to dramas of personal ambition, and then to domestic narratives about the pursuit of happiness and security. These narratives are held together by the imperial voice of the authors and the imperial will of their characters. Similarly, those who exercise power use it to control language, to impose fixed forms and definitions that subject the underclasses to their will. This domination leads to resistance as people reduced to the role of object strive to become the subjects of their own history. In Joyce's terms, in cunning and exile they forge the tools of a new consciousness. As imperialism disintegrates, they produce modernist narratives which dissolve the certainties of an external world. Continuing political and economic crises, however, undermine all concepts of authority and generate postmodernist texts where even the speaker disappears, leaving only a world of words where nothing exists outside the eternal play of signifiers. Yet, while these texts may constitute the ultimate form of resistance to the tyranny of language, they offer no satisfactory alternative to those who find themselves oppressed by race, class or gender.

The dilemmas of language were illustrated by two recent episodes. During his visit to the United States, Nelson Mandela was welcomed to New York with singing and dancing to chants in a language unknown to most of the performers and audience. Despite the contemporary argument that language lacks intrinsic meaning, both groups of performers were able to use it as a means of resisting and subverting authority. They were able to take a language structured by history, its meanings arbitrarily assigned by circumstance, and use it as a weapon of militancy, its meaning being the solidarity it produces. But while Mandela inspired this popular solidarity, he had also quite directly worked to destroy the spurious national solidarity imposed on the people of South Africa by its government.

The solidarity of the African people is like that of an army in wartime, based on the common action of its members rather than on the code imposed by its leaders. The unity of Afrikaners is similar, generated by their perceptions of themselves as the chosen people in the laager. The attempts of the government to extend this spontaneous unity of a minority to the whole state that it rules depends on a spurious unity imposed by a command structure operating through fear and coercion. It has attempted to construct a unified structure of nations based on arbitrarily defined racial groups, thus ensuring that its discriminations cannot be challenged by appeal either to universal principles or to alternative definitions and descriptions of people, race, class or nation. In defining people by race, the law assigned them their status within the whole society and allotted to each a circumscribed sphere of action. Any attempt to challenge the definition or act outside the permitted sphere became an attack on the state which maintained the definition. By thus subverting one of the principles of the common law, the principle of a common peace to which all have a right, the national law thus converted its other principle, the rights and responsibilities of the individual, to an instrument of tyranny. The simple act of speaking with others became evidence of conspiracy—an ironic if unwitting recovery of the word's etymology. Any attempt to fit words to experience or to subjective, rather than defined, reality became an act of subversion. With speech proscribed, any act sufficiently public to come to the attention of the authorities became presumptive as evidence of guilt. Thus, despite the efforts of some courageous judges to retard the process, the language of freedom in the law code came to be an instrument of oppression. By subjugating the meaning of words to their own authority, the authorities obtained exclusive legitimacy. Not only blacks, but any person or organisation that opposed the government was excluded from the community and became an enemy of the state.

Mandela was able to overthrow the moral ascendancy of this regime not by proposing an alternative, but by going beyond its imposed definitions to the suppressed meanings inherent in its expressed principles. If the law could hang people because it held them responsible for their own actions, it implicitly recognized their prior status as autonomous humans. Responsibility implies equality, for all people are equally responsible for their own actions, and freedom, for only people who are able to act freely can be held responsible for these actions and their consequences. Just as the development of the common law itself followed from the reasoning of lawyers and philosophers about the principles inherent in its precepts, so Mandela subjected it to intense speculation and scrutiny until he was able to develop from its own text the principles which contradicted its application in South Africa (Derrida, 1987). The meaning he discovered was immanent in the law, but came into effective existence only through his labour. Once expressed, it provided the criterion by which the government itself was judged. The language of the law, as expressed by Mandela at his trial, thus became an objective reality whose judgement the government could ignore only by active suppression. Mandela was cast into prison to suppress the meaning he had now built into his life. His history brings together three of the possible uses of language: to impose conformity, to create community, and to discover freedom.

At about the same time the South African government was recognizing the legitimacy of Mandela's stand by releasing him from prison and allowing him to travel the world, Chinese students mounted a similar challenge to imposed unity. Their demonstrations combined solidarity of the group and independence of thought to challenge the control exercised by the Communist Party over their language and thought. Arts students transformed the icon of the Statue of Liberty into a goddess of democracy who represented the desire to assert the self in a world subjected by old men to meanings they had constructed in their youth. The government sent tanks to drive the students from the space they had taken. The power of technology destroyed the freedom of art. Yet it was not enough to destroy the expression of freedom, for once asserted its memory continued as a challenge to authority. So even the memory had to be destroyed. Authorities in Beijing continue to insist that there was no popular uprising or massacre in Tiananmen Square in 1989, and that only the leadership of the Communist Party speaks with the voice of the masses. Unlike the African singers who created meaning, the Chinese authorities impose it. Yet they cannot efface memory. The viciousness of their actions was identified at the time by the writer and translator Fang, who in an interview broadcast to the world denounced them as bloodthirsty murderers. Their attempts since that time to cover up their crimes and write history in their own image have rightly been described by the physicist Fang Lizhi as an attempt to deny to the people their memory. His voice continues the conversations that began in Tiananmen Square.

The Maoist control of language, however, extends beyond the obliteration of history to the total suppression of individual and cultural autonomy that had been foreseen by George Orwell. Most societies attempt to impose some such controls over language, either through direct censorship or through court-ordered rules of libel and defamation. These rules try to restrict language to unambiguous statement, and to limit the denotations and connotations of words to those that arise from the experience of a particular class or social group. This control is evil to the extent that it prevents people on the margin from finding a language to express their experience, or shaping the language of society to accommodate their lives. Everyone is required to use language according to the rules defined by the powerholders of society, to use only the approved connotations and denotations of our common stock of words. By denying all members of a society full knowledge of their own possibilities, the suppression of language adds to social tension, alienates the individual, and thus leads to further brutality and suppression.

The Chinese authorities seek to go far beyond even this social control and rob language of the possibility of conveying any meaning, subjective or objective. Simon Leys has identified this process in the anecdote he cites from the writer Xu Dun (1889–1936):

> Once upon a time, there was a country whose rulers completely succeeded in crushing the people; and yet they still believed that the people were their most dangerous enemy. The rulers issued huge collections of statutes, but none of these volumes could actually be used, because in order to interpret them, one had to refer to a set of instructions that had never been made public. These instructions contained many original definitions. Thus, for instance, "liberation" meant in fact "capital execution"; "government official" meant "friend, relative or servant of an influential politician," and so on. The Rulers also issued codes of law that

> were marvellously modern, complex and complete; how-
> ever, at the beginning of the first volume, there was one
> blank page; this blank page could be deciphered only by
> those who knew the instructions—which did not exist. The
> first three invisible articles of these non-existent instructions
> read as follows: "Art. 1: some cases must be treated with
> special leniency. Art. 2: some cases must be treated with
> special severity. Art. 3: this does not apply in all cases."

The interpretation of this code requires, as Leys comments, the ability to decipher non-existent inscriptions written in invisible ink on blank pages. (*NYRB*, 11 Oct. 90, pp.8–9). When language is shorn of all fixed connotations and denotations, individuals are robbed of all security either in their own being or in the outside world.

Writers and artists serve the opposite function, using language not to control but to liberate. The extent to which they succeed depends on how well able they are to sustain the paradox of undermining all fixed meaning while insisting on the reality of the inner existence by which we interpret the world. In reading, viewing and listening to their work, however, we may find meaning in the performance or text, locate it in the historical effects of the performance, or assign all referential meaning to the subjectivity of each listener or reader. We can take this argument further and assert that words both construct an identity for us as we use them and simultaneously deny it. They suggest to us possibilities of being only to defer it indefinitely through the constant play of difference that makes us as one with the singers as it reminds us of our separation from them and from the world of which we and they are parts. But whichever approach we take, the existence of a text, fixed or spoken, involves us in a conversation with another in which we use our cultural codes to construct ourselves in the context of a material and social world beyond us. Our ability to profit from this conversation depends both on our freedom to join, like Mandela's supporters, in solidarity and celebration with others, and our ability to stand aside like Mandela himself and construct our own text from the language we are given. In other words, an objective world exists, even if we always construct it from a communal text which has neither origins nor ends.

The radical uncertainty of postmodernism offers no answer to those concerned with the material effects of human culture on the natural environment, nor to those who continue to be subjected to the violence of an oppression which makes even language an agent of tyranny. These issues become particularly urgent in the literatures of the new societies, which catch us between the orthodoxies of a western world in post-imperialist decline and a series of attempts to create useable identities from the shards of traditional and colonial pasts. These literatures now include not only those of post-colonial societies in Africa, Asia, and the Americas, but also works written in the last years of Russia's domination of eastern and central Europe. These works have in common a resistance to the political, economic and cultural domination of the imperial centres and the attempt to reach beyond imposed forms to discover an authentic tradition which can give independence and meaning to the present.

This sense of authenticity may be sought in a past which precedes imperialist domination or in the actual experience of settlement and colonisation. Writers from countries where the colonialists have never been more than a dominant minority characteristically seek to recover the traditions that have been displaced by colonisation, while those from societies which have displaced the original inhabitants commonly seek authenticity in the act of settlement and colonisation itself. Yet these two apparently contradictory processes follow the same pattern of alienation, abrogation and assimilation which has been ascribed to all post-colonial writing by Ashcroft, Griffiths and Tiffin, in their book *The Empire Writes Back* (1989). I differ from these authors only by asserting that the pattern is more general than they have recognized, and that it cannot be reduced to a "linguistic gesture." While all experience is mediated by language, the use of language is always a political act, dealing with realities that cannot be reduced to language and at the same time constituting a reality which makes possible new ways of living.

The term "post-colonial literature" is too limiting to describe the function of literature in the societies which now occupy the territories of the old European empires. It places the emphasis on the precipitating condition rather than on the emergent meaning. It also excludes work written during the period of domination, including that being written by Australian Aborigines today. I therefore prefer the term "new literatures," using the terms "post-colonial" and "post-imperialist" only when I wish the emphasis to fall on the act or process of rejecting colonial authority or imperial power. In discussing pioneering examples of these writings, I will use the term "new world literatures," as their distinguishing characteristic is their attempt, which continues to this day, to accommodate worlds new to European sensibility.

II

The very possibility of new literatures arises from the voyages of discovery which precipitated the European renaissance. While the significance of Columbus's voyages may be disputed by American historians, particularly those speaking from the point of view of the original cultures which are attempting to remake their identity, they are crucial in European history. The voyages of Christopher Columbus and Vasco da Gama turned the eyes of Europeans outward and started the plunder and enslavement which poured wealth into Europe, completing the destruction of feudalism and providing the surplus value which eventually provided the material basis of the industrial revolution. At the same time, these voyages commenced a process of global unification which means that no culture can now survive in isolation, but all must define themselves against worldwide systems of economic and cultural interchange and of political power.

Just as Europe was irrevocably changed by the consequences of the voyages, so were the voyagers and discoverers themselves. Henry the Navigator was motivated in his endeavours to find a seaway around Africa by the oldest of mediaeval ambitions, the desire to free the Holy Land from the infidels. After he and his brothers were defeated by the Moors at Ceuta, he turned to the ocean, trusting that his captains would find a way to the mythical kingdom of Prester John and form an alliance that would outflank his enemies and prepare the way for a successful assault on Jerusalem. Columbus similarly discovered America by accident in his search for a quick way to the fabulous riches of Cathay. Yet, in recording the success of these endeavours, the chroniclers show themselves already changed by their discoveries. In his letters and journals Columbus takes pains to vindicate his actions by forcing his observations into the pattern of his expectations. At the same time, however, the reality of the alien peoples he meets forces itself on him, so that his words start to reveal his growing inability to trust their accuracy to his experience. (Piedra, 1989). Similarly, in the *Lusiads*, where Camoens celebrates Vasco da Gama's voyage to

India by turning it into a Virgilian empire of empire and destiny, the triumphant idyll with which he concludes his work contradicts the Christian justification, leaving only nakedly materialist and sensuous ambition. (Camoens) Both Columbus and Camoens express the contradictions of hope and reality, and the denial of authenticity to the native experience, which become the substance of new world writing.

During the sixteenth century, Spain was of European states the most successful in extracting wealth from the Americas. As Columbus made clear in his letter reporting his discoveries and in his later proposals for settlement, extracted wealth, particularly gold, was the chief motive behind Spanish colonisation. He described the island of Hispaniola, or Espanola:

> The sierras and the mountains, the plains, the champaigns, are so lovely and so rich for planting and sowing, for breed- ing cattle of every kind, for building towns and villages. The harbours of the sea here are such as cannot be believed to exist unless they have been seen, and so with the rivers, many and great, and of good water, the majority of which contain gold. . . In this island, there are many spices and great mines of gold and other metals. (Jane, 1960, p.194)

Although he talks first of the delights the country offers to the senses and the prospects it holds for settlement, the culmination of the passage is the offer of gold and similar riches. Columbus continues his letter to Ferdinand and Isabella with a description of the docility of the natives and the efforts he has expended to ensure that they will "be inclined to the love and service of Your Highnesses and of the whole Castilian nation, and strive to collect and give us of the things which they have in abundance and which are necessary to us." (p. 196) Finally, he assures his patrons that he has only started to reveal the riches awaiting them:

> their Highnesses can see that I will give them as much gold as they may need, if their Highnesses will render me very slight assistance; presently, I will give them spices and cotton, . . . and mastic . . . and aloe . . . and slaves, as many as they shall order, and who will be from the idolators. I believe I have found rhubarb and cinnamon, and I shall find a thou- sand other things of value . . . (pp. 200–01)

Columbus's obsession with gold is even clearer in his Journal than it is in the letter, and contributes to the way he portrays the native Americans he encountered. These descriptions are further coloured by his belief that he had landed on islands off the shores of Asia. He records his constant attempts to find the whereabouts of the Great Khan, for whom he carried letters, and to reach the islands of Japan, or Cipangu, which he confused with the island of Cuba. The natives he actually meets, therefore, he considers as fringe-dwellers, outside the bounds of the major civilizations he was seeking. Because they offered him no resistance, and treated him and his men kindly, he writes of them as if they were children. This impression was encouraged by the fact that most of those he first met were naked. He therefore had no hesitation in taking possession of their land in the name of "the King and Queen his Sovereigns," thus denying any native political authority. Having made them subjects of Spain (or more accurately, of Castile and Aragon), he turned to their spiritual welfare, preparing them with kindness for conversion. "I," he explains, "in order that they might feel great amity to us, because I knew they were a people to be delivered and converted to our holy faith by love rather than force, gave to some among them some red caps and some glass beads, which they hung round their necks, and many other things of little value." (Columbus, 1960, p. 23). Yet this show of amity is, as he explains later to his sovereigns, merely a tactic to reduce the natives to subjection:

> these people are very unskilled in arms, as Your Highnesses will see from the seven whom I caused to be taken in order to carry them off that they may learn our language and return. However, when Your Highnesses so command, they can all be carried off to Castile or held captive in the island itself, since with fifty men they would be all kept in sub-jection and forced to do whatever may be wished. (p.28)

Later in his stay among the islands Columbus finds signs of authority in the form of "caciques," or chiefs, and he is also told that some tribes practise cannibalism. His interest in the people is, however, like his admiration for the beauties of the landscape, always subordinate to his search for gold. As he prays after two days when he and his company have been entertained by a great crowd of natives and their chiefs, "Our Lord in His Goodness guide me that

I may find this gold, I mean their mine . . ." (p.117). The effect of his narrative therefore is to construct a picture of a lovely countryside inhabited only by a gentle, timid, and docile people ready to accept Christ and give up their gold to Spain.

This letter portrays the new world as an inexhaustible resource to support the old, rather than as a place of value in its own right. True, in 1498 he reported to his sovereigns that he had discovered the site of the earthly paradise, but insisted that it was on a such a summit that no human could reach it, and so its existence was to all intents and purposes irrelevant to human enterprises. (Columbus, 1892, p.141) He set out the nature of these enterprises and the controls he believed should be exercised over them in a letter to Ferdinand and Isabella before his second voyage. In this, after asking for 2000 settlers to accompany him, "owing to the land being safer and better for farming and trading," he proposes a detailed structure of officials, regulations, and churches which is in effect an extension of Spain. The chief aim of this system is not the prosperity of the inhabitants, native or immigrant, but the control of gold. He intends that the profits from this should flow to his sovereigns and to him as their vice-regent. To ensure that others will get about their more humble but necessary tasks, he recommends that only licensed colonists should be able to engage in the gold trade, and that even their activities should be restricted:

> As, in the eagerness to get gold, every one will wish, naturally, to engage in its search in preference to any other employment, it seems to me that the privilege of going to look for gold ought to be withheld during some portion of the year, that there may be opportunity to have the other business necessary to the island performed. (pp.71–72)

Columbus's proposals were not entirely adopted, and their majesties in fact chose to use the new lands as a dumping ground for convicts, thus establishing another colonial tradition. However, they did set up a detailed system of official administration and control which repeated in the new world the forms of a Spanish feudalism already in decay. The economy of this empire quickly became based on the labour of slaves in mines and on plantations, so that rather than reproducing a feudal society they created a moribund society entirely dependent on the will of an absent monarch and his imperial representatives. The extracted wealth remained in the hands of the few, or drained to the bankers and craftsmen of northern Europe to pay for costly show, so preventing the development of a productive economy both in Spain and in its Empire.

Both the pretensions and the sterility of imperial Spain are captured by Cervantes in his masterpiece of the European renaissance, *The Adventures of Don Quixote*. This work portrays a society absorbed by dreams of a mediaeval glory and civility which no longer correspond with any economic or social reality. When, in the first part, the Don searches for a world which no longer exists outside his own imagination, he, like the conquistadores, has the strength of will and imagination to make his perceived reality correspond with his dreams. Yet, just as Cortes and Pizarro were able to create their empires only by ignoring the meaning—if not the politics—of the cultures they encountered, and making the people of these new lands pay in physical suffering the cost of their conquerors' glory, so Quixote pays for his dreams by the battering of his own body. There is no room for ideals in a society possessed by its own grandeur, but the cost of glory is paid by the powerless.

Cortes and Pizarro brought grandeur through ruthless conquest, and were then able to clothe their new domains in the mediaeval panoply which signified their own and their sovereigns' glory. The social structures their successes produced both in Spain and in America were, however, parasitical, serving none of the productive functions of the society from which they were copied. They depended not on even a notional exchange of duties and services, but on the power of the gun to enslave native populations and repel intruders. Cervantes again provides an exact image for this society in the second part of *Don Quixote*, where the knight's illusions are sustained by the hidden power and wealth of the Duke and his Duchess. The Duke and his wife also offer Sancho Panza a part in their game of power, but Panza, the common man, promptly exposes the pretensions of his superiors by proving himself an adept ruler. While power for them is a game, for Sancho it is a part of his lived experience and therefore a reality which he can manage. As a man without illusions, Sancho belongs in the new secular world which princes, conquerors and preachers were bringing into existence despite themselves. This new world would be ruled not by heroes and dreamers, but by artisans and merchants. Once Quixote realizes this, and recognizes also that there is no retreat from it into either

an heroic past or a pastoral present, he has nothing left to do but
to die.

Ironically, Spain had never properly been a part of the mediaeval
Europe of its renaissance dream. Under Arab rule from the eighth
century, the Iberian peninsula was the theatre of the great conflict
between Christendom and paganism that is commemorated in
narratives from the *Song of Roland* to *Orlando Furioso*. During this
period the Muslim kingdoms supported a flourishing civilization
that brought together the best Judaic, Christian and Islamic
scholarship. In 1479 the union by Ferdinand and Isabella of the
crowns of Castile and Aragon in 1479 established an absolute
monarchy which in 1492 defeated the last Arab kingdom of Granada,
expelled the Jews, introduced the Inquisition and despatched
Columbus to find a westward path to Asia.

Columbus wrote from within the same religious tradition as
Dante or Chaucer. This tradition emphasised the responsibility of
a person to act properly as a member of the community of church
and state. Columbus, like Ferdinand and Isabella, assumed that the
people he brought under the rule of Spain when he unwittingly
stumbled on the Americas would become members of this
community, just as those commissioned to rule them would receive
their rewards as servants of cross and crown. The new empire
provided the wealth that enabled the new monarchy to clothe itself
in a panoply of feudal splendour that concealed the basis of its
economy in imperial exploitation rather than domestic exchange of
goods and services. The empire of New Spain was thus from the
first an extension of the absolute power of monarchs dedicated to
their own glory as servants of God, a model which in turn Camoens
adopted in his Virgilian celebration of Portuguese conquests in the
east. In this model, the subject peoples of the new territories, once
their humanity was admitted, became the source of the glory of god
and empire.

By the time Hakluyt wrote his celebration of English exploits,
however, Europe had changed. Although absolute monarchs
continued to use the language of feudal obligation to assert their
power, Luther and Calvin had, by changing the relationship between
God and His creatures, decisively changed the relationships between
individuals, the world, and the community. Man was now
responsible not just for his behaviour, but for his salvation. The
world was not merely a place to be endured on our way to eternal
life, but the theatre where we must prove our worth through our

actions. On one level, this was the spirit of scientific pragmatism, taking the world as it was found rather than as an allegory in which we might read the will of God. But the assumption of personal responsibility also converted the devil from a tempter to a personal antagonist with whom we must wrestle to find salvation. The world thus became both a potential Eden and a wilderness where Satan threatened destruction from every thicket. The individual life thus became not simply a re-enactment of the eternally recurring drama of salvation memorialized in the mystery plays, but a chapter in a history leading to the end of time and the return of Christ to His chosen people. Hakluyt projected America as the theatre for this drama, and the English settlers continued to play it out in both its Edenic and its diabolical aspects.

III

Hakluyt's work represents the different and more practical spirit that was abroad in northern Europe when the English became interested in settlement, a century after Columbus. Certainly, the French, who under the leadership of Jacques Cartier were exploring the rivers of North America as early as 1534, and the English were as eager for gold as any Spaniard. The riches won by Spain from America dazzled the eyes of such ambitious English courtiers as Sir Walter Raleigh, whose dreams of El Dorado led him to absurdity in the jungles of Colombia and eventual death in the Tower of London. But more mundane enterprises were also commonplace. When Sir Humphrey Gilbert arrived in the harbour of St. John's in Newfoundland with his charter of royal authority to found a settlement, he encountered 36 ships already using the port as a base for their deep sea fishing expeditions (Hakluyt, 1927, p.16). His chronicler mentions also that as many as a hundred ships, chiefly Portuguese and French, were commonly come together on the banks during the season from April to July (p.14). Gilbert's own reasons for establishing the colony were to take advantage of the fishing and whaling and to exploit the potential trade in such commodities as pitch, tar, timber and hemp, as well as to forestall other nations (p.22).

After Gilbert's death on the return voyage from Newfoundland, Sir Walter Raleigh, who had furnished one of the ships for Gilbert's fleet (p.12), became the chief promoter of English settlement in

America, obtaining a royal charter for this purpose in 1584 (Hakluyt, 1927, pp.115–121). This charter grants to Raleigh, his heirs and successors, absolute authority in all lands he discovers and settles during the six years of its currency. Like the earlier charter granted to Gilbert, it uses feudal forms to confer capitalist authority. The form is that of letters patent making a grant of authority over lands to a subject in return for duties to be rendered to the liege lord. The duties to be rendered by Raleigh are not, however, those of government so much as of development. His title is absolute, to "have, holde, occupie and enjoy . . . with the right, royalties, franchises, and jurisdictions . . . in fee simple or otherwise" of all the lands he discovers, subject only to the law of England (p.116). He is granted, in other words, a monopoly which will guarantee his investment. In return, he is required to pay the crown a levy of one fifth of the value of all gold and silver "gotten and obteined" from his discoveries.

The Virginian settlements Raleigh promoted in discharge of this authority were mercantile enterprises led by practical men of affairs. But the lust for gold, and the desire for quick returns from piracy, continually got in the way of the longer-term planning and effort required to make settlement a commercial success. The boldest venturer of all, Francis Drake, financed his circumnavigation of the world with venture capital and expected to yield a fair profit from piracy. The final attempt to succour the Virginian colonists failed when the master of the chartered vessel insisted on engaging in piracy rather than proceeding in the shortest time to the site of the colony. Raleigh himself eventually went to the block not because his Virginian settlers vanished but because his search for El Dorado failed to discover the riches craved by his king (Naipaul, 1973). The dreams of Spain and the avarice of England thus continued to postpone the achievement of more sober goals.

The voyages of English settlers to the Americas also produced changes in the immigrants themselves. The first settlers at Roanoke in fact disappeared, so becoming part of American myth rather than of British history. But even before their disappearance the circumstances of the new land had created new forms of society. The organisation of the isolated settlements was military rather than feudal. Although Raleigh's royal charter gave him absolute authority to appoint a governor and officers for the colony, in fact the settlement seems to have followed the pattern already established in the navigations. Expedition leaders such as Drake were obliged to consult with their other captains about major decisions, and the representatives of the commercial backers also enjoyed authority. The ships engaged to convey supplies and settlers to the new colonies were also engaged in commercial privateering, or licensed piracy, which frequently interfered with their colonial obligations. In the colonies themselves, the unaccustomed circumstances made the settlers completely dependent on each other, so that authority became something earned rather than attributed. Social distinctions were maintained, servants and children forming parts of their masters' households and only the principal settlers enjoying separate dwellings. Nevertheless, although the records of the expeditions and settlements were written by the leaders, their hints at insubordination and mentions of dissent show that the wilderness was producing its own social order. Even the 1587 decision to abandon Roanoke and return with Drake was taken spontaneously as a response to an emergency rather than by command of Master Ralfe Lane, the governor (Hakluyt, 1927, p.161–62).

These successive attempts to found an English colony in Virginia were celebrated by Richard Hakluyt in *The Principal Navigations, Voyages, Traffiques & Discoveries the English Nation made by sea or overland to the remote and farthest distant quarters of the earth at anytime within the compass of these 1600 years* [1589 and 1589–1600], as part of his advocacy of English expansion to new worlds. The colony's chances of success were finally destroyed as a consequence of the advent of the Spanish Armada at home, an example of the way that colonial ambitions were inextricably interwoven with European religious and dynastic ambitions. But in becoming a subject of these European power struggles, the Americas contributed to the process which changed Europe from a single Christendom apportioned among competing overlords to a mercantile economy of warring nation states.

IV

Hakluyt's collection of travellers' tales constitutes the first major work of new world writing in English. One of its purposes is to establish the legitimacy of the English role in the new worlds, and consequently he starts his work with an account of the mythical journeys of King Arthur. The first edition is divided into three parts, dealing respectively with ventures to Russia and the far east, to

Africa, and to the new world of the Americas. This third part is a consistent piece of advocacy for English settlement in North America.

Hakluyt's selection and editing of the tales in this part emphasises not only the profit which the new world can bring to England but also the advantages it has for the settlers. It starts with another mythical tale, "The Voyage of Madoc the sonne of Owen Guyneth Prince of Northwales, to the West Indies, in the yeere 1170." This tale serves to establish the antiquity of Britain's interest in the new world, which is confirmed by another document ostensibly obtained by Ferdinand, brother to Christopher Columbus, from Henry VII, who pledged his patronage and authority to the projected voyage to America, and by the accounts of the voyages of the Cabots to the north American coast. After narratives of the voyages of discovery and warfare of such mariners as Francis Drake, Humphrey Gilbert, Martin Frobisher and Richard Grenville, Hakluyt offers a discourse by Sir George Peckham on the rightfulness and necessity of planting English colonies in the northern parts of America. These are followed by a series of narratives of the successive attempts by Sir Walter Raleigh to establish a colony in Virginia. These, with their sad coda on the failed attempts to find the lost colonists, constitute the centrepiece of this part of the work (Hakluyt, 1589).

Writing almost a century after Columbus, Hakluyt has a different kind of a dream. While he acknowledges the promises of wealth held by the new land, his central concern is with the possibilities it offers for trade and settlement. Even the charters he includes which give royal authority to Sir Humphrey Gilbert and then to Sir Walter Raleigh to establish colonies in North America are sober documents which provide for strong government while preserving royal prerogatives. In these, and more so in the reports of the venturers, America offers the possibility of a return to kind of mediaeval commonwealth where every man will have his place and his fulness. Certainly, treacherous savages and perfidious Spaniards threaten this rural idyll, but the narratives show their defeat by the superior force and firmness of the English. Ralph Lane in fact comments that "in deed tenne of us with our armes prepared, were a terrour to a hundred of the best sort of them": that is, of the "Savages" (Hakluyt, 1927, p.78). Yet these reminders of danger and accounts of battle do not contradict the peaceable ambitions of the settlers and their sponsors. The natives may appear in the

narratives as friends to assist them, in which case they are treated
as equals, as were Manteo and the two "Savages" and "lustie men"
brought home by Arthur Barlowe from his reconnaissance. Or they
may be enemies, to be treated with utter harshness, as Lane treated
the conspiracy of Pemisan (Hakluyt, 1927, pp.132, 152–59). But in
general, they remain as a part of the countryside, neither malign
nor benign, but scarcely credited with a reality of their own.

The nature of Hakluyt's hopes is suggested by a document he
prints from a Captain Carlile, written in 1583 as "A briefe and
summary discourse upon a voyage intended to the hithermost parts
of America" (Hakluyt, 1927, 6, pp.80–91). Carlile, writing to the
"Merchants of the Moscovian companie and others," argues that
the actions of hostile powers (Denmark, Holland, Turkey, Algiers,
Venice, Spain) make trade with Russia and the Mediterranean
dangerous and hostile, as well as injurious to religion. By contrast,
America above the latitude of 40 degrees offers safe sailing, freedom
from foreign powers, a wealth of commodities for trade, and the
advantage that resident factors, their servants and children, "shall
have no instruction or confessions of Idolatrous Religion enforced
upon them, but contrarily shall be at their free libertie of conscience,
and shall find the same Religion exercised, which is most agreeable
unto their Parents and Masters" (pp.83–4). Carlile admits that the
immediate supply of commodities does not equal that forthcoming
from Russia, but looks to the time when "it may have pleased God
to establish our people there" and the colony consequently will
supply "no less quantitie and diversitie of merchandize then is now
had out of Dutchland, Italie, France or Spaine" (p.85), as well as
providing a market for English manufactures, for "by the good
prospering of this action, there must of necessitie fall out a very
liberall utterance of our English Clothes into a maine Country,
described to bee bigger than all Europe, the larger part whereof
bending to the Northward, shall have wonderfull great use of our
sayde English Clothes, after they shall come once to knowe the
commodite thereof" (p.85).

Carlile foresees two advantages for the people of this new colony.
The influence of the English settlers will affect the natives, so that
"by gentle and familiar entreating of them, they bee made to see
what is better for them then they doe as yet understand of, and
. . . that they will daily by little and little forsake their barbarous
and savage living, and growe to such order and civilitie with us
. . ." as to provide the desired goods and markets the merchants

seek. But Carlile also points out that, as well as generating future profits, the merchants who venture their capital will be doing a godly service to the people from their own country whom they "plant" among the savages.

> Christian charity doth as greatly perswade the furtherance of this action, as any other that may be layed before us, in as much as thereby wee shall not onely doe a most excellent worke, in respect of reducing the savage people to Christianitie and civilitie, but also in respect of our poore sort of people, which are very many amongst us, living often times unprofitable, and often times to the great disquiet of the better sort. For who knoweth not, how by the long peace, happie health, and blessed plentifulnesse, wherewith God hath endued this Realme, that the people is so mightily encreased, as a great number being brought up, during their youth in their parents houses, without any instruction how to get their livings after their parents decease, are driven to some necessitie, whereby very often for want of better education they fall into sundry disorders, and so the good sort of people, as I sayde before, are by them ordinarily troubled, and themselves led on to one shameful ende or other, whereas if there might be found some such kinde of imployment as this would be, no doubt but a greater part of them would be withheld from falling into such vile deeds . . . (88)

As Hakluyt collected his tales from returning voyagers, they have a natural structure which moves them from hopeful embarcation, through dangers at sea and hostile encounters on land, to a return home which, if not always triumphant, is at least full of hope for the future. The source of this hope is not only the fact that a returning voyager has, by the fact of his return, overcome fate, but the peaceful achievements on land, which serve as a guarantee of success to future venturers. This pattern was to persist in the seventeenth century narratives of the pilgrim settlers in America, except that for them success is achieved not by the return home but establishing a permanent settlement. This permanency becomes itself evidence of the benevolence of the God they have served through their pilgrimage. The lost settlers of Roanoke may have harboured different ideas about divine providence.

These settlers provide a gloomy afterpiece to a sequence of narratives which begins quite auspiciously. Arthur Barlowe offers his patron, Walter Raleigh, a "briefe discourse" of his reconnaissance expedition of 1584 to enable Raleigh to "judge how profitable this land is likely to succeede, as well to your selfe, . . . as also to her Highnesse, and the Common wealth, in which we hope your wisedome wilbe satisfied, considering that as much by us hath bene brought to light, as by those smal meanes, and number of men we had, could any way have bene expected, or hoped for." (Hakluyt, 1927, p.121) In his discourse, Barlowe acknowledges the existence of "mortall malice . . . injuries and slaughters" among the natives (p.131), but the prevailing spirit of his narrative is of enthusiasm for a land of Biblical plenty:

> The soil is the most plentifull, sweete, fruitful, and wholsome of all the world: there are above foureteene severall sweete smelling timber trees, and the most part of their underwoods are Bayes, and such like: they have those Okes that we have, but farre greater and better.

> We were entertained with all love, and kindnes, and with as much bountie, after their manner, as they could possibly devise. Wee found the people most gentle, loving and faithfull, voide of all guile and treason, and such as lived after the manner of the golden age. The earth bringeth foorth all things in abondance, as in the first creation, without toile or labour. (Quinn, pp.7–8)

Just as the description of the land is of a place ready to accommodate a western society, so the organisation of the people is described in western terms, with kings and their advisers, people of the better sort, and lower orders. The potential of the land is realized, however, only by Europeans. The anonymous narrator of the following voyage, in 1585, describes a banquet in which Spaniards and English vie with one another in courtesy:

> In the meane time while our English Generall and the Spanish Governor discoursed betwixt them of divers maters, as of the state of the Countrey, the multitude of the Townes and people, and the commodities of the Iland [sc. Hispaniola] our men provided two banquetting houses covered with greene boughs, the one for the Gentlemen, the other for the servaunts, and a sumptuous banquet was brought in served by us all in plate, with the sound of trumpets, and consort of musicke, wherewith the Spaniards were more than de-

lighted. Which banquet being ended, the Spaniardes in
recompense of our curtesie, caused a great heard of white
buls, and kyne to be brought together from the mountaines,
and appoynted for every Gentlemen and Captaine that would
ride, a horse ready sadled, and then singled out three of the
best of them to bee hunted by horsemen after their maner,
so that the pastime grew very plesant for the space of three
houres, wherein all three of the beasts were killed, whereof
one tooke the sea, and there was slaine with a musket. After
this sport, many rare presents and gifts were given and
bestowed on both partes, and the next day wee played the
Marchants in bargaining with them by way of trucke and
exchange for divers of their commodities, as horses, mares,
kine, buls, goates, swine, sheepe, bul hydes, sugar, ginger,
pearle, tabacco, and such like commodities of the Iland.
(Hakluyt, 1927, p.16)

This passage has the idealized atmosphere of the mediaeval chivalry
affected at this time by the courts of France, Spain and England.
However, while the knights of mediaeval romance acted out in
ritualized form the real power struggles of their time, this courtly
encounter, while reminding the reader of the imperial contest
between England and Spain in which it is an interlude, diverts
attention from the common exercise of colonialism in which both
were engaged. The riches they exchange are not the surplus value
of their estates, but the confiscated wealth of the peoples they are
enslaving. The episode is a courtly entertainment like the games
played by Quixote's duke and duchess. Its irony in the context of
Hakluyt's narratives is that it celebrates the virtues of an age that
the venturers are destroying, in America as in Europe.

The image constructed of the Americas during the seventeenth
century is contradictory. It is on the one hand seen as an inexhaustible
source of wealth for Europe. This wealth in turn provides the
opportunity for new men, such as Columbus or Raleigh, to obtain
the power and standing of feudal magnates. But at the same time
commentators see Europe as possessed by greed and idleness, and
look to the new world as an opportunity for commoners to find
self-sufficiency in a renewal of the mediaeval ideal of commonwealth.
This commonwealth is, however, to be sustained not by feudal
allegiance but by commercial success. Farmers and traders will
produce the goods needed in their mother countries, and will at
the same time provide a market for European manufacture. This

free trade ideal is only apparently contradicted by the mercantile reality which confined trade to the ships and merchants of the home countries. In practice, this ideal was breached by the acts of piracy which maintained the open movement, if not free exchange, of goods on the high seas, and ensured that the wealth of the Americas was generally distributed through western Europe. But the ideal served also to guarantee investment in the new lands, and so offered the basis for the eventually successful settlement of Virginia, the Carolinas and New England.

V

Successful English settlement of the new world did not come about until the development of a further factor, slavery. This institution in its turn was responsible for the degradation of Africa and for the introduction to the world of racist ideologies. Yet the chronicles of the new world virtually ignore it, apart from occasional and incidental references to the value of slaves as booty or trade. It did, however, trouble some consciences. Peckham, for example, in his justification of the westering trade and plantations refers somewhat confusedly to slavery as a part of natural law, a necessary consequence of the freedom of the seas to trade and war:

> For from the first beginning of the creation of the world, and from the renewing of the same after Noes flood, all men have agreed, that no violence should be offered to Ambassadours: That the sea with his Havens should be common: That such as should fortune to be taken in warre, should be servants or slaves: And that strangers should not bee driven away from the place or Countrey whereunto they doe come. (Hakluyt, 1927, p.49)

The institution of slavery had indeed been a part of European society from the earliest times, but was not of major economic importance in feudal times, which depended rather on labour tied to the soil. The development of trade and manufacturing at the end of the middle ages, however, required further investment of free capital, and the timely expansion of Christendom to the east enslaved the people whose labour could provide the surplus value required. The Turks set up the trade, the Venetians profited and invested, and the Spaniards and Portuguese set up the systems (Davis). Everything was in place to exploit the vast new sources of labour discovered by the Portuguese in their explorations of the African coast.

The enslavement of Africa, however, required a more comprehensive ideology than the traditional one cited by Peckham. The numbers were just too great to be attributed to the fortunes of war. The need was supplied by the development of the doctrine of racial superiority based on the colour of the skin. This was the Portuguese contribution to European civilization and economic development (Diffie and Winius, pp. 80–81). So that the dream of America might be realized, a new image of Africa was constructed. The black became the inferior, the other, the exploited and ignored foundation of the modern colonial and industrial economy.

The treatment of Africa contrasts with the image of Asia which was simultaneously constructed, and even with the image of the native Americans. The newcomers had no alternative but to recognize the strength and richness of the states and cultures they encountered in Asia, and were thus forced to treat with their rulers as political equals, even if their pagan religion made them moral inferiors. In *The Lusiads*, Camoens distinguishes between the Indian rulers who were good and those who were treacherous—that is, between those who were friendly towards the Portuguese and those who remained hostile. In the American narratives, as we have seen, similar distinctions were made, although the settlers denied the natives the recognition of political sovereignty they had to the Indians. Yet, although the African states had a political structure as developed as that of the Incas or the Aztecs, this was ignored by the Europeans. They might recognize an individual chief as capable of trading slaves, they might even accept his allegiance to Christendom, as the King of the Congo gave to the Pope in 1513, but essentially they were regarded as outside the human race. Their enslavement therefore presented no problems.

VI

The theoretical implications of this process of discovery and description are clear. The India discovered by da Gama and celebrated by Camoens presented no real problems to Europeans. India and China had been connected with the west since antiquity.

Trade flowed in both directions by land and sea, invading armies had periodically marched from the east, Alexander had marched in the opposite direction and reached the Indus valley, knowledge had followed trade and war, and Marco Polo had brought back direct reports which had been widely circulated through Europe. In describing the exploits of da Gama and his successors, Camoens was therefore able easily to fit them into the imperial pattern established by Virgil. Portugal figured as the new and Christian Rome extending civilization to the furthest bounds of the world. The Indians were merely new kingdoms to be brought beneath the imperial sway. Their exoticism fitted them for the role of the other, but their strangeness was no greater than that of Egypt or Parthia in Virgil and the prose chroniclers of Rome. They were fit for the rule of proconsuls who would respect their difference while maintaining the imperial interest.

Africa and America were different. The Africa known to Rome and anticipated by Henry the Navigator was bordered by the Mediterranean and the Sahara. The southward extension and its peoples presented both a geographic and a cognitive problem. Da Gama overcame the first by finding his way around the Cape and across the seas to India, but in the process changed the object of Portuguese expansion from the known goal of Jerusalem to the east whose existence had hitherto been known but whose nature was largely imagined. The history of European expansion in the east is therefore largely one of experience displacing imagination. This experience has, however, always been shaped by the prior imaginings inscribed in language, so that the nature of the east as exotic other has never been entirely displaced. The other of Africa, however, from the beginning represented the unknown and hostile. The Africans did not fit into any prior European categories of imagination or cognition, and the first voyagers therefore seized on their most obvious physical feature, colour, to characterize them. This further enabled them to be assigned a place in Biblical mythology as the children of Ham, doomed forever to hew wood and draw water for the master races. Europeans displaced their own ignorance of black Africa onto the blacks themselves, their colour becoming a metaphor of their lack of any knowledge, culture, or morality which might be understandable to Europeans, and for their innate evil. The history of European penetration of sub-Saharan Africa has consequently not been one of coming to know another, however incomplete. Instead, Europeans have seen themselves as dispelling the darkness of ignorance with the light of civilization. Literally, it has been a matter of displacing the black people, firstly from their native lands to America, later from tribal lands in order to make room for white settlers. While language has been complicit in this displacement, its consequences have been real.

The displacement of the blacks to America in turn affected the history of perceptions of that continent. Columbus thought he had reached the Indies, and therefore called its native inhabitants Indians. Like da Gama, he anticipated a governing structure similar to the ones he had known, and when he found it lacking assumed that the people he actually met and their lands were outside the limits of rule and could therefore be claimed for Spain. The subsequent realization that America was a new continent caused even greater cognitive problems than had the discovery of black Africa. The Africans could, with an effort, be fitted into the universal history of the world that stretched from creation to the apocalypse, and centred on Christ's act of redemption. Christ had redeemed humankind, and had sent out the evangelists Peter, Paul, Phillip, and Thomas to save all the world. How, then, had he overlooked America? The eventual Catholic answer, reached not without debate and anguish, was that He had left the salvation of the Americans for the Most Catholic Majesties of Castile and Aragon. As a consequence, the term Indian, when applied to the inhabitants of the new world, lost its connotations of civilization, but retained the suggestions of childlike qualities attributed to them by Columbus. Instead of representing the innocence of childhood, however, they came to stand for its ignorance and amorality, manifested in the acts of savagery and treachery encountered by later venturers. So the notion of savagery was imported from Africa with its people.

All these ambivalent characteristics can be found in Hakluyt's chronicles, where they serve to justify English settlement. In Spanish America, they justified not only forcible conversions, but also the treacherous overthrow of Aztec and Inca empires. The existence of these states was not consonant with the perception of the Indians as childlike, but the Spaniards found alternative justification for their overthrow in the practice of human sacrifice. The native empires thus became mere sources of plunder rather than structures deserving respect in their own right.

The effect of defining the native inhabitants of these new lands, even those of Asia, as other was to place them outside the obligations of law and civility. At the same time, their lands became available for European exploitation. As the nature of this exploitation differed, so did the perception of the land. In India, the major form of exploitation was through trade; in Africa, by enslavement; in Spanish America, by plunder; and in English America, by displacement and settlement. These variations were determined both by the perceptions projected on the countries by the first European comers, and by the opportunities actually offered, which in turn shape the perceptions. As the reality of exploitation differed, so did the resistance offered to it in the literature.

VII

In Africa and in Asia, where the Europeans failed to destroy the native cultures, we can trace resistance to the time of the earliest encounters. In America the social structures and cultural patterns of the original inhabitants were largely destroyed, at least in the centre and south, and writing of or for them is a matter of the kind of reconstruction carried out by Naipaul in *The Loss of El Dorado*. But while it destroyed the structures of the native society, the colonisation of America introduced new cultures from Europe and Africa. In Latin America, the interaction between European, African and native has produced new cultures with roots in the three continents. In English America, the native cultures have been marginalised, while at the same time the centre of the dominant culture has shifted from Europe to America. The Pilgrim fathers, in completing the process of settlement foreseen by Hakluyt, closed the circle of hope. Instead of bringing it back to England, where it was always located in the future, they established it firmly in their American present, where it continued to mock their achievements. Yet as the evils of Europe returned with the success of settlement, the frontier moved continually westward, so maintaining hope even in the evidence of its collapse. This continual renewal and denial of hope shapes the frontier experience, and thus reshapes the culture it was expected to renew. At the same time, its validity is brought into question by the black slavery on which success is based and which the culture denies. Black writing directly confronts this suppression and denial, but even white writing, in confronting European domination with the American dream, is forced to confront the reality which denies the dream. (L. Marx, Fiedler). The development of American literature is a product of this dialectic between the dreams of culture and the realities of economics and environment.

The pattern of American literature is repeated in all other new literatures, except that the imperial domination they resist is now as likely to be centred in America as in Europe. The processes of alienation, abrogation, and assimilation are common to all, and in fact occur simultaneously in each. Alienation is common to all new literatures, but they differ in their efforts to overcome it. Their different histories impose different urgencies. In India and the countries of Asia the urgent task is one of recovering continuity as well as of confronting modernity. Alienation comes from the displacements of migration and industrialisation. The emphasis therefore falls on assimilation of old traditions and the new realities of secular democracy. In black Africa, where colonisation has alienated the people from their past, the writers abrogate European domination in order to build a new identity from their own past. In the settler countries of the Pacific and of white Africa, the initial alienation was between the newcomers and the land and its original inhabitants. The effort in these countries is to overcome alienation not by denial but by assimilation.

But while alienation was initially a product of imperialism, it may now be seen as common to all contemporary literature, or indeed as the condition of modernism itself. Much modern literature, however, by reducing it to a psychological phenomenon, removes it from the political. This distinguishes this writing from the literature of resistance in both the new worlds and Europe itself.

Alienation arises from the frustration of the desire for unity or communion. This frustration is, however, never purely psychological, but is rooted in the material circumstances of the individual. Language, which mediates physical experience and fashions the self, is itself a part of these material factors. While it is true that I can never have direct knowledge of the material universe, or fully possess the language and experience of another, the existence of language presumes the fact of the other. The solipsistic attempt to deny any knowable reality beyond language is a product of European anomie, itself the product of the end of imperialism. While the narrative structures of dominant literatures portray it as purely psychological, philosophers reduce it, with all experience, to language. This denies the reality of the history which brought both imperialism and Auschwitz. Writers of the new world cannot deny

the realities of the subjection of their societies and the foreign
domination of their land. Their alienation proceeds from precise
historical conditions which are embodied in their works. The process
of reading these works is hermeneutic. Their language involves us
in their history. As Derrida has said in another context, we admire—
that is, contemplate with astonished curiosity—a presentation of
the speaker which reflects both his historical moment and the
universal truths he reflects on us by speaking them (Derrida, 1987).

VIII

The new worlds were all conceived as objects of desire, as places
where the freedom, wealth, and community of the golden age might
be recovered. While this desire excluded the original inhabitants,
colonialism imposed on them its language, and therefore the same
patterns of expectation. The cultural history of the new worlds, for
both settlers and the native inhabitants, becomes therefore a
succession of attempts to fulfil desire through separation from the
imperial culture and unity between the new land, that is, the land
new to the imperial culture, and its people. While this history can
never be independent of the play of the words that signify it (Derrida,
1976), this play of the signifiers remains equally entangled in the
play of the signified, the material history of these new countries.

In all these countries, expectations and desire were denied to
settlers and natives alike either by the land itself, by their removal
from the land, or by the contradictions and inequities of colonial
societies whose inequities denied their aspirations of community.
The consequent alienation generates new attempts to create
community between the land and its people, which in turn generate
new contradictions and renewed alienation. These developments
can be understood in terms of the classical economic factors of
production, land, labour, and capital. Land is the basis of production,
labour the means, and capital the accumulated knowledge, skill
and surplus value which makes the labour effective. In terms of
literature, these factors become the issues of land, people, and culture
which generate its continuing dialectic. And, just as there is no
absolute distinction between the economic factors, so there is none
between those in literature. As the people shape the land they create
a culture which in turn further shapes them.

The relationships between the three elements of this dialectic are determined by history. In traditional societies, the accumulation of social structures and expectations dominates the individual and maps the landscape with its forms of ownership and use. The role of the individual can be changed only by such catastrophic events as invasion or plague, or a social breakdown followed by religious conversion or revolution. Only at such times do individuals and the land escape from the control of culture. In the new world, however, individuals are confronted by the reality of a land not governed by precedent. This imposes on them the task of converting the land to forms sanctioned by their culture. This ensures that the land will be a dominant element in the dialectic, but the form this takes will depend on the relative importance given by the culture to society and the individual. The different histories of the founding societies ensured that this relationship would differ diametrically in Latin and English America.

The development of Latin America was dominated by the political forms and cultural expectations of Spain. Columbus's instructions and comments emphasized the service he owed to his sovereigns, representatives of the accumulated social capital of feudal Spain, and consequently his reports and their actions were directed to using the new world to extend their glorious sway. The consequent imposition of the institutions of the old culture on the new land, and the uses of its resources to support an imperial order, produced a hierarchy which defined individuals by their relationship to a political power sanctioned from abroad. Even when political ties with Spain were broken, the new nations continued to be dominated by a culture of status rather than production, of power rather than individuality. The land is an object of contention, a mine of wealth and basis of power, rather than either a resource to be used or a source of life. Contemporary politics in Latin America is about converting it to resource, and contemporary literature about recovering the recognition of it as source of individual and social being.

English settlement in North America began a century after Columbus. Political and economic upheavals precipitated by civil wars, the dissolution of the feudal system, and the wealth already coming from the new world had in England already loosened the ties of feudal society. Healthy and unscrupulous men able to recognize the opportunity could escape their native station and seize wealth and power for themselves by piracy, plunder, soldiery, or clerical service. For the early venturers, North America offered such opportunity. They sought individual gain at least as much as they hoped to enhance the glory of their sovereign. While her charters insisted on the continuing obedience of her subjects, the business provisions made her a shareholder in their ventures rather than a monarch in search of wider realms. Thus from the start of settlement in North America the chroniclers recorded the conflict between the individual and the land. This conflict produced a culture which elevated nature and the heroes who subdued it, while suppressing from consciousness the sources of the labour they used and the capital they appropriated. The constitution of the United States is the direct cultural expression produced by the desire for individual wealth and freedom exercised on a land which appeared to offer unlimited opportunity. It is only in this century that this ideology of free men making their fortune in an open country has been challenged, both by those speaking for the minorities of natives and blacks whose land and labour produced the fortunes, and by women whose role and desires the ideology completely excluded. These challenges have not so far, however, affected the significance attributed by American culture to the centrality of the ostensibly autochthonous individual.

The conflict of land and people, which in the United States has produced the culture of the individual, has produced different cultural results in the other settler societies according to the differences in the history and success of settlement. In the colonial societies of Asia and Africa the conflict was not between individuals and the land but between cultures over the use and control of the land. This conflict produced a culture which defined individuals by their power, and by the origins and education which conferred power. The conflict in the successor nations is still over these cultural issues, and so individuals continue to be defined in terms of social rather than personal success. The literature of European modernism traced the efforts of the individual to find a place in a society whose structures of meaning had collapsed but which still denied a place to the human. The literature of postmodernism questions the possibility of either human value or individual knowledge. In the new worlds, however, land and culture are both open to possibility and faced with extinction. Consequently their literatures remain involved in a dialectic which seeks to produce from them an individual at home in both. It is in these new worlds that humankind still seeks the new world of desire.

CHAPTER 2

LANDS OF DESIRE: PATTERNS OF LITERATURE IN THE NEW WORLD OF THE UNITED STATES

Every new culture is engaged in a quest for identity, and must therefore continually seek for its point of origin, the moment or pattern which separates it from the imperial culture. Settler cultures are likely to place this point at the occasion of their declaration of independence, the occasion which defined them as independent entities. Subjugated cultures are more likely to reach back to the times before their subjugation, finding their new independence in an independent past. Both definitions of independence are examples of the movement from the historical present to a mythological past in order to create fictions which provide space to move in the present (Wieland, 1989). Cultures of neither kind can afford to ignore the period of colonial rule which has reshaped their cultural tradition, whether this tradition is indigenous or comes from the imperial source. Metropolitan cultures on the other hand find no need for this search, as their cultures seem to stretch without interruption to time immemorial. Only when this apparent continuity is interrupted, as it was in Renaissance Europe, and has been in Central Europe this century, is there felt a need to search for origins.

The declared origin of a culture and its literature is only one factor in determining the nature of the present it validates, which is shaped equally by the circumstances that initiate the search. By tracing their genealogy to Arthur, and beyond him to Brutus, the Tudors and their Plantagenet predecessors justified their own authority, but at the same time they asserted standards of royal duty by which they could be judged. By tracing the origins of human misery to Man's first disobedience to an inflexible law, Milton justified human rebellion and discredited God. Fascism in Italy constructed its national origins in a Rome shorn of the humanism that inspired the Italian renaissance. The Nazis in Germany appropriated from Wagner a Germanic mythology which had sung of the destruction of the gods and the futility of human endeavor, and used it instead to justify the brutal destruction of all human standards. More recent writers in Central Europe have, on the other hand, recovered the past of an enlightenment characterized by tolerance and respect for human rights. The United States was itself born from this enlightenment, which from the beginning gave it definition against the other of the older Europe from which its settlers had always sought escape. These promises of the enlightenment were already inherent in the definition given to the new land by the first venturers from England, and have remained central to its writers' understanding of their tradition. This tradition now finds its point of origin in the words of the Declaration of Independence. This document is the embodiment and the culmination of the hopes of generations of settlers at the same time that it grounds them, not in any historical moment, but in the immemorial past of human nature. It is literally impertinent to remark that this immemorial past is itself the product of eighteenth-century Europe.

The opening words of the Declaration of Independence move speedily from history, "the course of human events," to the absolute, "the laws of nature and of nature's God." This places the authors of the Declaration at the centre of their own history, dissolving the cultural bands even before the political bands which have connected them with their place of origin. The words of the following paragraph, "We hold these truths self-evident, that all men are created equal, that they are endowed by their Creator with certain unalienable human rights; that among these are life, liberty and the pursuit of happiness," are a declaration of metropolitan status. No matter that it would be a century before political and economic power would match the aspirations of the Declaration. No matter either that it was to take more than a century before the concept of man was effectively extended to include blacks or women, or that the culture continues to define the worth of the human in terms of property, the Declaration continues the work begun in the English Revolution of emancipating the human from dependence on inherited or attributed authority. The Declaration creates the moral authority it claims, thus destroying the merely historical origins of the United States in Europe and establishing itself instead as the author of its own being, the centre by which all else will be judged. From this moment, it is no longer simply a province taking its standards from Europe, but potentially a metropolitan centre producing its own traditions and imposing its own standards within its domain.

Yet, for all the confidence of the framers of the Declaration, the United States remained troubled both by its identity and its autonomy. Leslie A. Fiedler has argued that, like the modern novel, it is the child of a moment in the eighteenth century when the bourgeois were torn between reason and desire, and that it has never been able to come to terms with the split between the two (Fiedler, 1960). We can find this split in the Declaration itself. The "self-evident truths" were contradicted only too evidently by the state of the world, not only in England and France but also in the United States itself, where slaves were not equal and even free men were subject to the tyranny of money and religion. Benjamin Franklin's precepts are not an appeal to equality, but to an inequality grounded in achieved worth. More fundamentally, the Declaration's appeal to reason contradicts the implications of the pursuit of happiness, which is grounded in desire. The appeal to nature is similarly ambiguous or contradictory, for the promise of America is as much to subdue nature as to be at one with it. Further, as nature itself can be understood only as a human creation, or, if we wish to use deist terms, the human understanding of a divine creation, it is something to be brought into being by human efforts, not something on which these efforts can themselves rest. In starting from nature and desire as their standards, therefore, American writers were from the beginning locked into a contradiction. This contradiction produces the nostalgia for a simpler world and the fear of desire which Fiedler and others have noted in the American novel.

Nor could the Declaration, although it produced its own reality, contradict the reality of the history that had gone before it. The pilgrim narratives which reproduced and completed Hakluyt's hopes also told of encounters with the darkness of the forest and its native inhabitants, the Indians who had changed from objects of pity and conversion to subjects projecting hostility and fear. While they remained unseen they embodied the terror of anarchy and dissolution which contradicted the desire of the settlers for peace and harmony. When however their terror is realized in the narratives of Indian captivity, the experience of the white narrator moves her dark captives from the position of the inhuman other to that of human participants in her own history. These narratives show the Indians, like the English and French settlers, as capable of both brutality and succour, treachery and loyalty.

This ambivalence persisted after the Declaration of Independence. Although this brushed past history to the absolute, writers had to contend with a continuing present which could not be reduced to such certainty. While the Boston Brahmans around Washington Irving tried to ground a civil society on the absolute reason of civilized discourse, writers such as Nathaniel Hawthorne hurried back to the colonial past in their efforts to understand the contradictions of their time. Hawthorne found the source of evil in the nature of desire itself, which necessarily destroys its object rather than tolerate imperfection. Hester Prynne may have the courage to live her desire, but she overcomes the destructive zeal of the community whose unity she destroys only by denying her desire, refusing it any further expression in her daily life. She makes herself the prison she scorns when the Puritan godfellows her neighbours try to impose it on her spirit. Like them, she brings the contradiction of harmony with her from Europe in the desire which first generated it.

Hawthorne's contemporary Fenimore Cooper sought escape from this continual contradiction in the constantly receding frontier, only to show that the search for the frontier destroyed it in the act of finding it. The only harmony the Deerslayer finds is in the union with his Indian blood-brother, Chingachgook. But while this harmony overcomes the hostility of the dark forest, it recovers the object of desire only in the remembered simplicity of childhood, not in any promise of the future. Chingachgook and the Deerslayer are both people of the past, destroyed by the settlement they make possible. Similarly, Melville's Ishmael can find his harmony only from the high seas, from which he must return as a wanderer after the flawed commonwealth of the ship has been destroyed by its captain in his blind quest to destroy his own terror of nature. And the archetypal voyage of Huckleberry Finn leads only to New Orleans, Tom Sawyer, and the Widow Douglas. Twain may later despatch Tom and his allies to Europe to castigate the blindness and folly of the old world, but Huck can escape the American extension of these vices only by lighting out to the territories before Judge Thatcher destroys them.

American fiction tends to follow two mythical patterns. The simplest is familiar to us from dozens of westerns, where the lone stranger rides out of the wilderness into a troubled town, destroys the forces of evil and, after an entanglement with a woman trying to domesticate him, escapes again into the distance. The Deerslayer performs this function in Fenimore Cooper's work, and Hawthorne reverses it in *The Scarlet Letter*, where the stranger who proclaims virtue represents implacable evil. We can trace this pattern back to Homer and Achilles, who escapes from his wilderness of wounded pride to save the Achaeans from the onslaught of Hector. It is, however, *The Odyssey* which provides the other element of the American myth. In the last part of this, Odysseus cleanses the evil suitors from the palace and restores the domestic virtues. Later versions of the story take the parallel further, as he finds domesticity intolerable and flees once more across the ocean. The first parts of the epic, however, represent the other great American myth, the road story, which follows the hero on his travels until he finds wisdom or death.

The crucial use of these mythologies has been made in this century by the Southern writer, William Faulkner, whose novels deal with the agonies of the South where the failures of the American dream first became manifest. The fact of failure distinguishes him from most American writers, and adds to the Homeric mythology the deeper tones of Oedipal tragedy. The palaces of his heroes are thronged not just with suitors, but with the spirits of the dead, who will not be cleansed. His fiction thus includes not only the hopes and disappointments of the settlers but the guilt on which their enterprise rests. His Yoknapatawpha County is both a fully-created world of the imagination and a metonym for the whole of the American experience.

The genealogies Faulkner provides and implies trace the people of the South back to their origins in Scotland after the failed Jacobite rebellion of 1745, in Huguenot France, in Africa and in the prehistory of the American Indians. The South is the end of their journey, the mythical destination where they will remake their history. Yet this history is already written before the characters in the stories are born. Instead of being the heirs to Eden, they are lost in a world where they have failed to arrive, and where no new hero comes to show them the way or cleanse the evil. Like Benjy in *The Sound and the Fury*, they recognize the signs given by the world around them, but not the code that will make sense of the signs. They cannot find the pattern, the narrative of cause and effect in which each event is given its proper place in time. So they compulsively remake their myths of arrival and cleansing, telling their stories to each other, to their children and grandchildren, and to the readers, who have to join with them in the task of deciphering meaning from history.

While this is true of all the Yoknapatawpha county fictions, Faulkner takes it to its furthest extent in *The Sound and the Fury*, where the story is presented first through Benjy's inchoate impressions, leaving readers to make their own sense of them. Even the narratives supplied subsequently by other members of the household fail to provide final definition for this tale of decay and dissolution. While events like Quentin's suicide or Candace's (Caddy's) elopement are given complete clarity, their motivation and consequences remain blurred. The novel does not contain a history of the Compsons that the reader can decipher, but provides fragments of experience from which as readers we must each construct the history for ourselves. While this formal structure reflects the general emphasis of modern fiction on the reader's subjective construction of meaning, it also represents the specific circumstances Americans in the South found themselves in during the period from Reconstruction to the Second World War. Like other Europeans, they could find no meaning in a society of disintegration, but neither could they construct a new subjectivity from a past which implicates them in the guilt of settlement and slavery. In constructing a mythical county, Faulkner invites his readers to join him in an anticipatory reading of the past which would produce the potential meanings this history has destroyed.

The Sound and the Fury in any reading remains a story of darkness and confusion. The noble posturing of Southern honour cannot restore its social basis nor expiate the guilt of the slavery on which it rested. The gothic horrors of this and other novels are not incidental, but the consequence of the betrayal of reason by desire and the denial of desire by pride. These twin passions form the warp and weft of the Yoknapatawpha county that Faulkner creates through repeated revisitations of its families and their twisted histories. No story is ever finished because the

histories have neither beginning nor end. Like Boon Hogganbeck
the characters emerge into our ken already bearing their past
and their future with them. (*Reivers*, pp. 18–20). Thomas Sutpen's
pride denies the desire which carved his kingdom from the jungles
and swamps of the Mississippi, and which bred the slaves to
work it until he destroyed his son and desire and pride alike
dwindled down to the figure of Tennie's Jim. Yet Jim, ostensibly
a powerless figure merely doing the will of others, belongs with
those of whom Faulkner remarks at the end of *The Sound and
the Fury*, "they survived." Their history is still to come.

That history will not, however, commence until the whites
are able to come to terms with their own past. This, as old Ike
McCaslin foresees at the end of "Delta Autumn," will not happen
soon or easily: "Maybe in a thousand or two thousand years in
America. . . . But not now! Not now!" (*Go Down Moses*, p.361).
Until then, the Snopes, successful white trash, will control the
South on behalf of northern capitalism. Their lack of any
connection with either the land or its past, however, ensures that
while they may have success they will never build a present in
which they can live. They are the perpetual outsiders, even to
themselves. The Compsons, the McCaslins, the Edmondses may
destroy or exile themselves, but the land in its potential will
always be there. This is the subject of the series of shorter fictions
which culminates in "Delta Autumn." The resolution which Ike
McCaslin cannot foresee is necessary, because it is already built
into the past, and particularly his own past. As General Compson
exclaims to Ike's cousin McCaslin Edmonds while Ike is still a
boy, the land produces a knowledge which exists outside the
economics of growing and buying:

> You've got one foot straddled into a farm and the other
> foot straddled into a bank; you ain't even got a good hand-
> hold where this boy was already an old man long before
> you damned Sartorises and Edmondses invented farms and
> banks to keep yourselves from having to find out what
> this boy was born knowing and fearing too maybe but
> without being afraid, that could go ten miles on a compass
> because he wanted to look at a bear none of us had ever
> got near enough to put a bullet in and looked at the bear
> and came the ten miles back on the compass in the dark;
> maybe by God that's the why and wherefore of farms and
> banks. (p.76)

Ike, the boy, has just taken part in the hunt which finally slew the bear he had tracked three years earlier, and which has taken with it the dog that finally bayed it. As the hunters prepare to depart, Ike declares that he is staying beside old Sam Fathers, the half-Indian half Negro who has taught Ike all he knows and whom he recognizes is now dying, a final casualty of the hunt. Yet he is unable to share this knowledge with anyone.

Ike's role in this and the other stories is to be the one who knows, the one to whom the past has given itself with a knowledge he cannot share. In public terms, he is undistinguished, a landowner who on his twenty-first birthday gives away his land to become a small-town storekeeper. Yet this act of abnegation, of denial, is at the same time the redeeming point of both the tragedies of Sutpen's Hundreds, told in *Absalom Absalom!*, and of the tales of the wilderness and its destruction which begin with "The Bear." These two sequences are linked not only by Ike McCaslin, but also by the fact that Major de Spain built his hunting lodge amid the jungles of Sutpen's former kingdom. During the annual visits to this camp, the hunt for bear restores the unity of man and nature which Sutpen's mad plantation had broken. It does so by accepting violence itself as an expression of desire.

The story of the hunt, "The Bear," opens on the eve of the final hunt for Old Ben, the bear, but immediately circles back through the boy's memories of earlier hunting trips and the men's talk which took him past their lives to the wilderness itself:

> the big woods, bigger and older than any recorded docu-
> ment:—of white man fatuous enough to believe that he
> had bought any fragment of it, of Indian ruthless enough
> to pretend that any fragment of it had been his to convey
> ... the men, not white nor black nor red but men, hunters,
> with the will and hardihood to endure and the humility
> and skill to survive, and the dogs and the bear and deer
> juxtaposed and reliefed against it, ordered and compelled
> by and within the wilderness in the ancient and unremit-
> ting contest according to the ancient and immitigable rules
> which voided all regrets and brooked no quarter—the best
> game of all, the best of all breathing and forever the best
> of all listening, the voices quiet and weighty and deliber-
> ate for retrospection and recollection and exactitude among
> the concrete trophies. (p. 11)

The boy under the guidance of Sam Feathers becomes a woodsman, learning not just to listen to the men but to read the woods themselves. This reading is not a matter of interpreting the signs, the pragmatics of woodcraft, but of recognizing in them something he has known since before he was born. The woods literally give him possession of himself and the land, a possession symbolized by the bear to which he becomes, in a strange sense, the heir.

> It ran in his knowledge before he ever saw it. It loomed and towered in his dreams before he ever saw the unaxed woods where it left its crooked print, shaggy, tremendous, red-eyed, not malevolent but just big. . . . It was as if the boy had already divined what his senses and intellect had not encompassed yet: that doomed wilderness whose edges were being constantly and punily gnawed at by men with plows and axes who feared it because it was wilderness, men myriad and nameless even to one another in the land where the old bear had earned a name, and through which ran not even a mortal beast but an anachronism indomitable and invincible out of an old dead time, a phantom, epitome and apotheosis of the old wild life which the little puny humans swarmed and hacked at in a fury of abhorrence and fear like pygmies about the ankles of a drowsing elephant;—the older bear, solitary, indomitable, and alone; widowered childless and absolved of mortality— old Priam reft of his old wife and outlived all his sons. (p. 13)

The bear, symbol of the wilderness, dissolves all distinctions, leaving man alone with his own nature. Yet this nature is itself a product of culture, not only the violent masculine culture of the hunter but also the tradition of America as the other which promises even in its darkness to restore the golden age that existed before commerce and before cities. This culture produces the Major de Spain of the city office, "the short plumpish grey-haired man in sober fine broadcloth and an immaculate glazed shirt" as much as the Major de Spain of the woods, "in boots and muddy corduroy, unshaven, sitting on the shaggy powerful long-hocked mare with the worn Winchester carbine across the saddlebow and the great blue dog standing motionless at the stirrup" (*Big Woods*, p.82). It produces the mixed-bloods Sam

Feather and Boon Hogganbeck as well as the system of class and race which confuses their identity and denies them power over themselves except in the woods or the saloons. The backwoods culture of the huntsmen is a product of the same economic system which dooms the destruction of their hunting grounds. The railway that gives the hunters access is the agent of this destruction, and, in a final irony, Major de Spain becomes the executioner of the wilderness which gives his life its meaning. This wilderness is not rooted in the soil of the Mississippi, but in the culture transplanted from Europe. When Ike reads the wilderness, he reads himself. It can therefore offer no escape from himself or his times. The violence which is the only way these men know of expressing their love finally exhausts them, leaving them with no answer to those who continue to rape the land in pursuit of their loveless desires.

The wilderness is, however, only one part of Faulkner's landscape. It is on the margin, the boundary or frontier which offers hope of the escape it finally denies. The centre of his landscape is the town of Jefferson, surrounded by the myth-ridden homes of decaying gentry and the parched fields of negro sharecroppers. The landscape is the product of the labour of people exploited to supply the markets of Europe, to which it is symbolically linked by the wire that brings the local gamblers the latest prices of the cotton exchange. The town is the local branch of capital, where control is contested between the banks run by the old families of Sartorises, McCaslins, Compsons and Priests, and the unscrupulous parvenues, the Snopes. The action of the books is governed by the struggles of the inheritors of old wealth, the product of slave labour, to hold their place against the new class who seek control by financial manipulation rather than by direct involvement in production. The women who might have developed a culture of nurture are reduced to the status of either servants or ornaments. The people who produce the wealth, the Negroes, and the people who were dispossessed to allow its production, are generally excluded from the action, except when as objects of white desire they disrupt the orderly appropriation and possession of the land. Yet their endurance, whether as the apparent passivity of the Negroes or the ancient wisdom of the Indians, offers the only potential alternative to a white domination which destroys even its own values through its own contradictions.

As he looks back on his life in "Delta Autumn" Ike McCaslin reflects on the imperative the wilderness has placed on him, "himself and McCaslin juxtaposed not against the wilderness but against the tamed land, the old wrong and shame itself, in repudiation at least of the land and the wrong and shame...." (p.351) The shame is both the taming of the land and the means of its taming, slavery. But Ike has been unable to cure or repudiate either. He has given away his land to McCaslin, who has merely continued the pattern of uneasy exploitation. And in this story Ike makes himself complicit in the betrayal by McCaslin's son of the negro girl and the child he has had by her.

The story of "The Bear" finishes with an apparently unrelated episode, the hunting of a Negro slave by his Indian masters. The slave has been body-servant and companion to one of the last Indian chiefs, Issetibbeha. He is running from the sacrificial death to which he, along with the horse and the dog, has been doomed by the death of his master. During his flight, he recollects his childhood in an African society where people were supportive of each other. The story finishes with his capture and the last moments before his death. Yet this death, like the death of Sam Fathers and Old Ben, the bear, establishes a link between the land and the two peoples who have worked it. It implies that the third race, the whites who exploit it, can only overcome their own contradictions by recovering a culture which unites its peoples in unity with the land. The cost of this unity seems to be an acceptance of the violence generated by desire which contradicts the desire for life that drives the slave on his flight. But, through Ike, Faulkner suggests an alternative possibility. Ike may have failed in his own life, both in his marriage and in his repudiation of his kinsman's child. This is a double repudiation, because the child's mother is a great-granddaughter by a slave of Carothers McCaslin, progenitor of both Ike and the child's father, Roth Edmonds. Yet Ike does partially recognize the child by giving it General Compson's hunting horn, symbol of unity with the land. And earlier, in the momentary success of his marriage union, he saw in it an answer to the tragedy of the land, "that same wrong and shame from which he would at least save and free his son and, saving him, lost him" (p.351). Only in a love which seeks nothing from either its partner or its progeny, which is a desire for unity with all life, can there be an escape from the violence which is otherwise the expression of this desire. Yet, just as the desire for a unity with nature, with the wilderness, is a desire for escape from culture, and so from the only life we can know, so this desire for unity in love is a desire for death.

If the promise of the new world to restore a lost unity can be fulfilled only in death, it can recover its life only by asserting its otherness, by repudiating the desires projected on it by the old world. Faulkner attempts to do this through his images of the old order of the South, with the code of manners it taught each of its men: "to be gentle with his inferiors, honorable with his equals, generous to the weak and considerate of the aged, courteous, truthful and brave to all." This code rejects the injustices of the old world and the materialism of the new order, but it ignores the repression of both people and desire on which it is itself based and which generates the violence that destroys it. The wilderness offers only temporary sanctuary from this violence, and the older wisdom of Negroes and Indians remains inaccessible, cut off by the conditions of their suppression. Rather than becoming the basis for an independent new literature, Faulkner's work renews the metropolitan tradition in the new world. Rather than fulfilling its promise of an integration of personal and public, individual and social, the fiction reduces this world to a projection of the fantasies of private desire.

These desires can never be fulfilled either through nature or through love. Nature itself is alienated, crying for revenge on the men who have destroyed it. Or rather, as Ike McCaslin reflects at the end of *Big Woods*, it lies waiting for men to destroy themselves. "This land, said the old hunter. No wonder the ruined woods I used to know don't cry for retribution. The very people who destroyed them will accomplish their revenge." The wisdom of the old people has been destroyed and they themselves are merely a remnant. Nor is there any real hope of a new society built on a harmony of black and white. This is not only because, as Ike McCaslin remarks, American whites are not ready to accept blacks as equals, capable of marrying into their families. Rather, as Faulkner shows in the horrifying story "Pantaloon in Black" (*Go Down Moses*, pp. 135–59), the Americans for whom the sheriff speaks are incapable of recognizing them as even human.

This story tells of the frenzied grief suffered by Rider, a young Negro timberman after the death of his wife. Unable to find comfort in God, whisky, or work, he finds himself at a crooked dice game run by a white man, Birdsong. When he exposes the fraud, Birdsong pulls a gun on Rider, who responds by knifing the white man. Rider is arrested, but dragged from the gaolhouse by Birdsong's relatives and lynched. Looking back on the events, the sheriff reflects that he could do nothing about the lynching, as the Birdsongs command a decisive vote in the elections for sheriff and deputies. But his real justification is that Negroes are not human. He complains to his wife:

> Them damn niggers. . . I swear to godfrey, it's a wonder we have as little trouble with them as we do. Because why? Because they ain't human. They look like a man and they walk on their hind legs like a man, and they can talk and you can understand them and you think they are understanding you, at least now and then. But when it comes to the normal human feelings and sentiments of human beings, they might just as well be a damn herd of wild buffaloes. Now you take this one today— (p.154)

His evidence is the ostensible failure of Rider to show even hypocritical respect for his wife, "when a white man would have took the day off out of pure respect no matter how he felt about his wife" (p.156). The sheriff, disengaged from any values except those of authority, is unable to recognize, let alone share, the depths of desolation into which Rider had been plunged by the strength of his emotions. His wife, preoccupied with her club and her movies, is unable to take this much interest. This generation, lacking the common relation to the land which bound earlier whites together even in violence, lacks the capacity for any reparative start.

Even the love which McCaslin thought briefly might offer an alternative to the cycle of guilt and destruction is made impossible by the entrenched masculinity of the Southern culture which denies the possibility of mutuality between sexes as between races. Faulkner understands what Hawthorne had recognized before him, that no new land can heal a society and individuals whose violence stems from the deep divisions within themselves. Even in their sense of displacement, these people constitute merely another metropolis of the alienated modern world.

The literature of the white South is the clearest example of a regional literature in the United States, and therefore makes most evident the metropolitan status of this regional writing, involved as it is in the whole imperial effort to create a new society in a new world. However, just as the literature of the north-eastern states has become predominantly urban, dealing with the universal problems of industrial capitalism, so the South has become locked within its own boundaries, wrestling with the original problems of settlement with the possibility of change only in time, not in space. The frontier, however, has continued to shift westward, not stopping even at the coast but continuing to Hawaii, Japan, China, and Vietnam as Americans have sought the twin, and perhaps incompatible, grails of justice and prosperity. As the frontier has extended across the ocean, the object of confrontation has changed from the land to the cultures of the peoples already settled in these alien lands. For those living on the islands of the Pacific, the coming of the Europeans meant the end of Eden, and their hope of restoring it now seems to depend on the movement of either people or technology. For those people from the overcrowded countries of Asia, America became the Golden Mountain or the new land of the west, offering them the hope of fulfilling ancient dreams of escape from ancient oppressions. All of these people, whether they have migrated to America or remained at home, have contributed to the new literatures which endeavour to integrate traditional hopes and values with the realities of new societies.

Within America, however, the frontier has never completely closed. In *The Grapes of Wrath,* Steinbeck showed how the west continued to beckon people whose original settlements had literally been blown away by the winds to which they had opened the soil. The re-enactment, in films and novels, of the legends of frontier conflict represents, like Faulkner's work, a continuing attempt to establish the legitimacy of settlement. In this work the image of containment, whether in stage-coach, homestead or small town, repeatedly changes from a symbol of safety to one of an imprisonment from which only the wilderness offers escape. This hope, however, inevitably proves fallacious, as it has since the earliest narratives of settlement. The wilderness either menaces intruders with hostile outlaws and Indians, or swallows them in its mystery, like the first settlers of Roanoke. But these changes of the symbol represent shifts of reality. In the absence of the organizing hierarchies of the old world, the settlers impose their order by a force which demands the suppression both of the wilderness and of the desire for freedom which first drove them into it. But this suppression relocates at the core of their being the savagery they have tried by constructing their settlements to subdue, ignore, or deny. In the new world of the west, therefore, freedom itself is the threat, settlement is wild, and the only escape is through constant motion. The Easy Riders escape the city only to be gunned down by the settlers, Kerouac's bums have to stay on the road or find refuge in the other world of drugs, and the civilization from which Kesey's free spirits try to flee cripples them with lobotomy.

Recent writers have, however, started to explore another way of escape from a civilization which has become identical with both suppression and wildness. They have come to place new emphasis on the third element of the dialectic between humans and the land which has produced a culture of aggressive individualism. They are looking for a dialectic between land and culture which will produce an individual at home with both. This work is open to the cultures of the earlier peoples of the land, which grow from harmony rather than conflict between humans and nature, and place emphasis on the mutual use and stewardship of the land rather than its subjugation. The works of these writers start from a sense of place, and produce the new frontier of a wilderness to be learned rather than mastered. In the words of Gary Snyder, they perceive the wild as the truly ordered. The survival of human culture depends on its recovery of this order.

The movement to the west came to at least a temporary halt at the Pacific coast. Here those who came westering by land met European seafarers who had taken the route east to trade for furs, Chinese in search of their Golden Mountain, Van Diemonians in search of freedom, Japanese and Pacific Islanders looking for the good life. David Wyatt has described the object of this search in his book *Fall into Eden* (1986), where he remarks that the characteristic experience of California begins with rapture and finishes with loss.

> So great was the beauty of the land that it conferred on the completion of the quest the illusion of a return to a privileged source. As the sense of the ending merged with

the wonders of beginnings, California as a last chance
merged with California as Eden. It proved a garden but
briefly held. The city that rises like an exhalation, San
Francisco, burns and rises again and again. (Wyatt 1986,
p.xvi)

The illusion was that of an unmediated encounter with a
landscape which, according to the individual's reaction to it, could
either validate the self through artistic or scientific contemplation
or empower it through commercial appropriation. Appropriation
however, lays waste the garden which attracts. Rather than being
expelled from Eden, the new people continually raze it in order
to rebuild it. The assertion of self proves again to be a fall from
innocence that destroys the self it proclaims.

In his novel *Pinto and Sons* (1990), Leslie Epstein has attempted
to set the history of the movement west in a mythical rather than
a merely geographic context. He sees it as the culmination of the
scientific revolution that had as its highest aim the freedom of
humankind from contingency. The novel epitomizes contingency
in pain and disease, which its hero, Adolph Pinto, spends his
time seeking to cure. Pinto is an Hungarian Jew and heir to a
family that has travelled first east from Spain to the Ottoman
empire, then to Hungary and the establishment of a prosperous
soapworks. Their journey, which started at the same time as that
of Columbus, thus combines commerce and science, and Adolph
completes it by travelling to America to attend lectures at the
Harvard Medical School.

At Harvard, Pinto observes the successful practice of
anaesthesia and discovers its secret for himself. This discovery
culminates both his own youthful search and America's destiny.
As he reflects, "the idea of life without pain was itself American:
nothing done here before or since has proved of such worth to
the world." (p.33) Yet this discovery leads to the expulsion of
Adolph and his colleagues from Harvard, just as their later
applications of biological and engineering technology bring about
the destruction of Adolph's family and their community. The
battles and Indian massacres at the climax of the novel
demonstrate both the failure of technology and the fears and
violence bred by the attempt to use it to dominate the wilderness.
The inhabitants of the mining town of Yreka do not tame the
wilderness, they merely construct a moral desert as a town and
plant its savagery in their own hearts.

The source of this disaster is the inextricable mixture of idealism and greed, nobility of intent and ferocity of behaviour, that characterizes science, exploration and settlement. This mixture is first revealed when Pinto is interrupted by his companions as he dreams of the paradise that the discovery of anaesthesia has made possible. Responding to his friends' world-weary cynicism that everything in America is stale, borrowed from the old world, he exclaims:

> *Nein!* What happened this morning was new, new! *Life without pain!* Only America could think such a thought. And to bring it about—to make earth into heaven! . . . No more pain! no pain, friends! Paradise! (p.12)

In the event, none of the discoverers makes money, and Adolph himself is reduced to penury, but that neither dampens their enthusiasm nor destroys the contradiction at the heart of the dream of material progress. When the gold fever sweeps Boston. the Harvard men form their own company to tear from the west its treasures, and once more hit the road west to achieve the success that will compensate for past failure.

As Epstein's narrative moves west it gains in momentum in proportion to its loss of human interest, thus mimicking the history of America's attempts to escape from human problems into technological marvels. Like his characters, Epstein becomes fascinated by scientific and technological detail, reducing both Indians and white townspeople to objects for his observation. While his imagination fantastically multiplies the variety of their appearance and action, they lose differentiation and become merely members of particular groups: Indian police, dancers and whores, gamblers, Pinto's disciples of Bacon and Harvey. The novel thus moves like a wagon party, inexorably but tediously towards the frustration of the experiment with rabies, the destruction of the mine, and the catastrophic war of whites and Indians. Pinto himself prospers in the unheroic role of draper, but is denied either scientific achievement or children of his own. The sons of the title are the Indian disciples of his scientific mission, followers in his technological Odyssey, who eventually are either hanged by the white victors or live out their lives as convicted felons, incarcerated in Alcatraz for having asserted their moral independence. Thus, in a reversal of the history of Australia, the American dream of freedom finishes in the dread reality of prison. As the rule of law alternates between impotence and oppression, the epic of science and exploration ends, like the hopes invested in California, with the venturers destroying themselves.

CHAPTER 3

MYTH AND COUNTERMYTH
IN AUSTRALIAN LITERATURE

The development of new literatures is always a search for origins. In the United States, the Declaration of Independence provides a convenient, if flawed, point of origin. In countries such as India the new literature attempts to find its authenticity by establishing continuity with the traditions that were interrupted by colonialism. This is equally true of the writing of dispossessed peoples such as the American Indians, the Maoris of New Zealand, or the Australian Aborigines, who have been made dispossessed minorities in their native countries. Settler societies such as the Australian have a different problem. Like the Americans, white Australians have to come to terms with the land they occupy and the people they have dispossessed. Unlike the Americans, they can point to no moment at which they declared their independence of the nation from which their culture stems. Their search for origins therefore becomes an attempt to construct myths which will separate them from the sources of their culture and join them instead in a unity with the land they inhabit. The tensions in Australian writing and culture arise from the attempts to reconcile these contradictory ambitions.

These tensions were particularly evident during the Bicentennial year, 1988, and in the celebration in 1990 of the 75th anniversary of the landing of Australian and New Zealand troops, the Anzacs, at Gallipoli. The Bicentennial functions became the focus for protest by Aborigines and their supporters that the landing at Sydney Cove in 1788 of Governor Phillip and the convicts and soldiers who established the first colony should be recalled with sorrow rather than pride. They made this stand public on Australia Day with a peaceful march and demonstration which reportedly drew larger crowds than the official launching of the year's festivities by the Prince of Wales. These protests effectively changed the emphasis of the year from celebration to reflection.

The anniversary of Gallipoli was celebrated through the media and by the Prime Minister as the day "Australia became a nation." This in turn led to controversy, at least in the letters columns of daily newspapers, about the relations between the Australians and the British during the landing and the subsequent campaign. This controversy continued an argument which has raged since Keith Murdoch's critical reports to the Australian Prime Minister of the time, the treacherous and self-glorying Billy Hughes. Hughes staked his political career on his identification with the men of the A.I.F. (Australian Imperial Forces), the "Diggers." This enabled him to promote a contradictory nationalism of identification with the British Crown and Empire and repudiation of the incompetence of the British commanders. Australian troops were portrayed as the stalwart sons of Empire who would save the old country from its own weakness. This ran in the face of the facts, repeated in 1990 by more sober or anglophilic correspondents, that in Gallipoli, as in other theatres of war, the numbers of Australians and New Zealanders engaged and of their casualties were exceeded by the numbers from Britain and other parts of the Empire, including India. More seriously, the identification made at Gallipoli between Australian and British interests was viewed by other correspondents not as the foundation but as the betrayal of Australian nationalism. This viewpoint had been given its definitive expression by the historian Manning Clark, who wrote in the fifth volume of his *History*:

> Australia's day of glory had made her a prisoner of her past, rather than the architect of a new future for human-ity. The story of the heroism would be told for generations to come. The ideals of Australia had been 'cast to the winds.' (p.426)

Thus the mythical points of origin have been turned from symbols of unity to places of contestation. The contestation is not over the facts, but over the meaning we wish to attribute to them, the significations we want to attach to the signs. This is not a cause of disunity, but a process of national definition, a part of the history which establishes what makes Australia different.

The establishment of difference is both a necessary part of cultural development and a denial of the culture it thus defines.

There can be, as Derrida argues, no point of origin. Our identity always comes from language, and language always carries with it the trace of the other which it effaces as it declares our difference. As for humanity, so for individuals and nations. The ascription of a name or identity destroys our unique potential by establishing it within an existing structure of meanings and differences, an existing culture. However, contemporary cultures and nation states locked into a global economy which constantly threatens our independence, our felt differences, are under a compulsion to assert their identity. New nations, unable to find this identity in an immemorial past, seek for it in the point of origin, the event or time which makes them different.

The search for origins is inherent in the western cultural tradition. It goes back to the author of Genesis, who wrote that "In the beginning God created the heaven and the earth." God, the indistinguishable, enters time by establishing difference, heavens and earth. All else is created by dividing these two. The differences, however, if created by God are first recognized by man, who gives names to every living thing, and who receives from God the law which divides right from wrong. Man does not fully exist, however, he remains uncreated in his unity, until he is further divided into man and woman. Only through the difference can either know the self. Nor can they know right or good until they have tasted of the tree which establishes the difference and thus brings both into being. The divided self is the condition of conscious being. This was understood by the writer of the Gospel of St. John, who understood creation as the separation of God, of non-being, into the word which separates spirit from flesh. "In the beginning was the Word, and the Word was with God, and the Word was God. And the Word was made flesh, and dwelt among us." The word abolishes unity, establishes the difference which alone is life. It gives the speaker command over the world by the same action by which it creates the speaker. Yet in creating the speaker, it also produces opposition between speaker and world, word and thing. The uttered word writes each thing into place in a system of differences. In so doing, however, it does violence to its own feeling of uniqueness, and to its desire for the wholeness which can be fulfilled only in death, in a return to the uncreated God.

The act of producing a new nation or a new culture is the establishment of difference within this existing system. It is itself an acknowledgement that there is no already existing unity, no immemorial truth, only systems which exchange the words, ideas, and goods which produce and distribute power and privilege between people and nations. The modern age commences when the discovery of new worlds forces this system open, allowing people to make their own space within it, to choose their own difference. In "Paradise Lost," the epic of universal history which first recognizes that this change has turned man into God, Milton understands the flow of power from language.

> Of Man's first disobedience, and the fruit Of that forbidden tree whose mortal taste Brought death into the world, and all our woe . . . Sing . . .

The verb "sing" commands the grammar of the sentence, and thus the whole of the world history that the sentence comprehends. It is at the same time a command to the "heavenly Muse," that is, to the voice of God Himself. Milton, whose original ambition had been to write an epic of British national glory, writes instead the epic of western science and imperialism which has no less ambition than to bring the whole of reality into its control. Yet the control which he exercises in stating his ambitions wavers when he tries to explain human evil, or even the delights of the new world in which Adam and Eve find themselves. The imperial project was to founder on the same unchartable shoals of guilt and innocence. Its literary vehicle was not to be the epic, vehicle of certainty, but the journal, the novel, and the short story, wavering journeys into uncertainty. Yet Milton's ambition sets the standards against which new nations must revolt.

Rather than revolting against his vaulting ambition, the United States took it for its own. New England was the country of the Book which justified the violence done by the settlers in their attempts to overcome their own divisions and become as Gods. Australia, child of a more sceptical Age of Enlightenment and of a pietism which separated private from public, generated more secular ambitions. Rather than a land to be redeemed, it was a land which would itself punish and redeem the felons of the old world. Redemption was envisaged in the earthly form of rural independence. They were to become sturdy yeomen, like the rude forefathers of the villages from which their stock was sprung before its lands were enclosed and its people dispossessed.

The freemen who accompanied them, men like John Macarthur, had even loftier ambitions. They dreamed of planting in the new world agrarian fiefdoms as strong as those of the Scottish chiefs who had driven them from their native highlands and islands. It did not trouble them that this redemption and indeed transcendence of their origins could be achieved only through a further act of dispossession. When the prophet of this pastoral imperium, Thomas Mitchell, passed in triumph through the tracts of western Victoria, and later through the wide plains of the north, he assimilated the Aboriginal names to his grand vision. He saw himself in the image of a new Vasco da Gama, leading in triumph the expedition which would open the wealth of new worlds (Carter, 1989). His vision remained the dominant image of hope as late as the 1860s, when Henry Kingsley opened the Australian episodes of his pastoral romance with the cry, "A New Heaven and a New Earth!"

These Australian dreams were, however, contradicted by crude reality. The convict colonies became, not redeeming purgatories, but infernos of desperation. While the new world of America had been the projection of Europe's hopes, Botany Bay became a projection of its fears. The England of the industrial revolution felt threatened by the chronic lawlessness and periodic violence of the mob. The convicts were the tumours it purged, the bushrangers the continuing threat of their return, Magwich the realisation of this threat. Australian writers and singers reacted to this characterisation with a rejection both of England and of the system it had created. Governors became objects of vilification, newcomers of ridicule. But neither the hope of independent farmers nor the dreams of the pastoralists proved capable of sustaining an alternative vision. The land was unforgiving, reducing the most grandiose dreams literally to dust. Just as the harsh conditions of settlement kept Australia economically dependent on England, so its culture remained derivative until late in the century. The indigenous contribution was to replace the image of sturdy independence projected on the English yeoman with a culture which resisted power and adversity through mutual dependence. However, as in America, the conditions of the frontier meant that the central figures of the culture were masculine. In both countries, women were left at home to nurture the gentler virtues. The contrasting circumstances of the two frontiers led, however, to contrasting images of masculinity and femininity.

Mark Twain provides us in *Huckleberry Finn* both with the characteristic American images and their critique. At the beginning of the novel Huck and Tom provide us with essentially the same image of boyhood—outdoors, impatient of convention, eager for adventure or experience, anxious to maintain their independence of adults. Apart from the lack of sexuality, this is the image of the American male, with his obsession with the trappings of ritual and the exercise of independence. But in the course of the novel Huck grows up. The men he encounters along the bank reveal themselves as truly childish in their vicious codes of honour and their unscrupulous avarice. He discovers from Jim the reality of a love which finally shows Tom's games as tawdry and unworthy. Yet the love between Huck and Jim, their true mutuality, is possible only on a raft which removes them from reality as surely as it drifts them towards captivity. The slavery Jim has known is no more real—although more vicious— than that which Huck experiences among respectable adults, so that he has eventually to seek refuge in further flight, this time to the territories. But the imprisonment from which he flies is domesticity, symbolized by the Widow Douglas and enforced by Judge Thatcher. The woman becomes the emasculator and the man simultaneously her agent and her protector.

This pattern is repeated in the stories of the frontier where man regains his masculinity only through violence. Faulkner's hunters escape from their wives to the wilderness, but even here their role is to tame by violent assimilation those forces of nature which threaten their domesticity even as they renew the strength of the hunters to sustain it, or to endure it. The characteristic tale of American cinema—say, *Pale Rider*—is built around the figure of the lone rider who comes out of the wilderness to find its violence threatening the domestic order of the town. After a brief entanglement with a good woman who threatens to tame him, to take away the qualities which make him a man, he asserts himself again and, through superior violence, destroys the evil which has erupted into the civility of the town. He then rides once more into the wilderness to renew himself, confident that the women and their values are safe once more. A variation of this is where, as in *Stagecoach*, a fragment of community is carried into the wilderness and its dangers, and has to be rescued by the male who has the force needed in these surroundings. The pattern is the same. Women are the source of values, men the protectors. But men will lose their power if they succumb to the values they protect. They therefore can survive only outside society. Or, in other words, the conditions of the new world make it impossible to sustain the society it promises.

The characteristic Australian tale follows a different pattern. Again, the woman is seen as responsible for the domestic virtues, but she is shown as having to uphold them in the absence of the man. Far from being protectors who retreat to the wilderness to draw strength from nature, the men flee from their wives and the bush alike, seeking refuge in each other's company. The pattern is seen in Lawson's "Drover's Wife," who is left by her husband to protect their selection both from natural hazards and from itinerant males. This situation is developed in his sequence of Joe Wilson stories, where Mary Wilson represents the wife at an earlier and more hopeful stage of her life, and Mrs. Slater the final stage, "past carin'." At each of these stages it is the woman who provides support for her neighbours and, while he is home, for her husband. The man's inevitable flight from home is seen by all parties as failure, of the individual as well as the dream, a failure produced by the reality of the land and the structure of capital in defiance of the labour expended by the people. Thus, whereas the structure of the American narrative assimilates people to the land and the capital which exploits it, the Australian experience alienates them from both. Ironically, the assimilation produces a violence of resistance, while alienation induces rather a resigned indifference.

This indifference is the basis of the mateship which is frequently asserted to be the central characteristic of Australian literature. It is what Arthur Phillips has described as the taste for plain mutton and tomato sauce (Phillips, 1958, p. 40). This taste represents the attitude that in the face of the insuperable odds which are the Australian's normal lot, we must not only be satisfied with any little sustenance that is offered us, we must regard anything more with suspicion. To look for more is to risk not only the loss of what we have but to destroy our masculinity, our ability to survive without the pamperings of civilization. Women like the drover's wife and Mrs. Spicer try to keep their families and their sanity intact by putting out table napkins, dressing for Sundays and reading fashions in the *Ladies' Home Journal*. Women editors like Louisa Lawson and Mary Gilmore, both themselves familiar with the deprivations of the bush, encouraged this behaviour with their columns of advice on domestic politics and economy (Matthews, 1987; Wilde, 1989). Their husbands and sons, however, continued to go shearing or droving, forced as much by the need to prove their manhood as by the desperation of their land selections. Once away, they found refuge in the mateship of the track and the wayside shanty, where they could succour each other in a male society of mutual self-esteem.

The sources of these attitudes may be found in the land itself, which from the earliest settlement defied attempts to reduce it to European patterns of husbandry, and in convictism, the system of labour first imposed on the land. Russell Ward has shown how the code of mateship grew first among convicts as a defence against the system, the formal code and authority of convictism. Later, the same creed served small settlers and bushrangers as a defence against all authority. The convict System also, however, produced a nihilism which is the reverse side of the taste for plain mutton. The decision to plant the new colony in New South Wales was influenced by the optimistic reports of Cook and Banks. These in turn reflected the original European hopes for a new world, which continue as one strain of Australian thought through Major Mitchell's journals, emigrant narratives, particularly after the gold rushes, and William Lane's early utopianism, right down to the socialist realists of the twentieth century. The convict experience generated the first of the savage and sardonic backlashes to this optimism. It defined a point of origin which doomed the new world of Australia to an intensification of the evils of the old.

The actual literature of the convict period is largely confined to ballads, folklore and sensational or moralizing fiction. It was left for such writers of the following generation as Marcus Clarke, "Price Warung" (William Astley) and "Tasma" (Jessie Couvreur) to lay bare the meaning of the System, the way it operated as a total code to define and control every aspect of existence. Recently, historians have questioned the factual accuracy of the System portrayed in these fictions, pointing out that the convicts themselves came from a fragmented and demoralized criminal underclass, that many of them encountered propitious circumstances and were able to make good in the new land, and that the episodes of gratuitous cruelty described in the fiction were the exception rather than the rule (Robson, 1963). The importance of the fiction is, however, to describe not the normality but the structure which created the normality. This structure confined even those who were able to find some room within it to establish their own lives. In itself a grotesque parody of the class system of England, it assigned every person and action its meaning. By taking the extreme cases of the System, the novelists reveal its inner logic, which continues to impose its structure of meanings on even society after its legal basis has been abolished.

While the persistence of the values of the convict system is paralleled by the survival of some aspects of the slave system in the American South, the ideologies of the two systems were quite different. Racism reduces the black to less than human status. Any attempt he makes to assert his equality is thus a threat to his white masters, for whom he exists only as an instrument. The black woman can exist further as an object to be used as a substitute for white wife or mother. An attempt to build an obligation on this relationship, to include in it any mutuality, will, however, endanger the male sense of wholeness, of that self-sufficiency of which his white wife is merely an attribute. But although the slaves cannot aspire to be more than property, they can be cherished property, nurtured within the unity of the family. The convict system, on the other hand, identifies the convicts as humans fallen through their own evil nature. As all human nature is by definition liable to a fall, the convicts are a potential source of contagion, and must for hygienic reasons be excluded from any family bonds and for their own good be subjected to punishment harsh enough to purge their evil.

This leads to an atomistic but hierarchical society in which, while no individual is responsible for any other, authority has the only wisdom and the convict is responsible for all evil. It is a model of the totalitarianism which has been a characteristic of the world of the twentieth century. The most extended fictional study of it is in Marcus Clarke's *His Natural Life*, which traces the struggle of the unjustly condemned Rufus Dawes against the brutality which envelops him in its toils. The fiction shows how the System reverses its own values, shifting the values of the civilization its officers supposedly represent to the convicts themselves. However, because they are denied any autonomy, they are unable to make these values prevail. The success of the System therefore is to destroy the values which give it its only justification, and so to throw into question the validity of the civilization which has produced it. The new world thus returns not to correct the evils of the old but to reveal these evils as the very foundation of the imperialist social structure. Imperialism can subjugate the new world only by first denying its own subjectivity, making itself the instrument of its own purposes and thus subjecting itself to the evils it seeks to expel. It is not by accident that Rufus Dawes' experience of the System begins, not on his arrival in the new world, but on board the ship taking him there.

The practice of mateship which the convicts devise in defiance of authority is unable to save them. The only help it can render them is to force the System to grant the sole release in its power, death. This forms the topic of one of the novel's more horrifying episodes, as well as of one of Price Warung's stories. For officers there is not even this escape. They must either be brutalized or destroyed. The chaplain, the Rev. Mr. North, tries to escape into alcohol, but this causes him to fail at crucial points in his duty, so adding to his torments. These enable him to establish a link of compassion with Dawes, but this cannot release either from his fate. Release can come only from outside the System. Dawes finds it eventually by reawakening the love of Sylvia, the girl whom the System has taken from him. In the first version of the novel, this enables him to escape with the daughter of Sylvia, known in this version as Dora, and with her establish a new life as a shepherd in the bush. The new land is allowed for a time to perform its healing function, until an eventual encounter between Dawes and his persecutor, Frere, expunges all in a final episode of violence. In the revised version, however, Clarke recognized the impossibility of this resolution, and Sylvia perishes at sea with Dawes during their escape. The logic of the System destroys all values, and so can allow no other release.

We see a different aspect of the System in a story by "Tasma," "An Old-Time Episode in Tasmania." While the story is, like Clarke's, told in the third-person by an outside narrator, the centre of attention is not so much the convicts as Mr. Paton, the officer with whom their fate rests. He is written between the innocence and beauty of his child and the innocent love of the two convicts in his power. Although the System condemns both kinds of innocence, the officer is moved by an incipient love to soften his behaviour and allow the two convicts go free. When he discovers that he has been deceived, that their love is of man and wife rather than brother and sister, he rebounds into darker brutality, becoming one of those whose "name is inscribed among those 'who foremost shall be damn'd to Fame' in Tasmania." Even this last phrase demonstrates the way the System reverses all values. The love which could have lifted Paton from the System becomes instead his damnation.

Both Clarke and "Tasma" propose love as an alternative to the System. This is in itself, however, a form of sentimentality which contradicts their perception of its absolute brutality. This does not mean that love could not, as a fact of history, survive and even flourish in a convict colony, but that it could do so only by remaining apart, not in opposition to the System. In "Tasma's" story, even the image of innocent love, the child, is blighted in the author's eyes by the name she has been given, Trucaninni. This was the name of the last of the full-blooded Tasmanian Aborigines to survive white settlement. To give such a name to a child whose "straw-coloured, sun-steeped hair and clear sky-reflecting eyes" are the delight of nature is, in the author's view, an act of "clay-brained" irresponsibility, symbol of a society dead to true values. To the modern reader, the author's comment marks rather the blindness of even sensitive members of that society to the full horror of its origins. In either case, it destroys any claim the System might have to moral validity, and casts doubt on the apparently happy ending inscribed for the two convicts who escape its toils. While Clarke eventually erases such a possibility from his novel, even the love he allows comes from outside the terms of the System. Dawes resists because he comes from nobler stock than the run of convicts, and his fate is self-willed to save his family's reputation. This knowledge of birth and virtue gives him an inherent strength which is able to resist almost to the end the malevolence of Frere. But the System is even more just than Clarke allows. Dawes' defiant honour is rooted in exactly the same economics and politics which give Frere his guilty power. As imperialism is rooted in injustice, it can only reproduce in the new world the oppressions of the old.

Writers like Lawson tried to escape from this bind by discovering a point of origin which would be independent of this taint of imperialism. This involved constructing the new myth of mateship, but the work constantly contradicted its own premises. Once the belief in God is taken away, man is unable to command circumstances, and the myths dissolve under their own weight. So the Joe Wilson stories start, like the Declaration of Independence, with a reference to happiness, but in Australia Lawson's pursuit is accompanied by an acknowledgement of its impossibility.

> There are many times in this world when a healthy boy is happy. . .
>   I wasn't a healthy-minded, average boy; I reckon I was born a poet by mistake, and grew up to be a bush-man, and didn't know what was the matter with me—or the world—but that's got nothing to do with it. There are many times when a man is happy. When he finds out that the girl loves him. When he's just married. When he's a lawful father for the first time, and everything's going on all right—some men make fools of themselves then—I know I did. I'm happy tonight because I'm out of debt and can see clear ahead, and because I haven't been easy for a long time.
>   But I think the happiest time in a man's life is when he's courting a girl, and finds out for sure that she loves him, and hasn't a thought for anything else . . . Make the most of your courting days, you young chaps, for they will never come again. (p.3)

The style is that of the bush yarn, with general reflections such as might arise in conversation to introduce a story illustrating the point the speaker has been making. These reflections continue for almost another page, before Joe gets to his point, "I never told you about the days I courted Mary." (p.4) Even this is followed by more regretful reflections, finishing with the exclamation "Ah, well!" before he starts the actual yarn: "I was between twenty-one and thirty . . ." The happiness that the story promises is thus clearly defined by its contrast, not so much with unhappiness as with normality. Yet there is a further contrast: the writer is not normal, he is a poet, and therefore more sensitive and more liable to unhappiness. By implication, happiness is not only fleeting, but achieved only at the cost of some of our humanity. Anything which sets a man off from his mates can produce only unhappiness.

The sequence of stories bears out this implication. Joe Wilson does win Mary, after he has sacrificed some of his sensibility to the code of manhood by taking on the local bully in a fist-fight. But his achievement is overshadowed by his continual reminders to the reader that this marriage, like those of his mates, and even of the squatter, Black, is destined to failure. This failure is symbolized by the gaunt figure of Mrs. Spicer, neighbour to Joe and Mary when they take up their selection. It is symbolized by Brighten's sister-in-law, who is able to give desperately needed help to Joe's son only out of her own loneliness. But it is embodied most in Joe himself, who is sustained in his weakness only by Mary in her strength. This strength is in the end self-defeating, because by emphasizing Joe's failure it denies him the only role in marriage he believes he can play. Ultimately, beyond the momentarily happy ending, he must take refuge in the bottle, desertion, and the company of his male mates. Happiness is a temptation to the gods which man forestalls by not trusting in it. The domesticity that Mary offers is not so much emasculating as too good for him, too much to hope for. He retreats to his boiled mutton and tomato sauce, washed down with beer.

The mateship which Lawson proclaims elsewhere proves itself in his best stories as incapable of sustaining a fresh start, a new point of origin. The degradation of a male-dominated society, and the horror it brings on women, forms the theme of Barbara Baynton's stories. The code of mateship leads not only to the desertion of women, but to their destruction. "Squeaker's Mate" plays on the ironies of this situation in its portrayal of a man so weak that he does not have mates, only women whose promise of complete mateship he exploits and betrays. "A Chosen Vessel" takes the situation of "The Drover's Wife" or "A Double Buggy at Lahey's Creek" to its logical extreme, where the woman is left alone with her baby and neither son nor dog to support her against the attentions of swagmen "going to, or worse coming from, the dismal, drunken little township, a day's journey beyond . . ." (p.82) There are no neighbours to come to her assistance, or comfort her against the memory of her husband's sneering taunt at her fears: "'Needn't flatter yerself,' he had told her.' nobody 'ud want ter run away with yew.'" She is therefore in a sense already destroyed before the arrival of the particular swagman who is agent of her death. The actual murder is precipitated, however, by the arrival of another bushman, exactly the event which in Lawson would symbolize mutual assistance, the code of mateship extended even to the stranger. Instead, this stranger, drunk on spirits and religion, sees the desperate woman as a vision of God and leaves her to her fate. The Australian bush and the old world God conspire to destroy both life and hope.

Both Lawson and Baynton portray a country in which land and people combine to deny their characters the home which is at the centre of their cultural values. Or, to put it in another way, their investment of labour and emotion is exhausted by the immediate demands of survival, and so they are unable to accumulate any surplus to provide a permanent establishment in the country for themselves and their family. This becomes a common theme in Australian writing. In the celebrated opening scene of *The Fortunes of Richard Mahony*, Henry Handel Richardson shows how the land itself takes vengeance on those who rape it in their search for the wealth which will sustain them. The desire which drives their search is thwarted by the violence with which they pursue it, destroying their object even in its attainment. Although Mahony himself gives up gold-mining, first turning to business as a grocer and then returning to his profession of medicine, his life continues to be marked by the same uncertainty as that of the miners. As he restlessly crosses the seas to Britain and back, he learns that neither the new world nor the old can satisfy the desire for unity they have planted in him. The fortune the new world gives him merely generates further desire for the knowledge and understanding both worlds still withhold. When the fortune is taken away, he is thrown back on a self incapable of either maintaining itself or finding a sustaining unity with the world. His restlessness at the same time denies his wife the companionship she craves, leaving her only with his needs to justify her life. The bread of life promised by the new world proves to be stones that fracture the lives of those who trust to it.

In the interwar period and after, the social realists tried to fulfil the hopes of the land by reconstructing the tradition of Lawson to bring women within the bonds of mateship. In *Working Bullocks*, Katharine Susannah Prichard tries to build a unity around the partnership between Red and Deb, the trees and the working beasts. Life in the forests provides a model for the working harmony which in the mill is disrupted by the power of capital, which forces workers to labour according to the rhythms of profit rather than of nature. The millworkers find temporary unity during a strike, but ultimately management is too strong for them. The novel finishes with Red and Deb going off to make a life for themselves, but this resolution is purely personal. Further, it shows Deb as finding her unity by surrendering to the greater force of Red's desire. Both the individual and the social sources of disharmony are thus left unchanged. In a later novel, *Coonardoo*, Prichard traces the ultimate source of disharmony to the seizure of the land which dispossessed the original inhabitants. The whites who grow up in this new land learn to love it as the natives do, but the forces of racism and capitalism which place them in the land keep them apart from it. Unable to fulfil their desire, they are eventually destroyed, along with the natives whose unity of land and people the whites exploit and destroy.

The attempts of Katharine Susannah Prichard to build a unity of people on harmony with the land are destroyed by the incompatability between this harmony and the imperatives of capitalism. These imperatives also thwart the drifters in Kylie Tennant's novels. Tennant shows how these drifters build a mutual society of their own, outside the respectable life of both cities and country. The mutuality they establish depends, however, on the bonds which hold them together as outsiders, as people without the power to change society or even to control their own history. In Xavier Herbert's novel from this period, *Capricornia*, this powerlessness extends to the whole of society. The most eminent of his characters are made the most ludicrous by their inability to perceive the vanity of their endeavours, of their belief that they can control land or people. The land itself is possessed of the same destructive force that drives its people to destroy themselves and each other. Even the unity of the races does not promise to overcome this savagery. While Herbert shares with Faulkner an understanding of the originary act of injustice which has ripped man and land apart and set in motion the cycle of violence, he has no equivalent hope that, in however remote a future, this injustice may be repaired by a return to harmony with the wilderness. Only in his last work, *Poor Fellow My Country*, does he venture to portray a nature which offers any succour, a possible universal mother, but this possibility is literally and figuratively destroyed by the savagery of man.

The search for permanence is the central theme of Patrick White's early works, culminating in *The Tree of Man*. It remains as a trace in his later novels as his characters struggle to accommodate themselves to the fact that there is no permanence before death, perhaps not even permanence of identity. White builds on the recognition by his realist predecessors of the vanity of human hopes in the unyielding Australian landscape, but he goes beyond them in finding in the experience of this landscape a universal metaphor of the human condition. In White's novels, people overcome their inner divisions only by unity with a spiritual reality which can be found only in the dance, the desert, and the eye of the storm. His characters resolutely turn their backs on the harmony of achieved settlement and march into the wilderness whose obduracy is the only hope of salvation.

This Australian fiction constantly discovers in the exploitation of land and people which derives from the origins of settlement the injustice which contradicts the hope of permanency and harmony. Fiction is able neither to offer a vision of the future nor even a comforting image of the past. This may account for the popularity in Australian writing of autobiography, which locates the origins of the social in the perceptions of the individual. Where the country can offer no comfort, childhood may. The image of childhood offers a secure foundation for the myth of our own self.

Autobiography is one of the slipperiest of all forms of writing. Rousseau, who may be considered its founder in modern times, considered it an actual betrayal of the self it endeavours to make present in its words. The author's attempts to recover a real self from the evasions of language result only in the construction of a false image, a figure who did not exist before the writing and cannot exist outside it. Yet the way in which the writing brings the self into existence is an indicator of the relationship between the writer of the autobiography and the society which constructs the writer. While the autobiographical self may be a fiction, it proceeds from the history of its creator. The writer's perceptions of this history determine the autobiography.

One method of beginning is the genealogical, which follows the example of St. Matthew's Gospel, tracing the ancestry of the subject from the earliest times. Kylie Tennant opens her autobiography, *The Missing Heir*, in this way, starting with portraits of her father and grandfather. She thus prepares the way to convey a secure sense of herself as an actor within the continuity of time. More characteristically, Australian autobiographers have placed their beginnings in a context of time and place which determines the outcome. Thus Jack Lindsay opens his autobiography, *Life Rarely Tells*, with a chapter giving a "Glimpse of Brisbane" and placing the young narrator at its centre, amid the "sprawling mass of galvanized-iron and slated roofs" the echoes of drovers' songs, and a "vast herd of red cattle pike-horned and bony, wearily staring with a sullen gaze from behind the fences of wire and gum-sapling" (p.1). Although the autobiography goes on to present a life of constant activity, as its subject chases his father to Sydney and his hopes to London, building himself an identity, a politics, and a career as he goes, this opening casts him primarily as an observer, a person hemmed in by the fate of his times. He presents his experience as the basis for his subsequent art. The record of his career thus becomes a history of his escape from the imprisonment he is born into with those weary cattle in the yards of the Brisbane slaughterhouse. The autobiography, the record of the making of an artist, is the last episode of this escape, but it is also the ultimate prison, the prison of words which pins down his life for ever.

A variation of the contextual opening is the perceptual, which shifts the emphasis from the surroundings to the observer. The objects the writer recalls do not constitute a determining context, but furnish the building blocks of consciousness. Thus Hal Porter begins *Watcher on the Cast-Iron Balcony* with his recollection of his mother's body after her death. This recollection enables him to travel back to his birth and before, constructing himself from memories and speculation. The contemplation of his dead parents, the others who made him in some remote and incomprehensible moment of passion, defines the writer as the point of consciousness, that which is alive when all the time and the people who have made it are dead. The subsequent words of the autobiography bring them back subsequent to this fact of death, that is, bring them to life only as the already dead. The time that he opens for us is irrevocably closed. He goes back to the memories of his earliest years, of the view from the precisely identified 36 Bellair Street, Kensington, to the objects that filled the house and the people they visited from there, with the air of someone opening an old book of photographs to show us what is already written there. Finally, he brings himself in:

> ... I watch myself closely. It is hardly necessary. I have been
> watching myself, by this time, for too long, since the days
> of the cast-iron balcony. I have watched myself watching
> the small suburban creature, the uninnocent good boy. (p.20)

The apparently objective detail has been an illusion. The details
have not been those of Kensington or of his family, but of his
own consciousness. The object of his observation is not the view
from the balcony, but the watcher himself. This style, apparently
egotistic, shows in fact the most precarious sense of self. Porter
is only too well aware of the effort with which he must cling
to the world offered to him, make it a part of his being, lest he
dissipate himself on these scraps of existence.

Randolph Stow commences his autobiographical fiction, *The
Merry-Go-Round in the Sea*, in much the same fashion as Porter.
Rather than the dead, however, he builds his narrative around
the image of the merry-go-round:

> The merry-go-round had a centre post of cast iron, red-
> dened a little by the salt air, and of a certain ornateness:
> not striking enough to attract a casual eye, but still, to an
> eye concentrated upon it (to the eye, say, of a lover of the
> merry-go-round, a child) intriguing in its transitions. (p.1)

The image is at once stable and transient, the subject and the
object of our attention. Its significance is not in itself, but in the
child who observes it. The mystery of the book is to discover
the significance of the merry-go-round, to unravel the meaning
it gives to the child's life. In its flawed motion, it already has
written the story which is to come. This writing comes, however,
not like Lindsay's Brisbane from any history of its own, but from
its place in the boy's consciousness.

Each of these symbols—the parent, the cattle, the balcony,
the merry-go-round—is distanced both by time and space. They
are very different from the fragmentary memories Lawson
presented in his unfinished attempt at autobiography. Lawson
from the beginning felt himself alone in a world of poverty,
marked for destruction by his own difference. These later authors,
however, in their own ways control their worlds from the start.
Their moments of beginning provide stable points to control a
disintegrating world. The parent blusters but doesn't destroy,
the merry-go-round turns on its single pole. Even the cattle are

kept safely apart by their fence, their menace never realized. Death itself, the final disintegration, is controlled by the careful words of the watcher, who remains uninvolved as well as uninnocent. In each case, the myth of childhood provides a point from which we can safely negotiate the Australian experience.

The myth of childhood is, however, self-contradictory. It suggests the unity of the self to which we aspire, but it places that myth in the irrecoverable past. While Fiedler has noted a similar tendency in American fiction, it carries with it there also a sense of hope that the moment of security and harmony may yet be recovered on some future frontier. In Australia it provides no such confidence, but is pure nostalgia for qualities which cannot survive the reality of history.

In *Merry-Go-Round in the Sea*, Randolph Stow questions and tests this nostalgia, ultimately finding it wanting. The novel combines the personal quest for identity of the autobiography with the national search for origins and identity. Rob, the "boy" who is at its centre, is born into a Western Australian squatting family, which automatically finds its identity in the traditions of European gentry translated into pastoral traditions of the bush. As the book opens, just after the bombing of Pearl Harbor, these traditions are menaced from beyond the horizon by the threats both of the unknown and of violence, represented by Germans and Japanese (p.4). This violence is however also at the heart of the home which represents the boy's security within tradition. His grandmother's house, with its cellars of sweet- smelling apples and reminders of long-settled wealth, is convict-built. The family's prosperity rests on suppression, and beyond that on the displacement of the original inhabitants, traces of whom the boy finds later in his search for the meaning of the land. In this search he is at first accompanied by his cousin Rick, embodiment of all the family and nation stand for, but Rick is caught up in the violence, the other tradition which goes back to the Anzacs, and goes off to war. When he returns after serving as a prisoner of the Japanese, the war has taken his easy sociability. He is now no longer a guide so much as a part of the country to be searched. His experience has led him too far out of Rob's country for him to help:

> He sat down again, and went back to rolling cigarettes, while the boy watched him in the yellow light of the lamp. Rick was remembering something: he knew the signs. Rick's face

was changing, almost changing in substance, growing
clenched and closed, and his eyes had that dead look that
the boy hated, because there was nothing he could do about
it. (p.153)

The boy cannot find his own origins until he comes to terms
with the hatred and violent death Rick has known, and which
he discovers at the heart of his own country. Then when Rick
eventually decides "I don't want a family, I don't want a country,"
the boy is forced to recognize that the world he had believed
in "did not, after all, exist. The world and the clan and Australia
had been a myth of his mind, and he had been, all the time, an
individual." (p.275) He is left alone with the merry-go-round, a
symbol of another and another in a regress only finite in the
infinite change and sameness of the sea. The individual is left
alone, with no nation and no possible point of origin.

Stow is one of several recent Australian writers whose search
for an origin leads them only to the universal. The whole tendency
of Patrick White's work is towards the undifferentiated
transcendental. David Malouf, in *Harland's Half Acre*, tries to
project the security of childhood onto an artistic vision of the
future, but finds only paint and canvas and the bush. In his
earlier *An Imaginary Life*, he bypasses Australia entirely to find
a confrontation of the old world and the new in the Thrace of
imperial Rome, where Ovid is forced again to learn to speak, to
experience with the wild child the universal dawn of
consciousness. Even a nationalist writer like Rodney Hall, whose
Just Relations creates a mythic Australian community which tries
to preserve its past by insulating itself from the present, finishes
by collapsing its humanity back to nature.

Australian writers have found no heroic progenitors like
Aeneas of Rome or Arthur of Britain, nor revolutionary myths
of origin like those of the United States, France, or China. Nor
does nature supply the source denied by history. The poet Judith
Wright has worked her way back to the seeds of life in the
rhythms and powers of nature, but this contemplation leads
inevitably to a recognition of the violation of nature by white
settlement. Like others, Wright finds an answer to this violence
in the harmony that she finds between the culture of the
Aborigines and the land, but settlement disrupted this harmony
also. Xavier Herbert's savage depiction of conflict between the

races and between land and people seems truer to Australians' experience of their history, where hope has been continually frustrated by human malevolence or harsh nature. Thus the only secular myths of Australia lead either beyond the country or to *terra nullius*, the land of nothing, not as a legal fiction but as an historical fact. Those who were there have been dispossessed, their successors are still not at home. Australia is finally unable either to escape from its own reality or to redeem the hopes of Europe. Yet this situation is itself an image of contemporary western civilization as it reaches the end of the process of human and natural exploitation which commenced with the renaissance and the discovery of new worlds of apparently inexhaustible wealth and possibility. In learning to live without illusions, Australian writers are returning to Europe the reality it tried to escape by embarking on its course of infinite expansion.

Chapter 4

Canadian Voyagers and Garrisons

The cultural problem in the settler societies of Canada, Australia, and New Zealand is one of adapting imported traditions to local reality. This reality is produced by the new land, the hopes and expectations brought by the settlers with their tradition, and continuing domination by the original home countries or their metropolitan successors: that is, by land, labour, and capital. They resemble the United States in the importance given to the land among these factors in their development. Land, the physical environment, is the element which is new. For intending emigrants, it represents the opportunities denied in their homeland. Once in the new country, it constitutes at once the most obvious difference and the greatest challenge. Whether as frontier, wilderness or bush, the land changes the settlers and produces the kind of people they recognize as truly representative of the new society. At the same time, however, it challenges the values they bring with them, and so offers itself as a resource where the human spirit can be redeemed from evil. This feeling, originally cultivated in England by Wordsworth and his fellow Romantics, and incorporating Rousseau's view of civilization as necessarily corrupting, is developed explicitly by Thoreau in cultivated and urban New England.

The wilderness remains an insistent theme in new world fiction of the twentieth century. The myth of the true Australian as a battler pitted against the bush and the cities remains alive in Kylie Tennant's novels and Alan Marshall's stories, David Malouf contrasts the terrorism and blight of twentieth-century Europe with the untidy harmonies of the Australian landscape, and even as urban a writer as Frank Moorhouse celebrates the "Electrical Experience" by setting it against the ostensible simplicity of a country town. The same search for a return to nature can be found in the work of the New Zealand Maori

writers, or in writing from the Pacific North-West of America.
In America also, Jack Kerouac's *On the Road* inaugurates a whole
genre of novels and films about people trying to escape urban
complexity through continuous movement. This novel suggests,
however, a different wilderness in the new world, the cities that
the settlers have built and which represent a new fall, the evil
counterpart of the Eden they set out to find.

The cities in new world fiction are different from those of
the old world, which were built as monuments of civilization
and alternatives to rural poverty and idiocy. In Dickens or
Dostoevsky or Kafka, these cities become prisons that destroy
human hope. In the new world, the cities become jungles.
Although the hopes that John Dos Passos' characters bring to
Manhattan are thwarted, the city still has an energy which
promises a potential future. By *Last Exit from Brooklyn*, this
potential has vanished. Yet in Australia, where David Ireland
portrays the suburbs and their industrial plants as jungles which
trap their denizens in mazes of Kafkaesque fatality, people still
seek and find their Edens, in brothels amid the mangroves, in
pub bars, or in a solitary tree. The suburbs may represent the
perversion of the new world ideal, but they still offer a space
where the individual can create a life unburdened by the weight
of the old world culture. The cost of this freedom is, however,
the same brutalization suffered by rural settlers who found their
dreams destroyed by the hostile combination of land and capital.
So alienation, rather than being the product of a new land,
becomes universal. It is experienced differently in the new lands
because they lack the traditional structures which in the old world
supported the individual but which have now become the
mechanisms of the prison from which the only escape is through
the internal migration which deconstructs all meaning.

The settler societies continue to be engaged in a search for
the earthly home which constantly eludes them. The search is
complicated by the continuing arrival of new settlers, not only
from Europe but also from the poorer countries of Asia and Latin
America. These settlers challenge the culture of the older settlers,
which is in turn part of the environment the newcomers confront.
The frontier and its conflicts are thus constantly renewed, with
consequences that are explored in works as different as those of
Maxine Hong Kingston and Josef Skvorecky. Kingston writes of
the Chinese community of San Francisco, whose lives have been

intertwined with white society for more than four generations but who are still made to feel aliens in their own land. Skvorecky writes from the Czech migrant community of Canada, whose history is shaped by the double alienation of the imperial subjugation of their homeland and the strangeness of the community of their new home. For both writers, however, the new country offers the future their characters must construct. As individuals, they have been shaped by the culture of old worlds, but their expectations are given to them by the culture of the new. This leads them to join the other new world writers in the task of reshaping the landscape to provide unity for their conflicting desires.

I

Canada is both part of the shifting frontier of America and a separate entity which challenges aspects of the American dream. From its beginnings Canadian literature in English has been affected by the proximity of the United States, as well as by the existence of the separate society of New France, or French Canada. The Maritime Provinces are in some ways closer culturally to New England than they are to the rest of Canada, but British loyalties and economic conflicts have kept them apart from their southern neighbours. Similarly, geography draws the Prairies and British Columbia to the south at the same time that economic and political interests hold them to the east-west axis. The histories which separate Quebec and Ontario from the United States also separate them from each other. The result, according to Northrop Frye (1982), was the development of two voices in Canadian literature. The one, cultural nationalism, emphasizes a future built on the heroic achievements of the past. The other, heard in the regional literatures, places its emphasis on nature. In both he finds, however, a sense of the human isolated in a hostile environment, and in both a tendency to parochialism, whether of strident assertion or of complacency. These are both aspects of what he calls a garrison literature, where humans are conscious of the frailty of their puny settlements surrounded by a hostile and indifferent environment.

In "At the Cedars," the confederation poet Duncan Scott shows this sense of the precarious security which is the best the settler achieves in the home and family his skills protect. The poem opens with a salutation to the logger, Baptiste, and his children:

> You had two girls—Baptiste—
> One is Virginie—
> Hold hard—Baptiste—
> Listen to me.

The mention of the daughters, who are recalled again in the final verse, where the speaker says he does not know the name of the second girl, frames the story of their father's heroic clearing of the log jam and his insouciant greeting for death:

> As he floated along
> He balanced his pole
> And tossed us a song
> But just as we cheered
> Up darted a log from the bottom,
> Leaped thirty feet square and fair,
> And came down on his own.
>
> He went up like a block
> With the shock,
> And when he was there
> Kissed his hand
> To the land . . .
> (Brown and Bennett, pp.195–97)

But his daughter, who has been with some girls "Picking berries on the hillside," sees him fall, launches her canoe to go to him, and joins him in death. Baptiste's heroism thus encompasses the destruction of the little family for which he has worked. We are left to infer the home which the accident has left bereft of its garrison. Nature, which gives both berries and the death-dealing river, remains as indifferent as the crisp, almost banal, metre in which the poet encapsulates the images, excluding emotion. The human gesture becomes its own and only reward. Baptiste's existential stance is quite different from the heroic moments of United States literature, where hardship produces the virtues that build a nation and its prosperity.

Scott's poem combines the homeliness of the berries with the heroism of the logger, whose name associates him with the earliest

Canadians who conquered the wilderness before there was a nation. These French-Canadian *voyageurs* established the first garrisons, the agents' depots and, even further out, the solitary cabins of the trappers. Like the pathfinders of the United States, they provide the foundation for a national mythology which can transcend regional and cultural divisions. Setting out from Montreal, travelling in the bark canoes the Indians had taught them to use, they had before the War of Independence opened up the Mississippi basin and established the fur trade. Their traffic with Louisiana hemmed the English settlers in between the Appalachians and the Atlantic. The French Canadians were, however, doubly betrayed, first when they were ceded to England after the first Treaty of Paris in 1763, and then when they were cut off from their trade by the second Treaty of Paris which ended the War of Independence and ceded the Mississippi basin to the United States. Their consequent ventures to the northwest opened up the territory of modern Canada, but the profits passed largely to the British Hudson's Bay and North West Companies and their servants.

As settlement spread, the new regions were bound to the confederation by the garrisons of the Royal Canadian Mounted Police and by the English language which linked them to each other and to the capital. The voyageurs remained however as the link with the further past which gave Canada the icy north in place of the rich lands to its south. The northern cold offers Canada the same challenge and image of human frailty as the deserts of the centre furnish to Australia.

The exploits of the *voyageurs*, French and English, provided, with the Indian Wars and the rebellion of the thirteen old colonies, the points of origin for subsequent Canadian literature. From these points, boundaries could be drawn to distinguish Canada from both its southern neighbour and its European origins. When, after confederation in 1867, Canadian writing came to be characterized by an affinity with a demanding environment, pride in the achievements of exploration and settlement, and loyalty to its British institutions, trappers and agents could be used as symbols of the new nation rather than either its French or English components. Their personal alienation thus became a symbol by which later generations were able to assimilate their environment and overcome their differences.

While confederate Canada took pride in its British connections and its new world independence, it remained suspicious of both Britain and the United States. Their economic power and their indifference to Canadian interests threatened the ability of the new nation to prosper in its own lands. The response of Canadian writers was the development of a culture which asserted its difference. The *Canadian Magazine,* was established in 1871 as one of the organs of this cultural nationalism. In its first issue it published the opening episode of "Royalists and Loyalists," which expounded the issues in a serial set shortly after the American War of Independence. It condemns equally the perfidy of the French, the treachery of the American rebels and the pusillanimity of the British government in failing to crush them. The novelist, who is not named, attributes this failure to misplaced sympathy with fellow countrymen. He also, however, portrays the English at home as servile and oppressed, compared with the independent colonists.

The magazine's opening editorial explains the novel's serious purpose. All novelists, it asserts, have a responsibility to convey an accurate picture of reality. The reality portrayed in this novel teaches "a great political lesson—which many are slow to learn (and none more than our cousins across the line) that Canadians are Loyal but not necessarily *Royal*." The editor goes on to argue that Canadians "have a great mission of our own to accomplish" which will not be served by servility or blind obedience. He complains, in terms which anticipate subsequent English critics in Australia, that Canada lacks "those old, historical, and picturesque topographical associations and memories—those ancient mansions and castellated buildings, with their family histories and adventures" which enrich older literatures, but invites his readers to submit writing which will compensate for these disadvantages by attending to "the heavens above and the earth beneath and around us." Literary merit, he declares, can create a tradition from its own environment. (*Canadian Magazine,* vol.1, no.1, July 1871, pp.1–7).

The Canadian environment was, however, never simple. It included not only geographic but also social extremes. As well as the farming areas of Upper Canada or Ontario, which provided subjects for some of the earliest writings, there were the maritime provinces yielding meagre subsistence, the immediate obstacle of the Laurentian Shield and the further barrier of the Rockies, the harsh prairies and the wilds of the far north. The English-speaking communities were divided from each other not only by distance, but also by the proud French-speaking community of Quebec. These communities were strung out across the north of the expanding and confident democracy of the United States. The culture of tough independence engendered by this environment rested on the traditions of the isolated voyageurs, trappers and settlers. The writers of confederation described a Canada of natural beauty nurturing a people whose independence was underwritten by the values of the home and, behind it, the British and ultimately classical institutions which provided its ultimate guarantee. Their British institutions held Canadians together against the centripetal forces of geography and the southward pull of the United States, while their pride as free settlers countered the ignorance and indifference of England.

The new Canada looked to the old ideals of Eden to provide it with a national mission. The land provided in its emptiness new opportunities for individual freedom and prosperity, and in its harshness both a training in virtue and a direct encounter with nature unmediated by culture. The attempts of nineteenth century writers to develop from this experience a new understanding of human truth extend the work of English and American romanticism. As did Wordsworth or Thoreau, they found in nature a source of spiritual healing through which they could escape both the hardships of the frontier and the confusions of the modern age. Their poetry however tends to an affinity with the wild nature of Keats or Shelley that humbles humankind with its power rather than with the tranquility sought by Wordsworth. However, while this affinity may be valuable in itself, it is never sought for its own sake, but arises as a by-product of the struggles of exploration and settlement. This leads to a duality, similar to that found in American or Australian writing in the nineteenth century, which celebrates both the force of untamed nature that gives the individual access to ultimate truth, and the wealth of the cultivated landscape which nurtures a human society which unites in a single home the old cultures of England and America.

Charles Mair provides a vision of the latter kind in his elegaic "Summer" (1868; rev. 1901), where he imagines the wealth of the tilled fields yielding leisure in which the tillers can rest from their labours in dreams of romantic legend:

All the windrowed meadow's math,
Every note each small bird hath,
Every breeze by woods delayed,
Each cool place those woods have made!

So may I your treasures prove,
Richer still at each remove, . . .

Or, in quest of bygone themes,
Lapse into the realm of dreams,—

Dreams of old world chivalry,
Bout and joust and revelry;
Or, more suited to our land,
Dreams of forest chief and band . . .
                                                    (Klinck and Watters, p.81)

The quiet of the landscape exists so that the poet can escape into
his dreams of older myths. These myths, whether of Europe or
America, do not give meaning to the landscape, and so the intent
of the poem remains forced. It is the kind of poetry mocked by
Wilfred Campbell in "At Even" (1893):

I sit me moanless in the sombre fields,
The cows come with large udders down the dusk
One cudless, the other chewing of a husk,
                    . . . An old hen sits
And blinks her eyes. (Now I must rack my wits
To find a rhyme, while all this landscape reels.)
                                                    (Klinck and Watters, p.96)

The pastoral mode can be maintained only by ignoring the
necessities both of rhyme and of the mosquitoes and "June bugs"
which insist on disturbing our enjoyment.

The pastoral myth in Canada constantly collapses against
the reality of the Canadian winter which drives the settlers back
to their garrisons. Summer is not a time for enjoyment but for
the work of heaping up supplies, and relaxation comes, if at all,
only when adequate provisions have been stored behind safe
walls. Charles Roberts embodies these ideas in his poem "To an
Old Barn" (1893), where the security of the garrison is suggested
through the image of cattle that "in their shadowed stalls"

Nose-deep in clover fodder's meadowy scent
Forget the snows that whelm their pasture streams,
The frost that bites the world beyond their walls.
                              (Klinck and Watters, p.103)

The affinity of this world is not with the romantics, or even with
eighteenth-century pastoral mode of the two Oliver Goldsmiths,
but with the stark Anglo-Saxon poetry of *The Wanderer,* where
all human comfort is shadowed by the waiting storm and cold.
So Roberts symbolizes even the coming of spring with images
of darkness and uncertainty, the flight of the geese and

                     The sound
Of their confused and solemn voices, borne
Athwart the dark to their long Arctic morn . . .
         Charles G.D. Roberts, "The Flight of the Geese"
         (1893; in Klinck and Watters, p.103.)

The Canadian achievement has been to build these sanctuaries
for its garrisons, but its writers rarely forget either the cost of
their building or how precarious they remain. But if the protective
homes are the prize and the guarantee of settlement, paradoxically
the poets seem most at home when they step outside their walls
and discover from nature the truths that the culture of settlement
represses. In this poetry, nature is neither tamed nor hostile, but
provides in its vast indifference the opportunity for humans to
discover themselves.

Duncan Scott brings together these contradictory responses
in his meditative poem, "The Height of the Land" (1916), where
the speaker halts during a portage on the watershed between
Hudson's Bay and Lake Superior, posed exactly between the two
great facts of Canadian history and geography. The moment is
one of rest after the labour of the journey to this

. . . last portage and the height of land—:
Upon one hand
The lonely north enlaced with lakes and streams,
And the enormous targe of Hudson Bay,
Glimmering all night
In the cold arctic light;
On the other hand
The crowded southern land

With all the welter of the lives of men.
>   (Brown and Bennett, p.208)

The portage camp, where everyone else is asleep, is a temporary
sanctuary of security and rest. But stepping outside the camp,
the speaker hears the movement of primeval nature in the sound
of the "gathering of the waters in their sources." He broods on
the stress and welter of human life, but the place confers a peace
which makes life seem simple "as to the shepherd seems his
flock":

> A Something to be guided by ideals— . . .
> Making life lovelier, till we come to doubt
> Whether the perfect beauty that escapes
> Is beauty of deed or thought or some high thing
> Mingled of both . . . (p.208)

The Wordsworthian moment is, however, succeeded by
something far more savage, a vision of the rainbow as "The
ancient disturber of solitude" that

> Stirs his ancestral potion in the gloom,
> And the dark wood
> Is stifled with the pungent fume
> Of charred earth burnt to the bone
> That takes the place of air. (pp.208-9)

This nightmare vision is instantly linked with an incident from
the journey to the watershed, a stage when the travellers had to
force their way through a

> weird lakelet foul with weedy growths
> And slimy viscid things the spirit loathes,
> Skin of vile water over viler mud
> Where the paddle stirred unutterable stenches,
> And the canoes seemed heavy with fear . . . (p.209)

This image overshadows the conclusion of the poem, where the
speaker again works his way to peace in "The long light flow,
the long wind pause, the deep / Influx of spirit . . ." (p.210).
Nature can still our passions, but it cannot take away its own
terror.

The solitude which surrounds and dwarfs humans and their momentary refuges takes Canadian poetry back beyond the beneficent nature of the romantics to the bleaker world of Anglo-Saxon poetry. The myth of Canada is not Odysseus who finds his home, but the Wanderer for whom every home is merely a moment of warmth amid the surrounding darkness of space and time. In Scott's own poetry, the Wanderer appears in the guise of the paddlers on Lake Nipigon, singing "the hymns of the churches, while the dead water / Whispers before us," or of the Indian as a young mother who succours her child in the storm with her own blood, and in old age is left alone in the winter storm by her fellows

> Because she was old and useless,
> Like a paddle broken and warped,
> Or a pole that was splintered.

There she meets her end unmoving and uncomplaining, as she

> Saw two spangled nights arise out of the twilight,
> Saw two days go by filled with tranquil sunshine,
> Saw, without pain, or dread, or even a moment of longing:
> Then on the third great night there came thronging and
> thronging
> Millions of snowflakes out of a windless cloud;
> They covered her close with a beautiful crystal shroud . . .
>   (Klinck and Watters, p.153)

This is not the romantic unity in the mystery of nature, but the stoic acceptance of nature for what it gives and what it takes. In his prose story, "Labrie's Wife," Scott shows the tragic consequences brought on himself and others by the man who refuses to listen to nature, whose preoccupation with material concerns blinds him to the human truth in front of him. The land destroys even the desires of those who ignore it. The assimilation it offers to a wider nature remains, however, individual rather than social.

Unlike Scott and his fellows, Stephen Leacock is concerned with the vanity of the individual and the pretensions of local culture. He is the first Canadian to write in international terms, to take the land for granted and portray the established communities on their own terms. His writing is mid-Atlantic in its sensibility, his affectionate portrayal of small-town humours and characters in *Sunshine Sketches of a Little Town* (1912) secure in its regionalism. His urbanity is, however, that of the outsider, who achieves his detachment because his real commitment is to the entertainment of his city friends. Canada may be a mirror of the world, but the reflection itself is diminished. By ignoring the land which has shaped them, Leacock leaves his towns and their people detached from any reality but their own society.

Leacock's gentle mockery is quite opposite to the heroic visions of Hugh MacLennan or E.J.Pratt, who celebrate the triumph of Canadians over the wilderness as the culmination of the visions of the European renaissance. While Leacock attempts to assimilate Canadian reality into a greater Europe, these writers abrogate the heroic myths of Europe to celebrate the Canadian experience. Certainly, MacLennan takes a bleaker view of this experience in his novels, where he describes attempts to expiate the Calvinist guilt brought by the original Scots settlers. George Woodcock (1961) has suggested that in these works MacLennan provides variations on the theme of the return of Odysseus and his cleansing of his home, a further example of the new world finding its hopes mocked by its continuing involvement in old-world patterns of guilt and destruction. The main characters in these novels find the puritanism of the Canadian culture stifling, but their journeys of escape always lead them back home where the problems still wait. In his prose epic, however, he finds escape from the problems of actually constructing a life by chronicling the deeds of those who, then and now, have opened the wilderness to settlement.

The Seven Rivers of Canada (1961) is in form a travel book but in effect a celebration. MacLennan finds an escape from these betrayals of the present by his recovery of the stories of the earliest voyagers and settlers. He retells their history in tales of endurance in which heroic figures open up a vast new world, and the greatest of them all, Mackenzie, actually realizes the Elizabethan vision of a pathway to the Pacific. MacLennan however achieves this heroic escape from the stifling mundanities of the provinces by concentrating on the vastness of the landscape and consequently on the greatness of the achievements which overcame it. He shows the toil by which these achievements were won, but as it were at a distance and through a series of fixed portraits which place man in dominance at the centre of the landscape.

Similarly, in "Towards the Last Spike" (1952), E.J. Pratt keeps his attention on the larger view, the visions and achievements of the politicians, businessmen, surveyors and engineers who built the Canadian Pacific Railway and saved the union. He builds his poem from the dreams of the projectors, the visions and speeches of politicians, the magnitude of the feats of engineering and organization which bridged marshes and forced way for the rails through the mountains, and on the triumphal moment of completion. But as F.R. Scott suggests, this imperial vision omits the cost of the human labour which actually makes the empires:

> Where are all the coolies in your poem, Ned?
> Where are the thousands from China who swung
>   their picks with bare hands at forty below?
>   . . .
> Did they fare so well in the land they helped to
>   unite? Did they get one of the 25,000,000 CPR acres?
>   (1964) (Brown and Bennett, p.355)

The epic writers deliberately constructed a tradition from their vision of the interaction of man and nature combining to make a new world. By concentrating on the magnitude of the physical accomplishment, however, they lay stress on the importance of the land as an object of domination rather than on either the cultural structures of labour and profit the venturers impose on it or the changes the land makes to these structures. Scott lays stress rather on the interaction of land and people. In "Laurentian Shield" he suggests that an authentic tradition cannot be imposed, but must arise as the poet allows nature to shape its own words:

> Hidden in wonder and snow, or sudden with summer,
> This land stares at the sun in a huge silence
> Endlessly repeating something we cannot hear.
> Inarticulate, arctic,
> Not written on by history, empty as paper,
> It leans away from the world with songs in its lakes
> Older than love, and lost in the miles.
>
> This waiting is wanting.
> It will choose its language

When it has chosen its technic,
A tongue to shape the vowels of its productivity.

A language of flesh and of roses

Now there are pre-words,
Cabin syllables,
Nouns of settlement
Slowly forming, with steel syntax,
The long sentence of its exploitation.

The first cry was the hunter, hungry for fur,
And the digger for gold, nomad, no-man, a particle;
Then the bold commands of monopoly, big with machines,
Carving its kingdoms out of the public wealth;
And now the drone of the plane, scouting the ice,
Fills all the emptiness with neighbourhood
And links our future over the vanished pole.

But a deeper note is sounding, heard in the mines,
The scattered camps and the mills, a language of life,
And what will be written in the full culture of occupation
Will come, presently, tomorrow,
From millions whose hands can turn this rock into children.
                                    (1954) (Brown and Bennett, p.353)

Although this poem apparently starts with the Canadian landscape, it quickly reveals that its concern is with the landscape as language. The land waits to "choose its language," which it does by first choosing its "technic": the human arts and skills which produce the language as they shape the environment. However, as both Pratt and MacLennan have shown in their epics, the land itself chooses, by selection of the fittest, the technic—the art and skill—which will work in its harsh conditions. In this sense, the land itself produces the language. In another sense, the settlers and venturers, and the poets who follow them, learn to read the land as language, and this language in turn produces humanity, the "full culture of occupation" which will fulfill the new world's destiny. Both senses are aspects of the process by which language overcomes alienation so that land and people are assimilated to each other. But without the initial alienation, the people would not distance themselves sufficiently to see the land in its own terms rather than only in the terms imposed on it by the old world culture. This distancing is similar to the effect Ricoeur (1981) describes as a necessary part and effect of the process of reading. Without it there can be no assimilation.

In Scott's poem, abrogation follows assimilation. Rather than following the epic writers in finding a point of origin in an historical event, or the confederation poets in locating identity in the land, F.R. Scott locates Canada's identity in a future which will be produced by human effort. This effort abrogates the hopes of the new world by producing for the makers the physical capital—farms, railways, mines and mills—and extending through their work the cultural capital—human lore and language—which together enable people to inhabit the new lands and build a community in them. This culture of occupation will be fully itself, "a language of life," only if the people share fully in the wealth they have created. In this way their hands will "turn this rock into children." The desire of the settlers, rather than finding a mystical union with nature, is fulfilled through the children, symbol of both creativity and the future. In economic terms, labour, the settlers, bring their culture, or capital, to work on the land and produce not merely wealth but a new society or commonwealth: the hope of the middle ages now fulfilled in the new world.

Scott's vision is, however, still a part of the garrison culture. The plane "scouting the ice" can weave links between the "scattered camps and the mills," but it is too fragile, too small in the vast space, for us to believe that it "Fills all the emptiness with neighbourhood." The culture we find in Canadian writing is one of particular places, filled with human warmth maybe, but always looking out on emptiness, not yet offering a "full culture of occupation." In the work of Hugh MacLennan or Ethel Wilson these places may be cities like Halifax or Vancouver, or they may be the tiny cabins that keep the prairie at bay in the work of F.P. Grove or Sinclair Ross, but always we are aware of the land beyond them, indifferent to their concerns. Although this hinterland is like the Australian outback in its emptiness, even in its indifference it seems to have an heroic scale that lends grandeur to those who battle it. The Australian bush, on the other hand, seems rather to reduce or brutalize those who try to subdue it. This contrast represents a difference in distance. Although the success of settlement in both countries has depended finally on foreign markets, Canada is much closer to these than is Australia. Wealth has always returned to Canada in response to the flow of goods east down the St. Lawrence to Europe, or south through plains, rivers and lakes to the United States. The garrisons consequently have always been confident of their ultimate security. They are the furthest outposts of the new world of Europe.

The alienation of the Canadian landscape is nowhere expressed as strongly as in the works of Frederick Philip Grove, himself an immigrant who grounded his identity on a fiction of a romantic and aristocratic European past. However, his earliest published work in English, *Over Prairie Trails* (1922), is a grimly realistic account of the individual pitted against the wastes of northern Manitoba. The chapter "Snow" provides the dominating image of a man struggling through a virtually trackless waste of snow between tiny and isolated points of settlement which keep alive the light and warmth of home. The same image opens his first novel, *Settlers of the Marsh* (1965), with the further intensity that the two men struggling through the blizzard are migrants and strangers who are turned away at gunpoint from the first dwelling they find. One of these migrants, Niels Lindstedt, becomes the main character of the novel. The prairie marsh eventually yields him the material prosperity he has dreamed of in compensation for the poverty of Europe which destroyed his mother, but the marshes also destroy their people. The hardship of their lives turns the families in on each other, allowing prosperity to come only at the price of conviviality. The resulting tensions lead to brutal sexual exploitation and suppression, which in turn destroy Niels' life and drive him to murder. With savage irony, material prosperity leads to complete alienation, individual and social, which is scarcely redeemed by the new start Grove allows Niels in the concluding chapter.

Isolation and alienation provide the structure also of Grove's last novel, *The Master of the Mill*, although this is set in a small mill-town linked directly to the wider world by ties of money and politics and by the railroad that brings its supplies and carts away its products. The dominating image is the mill itself, a vast pyramidal structure bathed in white light from its own electricity plant. The mill is a symbol of the power that man creates and which then controls his life. But the mill is set against the empty prairie, and in the climactic scene both mill and town are isolated by blizzards. The wintry weather is central to the owner's plans which conclude the action of the novel, but they also symbolize its theme, as the machines finally drive the men who work them back into the cold. For a while, the novel suggests, the machines will continue to feed them, but eventually humankind will dwindle to a remnant living in the wastes from which they first came.

The theme of the novel is not specific to Canada, but rather uses a Canadian mill as a symbol of the whole industrial process. Although the isolation of the town is a symbol of the alienation of its people, the agency is the mill which is a metonym for the machinery which frees humanity from work only to deprive it of function. The new world of the novel is not geographic but historical, a world in which the industrial revolution has finally created a system of production and finance which centralizes all power in the hands of the ruthless few. Although Grove gestures in his conclusion toward a collective alternative to this process of destruction, the logic of his novel leads to the fascism of total authority, of society made over in the image of the machine. Yet, although this theme is universal, the culmination of the European renaissance, the emptiness of Canada and the absence of resistant social structures makes it the appropriate place for the disastrous fulfilment of all the hopes of the new world. The mill owner indeed builds a new and mechanical Eden, but it is one from which Satan expels the human laborers, leaving himself in sole possession. The death of the Satanic plotter at the hands of the strikers he has provoked is the only slender hope of escape that the author allows us. His study of modern alienation thus becomes an abrogation to the new world of the culmination of all world history. The bleakness of his work seems at home in Canada, but it is a product of global rather than provincial reality.

Toward the end of this century, the Czech-born writer Josef Skvorecky has brought a different sense of global reality to bear on the Canadian experience. The title of his novel *The Engineer of Human Souls* is taken from Stalin, who used the expression to define the task of the writer or intellectual. Skvorecky's work shows, however, that no writer can hope to control the reality of a world which produces Stalinism and Nazism. His protagonist has grown up in Czechoslovakia, where he has known first democracy and then Nazi and Communist domination. He has experimented with painting and music as a student, worked as a forced laborer, attempted sabotage to the German war effort, seen his friends betrayed by Nazis and communists, enjoyed the Prague spring and finally escaped to Canada, where he works as a lecturer in English. The novel consists of his reminiscences of his life, punctuated by the epistolary biographies of several of his fellows, and juxtaposed with his involvement in teaching and in the emigre politics of Toronto. Behind these activities looms the Canadian landscape, and within them is entwined what he perceives as the extraordinary naivete of his students, citizens of a new world. Although his task as a teacher is to involve the students in the ironies of the writers who have created the new world tradition—Poe, Hawthorne, Twain, Crane, Fitzgerald, Conrad and Lovecraft—he finds their detachment from these worries offers hope of a new start, of a world which, by hoping only for love and happiness, may escape at last from the age-old cycle of guilt and revenge. The novel ends, however, not with this hope, but with a return to the confusions of the emigres, new disasters in Europe, and the last communication from the only true innocent in the book, Lozja, the peasant whose moral blindness has given him wealth and power in an inhuman regime. The attempt to abrogate the old world ends by merely embroiling the new world more deeply in its deceits. Yet hope may lie in the very fact that these can now be seen from the detachment of a new world. Unlike Kundera's characters, Skvorecky's protagonist is engaged in the real work of building a new society among the young.

Both the visions by Canadian writers of a future and their awareness of continuing entanglement in the guilts of the past escape from the need for an originary justification and from Derrida's strictures against presence. The landscape and the nation are not things present which we constantly fail to invoke by a language which destroys them as it names them, but things brought into being by the act of naming, of differentiating them from the speakers and from other histories. Desire escapes from the yearning of Rousseau or Keats for the undifferentiated unity which is supposed to belong to infancy and is in fact attainable only in death. Instead, as in the works of Melanie Klein and her followers, identity is described as arising from the moment of differentiation. Identity does not come from the unattainable I, the self for the self. Rather, the self is a social product, born only in the recognition of the I-thou. It creates and is created by a language of distinctions arising from a society which, as Levi-Strauss argues, is itself to be understood as a system of exchanges which constantly produce both its structures and their constituent units. We need to recognize that these exchanges are both symbolic and material, and include the constant exchange of work for goods which subdues the landscape, and produces the culture which defines the individual.

When the structures of exchange are transposed to a new world like North America, the exchanges are interrupted or distorted, and new patterns arise. The conditions of the new world frustrate some expectations of the old system, enable others to be fulfilled. As the individuals in the new land strive to establish equilibrium, they have an opportunity denied them in older lands to create the patterns which will fulfill their desires. These structures of desire and its fulfilment determine the identity of the new world cultures.

Canadian literature presents the history of a new culture growing from the conflicts between a particularly unyielding environment and a highly determined structure of imported institutions and expectations. These tensions are embodied in the geographic tensions between the drive to the north and west and the pull toward the south. The former represents manifest destiny, the opportunity to carve out of the harsh terrain a new domain for free people. The latter represents the other part of the hope, the golden dream of prosperity. The conflicts between French and English speaking Canadians, and between European and native cultures, are an expression of the contradictions imported from Europe with the original hopes, where freedom for one meant oppression for another. These conflicts are embodied in the languages of Canada and their literatures, but their resolution depends on a future which will reconcile their conflicting messages. The resolution is made easier, however, by the security of Canada's place in the new world of European culture. In Africa, by contrast, the resolution of present conflicts depends on the recovery of a past from which European culture has alienated contemporary African societies.

CHAPTER 5

LANDS OUTSIDE EDEN: THE CASE OF AFRICA

The writers of the new nations of Africa and Asia are in a quite
different political and cultural situation from that of either the
settlers of America, Australia and New Zealand, or of the native
peoples that the settlers dispossessed and made a minority in
their own lands. In Africa and Asia the settlers themselves have
always been the minority, but have been able to impose, with
greater or less success, their own institutions on the original
cultures. In Africa, even national boundaries represent colonial
interests rather than indigenous languages, cultures or societies.
For the rulers, the land was an object of desire, to be cut up and
used for their own purposes. When, as in India, the indigenous
political structures were too strong to allow this to occur, the
structures themselves were appropriated to the purposes of the
new rulers. But whereas in the Indies or America these purposes
had been the planting of a new Eden, from the Portuguese onward
Europeans viewed Africans as a fallen race, excluded forever
from Paradise.

   In both Africa and the Indies, a literature of imperialism was
produced from the ruling minority by writers like Conrad, Kipling
or Maugham. These writers perceive the land as the hostile factor,
and deprive the native people of any separate identity, either
reducing them to colorful adjuncts of the land or showing them
merely as agents of imperial domination. In the literatures of the
majorities, by contrast, the primary elements of the dialectic are
the people and their masters. The masters impose their desire
on the people, whose labour is necessary to fulfill it. The
individuals may acquiesce in their loss of identity, or draw on
their own culture for the strength to resist. Whichever option
they choose, the desire active in history remains that of the rulers,
which exerts itself against the traditional culture. In this struggle
the land ceases to be an independent element in the dialectic and

becomes instead an object of contention. The struggle pits the subjugated people against the culture which dominates them. It is not ended by political independence, but only by full possession of the land and its culture, that is, of the economic, political and educational institutions which determine its production of its material future.

In Asia, European imperialism largely maintained indigenous social, and even political, structures as the basis of its own power. Native rulers and intellectuals maintained the high forms of traditional culture, even if they were devalued by comparison with imported forms and became divorced from everyday life. The task of contemporary writers has been to make new these traditions by reconciling them with the political, economic and educational realities of the new nations which have succeeded the colonial states. In the work of R.K. Narayan this reconciliation takes the form of giving a wider voice to local ways. Raja Rao, on the other hand, attempts the more ambitious task of reconciling the high cultures of India and Europe. Both, however, belong with their fellow writers in English to a wider literature which encompasses work in all the languages of the sub-continent.

Writers from the native cultures of Africa confront a deeper dislocation and therefore a more difficult task. The resolution of present conflicts in their countries depends on the recovery of a past from which European culture has alienated their contemporary societies. To establish their cultural independence they must join the postcolonial present in continuity with the precolonial past. While this joining is as much a political as a cultural act, it is itself subject to the more urgent imperative of resisting colonialism in the present. Writing is perceived less as personal expression than as a call to national solidarity and action. The recovery of their past which this entails is at the same time an assertion of their right to the future which was the first of their property to be usurped by imperialism. Whereas in America and the Pacific, the invaders at first placed the natives outside history as noble savages, in Africa the slave trade placed them outside the bounds of humanity. Slavery denied them the right not only to history but even to compassion.

But while the slavemasters could suppress their slaves' human identity they could not obliterate it. It returned as the image of an innate savagery which threatened their civilization and even their identity. This fear of the savage who jeopardizes our society, our home and our womenfolk is intensified by our recognition of the same forces in our own nature. These fears were projected by later settlers also onto the Indians of the American woods, who came to represent not noble savages but the dark otherside of nature. Even more, however, Africa itself became the image of the other, the dark continent which must be subjugated to European civilization lest it overthrow all values. The first act in this subjugation was the denial of any reality to the Africans' experience and knowledge of their own world.

In the introduction to his anthology of twentieth-century African literature, Chinweizu writes that "African popular literature, being mostly 'folk-tale' is an unabashedly functional literature through which the outlook and values of its makers are manifest, and through which those of its hearers and readers are shaped" (Chinweizu, 1988, p.xx). His anthology serves the same function, taking modern African literature out of the context of "Euromodernism" and establishing it instead on the foundations of an indigenous tradition stretching back some 5000 years. In making his selection, he excludes not only all work from European and Arab settler societies, but also anything that he views as assimilationist, as trying to reduce African experience to the supposedly universal, which he identifies as actually Eurocentric. The resulting anthology is not a manifesto, but a testament of black cultural independence. It simultaneously proclaims and establishes a tradition.

This black tradition is necessarily quite alien to even the most sympathetic white writers working in Africa. Although their work is as political as the black writing, it belongs in the literary tradition of imperialism. They view life from a point of privilege, however courageously they may work to undermine that privilege. But while the earlier writers of imperialism were able to restrict their attention to the moral dilemmas of individuals in an enclave detached from its supporting society, contemporary white writers in Africa, and particularly in South Africa, are enmired in the politics of their society. This gives their work a dimension of realism lacking in the imperial writers but already clearly present in Olive Schreiner's apparently non-political novel, *Story of an African Farm*.

In Schreiner's novel, the separation of the white characters from the land and its people is absolute. Rather than being an Eden of peace or productivity, the farm is a place of privation and bondage. Tant'Sannie, a gross and ignorant Boer isolated from other people by her insensitivity and selfishness, nevertheless has total power over the lives of those who live on the farm. Her ignorance gives her into the clutches of the English confidence-man, Bonaparte Blenkins, and together they crush the generous spirits of the children and of the German farm-manager who has given them such education as they have had. In desperation, Lyndall, the orphan under Tant'Sannie's control, vows that when she grows and is strong, she will "hate everything that has power, and help everything that is weak." This time however never comes, and at the end of the novel she is left only to the care of a man himself too weak to gain her love and unable to preserve her life.

Although the children in the novel are at home in the harsh landscape, and even respond to it with love, they lack any language with which to express their feelings. The natives, who had a language shaped by the bush, appear in the novel only as dumb figures watching from the margins. The Kaffers (sic), from whom the whites might have learned understanding, are excluded from Sunday service because "Tant'Sannie held that they were descended from apes, and needed no salvation" (p.40). We hear only Tant'Sannie's Hottentot maid, and her few words serve merely to express the bitterness of her suppression. She rejoices in the dismissal of the old German manager because "It was so nice to see the white man who had been master hunted down" (p.66). The children therefore are left to find their own words, to shape their own meanings from the landscape. Only Waldo succeeds, as he comes to recognize that the native peoples understood the land in the way he can only feel, and which the European concepts he finds in his books are unable to unable to express. He responds to Lyndall's remark that books do not tell everything with the observation that "What you want to know they never tell" (p.17). He then shares with her his meditations on the landscape and its paintings:

> "Sometimes . . . I lie under there with my sheep, and it seems that the stones are really speaking—speaking of the old things, of the time when the strange fishes and animals lived here that are turned into stone now, and the lakes were here; and then of the time when the little Bushmen lived here, so small and so ugly, and used to sleep in the

wild dog holes, and in the 'sloots,' and eat snakes, and shot the bucks with their poisoned arrows. It was one of them, one of these old wild bushmen, that painted those," said the boy, nodding toward the pictures—"one who was different from the rest. . .

He used to kneel here naked, painting, painting, painting. . . . Now the Boers have shot them all, so that we never see a little yellow face peering out among the stones. . . . And the wild bucks have gone, and those days, but we are here. But we will be gone soon, and only the stones will lie on here, looking at everything like they look now." (pp.18–19)

Although he thinks him ugly, Waldo can identify with that naked Bushman and the countryside until he too is able to carve a stick to express a dream of humanity's search for truth and wisdom. Yet, despite this communion with the land and its people, Waldo, like Lyndall, eventually fails in his quest for a reason for living. They are destroyed not by the harsh and unforgiving bush in which their lives have been led, but by people who use power without understanding, and by their preachings of a God Who knows only vengeance without love. This God Who separates people from the land and from their own feelings is also the one Who separates them from each other. Lyndall, who does not hear the stones speak, has only her will to draw on. This takes her on a path of her own, to a man who equals her in strength, but her inability to share her life keeps her alienated from the land and brings her ultimately to destruction. Waldo is able to share his vision with only one other, a stranger who stays only long enough to comprehend the vision, and then Waldo too is left alone, unable to realize the unity he alone of all the characters feels with the land.

In its treatment of the fate of women trapped by the land in an isolation from which marriage or money offer the only escape, *The Story of an African Farm* is a variation on the theme of Miles Franklin's Australian work, *My Brilliant Career*. Franklin however leaves Sybil's story unfinished, leaving open the possibility of a third avenue of escape, through using her intelligence as a writer. This was in fact the route that Schreiner herself took, but it is not available to her heroine, Lyndall, who is as strong and as intelligent as Sybil. Lyndall decides early that the only thing that can help her is "to be very wise, and to know everything—to be clever" (p.13). But while knowledge can give her strength, it cannot bring her into harmony with the land and people that surround her. Sybil is similarly alienated by the coarse or brittle materialism of the people who surround her, but she finds some individuals who offer her at least partial understanding. Sybil's resilience in adversity allow the reader to infer that she will find a way of escape, and that if only men could recognize their foolishness all women could find their freedom. Lyndall, however, finds understanding only from Waldo, who is himself unable to find any avenue of escape. The Stranger who impregnates her and causes her death matches her strength but offers her no understanding. The only life they can lead together is therefore away from her place and her people. She is trapped in an isolation as complete as that of the plantation widow in the *Wide Sargasso Sea*, Jean Rhys's study of the woman trapped by gender and race in the West Indies after the ending of slavery. In each case, the structures which separate people in the old world are intensified by the circumstances of the new, which destroy the possibility of people working together to create a culture that will join them with each other and the land. The land—bleak in Schreiner, fecund but corrupting in Rhys, but in each case offering the possibility of fulfilment to those who learn to love it—becomes instead a prison which denies them any possibility of liberation.

Joseph Conrad's *Heart of Darkness* crystallizes this image of Africa as a prison, a dark continent utterly alien to the white man and his values. Significantly, the novel does not begin on the Congo, the river that, "its tail lost in the depths of the land" (p.30), penetrates the last unknown and thus offers the narrator of the main story, Marlow, the opportunity of adding to his experience. Instead it starts on the Thames in London, and moves from there to a city in continental Europe, presumably Brussells. Both cities are centres of imperialism, but whereas Marlow's listener recalls London as the home of navigators and adventurers, Marlow portrays Brussels as a "whited sepulchre" where, in front of a map covered with all the colours of imperialism, two attendants guard like fates the "door of Darkness." The difference between the two cities is that, whereas the English navigators dared to follow some sort of vision, the directors of Belgium sit at home concerned only with profit, completely indifferent either to the welfare of their colonies or the fate of their agents. The distinction Conrad makes may be coloured by his national preference: he might equally well have chosen to portray English colonial officials and Belgian adventurers. Their contemporaries did, however, undoubtedly see the Belgian colonists as peculiarly cruel and avaricious, and the Congo offered the naked spectacle of colonialism stripped of the ceremony and efficiency which concealed its economic foundations in more established empires. The images of London and Brussels therefore serve as a contrast of imperial ideology and reality.

Africa offers Conrad, or Marlow, nothing but images of the brutality and destruction wrought on the land by colonialism. His first images of the continent are of a barren shore, scattered outposts of idle soldiery, and a lone French warship, its interior poisoned with fever, aimlessly firing shells into the jungle. Arrived at the river, he encounters black convicts chained in workgangs, passing him with "that complete, deathlike indifference of unhappy savages" or lying in the shade, waiting "in attitudes of pain, abandonment and despair" for the death which is their only relief. He links the fate of the natives explicitly with the aggression of imperialism, reflecting that "They were called criminals, and the outraged law, like the bursting shells, had come to them, an insoluble mystery from the sea" (pp.35–7).

Behind the tyranny of law in this colony lies a moral indifference more evil than active vice:

> I've seen the devil of violence, and the devil of greed, and the devil of hot desire; but, by all the stars! these were strong, lusty, red-eyed devils, that swayed and drove men—men, I tell you. . . . But as I stood on this hillside, I foresaw that in the blinding sunshine of that land I would become acquainted with a flabby, pretending, weak-eyed devil of a rapacious and pitiless folly. (p.36)

Imperialism in the high age of capitalism can no longer carry on its task of plunder in the guise of adventure, but Conrad attributes this moral decline not to capitalism itself but to a darkness at the heart of Africa which corrupts the people who come to lift it. When Marlow looks at London, he sees behind its present prosperity a darkness first lifted by the Romans who came not as colonists but as conquerors, bringing

> robbery with violence, aggravated murder on a great scale,
> and men going at it blind—as is very proper for those who
> tackle a darkness. The conquest of the earth, which mostly
> means taking it away from those who have a different
> complexion or slightly flatter noses than ourselves, is not a
> pretty thing when you look at it too much. What redeems
> it is the idea only. An idea at the back of it; not a sentimental
> pretence but an idea; and an unselfish belief in the idea—
> something you can set up, and bow down before, and offer
> a sacrifice to . . . (29–30)

This is a form of social Darwinism, the justification of pain and
suffering by the survival of the fitter to build a higher civilization.
Conrad avoids racism, but surrenders to the ideology of
imperialism. The historical mission of Europe, beginning with
the Romans, is to impose its standards on new worlds and so
lift them out of darkness. Kurtz, as Marlow discovers, differs
from the other officials of his company, mucking around in the
dirt in pursuit of their own sordid gain, because he has come
to Africa with just such an ideal, to make each station "like a
beacon on the road towards better things, a centre of trade of
course, but also for humanizing, improving, instructing" (p.47).
But Africa has corrupted him as he has pursued his dream. He
has taken part in its dark rites, consumed the flesh of its people
literally as well as metaphorically, and its darkness has consumed
him. Marlow returns defeated to Europe, covering his and Kurtz's
failure with a sentimental fiction. Yet in exposing this fiction to
his companions, he also reveals the hollowness of the claims of
imperialism and the vulnerability of its own standards. The whites
are thwarted in their desire to impose their culture on the land
because they ignore the people whose culture already possesses
it.

    These standards become the central issue in later white
writing in Africa, and particularly in South Africa, where realities
of politics have forced the fiction into a pattern which combines
the isolation of privilege against its own claims to authority.
Whites enjoy the fruits of black labour, but this enjoyment denies
them their desire for involvement with the land and its native
community. Whatever lives they find or make, their values
eventually force them into conflict with the barriers erected
between the races. The suppression of the blacks denies to all
races the possibility of full humanity or autonomy. Even in an

historical novel like Andre Brink's *An Instant in the Wind*, the social imposition of racial distinctions contradicts what its two characters learn from the land and each other about their true selves. We know from the beginning that the woman is doomed to betray the slave on whom she depends for survival, but she is equally destroyed by the knowledge she has gained of their common humanity. When she enters the city that represents safety, she loses the self she has found in the bush.

Conrad uses a number of voices to lead us to the heart of Africa's darkness. These voices all come to us quietly, through the other darkness that surrounds a boat on the Thames in the moments between the full flood and the ebb of the evening tide. They are brought directly to us by the unnamed narrator, who allows us to listen with his companions as Marlow recalls his voyage to Africa and up the river, brings to our inner mind the images of what he has seen, and at the centre of them places the enigma, the voice and finally the figure of Kurtz. Then, having finally brought him into the action, he kills Kurtz in two now-famous phrases: "The horror! The horror!" and "Mistah Kurtz—he dead!" (p.72) Kurtz's last words condense the reality of his experience of the Africa into which the broken English of the announcement of his death assimilates him. Yet at the same time the multiplicity of voices, and the careful choice of images which will enable us to see through Marlow's eyes, make it evident that we are encountering a particular Africa, an Africa produced by the whole European culture represented by Marlow, by the Belgian trading company, by the English navigators, and by the successful men-of-affairs listening in their boat on the Thames. But although this Africa may be produced by the voices of Europe, its truth remains outside them, pointed to but not captured by that elusive epithet, "The horror!"

The white writers of South Africa live in the midst of this horror produced by their predecessors. It presses on them daily as a political reality which shapes their personal lives, their careers as writers, the language available for their use. Even a simple love story is changed by the involvement, potential or actual, of the lovers in the politics of division which force on them choices incompatible with the unity which is the end of desire. In *States of Emergency* (1988), Andre Brink engages quite directly with this complexity in a novel whose twin starting points seem to be Derrida and Conrad. The book, described as "Notes towards a love story" begins with the receipt by the narrator, a writer, of a manuscript story of love sent to him by a girl of whom he knows nothing except her name, Jane Ferguson. This prompts him to reflect on her existence, on his own stories, on possible stories and how they come into existence:

> Beginnings fascinate me no end. That disquieting moment when the writer becomes witness to the translation of mere possibility into the signs of a new system, branding the paper. Suddenly, instead of unlimited potential, there are facts— a presence, a thereness—to be respected; or at the very least, graces to be acknowledged. Through words relationships are established which conjure up awesome horizons; suddenly one has to take responsibility for whatever tracks are followed to whatever horizon. No matter if it remains an eternally elusive horizon. The tracking process has begun and must be followed through. (p.17)

The first sentence explicitly opens the argument with the epistemologists, particularly Derrida, that he conducts throughout the book. Here, he takes issue with Derrida's insistence that there can be no beginnings by examining the consequences which flow from any beginning. This examination opens the central issue of the novel, the responsibility for our actions, including our words, which makes sense only if these actions affect a reality beyond themselves, even although this reality comes into existence only through the words. This reality is implied in the first sentence, where beginnings fascinate the writer "no end"—once begun, they cannot be contained. Yet, as he also acknowledges later, the beginning opens up a past as well as a future. Just as his lovers compulsively exchange their pasts, so, as their love becomes his narrative, they produce both the whole "weight of history": "the presentness of all . . . past selves" and the "mythology" which "'represents' humanity" (p.69). When the lovers proclaim, "I love," he asks,

> do they not already include all my own previous experience of love, and yours, and of all others who have been involved with it? An entire history and literary tradition converge in us. . . . At every moment meanings tumble into *this* love from outside, while at the same time, from inside, it keeps spilling over its own boundaries. (p.103)

He then quotes Derrida to the effect that the *hymen* that signifies the boundary implies both transgression and celebration of unity. But just as lovers cross the boundaries of their own being, so the text also transgresses its own borders. When Derrida says "There is nothing outside the text," he also implies that the text itself is boundless. Love and its story cannot be separated from each other, or from the whole of history of which they are part.

To immerse ourselves in a text, either as writers or readers, is thus to change ourselves by absorption in another reality. Paraphrasing Gadamer, he suggests that the text "demands a moment of alienation, a "losing" of the I in the text in order to find it: in this way appropriation also becomes divestiture. Or, adapting this to his own view of literature, the writer explains that

> just as the text detaches itself from the world in order finally
> to be restored, in changed form, to the world, the reader,
> through the process of reading, is also first withdrawn from
> the world, transformed, and then restored. In this resides
> the element of risk which lends the adventure its sense of
> 'value': it is *worth while* running this risk. (p.75)

Detaching these theoretical comments from their context in the narratives of Brink's novel distorts their sense, for they are not presented as a connected theory but as meditations the writer's work compels him to. The narratives create characters and histories for which the writer must take responsibility. But if every text is linked to the whole of reality, if any history involves all history, then the writer's responsibility for his narrative makes him responsible for this moment of his life in which the whole of history is present. By entering into this text, the reader takes on this responsibility. The change which he risks is a change not only in himself but in the world for which he becomes responsible. The text becomes a part of his history, his cultural capital, and so produces a new self in new relationship to the land and its people. This textual obligation is made more urgent by the recurrent interpolation of history, in the guise of the violence of the South African Emergency of 1985, into fiction until the boundary between the two is destroyed. The first of these interpolations comes just after the narrator has written that "nothing can invade this little room" where his dream character has escaped the mysterious harassment of the strangers in the van. Then, knocking at the writer's real door, comes the black activist, Milton Thaya. "Mister Mtzuze, he said, was dead; 'necklaced' the night before" (p.8). The horror that Conrad found in the jungle now strikes at the blacks, but the responsibility for it has now shifted to the whites who have produced the history which generates it.

This horror is one of the possibilities produced by history in the multiple narratives of Brink's novel. Its frame is given by the writer's own problems in producing a narrative. Within this we have the two stories of Jane Ferguson: the love story she has written, and the story of her own love that the narrator reconstructs from her diary. These are involved in the politics, and therefore in the horror, through the figure of her lover, the white activist Chris de Villiers, who is on another level of fiction the real person behind the fictitious persona of Clive de Vos. Jane's fiction in turn provokes the narrator to construct a fictitious love story of Philip and Malan, a story for which he offers four possible beginnings. This story is interrupted by Milton's incursions, but the writer then chooses to involve Milton directly in his fiction by including Melissa and Philip separately in his covert acts of resistance. But Milton himself is, of course, real only in the world of the narrator, himself a fiction of the author. Yet, just as he represents real forces of historical resistance, so the fiction is constantly interrupted by incursions of the documented suppression of this resistance by the instruments of the Emergency proclaimed by the government.

The multiple narratives of Brink's novel have the same effect on the reader as looking at an exhibition of pictures and words in an unknown language. We can recognize images, give them meaning from our own experience, but the context, the linguistic and cultural grammar which would link them to their author's history, is lacking. We are forced instead to make our own narratives, to incorporate them in our own lives. The changes we make to ourselves in order to do this determine our own history. The process of sorting out its images and narratives into patterns of history and fiction is a matter of deciding truth and value. Although these choices are made with words, we are not free to make them without regard to the realities of the world the words signify. Thus, in constructing our own narrative from his work, we shape the history of which it makes us a part.

The individual narratives repeat a characteristic structure of white South African fiction, as the characters' private careers and loves shatter against the blind powers of oppression, symbolized by the interrogation rooms of the police and the tanks and guns of the army. So Chris de Villiers's work as a doctor brings him against the casual brutality of the system and forces him to make the choice between acquiescence and resistance. His love involves the hitherto unpolitical Jane Ferguson in his commitment, and leads both of them to their deaths. This story, which the narrator tells from her diaries, runs parallel, even in place and incident, to the story he constructs of the affair between Philip Malan and Melissa, which reaches its climax, or its end, when they take part together in university demonstrations against police suppression. Yet the narrator insists that these stories do not constitute a novel, but are merely "Notes towards a love story," as he heads his text. Although by disclaiming the certainty of the novel he reflects the general postmodernist distrust of authority, his fragmentary structure, which lacks even a determinate ending, is also a response to the specific situation of South Africa. The glimpses of the moral abdication of the State President, and intrusions of guns and police, which kill three of the novel's major characters as well as children and wayfarers who just happen to be in the wrong place, bring history directly into the fiction in the way that politics comes directly into the private lives of South Africa. Where it is impossible to keep things apart, it is also impossible to combine them in a rational pattern. Thus structuralism is impossible, as much an affront to reason, as apartheid:

> To keep things apart, distinct, separate (man and woman; life and death; beginning and end; the inside and outside of a text; life and story), to define them in terms of their exclusivity rather than in terms of what they have in common, must end in schizophrenia, in the collapse of the mind which tries to keep the distinctions going. In this lies the failure of apartheid, and the failure, as I see it, of structuralism. What is suppressed, Jung said somewhere, comes back to take its bloody revenge. And surely the most terrible revenge must come from the denial of the fluid oneness of things in favour of the principle of isolation. (pp.195–96)

This is also the failure of Philip Malan, whose attempt to keep separate his career and politics, his love and his marriage, leads eventually to the collapse of them all. His love gives him only a vision of happiness, of unity, which remains unattainable, because only for brief instants—during one concert, one demonstration, one orgasm—is he ever completely one. Jane Ferguson and Chris de Villiers find unity only because they sacrifice their lives to it. The book implies that only such sacrifice, which makes the personal totally public, can provide a basis for a new Africa.

A recurring image in the novel is the ruined garden of the hotel or rural guest-house where the lovers are alone with each other. The garden, like the island of woodland in the city, is threatened by fires which injure its beauty and bring the police to destroy its calm, but it remains a symbol of the possible recovery even in Africa of an Eden which will unite nature and art, land people and culture. This possibility is invoked by the last words of the book, which presumably are those of the narrator, but could be spoken by any of the lovers:

> If ever we wander through that deserted garden again, in a dream perhaps—the cries of ghost peacocks, of hadidas, of Valkyries, of mountain eagles soaring over the cliffs—and an autumn leaf drifts down to settle on your head and you grant me the wish that should by rights be yours, what shall I ask? I don't know. I honestly don't know. Perhaps only the freedom, the openness, the endlessness—the silence, as you called it—of a country for which the future is still possible, a love not yet circumscribed, a story not yet written. (pp.243–44)

The story not yet written will turn the wilderness of Camoens and Conrad into a garden, and will welcome into it the native peoples whom the chroniclers condemned or disregarded. In their own literature, however, the writers of these native people see the land as already a garden, hallowed by the creating mother and by generations of use. The only wildernesses are areas left for the gods to continue their sustaining activities, or places made barren by European despoilers. Chinua Achebe shows how European government and religion drove a division between the people and the practices which had sustained them on their land. In "A Wind and a Boy" (Malan, 1988), Bessie Head dramatizes this division in the image of the boy free as the wind in his land until he is killed by a truck that fails even to stop. A writer like

Mtutuzeli Matshoba, who grew up in Soweto, shows how the collective life of its people makes even an urban wasteland into a place of life and sanctuary for those who make it their home. This possibility is contradicted in the extensive prison literature, where the attempts of individuals to construct meaningful lives for themselves and their families lead inevitably to the ultimate segregation and degradation of prison and forced labour. These writers show, in their various circumstances, the struggle the native people are forced to take up against the conquerors of the land and their culture of division. This remains true even in work written in the African nations which have been given political independence only to fall into the hands of rulers concerned only with their own power and material prosperity. Achebe's 1987 novel, *Anthills of the Savannah*, examines the corruption of those who exercise power, while Wole Soyinka's prison notes, *The Story of A Man*, show how the new military caste, separated from their land and people, uses the same methods as its racist counterparts to uphold its power. For all these writers, the central need is the integration of the modern commercial and industrial world with both the traditional and the universal cultures and values that support the individual identity that imperialism denies.

The struggle against imperialism begins in the language and form of the works of black writers. The act of writing in English itself establishes their claim to be heard, to speak from their own experience rather than be confined to the stock responses allowed by the colonial masters. But as they use English they must also change it, not only to fit the vernacular but also to shape its grammar to bridge the quite different worlds which co-exist in modern Africa. This shift is most evident in poetry and drama, which can readily accommodate everyday speech, but even prose narratives can subvert the forms of imperialism both in their use of direct speech and by recovering traditional tales, constructing alternative histories and creating new fictions. Amos Tutuola develops a form of direct, idiomatic English which uses the rhythms of the colloquial to establish a dignity of its own quite different from the ordering of standard English. Within this language he brings to the reader narratives which seem to move freely in space and time, presenting myth as colloquial fiction and then turning the fiction again to myth. Wole Soyinka uses a similar technique in his autobiographical *Ake: The Years of*

Childhood, which begins with Christian and pagan spirits mingling among the mission buildings and finishes with a report of a demonstration in which the women put to confusion both their traditional subordination to men and the authority of the District Officer and his minions. Appropriately, the critical moment in their triumph is Mrs. Kuti's response to the officer's exasperated injunction: "SHUT UP YOU WOMEN!" Their victory is grammatical, and reported as such:

> In the sudden silence which fell over the shocked women, Mrs. Kuti made the response which flew round Abeokuta for weeks afterwards, as the 'grammar' which hammered the ill-starred District Officer into submission. It was referred to sometimes as the grammatical TKO of the entire uprising. ... It was undeniable that the District Officer was rendered speechless by Mrs. Kuti's angry riposte which rang through the hush:
>
> You may have been born, you were not bred. Could you speak to your mother like that? (p.211)

The language used by the official to control the natives is turned back against him as a weapon. Although the disturbance continues, he is defeated from this moment, and the episode ends with his removal and the coming together of African men and women to reach an agreement that meets their immediate needs. Colonialism is dead, although its death throes will take many more years.

The form of the novel, which originally evolved to evoke the patterns of domestic life in early capitalism, had been quickly extended by the historical romances of Walter Scott and Victor Hugo and the fiction of the American frontier. In *Things Fall Apart*, Chinua Achebe translates this form into the setting of an African village. The portrayal of the coming of the imperialists from the viewpoint of the villagers turns the heroic romance of exploration and settlement into a tragedy of resistance and destruction. The setting for this tragedy is not the trackless jungle of Conrad but a prosperous village with its own fully realized emotional, social and cultural life. The rhythms and ceremonies of village life provide the same kind of firm framework for a story of ambition and tragedy as rural traditions provide in the novels of Thomas Hardy. The clear expectations of the characters are similarly upset by an intrusion of strangers, in this case the missionaries. However, while Hardy's characters embody the fate of individuals caught in a time of social change or collapse, that collapse becomes itself the theme of Achebe's novel. His main character, Okonkwo, is a tragic figure both because he is unable to accommodate to change and because his courage is vitiated by the fear of failure which drives his ambition and turns valour to aggression. His son abandons his father and his tribal name for the Christian religion and the baptismal name of Isaac, the Biblical son offered as sacrifice for the future. This Isaac, however, offers himself to the new life in atonement for the violence which characterized his father and the traditional religion, with its human oppression and sacrifice. These divided loyalties of family and his village act as a metonym for the state of the country, which can be healed neither by a return to the past nor by surrender to the new practices of imperialism, nor by the politics of self-interest which have now succeeded them.

Achebe shows clearly how imperialism is based on language. The traditional life of the village is maintained by the stories told by mothers to their children, and by the words of the ancestors invoked in village ceremonies. Okonkwo maintains his own character by the stories he tells of his own heroic past and of his father's weakness and ineptitude. His "masculine stories of violence and bloodshed" (p.55) contrast with the gentler stories his wives tell, and which provide the basis for the rebellion of his son, Nwoye. But, unlike his friend Obierika, who puzzles over the contradictions of life even while he fulfils his duties as a traditional leader, Okonkwo's fear of himself leads him to suppress any gentleness, any attempt to understand himself or others. He has a stammer which makes him impatient of words, trusting only in physical action: "whenever he was angry, and could not get his words out quickly enough, he would use his fists." (p.4) This leads him to despise his father, Unoka,who was a failure as a provider and a coward who "could not bear the sight of blood, but who could create an idyllic world of music which harmonized the contradictions of life:

> He could hear in his mind's ear the blood-stirring and intricate rhythms of the *ekwe* and the *udu* and the *ogene,* and he could hear his own flute weaving in and out of them, decorating them with a colourful and plaintive tune. The total effect was gay and brisk, but if one picked out the flute

as it went up and down and then broke up into short
snatches, one saw that there was sorrow and grief there.
(p.7)

But Unoka's physical failures, as warrior and farmer, leave him
incapable of handing on the harmony he evokes in his music.
This leaves Okonkwo similarly unbalanced, able to achieve fame
and wealth but subject to fits of rage which leave his wives and
children in fear of him. His insistence on taking part personally
in the slaying of the hostage who has become a part of his family
and boon companion of his son Nwoye breaks the harmony they
had achieved momentarily as they worked together on a common
task. His grief at this slaying alienates Nwoye from family and
village, and lead him eventually to adhere to the church whose
hymns offer a vision of the harmony he has lost. The harmony
Nwoye finds as Isaac does not, however, extend to the village,
to which the church brings division. The novel finishes with the
failure of the missionary or the District Commissioner to hear
what the villagers tells them, and Okonkwo's consequential
suicide when his attempts at resistance prove futile. The village
loses its own history and culture as it is made merely the object
of the Commissioner's projected book, *The Pacification of the
Primitive Tribes of the Lower Niger*.

While Unoka's music symbolizes a language which will go
beyond the divisions of words to create unity, the title of the
District Commissioner's book symbolizes the power of language
to write us apart in mutual incomprehensibility. As it happens,
the copy of *Things Fall Apart* that I have been reading offers a
further example of the way our language determines our
perception as it assimilates the alien to our accustomed ways of
thinking. The marginal notes added by a previous reader identify
every allusion to traditional beliefs and practices with the
contemptuous epithet, "superstition," and welcome the tribe's
abandonment of subsistence for commercial farming with the
equation of Christianity and "better economy." Like the District
Commissioner's book, these remarks translate a story of
disintegration into a history of progress. This translation depends
on the equation of black with darkness, superstition and evil,
opposed to the light represented by Christian civilization. The
ultimate development of this grammar provides the logic of
apartheid.

Throughout contemporary African writing we find an insistence on the apparently contradictory facts that language is at the heart of oppression and that language can make us free. The language which divides all people into black and white characterizes the black as objects who can intrude on our consciousness only as agents of our will or as threats to the order we have constructed to contain and fulfil our desires. In a witty variation on this, Bessie Head shows, in "The Man who Wore Glasses" (Malan, 1988), how this guilt can be turned back on the white master by forcing him to acknowledge the commonality of our desires. Most commonly, however, the black is automatically construed as guilty. In Brink's novel, if a fire breaks out, the Kaffirs are responsible; if a black man gives shelter to a stranger, he is hiding terrorists; if a black man walks down the street, he is an insurgent and can be shot. In Matshoba's stories, the black is automatically the victim in every encounter with white authority. If he tries to speak, he is insubordinate, and if he remains silent he is rebellious. In "The Bridegroom" (Malan, 1988), Nadine Gordimer shows how this guilty characterization of the black prevents a white foreman even from accepting the unity implicit in his workers' offerings of the songs, which are like the "first music men ever heard, when they began to stand upright among the rushes at the river" (p.42). For a moment the music, "As if it had been made audible out of infinity and could be returned to it at any point" breaks the "barriers of tongues" and unites the man with his companions and the land, sitting in perfect harmony "just as he had for so many other nights, with the stars at his head and the fire at his feet" (p.44). But this harmony cannot endure against the fear of the blacks which forces him to separate himself from them, to keep his forthcoming marriage inviolate and so destroy the completeness it could offer.

The divisions of language can be overcome only by deliberate action to create a new grammar based on the mutuality of obligation rather than the subjugations of power. In Brink's novel, Chris de Villiers adopts this grammar when he chooses to remain in South Africa and work with the resistance. By this choice he abandons his white classification and privileges and joins the victims. In the grammar of the police, he is now an enemy, an object to be constrained, beaten, exterminated. The subjects of Matshoba's stories are born into this condition, but although they cannot escape it they can find ways, through crime, work or resistance, of refusing it, of asserting their status as humans. In "A Pilgrimage to the Isle of Makana" he shows how this assertion can cross even the boundaries of class, creating the potential of a unified Azania from the fragments of a divided South Africa. Finally, however, the success of this story, which establishes a political geography of South Africa, lies in its renaming of Robbens Island. The Africans convert this island, the political gaol which symbolizes the basis of apartheid, into the shrine of a new people who take their hope from Makana, the Zulu warrior who escaped its bounds by swimming from it to his death. By renaming the island after this nineteenth-century leader, the blacks change it from a symbol of tyranny into a source of faith and hope.

While all imperialism depends on the distinction between metropolitan powers and provincial subjects, the renaissance imperialism of which apartheid is the ultimate grammar differs from its Virgilian model by using race as the basis of this division of the active subjects of history from its objects. The black African, like the European Jew, is defined forever as the object of other people's power. The state, defined by this division, exists only to uphold it, to embody it in legal codes which define not individual rights but social and personal existence. By defining the individual in terms of his birth, the language freezes the culture, excluding it from the dialectic by which individuals constantly change it as they enter into dialectic with others and with their environment. In such cases as the Australian constitution, which originally excluded Aborigines entirely and now includes them only as people needing special attention, or the treaties which established the relationships between Maori or American Indian peoples and the imperial governments, the wording is loose enough to allow challenge and interpretation, and thus change, although only from within the conventions of English language and law. Before the Civil War, the Supreme Court of the United States attempted, in the case of Dred Scott versus Sandford (1857), to extinguish this possibility by excluding all descendants of slaves from recognition as legal beings. In South Africa, the ideology of apartheid achieves this exclusion by building racial distinctions into the legal code and justifying the use of state power to exclude blacks even from such limited protection as the consequent laws still offer. In all except the rarest of cases, the black man and his allies enter the courts already judged guilty.

The logic of apartheid can be challenged only by a new grammar that accepts all people as both subjects and objects in the complex interchange between themselves, their culture and their environment. Independence alone does not, as Soyinka shows, bring this new language, for the new masters easily appropriate the old language of division for themselves. Nor does the language of terrorism, which merely reverses the categories without altering the structures of the grammar. The new language cannot be brought together solely by political action, although political change may be a prerequisite for empowering its use. Nelson Mandela helps to bring it into existence when, by speculating on the law used to oppress him, he discovers in it the principles which free him from its control and enable him to use it as an instrument of further liberation. In other words, by refusing to be an object of the law, by using it as his object and entering into a dialectical relationship with it, he constructs a new grammar from the contradictions of its present grammar. In much the same way, the black writers who use the English language to write their own myths and histories, to produce fictions of their own condition, extend the language to construct themselves as subjects and enter into dialogue with all other subjects. In thus calling into being a new community of their own people, in touch with both its own traditions and the politics and economics of the contemporary world, they contribute to a new grammar of global writing which is constructing a new world by joining diversity in equality.

CHAPTER 6

ISLANDS OF FREEDOM: THE PACIFIC DREAM

From the time of their first discovery, the islands of the Pacific have stirred Europeans with dreams of a paradise of freedom and sensual delight. This dream was, however, an offence to puritans who equated delight with sin and who saw in the apparently indolent lives led by the natives a denial of God's command that humankind earn its bread by the sweat of its brow. Over the last two centuries, the joint assault of sin and censure, capitalist enterprise and individual escape, has destroyed the subsistence economies of the islands and replaced their often bloodthirsty paganism with the rites of Christianity.

I

Gavan Daws, in his *Dream of Islands* (1980), observes that Europeans thought of the Pacific, and particularly the South Seas, as "the other side of the white man's world." Among these islands they could find the other side of their own civilized humanity. As well as finding in the Pacific knowledge of themselves, however, they found also peoples to subjugate to God and Empire. As they sought to escape civilization, yielding to "the great oceanic pull, away from continents, from civilization, towards ease, voluptuousness, warm beauty of place and people," they took also civilization with them in the form of trade and the cross (Daws, pp.xi–xiii). The earliest European "dream of islands" in the southern seas is painted by Camoens in his *Lusiads*, first published in 1572. In Canto Nine of this epic, Venus rewards Vasco da Gama and his followers for their successful discovery of a seaway to India by taking them to an island of love where the nymphs lead the mariners a merry chase into the woods until

"all was forgotten in the ecstasy of love" (Camoens, 1952, p.214).
In the final stanza Camoens tells us how, after the venturers
have exhausted the island's carnal delights, Tethys grants da
Gama a vision of a future in which the Iberian domain will extend
as far as "that Terra Incognita over which the South spreads its
icy wings" (p.246). Power succeeds love. But, as Daws points out
of later venturers, the islands also take possession of those who
come to possess them.

In practice, power came first. Magellan, the first European
to cross the Pacific, set course from Patagonia straight for the
Spice Islands and made landfall at Guam in the Marianas, which
he names the Ladrones, or islands of thieves. The chronicler of
the expedition records the first European experience of Pacific
islanders:

> ... the people of those islands entered the ships and robbed
> us so that we could not protect ourselves from them. And
> when we wished to strike and take in sails so as to land,
> they stole very quickly the small boat called a skiff which
> was fastened to the poop of the captain's ship. At which he
> being very angry, went ashore with forty armed men. And
> burning some forty or fifty houses with several boats and
> killing several men of the said island, they recovered their
> skiff. (quoted Dodge, 1976, p.4)

Their experience in the Philippines was initially more fortunate,
for here they encountered a friendly sovereign who provided
them with fresh food, attended mass, and kissed the cross. Then
in Cebu, the raja, after accepting Christian instruction from his
visitors, entertained them with comely naked dancers. After two
days trading in gold and iron, the raja was welcomed into the
church. When his people demurred at following this example,
Magellan offered them the choice of conversion or instant death.
However, on a killing expedition to a neighbouring kingdom
whose ruler refused to pay homage to the king of Spain, Magellan
was mortally wounded, and on the expedition's return to Cebu
a landing party was ambushed and 24 Spaniards slain. The pattern
of love and trade, religion and death was thus quickly established
as the form of European presence in the islands.

While Magellan, like Vasco da Gama, was interested in
finding a seaway to the Indies, his successors were captivated
by the idea of the islands as the place where Europe might recover

her soul. Pedro Fernandez de Quiros sailed on three expeditions (1567–59, 1595–96, and 1605–7) that were in inspiration a part of the Franciscan mission to discover the unknown Southland and to make it the place of renewal for God's kingdom on earth. The first two of these, led by Alvaro de Mendana, were particularly bloodthirsty. Mendana's men established the burning of houses and canoes, seizure of property, and gratuitous slaughter as the normal ways of dealing with the natives. The Europeans were horrified, however, not by their own conduct, but by the natives' offering of "the quarter of a boy surrounded by taro" as a pledge of friendship. The natives were equally upset when the Spaniards buried the human morsel instead of eating it. (Dodge, 1976, p.16).

Quiros remained determined to convert the heathen, and in 1605 was given command of his own expedition. The expedition had with it as chaplain and vicar the Franciscan, Fray Martin de Munilla, whose journals record the peculiar mixture of devotion and disdain that characterized Spanish attitudes to the Pacific islanders (Kelley, 1966). These attitudes are expressed in Quiros' actions on the island in the New Hebrides (now Vanuatu) where he landed. Believing it to be a part of the elusive continent of Terra Australis, he dedicated it to Christ with the name La Austrialia del Espiritu Santo, the Southland of the Holy Spirit. The impressive ceremonies of dedication established all the institutions of Spanish colonial government, including provision for the care of the natives. Yet these ceremonies could be carried out only because Quiros' men had killed the native chief and driven his men away by force of arms.

In his instructions to the captains of the fleet, Quiros had insisted that the members of the expedition should be godly and devout in their behaviour on shipboard, and proper in their dealings with the natives, who were to be "loved as sons and feared as deadly enemies." In this he reflected the experience of the voyagers since Magellan who had found the natives both avaricious for European goods and hostile to European presence in their homes. Yet when the voyagers reached land they paid far greater attention to the instructions about their own safety than to the injunctions to respect native rights. They landed in force, seized hostages, and appropriated the native stock for their own use. When the islanders resisted, they retaliated with volleys of shot. Both by their conduct and by their narratives of the events, they distinguished the natives as beings of another kind who must be reduced by force to obey the European will.

Although Quiros attempted to establish friendly relations with the natives on their first meetings, these quickly gave way to mutual distrust and armed encounters in which the firearms of the voyagers necessarily bested the locals. Munilla describes the splendid ceremonies with which Quiros sanctified the new land in the name of God and the King, and allotted to "all the knights who may serve in these parts . . . the whole divine and human administration of the natives" (Kelley, p.221). The natives did not, however, appreciate their new status, and repeatedly attempted to repel what appeared to be a Spanish invasion in force. Munella tells his readers without pity of the repeated acts of vengeance taken against native attempts to protect their lands and goods. So, immediately after the ceremony of possession and the appointment of a "diversity of knights" to "all the offices, which a well organized city should have," Quiros and his officers "marched a league or so inland with eighty arquebusiers and shield-bearers." There they came across the realities of their new dominion.

> At length the voices of many natives, who were apparently gathered at an orgy, were heard. They were feasting noisily but could not be seen at all on account of the great density of the bush. A few arquebuses were fired off in the direction whence the sounds came, and the report of our arquebuses silenced the natives at once. Then the *maese de campo* [Torres] gave orders to the party to halt, as he was uncertain of the whereabouts of the natives. He told them to retreat the way they had come; whereupon the Father Commissary asked why they should not go forward since where the natives were they were sure to find what they sought, which was some food of which we stood in need. So marching forward, quite near the place, we found four native huts within which were tied a dozen pigs, large and small, and one was found roasted on a barbecue. And straightway the said sailor-knights made off with their spoils. (Kelley, pp.223–24)

The European ceremony is ascribed the greatest dignity, while the native feast is described as an orgy. The natives are thus not merely reduced to subjects of the Spanish power, but to others to whom there is no need to attribute human motivation or dignity. The subsequent events, including the kidnapping of three boys, "the eldest being about eight years of age," the attempt to trade them for pigs, the condemnation of the natives for their refusal, and the shooting of a further number who are "left behind wounded or dead," follow from this exclusion of the native population from any reciprocal human status. This exclusion is maintained through the remainder of the narrative, which continually describes the Spanish actions in terms of response to bad faith on the part of the natives. So we are told of their apparently effective guerrilla resistance that they "made this sally cunningly," that they tried to "lure us to the high ground," (p.228); disapprovingly, he informs us that "These blacks must spend all their time dancing" (p.229); and, of their attempt to retaliate for the taking of their children as hostages, that the Spaniards recognized "their evil designs and cunning" and were "finally convinced how little these natives were to be trusted and what vile people they were" (p.236). The narrative thus contradicts the noble purposes it has ascribed to the projectors of the expedition.

II

Fray Martin de Munilla concentrates his narrative on its holy purpose, ignoring the appeals that Venus and Mammon no doubt had for the sailor-knights to whom he preached the word of the Spanish God. The sea to him was a path of duty by which he carried this word to peoples awaiting salvation. The ingratitude with which they received the messengers of the cross did not shake his faith. The successors of the Spanish navigators, however, brought quite secular ambitions. From the privateers of the seventeenth century to the fur-hunters of the eighteenth and the whalers, traders, and blackbirders of the nineteenth the Pacific became a place for indulgence and exploitation. While the overlanders pushed the American frontier to the Pacific coast, the Pacific Ocean offered a different kind of frontier where the islands continually offered the illusions of both freedom and security. These sea-frontiersmen carried with them both the Spanish distrust of the natives and Camoens' dream that among them they might find a haven of prelapsarian delight.

After the Spaniards, the English explorers Wallis and Cook and the French Bougainville made known to Europeans the islands of the Pacific and particularly the delights of the archetypical South Sea Paradise, Tahiti. Their journals record the delights their men found with the Tahitian women and the difficulties the captains had in maintaining discipline among their crews, or even in keeping their ships together when iron nails became the currency of love. The leaders of these expeditions were, however, already showing, alongside their ambitions to serve their sovereigns by adding new lands to their domains, the scientific ambition to observe, chart, and classify. By the time Charles Darwin and Robert Fitzroy arrived in Tahiti on the *Beagle* in 1835, the ravages of disease and the missionaries had reduced the islanders to sobriety, at least in their public conduct. For both men, the islanders were the objects of scientific curiosity rather than of lust. They record their admiration for the figures of the men, Darwin noting that even their tattoos "so gracefully follow the curvature of the body that they really have a very elegant and pleasing effect." On the other hand, they both found the women disappointing, "far inferior in every respect to the men," with "no charm for me . . . no beauty among them" (Stanbury, 1977, pp.290–91). These remarks may of course reflect the authors' awareness of the decorum required by English readers increasingly influenced by evangelism, but they show also the displacement of religious or amatory fervour by scientific detachment. This detachment however generated a new kind of fervour, the enthusiasm for the contemplation of nature's work. Whereas Cook had subordinated the admiration for new places to the needs of surveying and navigation, and Banks to the requirements of scientific description, both Fitzroy and Darwin are moved by the variety of nature to contemplation of the magnificence of its creator. For Fitzroy, this creator remains firmly divine. Meditating on the remarkable adaptations of the small birds that thrive on the Galapagos islands, he remarks that their design "appears to be one of those admirable provisions of Infinite Wisdom by which each created thing is adapted to the place for which it was intended" (Stanbury, p.287). Darwin, considering the same evidence, turns this proposition on its head by omitting the assumption that intent precedes design. His remarks about the Galapagos conclude with the observation that was the genesis of his theory of evolution:

The natural history of these islands is eminently curious, and well deserves attention. Most of the organic productions are aboriginal creations, found nowhere else; there is even a difference between the inhabitants of the different islands; yet all show a remarked relationship with those of America, though separated from that continent by an open space of ocean, between 500 and 600 miles in width. The archipelago is a little world within itself, or rather a satellite attached to America, whence it has derived a few stray colonists, and has received the general character of its indigenous productions. Considering the small size of these islands, we feel more astonished at the number of their aboriginal beings, and at their confined range. Seeing every height crowned with its crater, and the boundaries of most of the lava-streams still distinct, we are led to believe that within a period, geologically recent, the unbroken ocean was here spread out. Hence, both in space and time, we seem to be brought somewhere near to that great fact—that mystery of mysteries—the first appearance of new beings on this earth. (Stanbury, pp.287–88)

The strangeness of the Pacific detaches Darwin from the preconceptions to which Fitzroy remains wedded, and so generates a conception of nature as a text from which we can learn, rather than a gift of God to be exploited. The full implications of this attitude were not to be realized until the development of the environmental movement in the next century. In the meantime, it was to lead to Darwin's theory of evolution which, when applied to the native peoples, and even to the lower classes of European society, was to justify the repressions of both capitalism and imperialism.

Although the text of nature gave Fitzroy and Darwin cause for admiration, the human variety they observed merely reinforced their assumptions of the superiority of their own civilization. The scientific habit of classification, rewarding when applied to fauna and flora, became a means of making distinctions and concealing commonalities when applied to humans. Different cultures thus became interpreted as different species. The otherness that Darwin and Fitzroy observed in the native cultures of the Pacific was interpreted as evidence of their own nature rather than as learned behaviour or a product of their environment. By describing them as if they were of a different species, the diarists robbed them of subjectivity and rendered them as appropriate objects of science, government and evangelism.

These distinctions became most apparent in New Zealand and Australia, where Fitzroy and Darwin saw the beginnings of white settlement alongside natives still living to some extent in their original cultures. On his first sighting of New Zealand, Fitzroy was delighted to note the Union Jack that, flying as the sole protection of a "single English house," in marked contrast to the fortified native villages, "forcibly impressed one's mind with a conviction of the great influence already obtained over the formerly wild cannibals." In describing the natives as cannibals before he even encounters them, Fitzroy is employing the same category Columbus had used to justify exchanging American Indians for Spanish cattle (Greenblatt, p.71–72). In the Pacific, the horror of cannibalism became an excuse for both the vicious treatment of the natives by settlers and traders and the suppression of their culture by the missionaries.

Fitzroy's response to the Maoris' cannibal reputation is reinforced by his disappointment at "seeing the natives so dirty, and their huts looking little better than pigstyes." These observations form the context of his more scientific attempts at description, where he places them as "a race intermediate between the Otaheitans and the Fuegians," explaining that "To me they all seemed to be one and the same race of men, altered by climate, habits and food; but descended from the same original stock" (Stanbury, pp.314–15). His further observations, although paying tribute to the artistry of Maori crafts, and even their tattoos, nevertheless emphasize the savagery of their culture, their desired appearance of "demon-warrior" and "untameable ferocity" (pp.315–16), which is only slowly being tamed by the missionaries. Although he accepts that white occupation is inevitably diminishing the native population, he regrets only that, apart from the missionaries, many of the settlers are themselves from such poor stock, "strongly prejudiced, deaf to reason, and too often habitually vicious; run-away convicts, . . . and democratic seceders from regular convicts, [who] cause the principal difficulties against which honest, upright settlers, and the whole missionary body, have to contend" (p.323). These scientific classifications of both natives and Europeans reinforce moral distinctions and so serve to make natural the authority of the missionaries and settlers from better backgrounds.

Fitzroy's impressions of native savagery and European degeneracy were reinforced during his visit to the Australian colonies. Certainly, he found that the prosperous settlement at Sydney justified the optimistic prophecies of Darwin's grandfather that a new Britannia would arise in the south, bringing "Joy's . . . graceful steps," where "Peace, and Art, and Labour" joined her train. But he doubted that this prosperity would last. In this case, he looks not to God but to the physical and moral, or cultural, environment, to explain the likely course of history.

> It is difficult to believe that Sydney will continue to flourish in proportion to its rise. It has sprung into existence too suddenly. Convicts have forced its growth, even as a hot-bed forces plants, and premature decay may be expected from such early maturity. Other rising colonies have advantages in point of situation and climate, which the country about Sydney does not possess . . .
>
> There must be a great difficulty in bringing up a family well in that country, in consequence of the demoralizing influence of convict servants, to which all children must be more or less exposed. Besides, literature is at a low ebb; most people are anxious about active farming, or commercial pursuits, which leave little leisure for reflection . . . (p.335)

The degeneracy of the convicts was matched by the savagery he and Darwin observed when the local Aborigines were persuaded to put on a display for them during their brief stop at Albany, Western Australia. Fitzroy found their corroboree, performed by "a hundred prancing demon-like figures" a "fiendish sight, almost too disagreeable to be interesting." The sight led him to reflect on the "pains savage man takes, in all parts of the world, to degrade his nature; that beautiful combination which is capable of so much intelligence and noble exertion when civilized and educated" (p.340). Darwin was more appreciative of the high spirits and ease of the dancers, but, like Fitzroy, he saw the dance itself as evidence of difference rather than of common humanity: ". . . the group of nearly naked figures, all moving in hideous harmony, formed a perfect representation of a festival amongst the lowest barbarians." At the end of the

dance, Darwin rewarded the performers by distributing boiled
rice and sugar "to the delight of all" (p.341). The exchange is
symbolic of the imperial mission. The natives give the best of
their culture, the Europeans the surplus of their economy. Yet
this simple economic provision, by developing the taste for
European goods, was to undermine both the health and the
culture of the native communities throughout the Pacific. This
induced decay became evidence for the truth of the scientific
theories that justified the colonialism that caused it.

III

During the nineteenth century, the United States joined, and
in many cases superseded, the European nations as the main
navigational presence in the Pacific. While in some ways American
movement into the Pacific was a natural extension of the ever-
moving frontier after it had reached the western coast of the
continent, the source of the maritime enterprise was among the
merchants and mariners of New England rather than in California.
The ocean, moreover, promised a different kind of freedom from
the landward frontier. While the land offered the individual the
opportunity to find independence, the sea promised freedom,
the opportunity to escape from society. In fact, it offered only
membership in the smaller, and more constricting and disciplined,
society of the ship's crew. Certainly, if this became intolerable,
there seemed to be the further possibility of escape to one of the
multitudinous islands. Here too, however, the promise of freedom
was contradicted by the twin threats, already noted by voyagers
like Fitzroy and Darwin, of cannibalism and degeneracy. These
become the stock themes of Pacific romance.
    The archetypal American writer of the Pacific is Herman
Melville. His earliest works deal with its offer of escape. In *Moby
Dick* it is the arena of conflict and, as manifested in the great
whale, the limit set on man's ambition to dominate the globe.
Finally, in the novellas, the ocean that isolates becomes the agent
of the kind of degeneracy that Darwin and Fitzroy had observed.
Where in the Galapagos islands the voyagers on the *Beagle* had
found evidence of nature's profligate creativity, Melville saw men
destroyed by the vanity of their own ambition. Rather than
offering man freedom, the Pacific becomes his judge.

Melville's only landfalls are in New England and on the Pacific islands. The Pacific for him is not a frontier to be tamed, but a realm that remains forever free from the constraints of the land. "Call me Ishmael" he asks us in the first line of *Moby Dick*, and as Ishmael the outcast wanderer he joins the crew of the Pequod in their voyage to destruction. Yet, for the first twenty chapters of the novel, Ishmael's wanderings are confined to the land. He tells us of the derivations and connotations of his chosen signifier, the hwal or whale, and then of the journey from New York to New Bedford and Nantucket, of his sojourns in Peter Coffin's Spouter Inn and the harpooneer Father Mapple's chapel, of his near-marriage with another harpooneer, the tattooed savage Queequeg, and of the first rumours of the Pequod's master, Captain Ahab and his missing leg. From this beginning the narrator imbricates his voyage in omens whose significance he promises will be revealed through the voyage. The land furnishes the problems, including the unstated reasons for Ishmael's seaward flight, but the sea holds the answers. Ishmael finds himself thwarted in his first attempt to reach Nantucket and find a berth on a whaler. Instead, he is forced to seek lodgings in New Bedford, where the name of his landlord, Peter Coffin, serves to turn the hostelry into a place of death. Father Mapple's sermon further suggests that the whalers are engaged in a voyage away from the deadly attractions of carnal delight, already signified by the scenes of debauchery Ishmael passes through as he enters New Bedford. He enjoins the voyagers to emulate him who "gives no quarter in the truth, and kills, burns and destroys all sin" (p.64). The struggle against the whale is like the struggle against sin. This opposition suggests the sea as freedom, the land as death. Yet the whale, the apparent image of the sin that must be destroyed, is also the creature of the sea, and it is on land that Ishmael encounters the strange scene in the Negro chapel, where his colour excludes him from the devotions of the blacks, and thus confirms him in unfreedom. It is also on the land that he escapes this tyranny of colour as Queequeg woos him from the Manichean divisions of his Presbyterian upbringing. Sharing a bed and a pipe of peace with the savage brings him to a recognition of a common humanity that unites them and their different gods. Although the whaling voyage appears to offer freedom from the vices of the land, the sole motivation of the voyagers and their backers, until Captain Ahab subverts them,

is greed. The white whale that becomes the object of their eventual
ambition is presented at first as a symbol of evil but finally is
revealed as an image of the anarchic freedom that the voyagers
seek but which is incompatible with their destructive aims. These
aims, grounded in the desire for dominion, convert Ahab, the
puritan venturer striving to prove himself to his God, into a
Satanic agent seeking only to bind the world to his own ambitions.

The ambivalent significance of the ocean and the whale is
repeated in Melville's other writings of the Pacific. Although his
earliest work repeats the ideal of the islands as a paradise
embodied in the dusky maiden Faraway, her image is
overshadowed with hints of the cannibalism. In his later work,
however, it is the white settlers who are destroyed. The
enchantments of the Galapagos islands, the "Encantados," prove
to be evil spells that destroy the dreams of their white settlers
and reduce the dreamers to bestiality. The crippled slaveship *San
Dominick*, in *Benito Cereno*, proves to be the site of treachery and
murder beyond the comprehension of the bluff Yankee captain
who offers it succour. In this story, the ship, normally the symbol
of civilized humanity, is presented instead as a mystery. The
narrator emphasizes both its strangeness and its isolation from
its surroundings:

> Always upon first boarding a large and populous ship at
> sea, especially a foreign one, with a nondescript crew such
> as Lascars or Manilla men, the impression varies in a peculiar
> way from that produced by first entering a strange house
> with strange inmates in a strange land. Both house and ship,
> the one by its walls and blinds, the other by its high bulwarks
> like ramparts, hoard from view their interiors till the last
> moment; but in the case of the ship there is this addition:
> that the living spectacle it contains, upon its sudden and
> complete disclosure, has, in contrast with the blank ocean
> which zones it, something of the effect of enchantment. The
> ship seems unreal; these strange costumes, gestures, and
> faces, but a shadowy tableau just emerged from the deep,
> which directly must receive back what it gave. (Melville,
> 1960, p.42)

The ship is itself an island, an *isola*, separated like Ishmael or
Ahab from its fellows and from its environment, which

nevertheless must inevitably reclaim it. The aspiration to human dominion is doomed from the start.

The same image appears in *Moby Dick*, except that the natural island, as opposed to the man-made island of the ship, offers refuge. For Ishmael, the sea that he had turned to earlier as a way of escape, becomes an "appalling ocean" contrasting with the "green, gentle and most docile earth." These he explicitly likens to the "soul of man" where "there lies one insular Tahiti, full of peace and joy, but encompassed by all the horrors of the half known life" (Quoted Daws, p.91). The quest for knowledge, a central motive of imperialism, becomes the cause of destruction. Western man is not content with either the island of his self or the natural islands that he finds. The whale is the symbol both of the unattainable island and of the ocean itself. Among the epigraphs to *Moby Dick*, Melville quotes both Isaiah, for whom Leviathan is "the dragon that is in the sea," and Milton, for whom he "seems like a moving land" (pp.x, xiii). The voyage that Ishmael embarks on with Ahab is thus simultaneously an expression of the desire to comprehend, to take into himself, the spirit of the ocean, of life itself, and of the need to destroy the creature that, in its absolute otherness, mocks our delusions of both power and knowledge. Ahab, both Moses and Odysseus, represents the drive of western man to create the kingdom of heaven by making himself God. Like Odysseus, his quest draws his followers insistently to their destruction. But just as the Promised land beckoned to the Israelites in the desert, so the islands of the world's great ocean continue to lure the westerners who destroy them as they are themselves destroyed. The white whale, Moby Dick, the symbol of evil that demands destruction, becomes instead the figure of the vengeance that follows our attempts to impose the dominion of industry and technology even on the oceans.

IV

Robert Louis Stevenson fled to the Pacific to escape Britain's climate rather than its civilization. Nevertheless, like so many colonials, he exerted himself in his new country to create an idealised replica of the old. At least until the cyclone of 1991, his house, Vailima, still stood in Western Samoa as a South Seas counterpart of a Scottish chieftain's mansion, a weatherboard memorial to Stevenson's baronial ambitions. The house has been maintained as a government guesthouse, and on the peak of the nearby Mount Vaea, Stevenson's grave is marked with a tombstone bearing the lines of the epitaph he wrote for himself:

> Under the wide and starry sky
> Dig my grave and let me lie;
> Glad did I live and gladly die,
> And I lay me down with a will.
>
> And this be the verse you grave for me,
> Here he lies where he wants to be;
> Home is the sailor, home from the sea,
> And the hunter home from the hill.

In death Stevenson has created himself as the solitary man of action who is still thoroughly at home in his adopted country. In that country he had also created a role for himself, as an adventurer, as the head of his family clan, and as Tusitala, the man of stories.

This image is in keeping with the heroes of the romances with which he had made his name before coming to the Pacific. Yet from the beginning his work had a darker side, most clearly designated in *Doctor Jekyll and Mr. Hyde* but present in the romances in the driven characters of *The Master of Ballantrae* or the last, unfinished, *Weir of Hermistoun,* and even in the ambivalent figure of Long John Silver in *Treasure Island.* His heroes appealed to the Victorian belief in individual achievement and the essential heroism of the imperial enterprise, but Stevenson himself was aware of the destructive force at the heart of this drive for freedom and power. His house in Samoa represents the ambition of Empire, but the true subject of his Pacific stories is the destruction it brings.

Unlike Melville, Stevenson dramatizes the inner turmoil of his characters in outward action. Although Melville's characters move in real danger of death, at the hands of cannibals, mutineers or the sea itself, their central concern is to understand themselves and the world in which they find themselves. The main concern of Stevenson's characters is with their own survival, and their actions are driven by the need to control fate rather than to understand it. He skilfully controls his stories so that we read on to find out what happens next, how the hero escapes the traps laid for him, rather than to find out what it all means. Nevertheless, these actions arise from the same conflict of good and evil, the same need to find a moral framework, that we find in Melville. For both writers, the Pacific forces men back to their essential moral foundations, and destroys those who can find there no base firm enough to sustain them in a world devoid of the guidelines of our accustomed society.

In "The Beach of Falesa" Stevenson shows us this conflict through the eyes of a narrator who does not really understand what is happening to him. The beach of the title is the community of traders who stand between the natives and the outside world, belonging to neither and forming a community of their own. This community is threatened by one of the traders, Case, who, in a parody of both missionaries and governors, has established a superstitious cult that gives him complete power over the natives. He entraps the narrator, Wiltshire, into a supposed marriage with a native girl who has been declared taboo, thus extending the taboo to Wiltshire and his trade. The story's suspense is created by Wiltshire's attempts first to find the cause of the blight on his business, and secondly to destroy its source and Wiltshire's power. The story culminates satisfyingly in a gunfight.

The driving force behind his actions is, however, not so much Wiltshire's business ambition as his only half-comprehending refusal to acquiesce in the evil represented by Case. This refusal leads him directly into battle with Case, but more significantly it brings him to reject the central tenet of white dominion, that the blacks and their women are there for the use of the whites. He is horrified by the deception practised by Case on the native girl, Uma, whom he has fobbed off with a phony and blasphemous marriage certificate in which she places her whole trust. Wiltshire, sensing the evil in this, finds himself, against both his will and his instincts, falling in love with Uma. If the climax of the story comes in his gunfight with Case, the culmination of the moral redemption that leads to it is his use of the despised missionary to join him to Uma in legal wedlock. Case, using power to subjugate the islanders, finds himself trapped in the evil he practises. Wiltshire, grudgingly giving himself in love, makes a commitment to the islands that fulfils him. The end of the story is not the destruction of Case but Wiltshire's grudging acknowledgement of his legitimate half-caste children, product of the union that takes him from the in-between world of the beach to a completeness that unites European and native as equals.

In the more complex "Ebb-Tide," Stevenson presents a similar choice of life or death, but this time the central character can find life only by escaping from the islands and their governing power. This character, with the ironically pastoral name of Robert Herrick, has wandered through the islands of drink and penury. At the opening of the story he finds himself destitute in Tahiti, with only the vicious clerk Huish and the dissolute Captain Davis as companions. Here on the beach and in the prison of Papeete, in the French Tahiti where Melville had earlier been a deserter and prisoner, Herrick faces the final dissolution of his values. He is temporarily saved when Davis gains command of a schooner whose captain has been killed by the plague, but the escape proves deceptive. He is forced to become an accomplice in Davis's plans to abscond with the ship and its cargo and sell both in Peru. Yet the voyage restores some of his self-respect. While his companions prove unable to keep faith even with their own treacherous scheme, broaching the cargo of California champagne that they intend to sell and drinking themselves into a stupour with it, Herrick busies himself with the duties of navigation. When they find they have been deceived by the previous captain, who had concealed a worthless cargo of bottles of spring-water beneath a layer of champagne, they are forced to seek refuge on an uncharted island. This proves to be inhabited by a solitary planter and four native servants, and Herrick has a last chance to redeem himself when his companions plot to kill the planter and steal his fortune in pearls.

Herrick is, however, offered no simple choice. The planter, Attwater, is a misanthrope who exercises absolute and inflexible rule in the name of Christianity. Like Case, although in his case with a fanatical sincerity, Attwater combines the moral authority of religion and the absolute power of the gun, but unlike Case he intends to use the wealth he acquires in order to return home and make a good marriage. His rule, which, in both its nature and its motivation epitomizes imperialism, is characterized by the images of the helmeted divers and of the hanged man in the tree. Like Attwood, the divers bob up and down in the lagoon, obtaining wealth from its depths but untouched by the reality of the waters. The hanged man is the victim of Attwood's punishments, which allow neither remorse nor explanation. When Attwood discovers he has been deceived, his victim is joined by another:

> He was hanging in a cocoa-palm. . . . His tongue was out, poor devil, and the birds had got him; I spare you the details, he was an ugly sight! I gave the business a good six hours of thinking on this verandah. My justice had been made a fool of. . . . Next day, I had the conch sounded and all hands out before sunrise. One took one's gun, and led the way. . . . Presently the tree came in sight, and the hanged man. . . . Obsequiousness was the loudest of the mourners. . . . Well, presently—to make a long story short—one told him to go up the tree. . . . He was obedient to the last; he had all the pretty virtues, but the truth was not in him. So soon as he was up he looked down, and there was the rifle covering him; and at that he gave a whimper like a dog. You could hear a pin drop; no more keening now. They were all crouched on the ground with bulging eyes; there was he in the tree-top, the colour of lead; and between was the dead man, dancing a bit in the air. He was obedient to the last, recommended his soul to God. And then . . .
>
> . . .
>
> 'Shot,' said Attwater. 'They came to the ground together.'
> Herrick sprang to his feet with a shriek and an insensate gesture. (Stevenson, p.268)

The anecdote makes its point not only by its horrific imagery, but by the absolute inflexibility of its narrator's voice, the unmoved notation of details like the type of tree, the victim's whimper falling into the silence, or the two bodies hitting the ground together. It is the inflexibility of a colonialism that has its genesis elsewhere and is unable to give anything to circumstance, least of all to the reality of another's being. Herrick gives it its true name, "murder."

Yet, just as his companions are held by the bonds of Attwater's will and the form of his hospitality, so Herrick is unable to break either from their avarice or from Attwater's tyranny without betraying the moral standards he has discovered in his condemnation of the murder. His only alternatives are to surrender himself to Attwood, or to betray Attwood to his companions. Only chance eventually grants him a third way, when Attwood shoots Huish and Davis chooses to stay on the island, abandoning his past and subjecting himself to Attwood's absolute rule. This leaves Herrick free to leave on the trading vessel, but the story has no clear ending. Herrick's future remains unclear, and we must assume that he continues to roam the islands like a Lord Jim, trapped by a weakness that irrevocably cuts himself off from the past that alone gives his life meaning.

Stevenson's roaming figures, detached from both past and present, form a parable of imperialism. If they abandon themselves to the islands' promised freedom, they become dissolute, losing any common humanity; if they try to preserve the standards of the homeland, they become tyrants. The only alternative, which Stevenson tried to find for himself in Samoa and Wiltshire found on the fictitious island of Falesa, is to give themselves to the future by casting in their lot with the islanders to generate a new people from the integration of the two cultures. This course, however, contradicts the premise of imperialism, which is the attempt to use the new land to find freedom for the fulfilment of an alien culture. Attwood and Case are the products of this dream.

V

Finally, to put Melville and Stevenson in perspective, the work of Louis Becke expresses almost ingenuously the popular attitude to the Pacific. Unlike these authors, Becke became a writer almost by accident when, after twenty years roving the Pacific, he found himself in Sydney and in need of an income to support a wife and family. He accepted the suggestion that he should write for the Sydney *Bulletin*, which specialized in fiction that appeared to be the unmediated product of experience, preferably in a bush or frontier environment. For the rest of his life Becke supported himself by his pen, providing his readers with tales from the last frontier, the Pacific islands. His work is designed not to impress but to entertain, not to join his readers by writing of experience they have in common, or even to provide them with an heroic national mythology, but to enable his readers to escape vicariously from their drab quotidian existence. Neither

Henry Lawson nor Jack London, he becomes a kind of Pacific Bret Harte, writing tales of sentiment and humour about colourful characters in exotic places.

In this style, the importance of the setting is not its beauty but its difference, its apartness from our own experience. While Stevenson and Melville force the reader to enter into the moral dilemmas faced by their characters, Becke keeps them at a safe distance. He does not invite us to join him in the search for freedom, but rather to admire those who are prepared to pay the cost of placing themselves in a world outside the law. The natives who pay the real cost of these ventures, however, remain outside the stories, figures of colour or fun, not subjects who act on their own initiative.

The tone of Becke's work is set in the story of "Mrs Maclaggan's Billy" where he tells us that Samoa "in those days was the Land of Primeval Wickedness and Original and Imported Sin, Strong Drink, and Loose Fish generally" (Becke, p.26). His characters include the historical Captain Bully Hayes, the notorious scoundrel with whom Becke was associated in his Pacific days, but who appears here, as in other stories, as a likeable rogue rather than a figure of evil. The Pacific setting of these stories is important only because its ports bring together diverse characters united only in their remoteness from the constraints of the lands of their origin. Power is represented by the consuls, the gunboats they can command, and the guns and fists of the seamen and traders who use the ports. In "Mrs. Maclaggan's Billy" this power is used only to discomfit the respectable, but in others it furthers exploitation and brutal crime. The stories clothe these aspects of Pacific life in either knockabout humour or romantic mystery. Thus, even the story of "The Shadows of the Dead," which deals with murder, mutiny and attempted massacre by both whites and blacks, subordinates these to the romantic story of the "big white man" and his island bride, and wraps the whole event up with the text, "He that sheddeth blood—by man shall his blood be shed" (p.78). The actuality of bloodshed is diminished to a tale told on an idyllic tropical night and kept safe for us by comforting Biblical allusion. The reader need neither worry nor feel involved.

Yet Becke is not entirely insensitive to the dark side of the apparently carefree and certainly shameless lives his characters lead. In stories like "A Dead Loss" and "The Obstinacy of Mrs.

Tatton" he credits the native women with feelings of their own. The first of these condemns the callousness with which the white men treat these feelings and the bodies of the women they use, while the second shows how the native woman can tame—we might even say civilize—her white husband. Although his narrator accepts the blackbirder Bully Hayes as a friend, his references to the practice of blackbirding—the forced recruitment of islanders as indentured labourers in conditions little different from slavery—is consistently condemnatory. The story "Collier, the Blackbirder" in fact departs from his usual style to give a brutally realistic account of the carnage resulting from a blackbirding trip. Even here, however, our sympathies are directed to the white men resisting the attack their actions have provoked, and the whole is framed in the story of the love affair between the seaman who tells the story and his Tahitian bride (pp.79–86).

It is in such accounts of sexual relationships that Becke departs most dramatically from the romantic conventions, while remaining true to the tradition of Pacific romance. Like their predecessors, his characters are overwhelmed by the beauty of the Pacific islanders, but unlike the majority of these earlier voyagers, including Melville, they are in most cases not prepared merely to use the women and abandon or discard them when they are no further use. Most of his traders have what are referred to as "island wives," and several stories turn on the devotion they show to these women. The mixed-blood offspring of these marriages provide crew and officers, although not captains, to the trading vessels, and generally mix in white company on terms of near equality. A new society of migratory mixed-bloods thus seems to be emerging from the initially exploitative and bloody encounters of Europeans and islanders.

The migratory nature of this new society, however, denies it any substantial basis from which a comprehensive social structure could emerge. The people Becke describes are destined to remain on the beach, people moving between two worlds, not building one of their own. They are part of the age-old tradition of merchants, linking the world together and preparing the way for the imperialists, rather than colonists themselves. They work hard, but their work is organizing the labour of others and appropriating wealth that is already there. The contradiction of their lives was that they lived for themselves, beyond society and its laws, yet depended on the markets and capital of western societies and the power of its gunboats to maintain their existence. Like their enemies the missionaries, they were doomed to pass, having undermined one culture but leaving the task of building another to the planters, colonial officials and politicians who succeeded them. The construction of this culture forms the subject of contemporary writing in the islands of Pacific.

PART TWO

WILDERNESS IN ENCLOSURE

REGENERATIVE VIOLENCE: NATURAL MAN AGAINST SOCIETY

By the end of the nineteenth century the frontiers around the globe were effectively closed. During the twentieth century, migration has been from the country to the cities, and from the cities to extermination and refugee camps. Although romantics, and those who exploit the romantic ideology for material profit, may still search for new frontiers in the depths of the sea, on the peaks of the Himalayas, or the icy stretches of Antarctica, or on the face of the moon, these places will always be outside the boundaries of effective settlement. The greatest extension of settlement will continue to be the expansion of cities to consume what was previously wilderness or farming land. The attempts that have been made to extend agricultural settlement by razing forests or watering the deserts have generally led to disaster. They have brought about the misery of Manchuria, the dustbowls of Oklahoma or the Victorian Mallee, the destruction of rainforests in Borneo and Brazil, the salination of the Murray River basin. At the same time, the displacement, repression and exploitation of people which allowed Europeans to subjugate new worlds has bred violence and disorder which contradict the hopes of peace and plenty that first led them into these worlds. Both forms of disaster come together in Africa and the Middle East. But with the closing of the frontiers to further settlement has come also a new recognition of the power of nature and the need to seek accommodation rather than domination. This has led to a literature which seeks to produce a culture based on a relationship of partnership between humans and nature, and which looks at wilderness not as a resource to exploit but as a place where we can return to the sources in nature of our human cultures and conscious existence.

Much of this wilderness literature arises from a disgust with cities and the material culture they breed. Like the romantic poets, these writers seek in nature a renewal of a primal energy from which we have been separated by industrial capitalism, but rather than seeking this renewal through contemplation they seek an active partnership which will restore a unity of word and action they associate with the earliest societies of hunters and gatherers. Implicit in much of this work is the idea of man as the lonely hunter. These hunters share the self-reliance which made the frontier hero superior to those who relied for survival on the artifacts and social supports of the cities, but unlike the frontiersman they do not try to impose their will on the wilderness or make a path for others to follow. Rather, they seek the kind of wisdom that Faulkner's Ike McCaslin learned from Sam Feathers and the bear. But while Faulkner portrayed the wilderness as the image of a sullen continent waiting its revenge on those who had ravaged it, more recent wilderness writers see the land as still offering the strength and wisdom men need to live fully in harmony with the nature that is both inside and beyond them.

While Faulkner finally recognizes that his people are irrevocably tied to metropolitan industrial society, the wilderness writers are still intent on escape, on making an alternative. This search for an alternative has been particularly important in writings from around the rim of the Pacific, the provinces or regions of Australia, New Zealand and the Pacific Northwest of America. In all these regions there are still places where the wilderness is still sufficiently untouched or regenerated to offer a connection with the pre-industrial and pre-agricultural past. At the same time, the lives of the people in the provinces are subject to the control exercised from the remote metropolitan centres of political and economic power. The global economy spreading from these centres simultaneously generates demands for more resources and control over the process of production, which becomes steadily more mechanical and impersonal. Capital is preferred to labour, and the jobs which remain are more tightly organized and controlled. People therefore lose at the same time power over their work and over the goods and the environment they produce. The consequent disputes within the provincial communities over the use of resources are ultimately the local expression of a conflict between the metropolitan centre and the provinces. Because the regions still have areas which by their nature cannot support settlement, although they can be destroyed by attempts to exploit their wealth, it is in the writing of these regions that we can expect to find the search for the new balance between land, culture and the individual which the closed frontier of a finite world demands.

The distinctive literature of these places begins when expansion and settlement have finished, and humans are left alone to contemplate their puny culture against the immensity of land and sky. The land which had been the enemy, an object to be subjugated to human will, reveals itself as the continuing subject which ultimately controls all human activity. Individuals can realize their desire only by learning to accommodate its demands. As in the earlier phase, the dialectic continues between the individual and the land, but now its aim is the construction of a new culture of harmony rather than the imposition of established ideas of dominance.

In his autobiographical *A River Runs Through It*, Norman Maclean takes us with him in search of this new relationship. The book begins with his early childhood, when his clergyman father introduced him to fly-fishing and God, and God, man, and nature seemed linked in a single unity of love. Two later stories deal with an adolescence in the logging camps, brothels and bars of the mountain country, but the first, and title, story brings the author back to fly-fishing with Paul, his reprobate brother, and their now aging father. In this episode, when the family comes together for what proves to be the last time, the ritual of its solidarity is challenged externally by the amoral outsider, and internally by Paul's wild ways. The brother-in-law who profanes the river by screwing instead of fishing, and commits the ultimate solecism of drinking his hosts' beer, suffers not only a sun-blistered bum and body, but also exclusion from the healing communion of rivers and mountains. Although Paul returns to the urban world where his passions lead to inevitable conflict and death, his short life is redeemed, given meaning, by his understanding of the mountain waters and the art of fishing which unites desire, action, and nature in complete harmony. The story is a loving elegy for the author's father and brother, and a comedy of the manners and mores of a Scots-American family, but its true subject is how the mountains nurture in the author an understanding which allows him to contemplate steadily the violence and treachery which contradict the unity they symbolize.

The whole story is built around the art and practice of fly-fishing, both as the subject of the narrative and as a metaphor for the lives it brings together. However, although the story celebrates an achieved unity of family and nature, it is about exclusion as much as inclusion. The art of fishing separates the community of the elect from those outside: from the feeble of spirit who have deserted the mountains for the easy life of the coast, from folk who fish with bait, from the brother-in-law who does not even recognize the rituals of holiness. It also separates the men who fish from the women who stay at home. Yet these women form a part of the community. Their role is to indulge the weakness of the men who need to actually practice the art to become part of that harmony of humans, waters, and mountains that it produces and confirms. Scottish mothers, more than most mothers, "have had to accustom themselves to migration and sin, and to them all sons are prodigal and welcome home" (p.11). Hope and fear are a normal part of their lives, and they do not need to indulge in the further dialogue between them that fishing involves in order to nurture a community which, the narrator is sure, already includes Christ and his disciples, fly-fishermen of Galilee. The fishing both symbolizes a possible grace and generates division.

Maclean's book thus is at once an invocation of Eden and a recognition of the impossibility of reaching it in our actual circumstances. The culture produced by men's work in the mountains can bring them glimpses of immortality, but it cannot sustain a community outside its immediate bounds. The logging camps sublimate sexuality through work or contemplation, but when the men return to society they can release their pent-up energies only through violence. Neither the comradeship of the camps nor the simulated family of the brothel can provide a community which can sustain people beyond the needs of the moment, and they thus remain subjects of the history their work produces. Paul Maclean lives fully only when he is fishing, and beyond that is unable to bring into any unity his work, his casual lusts and his craving for the excitement of gambling. Eventually, he is found dead, beaten to death in an alley. Even the author has to leave the mountains to find fulfilment in work and family elsewhere. The culture of fishing, expression of the highest elements of human work and desire, can be only a vacation activity. The book's memories of Eden and evocation of what human life might be are held within the recognition that beyond the mountains there are bastards, and only the tough survive. Although the writer captures the world of the mountains in his art, nature, like the fish which escapes his greatest skill, remains outside the best his culture can do.

Yet at the heart of the story the author creates a complete harmony of culture and nature. He has caught some fish, and sits musing on the puzzles in which he is embroiled. These include Paul, the brother who is a great artist with rod and fly but enjoys trouble too much to bring the other parts of his life and ability together in the same way. They also include the brother-in-law Neil, whose life seems nothing but lies but who enlists the sympathy of a succession of women who protect him from a reality his prevarications transform from tragedy to farce. As the author muses over these problems his mind merges them with the pattern it discovers in the river itself:

> Eventually the watcher joined the river, and there was only one of us. I believe it was the river.
>
> Even the anatomy of the river was laid bare. Not far downstream was a dry channel where the river had run once, and part of the way to know a thing is through its death. But years ago I had known the river when it flowed through this now dry channel, so I could enliven its stony remains with waters of memory.
>
> In death it had its pattern, and we can only hope for as much . . .
>
> I also became the river by knowing how it was made. The Big Blackfoot is a new glacial river that runs and drops fast. The river is a straight rapids until it strikes big rocks or big trees with big roots. This is the turn that is not exactly at right angles. Then it swirls and deepens among big rocks and circles back through them where big fish live under the foam. As it slows, the sand and small rocks it picked up in the fast rapids above begin to settle out and are deposited, and the water becomes shallow and quiet. After the deposit is completed, it starts running again.
>
> On a hot afternoon the mind can also create fish . . .
>
> Fishermen also think of the river as having been made with them partly in mind, and they talk of it as if it had been. They speak of the three parts as a unity and call it

"a hole," and the fast rapids they call "the head of the hole"
and the big turn they call "the tail of the hole," which they
think is shallow and quiet so that they can have a place to
wade across and "try the other side."

As the heat mirages on the river in front of me danced
with and through each other, I could feel patterns from my
own life joining with them . . . (pp.61–63)

The author does not enter into some mystic communion with
nature, but employs language to describe with absolute precision
the geological origins and patterns of the river. He then moves
from the detached observations of science to the language of
fishermen, which orders this natural pattern to fit their desires.
He thus imposes on apparently random nature an order which
enables the river to enter into his consciousness and so take over
his mind and bring order in turn into the confusion of his personal
worries. The work and play of words produce the fusion of nature,
culture, and the individual in which each part, enhanced by the
others, still retains its own integrity, is simply itself. This
momentarily achieved Eden offers not only a model by which
to judge the other parts of life, but a strength with which to
endure them. The pattern of the river provides a story giving
meaning beyond time.

Just as the rocky obstacles the river encounters divert its
course without stemming its flow, so the violence of Paul's life
does not destroy the essential truth he found in the grace of his
Indian girl's dancing, in the mountains, and in the fusion of self,
art, and nature that constitutes the high moments of fishing. Nor
can Neil's graceless state destroy the truth embodied in the family
whose love and protection he exploits. For finally the story is
not about fishing, or even about mountains and families, but
about the need of people for each other, and the need to accept
their incapacity to solve some problems, their inability to give
of themselves to somebody who needs their help badly but is
unable to accept it. Watching Paul's triumph and tragedy, the
author comes to understand his father's words:

So it is . . . that we can seldom help anybody. Either we
don't know what part to give or maybe we don't like to give
any part of ourselves. Then, more often than not, the part
that is needed is not wanted. And even more often, we do
not have the part that is needed. (p.81)

This acceptance is the reverse of the ambition to subjugate the land and its people to human desire which drove the frontier west. It is a recognition that nature is finally beyond us, but not outside us.

Paul and Neil are both black Scots, rocks which divert and enhance, with comedy or tragic beauty, the river of life that eventually sweeps past them. This river runs through all our confusions, turning them into a story that gives assurance that humans can eventually learn to rise above the violence they perpetuate to achieve the harmony with nature of which fishing is a symbol, and which the human mind alone can conceive. This conception comes neither from the individual nor from nature, but from finding the source of culture in nature, from learning that "if you listen carefully you will hear that the words are underneath the water" (p.95). Reality is beyond us, but we know it through language.

In the novel *Hook's Mountain*, James McQueen describes the partnership of man and nature in a similarly remote area of Tasmania. But whereas the people in Maclean's work are destroyed when they leave the wilderness, McQueen brings destruction into the heart of their fastness. The crucial episode in the novel is Section 5, when Hook finally takes his rifle and with his neighbour Arthur goes off to defend his mountain against the loggers who want to destroy its forests and the agents of law and order who protect their assault. This section could be read on its own as a novella, a tale of individuals pitting their wits and skills against organized force, of overcoming their fear in order to achieve a true integrity of manhood, symbolized by the ease with which they move through the bush and by the phallic power of their assertion through the rifle. The episode gains its significance, its meaning, however, from the memories of wartime violence which it repeats and expiates, and from the action of the earlier episodes in which Hook has revealed himself to Arthur and has had one last attempt to encounter with love and family.

Hook comes to the mountain as a solitary. Because his wartime experiences make him incapable of emptying his own shitcan, he is forced to employ his neighbour, Arthur, another solitary, to perform this service for him. Arthur has compensated for his size by his physical strength, his knowledge of the bush, and an intellectual stretch which took him beyond his schoolfellows and gives him continuing access to the world of books. The community which is unable to understand him contains his unsettling presence by classifying him as crazy and allotting him a place on its margins, where it contemptuously throws him scraps of charity and employment. By allowing him to share the secret of his coprophobia, Hook breaks the solitude in which each has been enclosed, and so creates an alternative community of two. This community poses a greater threat than either could alone, and provokes Kevin Monson's verbal, and then physical assault on Arthur. Arthur's violent response seals his alliance with Hook and marks his rejection of his allotted status, his first attempt to assert himself, to claim a space within society rather than a refuge outside it.

During the novel Hook gradually reveals that his bitterness arises not just from the horror of the war, but from the ease with which the establishment discarded him once the war came to a finish. By denying him value, authority also denied value and meaning to the suffering and sacrifice of his fellows. Although during his later life he goes on to work for intelligence and as a mercenary, and for a time becomes a successful and wealthy businessman, he remains the outsider, unable to recover from his rejection. By building his house near the mountain he achieves a sufficiency outside society, and from Arthur he receives a shared knowledge of the land. But he is unable to escape from authority, which intrudes first in the person of his former commanding officer, and then of the foresters who come to take from the mountain its covering bush, to subject it to the material demands of society.

First, however, Hook becomes involved in a love affair which promises to extend the outcast society of two and provide an alternative to the bitter isolation which eventually drives him to his death. By picking up the hippy girl, Ellen, and her son, Stephen, Hook allows strangers to enter his life. By letting them stay with him, he accepts responsibility for others. By surrendering himself to her in love he admits his own incompleteness and so completes a self-contained world of domesticity in harmony with the surrounding world of nature. But his surrender is never complete. His wartime experiences have wounded him too deeply, and although he admits Ellen to his memories he continues to draw a circle at the centre of his being that he allows no-one to violate. Ellen recognizes that she cannot heal this bitterness, that Hook can free himself only by completely separating himself from society and returning its violence on itself. She realizes also that this complete separation can lead only to his death. Rather than wait to be discarded with the rest of his life, Ellen chooses to leave first. She ends the affair after the day's walk on the mountain has brought them closer to each other and to nature than ever before. The small stone that Stephen finds, "covered with a growth of delicate fan-headed clubmoss" (p.136) is a symbol of the unity they find in the beauty of time and place, but it also marks the end of the distance they can travel together. Ellen knows "how, she could not tell—that they would never climb to the top of the hill" (ibid.). She has no power to turn Hook from his fate, and, as she explains to him through Arthur, "she couldn't stop and watch you hurt yourself" (p.139). Stumbling through the empty house after she has gone, Hook comes across "the cold feathers of clubmoss on Stephen's stone." It has become a symbol of loss: "he picked it up, sent it skimming viciously into the night" (p.140). By the action, he accepts his fate. "Now nothing." Only a final act of violence can fill his void.

With Arthur, Hook retires to the mountain to wage guerrilla war against the loggers and their police protectors. For Hook, this struggle is the culmination of his determination to assert his individual values against those that authority seeks to impose on him. For Arthur, it is an opportunity to obtain the value as an individual, as a man, which society has denied him. For, despite the consummate bushcraft which makes him completely at home with the land, his social alienation has robbed him of value in his own eyes. The struggle inducts him into the knowledge of warfare and violence that he feels has separated him from the only people who have mattered to him: his father and uncle, victims of the first world war, and Hook, victim of the second. Eventually, however, even Hook's death cannot give him the place he seeks, and he is forced into the same course of action. The novel closes as he declares his value as a person by taking Hook's rifle in a futile act of defiance against the spoliation of the last of the mountain.

Hook himself is driven to his final, homicidal and suicidal, act of defiance only when authority brings Ellen and Stephen back to tempt him down from the mountain. Until this moment, he has held back from killing, resisting only by threatening and wounding. The use of the family he has adopted is the ultimate betrayal, although the novel leaves it unclear whether he blames

them or authority. Yet this final act of defiance, although inevitable
in terms of the novel's action, seems inadequate to its theme. Just
as the novel opens and closes with the image of a rifle, the deaths
of Hook and then Arthur seem to reduce their lives to these
single acts of phallic aggression. The original imbalance in their
lives comes from the failure of the culture which has produced
them to accommodate to the nature to which they belong. The
forests that clothe Hook's mountain, the homes where he and
Arthur nurture family love and literary culture, and the ease
with which they both learn to move through the bush, symbolize
the ideal balance of nature, culture and the individual. The
violence of war and deforestation arise from the destruction of
this balance, but Hook's resistance leads only to the ultimate
destruction of violent death. This death not only fails to save the
forest, it denies the value of what he had produced through the
work he had put into his home and into the brief family Ellen
had given him. By ensuring that Arthur follows him, Hook denies
his death even the meaning it would have in the memory of his
witness. The novel thus finally denies its own central theme,
asserting that there is no escape from violence into nurture, and
that the only value the individual can achieve against society is
self-destruction.

Each of these narratives demonstrates the kind of love which
could renew in the family the connection between culture and
nature that has been lost in industrial societies. Neither, however,
deals with the kind of work needed to build a culture that joins
individual and nature within a larger society. Norman Maclean's
work in the forest camps is vacation work that enables him to
get the qualifications for his real work as an academic. The men
that he works with are separated from the rest of society by the
nature of their occupation, and can relate to it only by violence.
In McQueen's novel, Arthur works on the periphery of the
community and Hook works only for himself. Arthur is linked
to a wider culture through his books, but these bear no
relationship to his work and have no meaning for others in the
local community. They therefore serve, like the forests, to provide
a refuge from the immediate, and so remove him further from
his actual community. Like Maclean, McQueen, by pushing work
to the margins of his narrative, apart from both culture and nature,
shows more clearly the imbalance that leads to the violence that
characterizes relationships between society and nature and society

and the individual. Like Maclean, he is unable to find any way of escape from this violence. By rejecting society's adversarial relationship to the land, Hook and Arthur merely place themselves in an adversarial relationship to society. They are oblivious to their dependence on society not only for the technology which enables them to oppose it, but also for the ideas of nature and of individual worth which drive their opposition. Consequently, rather than offering an alternative to a culture of destruction, their rebellion merely compounds it.

CHAPTER 8

TAMING THE WILDERNESS

Wilderness writing like Ken Kesey's *Sometimes a Great Notion*, set in Oregon, or Rodney Hall's *Just Relations*, set in Australia, goes beyond the idea of man as a hunter to show him as part of a network which includes the past which has produced his culture and the environment with this culture has tangled to produce the present. Nature is neither merely a primitive source of strength nor a resource to be exploited, but an element to be both controlled and respected. Nature creates the possibility of love, but it also provides the means of power. These books deal with the struggle between power and love to create a community which will satisfy the needs and desires of all those who work and live in it.

In *Sometimes a Great Notion*, Kesey builds his stories of a town on the Oregon coast around a family of lumbermen and the work which unites and divides their community. Kesey shows us this community and its history through his puzzled narrator's voice and through the eyes of equally confused businessmen, unionists, lumbermen, drunkards, lovers, and whores. Leland, or Lee, younger son and son of a young wife, is caught in the midst of these. As a child he leaves home with his mother to get a decent education. After his mother's suicide he aborts his education at Yale and returns home to help the family through a crisis and seek vengeance on Hank, the older brother who has shamed him. To his amazement and annoyance, however, he finds that his work with the lumbermen unites him in a community that embraces the whole family in a single world of nature and of the culture that grows from it and the men who work with it, rather than from books:

> "Oh! Hey by golly." Joe Ben laughed, pounding Hank on the knee. "You know what's happening? You see what's

coming over this boy? He's getting the *call*. He's hearin' the
gospel of the *woods*. He's forsakin' all that college stuff and
he's finding a spiritual discovery of Mother Nature." (p.221)

Hank disagrees, claiming that it's just the work getting Lee into
condition, "making a man out of him," but Joe Ben persists, and
Lee is forced reluctantly to agree.

> And, shifting himself to a more comfortable position, Joe
> Ben folded his hands behind his head, gazed happily at the
> clouds overhead, and launched into an exuberant theory
> involving the physical body, the spiritual soul, choker chains,
> astrological signs, the Book of Ecclesiastes, and all the
> members of the Giants baseball team, who, it seemed, had
> all been blessed by Brother Walker and the whole
> congregation at Joe's request the *very day* before their current
> winning streak!
>   Lee smiled as Joe talked, but gave the sermon only a
> part of his attention. He rubbed his thumb over the knobs
> of callus building in his palm and wondered vaguely at the
> strange flush of warmth he was feeling. What was happening
> to him? He closed his eyes and watched the last rays of the
> sun dance across his eyelids. He lifted his chin towards the
> color. . . . What was this feeling?
>   A pair of pintails flushed from the rushes, started up
> by Joe Ben's joyous arguments, and Lee felt the drumming
> of those wings beat at his chest in delirious cadence. He took
> a deep breath, shuddering . . .
>   *The river moves. The dog pants in the cold moonlight. Lee*
> *searches his bed until he finds the book of matches. He relights*
> *his minuscule cigarette and writes again, with it burning between*
> *his lips:*
>   And . . . as you shall hear, more than memory is affected
> by this country: My very reason was for a time debauched—
> I was beginning to *like* it, god help me. . . . (pp.221–22)

The changes in typeface mark the changes in time and viewpoint
which the narrative nevertheless unites in a single pattern. These
thoughts about Lee's experience conclude the description of a
day in which everything seems to have come together. It has
begun during the journey to the logging site, when a deer offers
itself as a gift of nature to Joe Ben's rifle. It continues through
a morning when men, logs, and machinery—people, nature and

culture—for once work in harmony. The lunchtime break comes as an earned period of rest. The loggers relax, their bodies worked and fed and their thoughts free to wander through the morning's events, linking them in patterns of meaning. Joe Ben offers his words as a tribute to the moment and to his realization that Lee has made himself a part of it by his work. Hank's response reduces the wider implications to the single image of natural manliness which is at the centre of his woodsman's culture, but Joe Ben builds this out again into a network linking body, mind, and spirit: another variation of people, culture, and nature. This linkage is not the intellectual taxonomy of the academic, but a bricollage starting from the immediate and building out with whatever comes to hand or mind. Without fully listening, Lee surrenders to the same mode of consciousness, allowing the immediate to soak his tired body and seep into his senses until, bringing his thoughts later that night into the quite different order of writing, he wonders at the changes in him, and thereby resists them, breaking the mood.

Lee's resistance to the integrating warmth of his family leads back to the disintegrating and destructive aspects of the work and love which generates it. The work of the family unites them in bitter hostility toward the union and the loggers who are not members of the family. This hostility erupts at the meeting where the unionists demand just a "fair share" of the product of their labour, and the contractors scream at them their demand for the right to run their businesses as they choose. Their attitude is that of old Henry, who built house, mill, and business by brute force and intends to keep it that way. As he shouts at the union official who ferrets out the family secrets *"I never yet rose to see the GODDAM day I weren't up to RUNNING my own SONOVABITCHING affairs and if any BASTARD thinks.* (p.94) There is no need to finish the sentence, but in fact neither unionists nor owners run their own affairs. They and their product are ultimately controlled by the big mills like the Wakonda Pacific Lumber that Hank sells his logs to to break the strike. The unity which work can bring locally between men and nature is broken by the wider culture of money which dominates both. Yet men continue to resist this domination with the bawdy and violent integrity that marks the Stamper family. While they fail to make the world their own, they succeed in making their own world.

This world however remains vulnerable both to the divided culture of work and to the disrupting force of passion, of Eros. This force is by its nature duplicitous, generating both the nurture which binds people together and the violence which destroys them. Old Henry embodies this force in his fierce individualism, which drives him to dominate or destroy the forest, the townsfolk, and his women. Hank inherits this force, and Leland tries to escape it, but both are implicated. Both are heirs to the constant movement west which first brought the Stampers to Oregon. Hank first completes this journey by way of the war in Korea and the return across the plains where he meets and marries Vivian. Leland's mother tries to remove him to safety in the east, but after her suicide he responds to his brother's invitation, making his return journey in a drug-crazed trip by bus. Once back together at home, there is no further for either brother to go. Just as there are no new lands to find, only old forests to continue logging and old conflicts to resolve. Their grandfather had fled back east, their father had stayed to build the business, but the brothers must resolve its future. At first, Hank is able to use his strength to hold everything together in the old ways despite the challenge of new men and new ideas. The family keeps the business going in defiance of the union, Hank sustains the house for his father, wife, cousin, cousin's wife and cousin's children. Lee's return seems to him to complete this community, but in fact proves that its solidity rests on an illusion.

First, it is revealed that Hank's apparent lonely defiance rests in fact on the contract he has entered into with Wakonda Pacific to break the union. This contract weakens the unity of the family as its members are torn by competing loyalty to the neighbours who constitute the community in which they live and which the completion of the contract will destroy. The ties of kin are finally broken when Hank rejects the union's offer to buy them out, to trade money for independence. Caught between big union and big business, Hank's appeal to family solidarity is anachronistic. It is destroyed by the same aspirations to wealth which created it. In surrendering to these aspirations the family side with the fragmented individualism of the townsfolk rather than with Hank's vision of the family creating its own community through the labour that gives it prosperity.

The family is, however, destroyed from within as well as from without. Its emotional centre is not the bedroom but the

kitchen where men women and children come together for the
festivals of warmth sustained by the labour of the men and
supplied by the labour of the women. But this domestic harmony
depends on the family maintaining its oblivion to Hank's
seduction by Leland's mother. This act, so far in the past,
destroyed the image Old Henry had built of himself as the sure
cocksman, able to do what he liked to man, woman and nature.
Instead, he is cuckolded by his own son, a judgement on his
insensitivity to the needs even of those who share his bed. But
while the cuckoldry destroys Henry's authority, it destroys
Leland's security. His return home cannot complete the family,
because the family is the source of his division from himself.
Instead, his return brings back the Oedipal rivalry which has
rotted its centre.

Until Leland's return, the tolerance of the women and the
space of the frontier have largely allowed this destructive force
to dissipate itself harmlessly. Henry's illusions have been left
intact, Hank's strength has been unchallenged. But as the frontier
shrinks and closes, male strength and female love prove no longer
adequate. While old Henry's ferocious desire built the business
and the family it supports, he brought it no love of his own to
complement his work. One wife escaped him through death, and
the other by flying back to the east. Hank and his wife Vivian
for a time maintain a stable core by supplying the want of love
left by Henry. Hank however allows work to introduce division
by accepting the strikebreaking contract with Wakonda Pacific.
Leland drives this fissure open when he rejects the nurture of
the family and follows instead his own desire for vengeance.
Where Hank has played the cuckold with Leland's mother, Leland
will perform the same service with Hank's wife.

Hank represents the older America, based on individual
achievement and the power of the will driving the body. Yet he
himself knows that willpower and strength are not enough. His
life is a search for the completeness of love which he knew as
a child when he found the three bobcat kittens in the woods and
nurtured them by the river. But the river, image of the destructive
as well as the nurturing powers of nature, takes them away from
him, drowning them in its flood. This is the first, decisive step
toward making Hank the man he becomes. He lives every moment
of their drowning with them:

> *he forces himself to imagine exactly what it must have been like—*
> *the crumbling, the cage rocking, then falling with the slice of earth*
> *into the water, the three cats thrown from their warm bed and*
> *submerged in struggling icy death, caged and unable to swim to*
> *the surface . . .* (p.108)

The almost unbearable pain of the incident, the boy's memory of the love which has betrayed its objects to their death, and his ability to contain his grief help to build the solitary strength which sets him apart from his fellows. The episode also foreshadows Joe Ben's later death in the same river, betrayed by his zeal for life which makes him an enthusiastic accomplice of Hank's plans. But more than these, it symbolizes the strength and vanity of human desire which is at the heart of the novel. Just as the river destroys the cage with its bobcats, so it will eventually—although not within the time of the novel—take away the house which old Henry has built defiantly on its banks. Within the novel, the river of time will invade the loving community that Hank has nurtured within this house, leaving only the two brothers, the river, and the logs with which they trust and defy it.

Leland represents a newer America, literate and educated, compassionate but manipulative, scornful of the older crudities and naiveties, but finally standing for nothing. At first, the action of the novel seems to endorse his stance. Leland wins Vivian, Hank loses cousin, father and contract, and is left isolated in the house that had been the centre and source of both his commercial and his domestic energies. Lee conquers through the weakness that wins Vivian and exposes his brother as a bully and blusterer.

This resolution, however, fails to accommodate either the cowardice or self-contempt with which Leland has rejected the opportunity to work with brother and cousin as one of a community, or the generosity of spirit with which Hank treats everyone who deals with him. In recognizing the limits of his strength, Hank has in fact become stronger than Lee, who knows only that there is no magical SHAZAM to turn him into his brother, but has still to learn to be himself. He has destroyed one community by exposing its illusions, but he has not found the basis for another.

The hollow simulacrum of community offered by the union and the town, presided over by the croaking of Boney Stokes

and bluster of Floyd Everwrite, offers no alternative. Although
the culture of town and union have grown from logging, they
have outlived any organic connection with the industry, which
has become merely a means of providing employment or business
opportunities. The loggers are left therefore with only their
physical skills and the businessmen with their narrow ambitions.
The dominant emotion is not greed, but fear. They fear the outside
forces of government and business which frustrate their ambitions
or threaten the only way of life they know. Above all, they fear
themselves and their own inadequacy. The hotwire estate agent
keeps his fears at bay by gloating over the only smart deal he
has made, selling a fleabag cinema to his brother- in-law, while
the victim plots ways of escaping from the deal and his joyless
marriage. Bigger Newton rejoices in the strength that enables
him to beat up anyone who crosses him, until everybody takes
care to keep out of his way. Deprived of the opportunity to use
his only talent, he finds himself senselessly angry at insignificant
blockheads like Les Gibbons, terrified by the incomprehensible.
Only Teddy, proprietor of the Snag Saloon, has been able to
quiet his fears by buying up all his competitors and learning to
watch and listen to his customers from the shadows, unafraid
because uninvolved. This is why he admires Jonathan Draeger,
the professional unionist for whom the dispute is merely a
problem to be solved. Teddy recognizes in Draeger a man who
has learned not only to escape fear, but to use it. "This is one
thing, Mr. Draeger, that sets you apart from me and the
muscleheads both . . . I can just escape fear; you can create it"
(p.389). Floyd Evenwrite, however, can do neither, and therefore
remains a victim. Driven by the need to escape from toil and
poverty and a lingering desire for justice implanted in him by
his IWW father, he fails to achieve either. Draeger's smooth skills
outwit his political skills, and Hank refuses to be cowed when
he retreats to the violent methods with which alone he feels
comfortable. Like the businessmen and loggers, Floyd is thus
reduced to being another actor in somebody else's drama, forced
to await for an end he fears but cannot understand.

The Stamper homestead provides the carnival to subvert this
official culture which tries to control fear by rules and sanctioned
violence. Hank Stamper fears nothing, and celebrates in his life
a union of the human and the natural, mind and body. His
enemies are Draeger and his own brother Leland, who try to

subjugate him to a regime of words and figures. They use Hank's own lack of confidence in his mind in order to defeat his physical control over nature. It is, however, nature which brings him close to defeat. His attempt to impose his will on nature brings the nemesis of death. In one catastrophic incident a saw amputates old Henry's arm and a runaway log pins Joe Ben in the river, which drowns him in its slow rise as Hank desperately tries to breathe life to him. While this is happening, Leland jibs at his attempt to seduce Hank's wife, only to have her yield to his weakness. While his strength of will and body brings Hank to disaster in the woods, at home he is defeated by the weakness which is its opposite. In despair, he gives up the struggle with the union.

This defeat, however, leads to at least partial victory. Old Henry's death and Hank's defeat take away the scapegoat on which the town has projected its own fears and hatreds, and leave it face to face with its own terror. Floyd Everwrite, who has sent thugs to beat him up, attempts to take away his last hold on independence by burning down his mill. Leland is not content just to go away, leaving Hank to wallow in his defeat, but tries to take away his last dignity. He taunts him about how the town is now taking pity on him, making him an object of charity. This faces him in front of Viv with the alternatives of backing down and condemning himself as a craven, or fighting and proving himself a bully. Hank recognizes the trap but is unable to avoid it: "He's built it like the hanging nooses we useta build as kids, that can't get any way but tighter . . . whipped if I fight and whipped if I don't" (p.610). As the river also turns on him, washing out a "rumbling of heavy earth" and making "a great section of the bank pitch out from the foundation and slide crashing onto the boathouse" (p.609), Hank turns at bay, forced to fight and determined to kill.

This fight is the culmination of the tension that has been building between the brothers throughout the novel. This tension is in itself representative of the imbalance between culture and nature, which in turn leads to divided and warped consciousness in the individual. Hank lives an instinctual life, in tune with nature but not able fully to understand either it or himself. Leland lives by the word, not as a means of understanding but as an instrument of control. Each brother therefore completely misunderstands everything the other does. Hank welcomes Lee's return to the Wakonda as an opportunity to get to know him in a way he had not been able to do when they were younger, to teach him his own skills and share his own strength, and to integrate him once more into the life of the family. Lee returns home with the intention of using his superior intelligence to avenge himself on Hank for perceived childhood slights and for taking his mother away from him. At first, he is diverted from his intentions by the warmth he finds in the family, and which he correctly associates with the fecund generosity of Hank's wife, Vivian, and his cousin, Joe Ben. He even allows himself to enjoy the development of his physical skills as a logger, to take pride in himself, until he reaches the point where he resolves to "bury the hatchet" and love his brother Hank as himself (pp.228–29). This is, however, the problem, for he finds himself completely unlovable. He can neither rest in the warmth and contentment of the family, "my stomach heavy with Viv's cooking and my head light with Hank's praise" (p.228), nor pursue revenge, until he finds something in himself to respect. Winning Viv's love does not do it, for he earns this by weakness, not strength. Destroying Hank does not do it, for this again is the product of weakness. Only when he eventually stands up to Hank, matching him on physical terms and choosing to accept defeat, rather than accepting the weapon of weakness because he has no choice, does he take possession of himself. He releases himself from the passivity which has denied the strength he also has inherited from old Henry. Ironically, his acceptance of the need to fight also gives Hank back his respect. He starts the fight from frustration, because Lee has left him no way out. He is determined to kill his brother, even although this will complete his own destruction. Only when Lee hits back is he released from this determination and freed to be himself. He chooses not to kill Lee, just as Lee chooses to fight a battle he cannot win. So they both win themselves, and find the unity they have both sought.

The ostensible reason for their fight is for the love of Vivian, but she is in fact a surrogate for Lee's mother, the stepmother who introduced Hank to the instinctual life and so betrayed her son's love for her. Her betrayal of Lee however goes beyond cuckolding his father. The gift of instinctual life she gives to Hank she withholds from her own son. While he is a child, she keeps him from venturing either to the forests on one side or to the river on the other side of their house, confining him to the world of words that her eastern upbringing and education hold superior. As he enters adolescence, she takes him away from family and forest and back with her to the east to receive a proper education. Before he completes this education, she further betrays his love by committing suicide, symbolically leaping from a high window to the earth she has always denied. When he returns, and after he appears to have succeeded in avenging himself, he finds that she has given as a love gift to Hank the poems Leland had carefully written out for her birthday. The highest verbal expression of his love becomes a tribute to the power of instinctual, physical love. His betrayal is complete, and can be overcome only by recovering the instinctual, physical life that Hank offers. He recovers this in their fight, and the two brothers together ride off on the log rafts, the success of their mission uncertain as they fight now merely to keep their balance on the logs riding down the river. Mind, body, and nature are finally united through balance rather than by subjugation to any one.

The novel, however, remains open-ended. There is no certainty that the brothers will get the logs to the mill in time to meet the contract and defeat the union, nor even that they will survive the attempt. Also, while they have achieved an integration of their mental and physical being, the family and the love within it have been destroyed. Joe Ben is dead, the house is empty, and Vivian is leaving them both. While she loves them both, she realizes that she cannot give what they demand. They need her love to restore their wholeness, but in using her they would destroy her. She needs "Someone who wanted the real us, me, who wanted—truly—what I am—was. Yes. Not a Someone who just wanted what they needed me to be . . ." (p.626)

The significance of this wholeness is perhaps indicated in the epigraph, or prologue, which the author speaks in his own voice for the last chapter. This tells an apparently unrelated story of the man he met in a mental home, a "nuthouse." This man, Siggs, a self-taught loner from eastern Oregon, had tried to live in complete solitude, but after a month and a half committed himself and took on the position of ward public relations officer. He explains that only by succeeding in this can he make solitude a real option, an act of choice rather than of flight. Once he has made this choice, he is able to go back to his solitude, where he is perfectly happy with himself and able to get on with the main task, to deal with the "main party . . . Nature or God. Or . . . Time. Or Death. Or just the stars and the sage blossoms" (pp.574–75).

The novel ends with a certain balance achieved between culture and nature, and its three main characters, freed of emotional tangles, now able to get on with this "main task." It resolves none of the fundamental problems of sustainable balance, but it does point the way to a balance based on love and work by people at harmony with themselves and therefore not seeking domination over nature or others. The open form of the novel is itself a part of the carnival it celebrates. Carnival is the rebellion of the lower orders, the instinctual people like Hank, over the upper orders like the professionals of the union and the logging company. It is also the rebellion of the lower parts of the body, of fucking, eating, shitting and drinking, and even of praying and singing, over the controls of mind and language. The multiple voices of the novel, its refusal to allow events to be subjugated to any single viewpoint or authorial control, not only suggest the impossibility of imposing any single meaning on nature, but shift the obligation of trying to find a meaning from author to reader. At the same time, its celebration of the unity of the senses, and their unity with nature, its admiration of rascals like old Henry or timid rebels like the cinema owner who finally gives all to his black mistress, thwart our attempts to reduce it to any easy morality. It celebrates the power of work and love to produce unity rather than division and subjugation. In its unending dance of symbols and senses, it breaks through the solipsism of language and returns us to a nature which encompasses and engenders them all. Yet although Kesey concedes nature, both as wilderness and as female sexuality, an autonomy which cannot be breached without incurring disaster, it remains essentially the object of male desire. The most potent images in the novel are those of the fecund household where all participate in the festival of domestic love prepared by Vivian, and the team of men working as one in the woods, rejoicing in the unity of man and nature created by work. Both of these scenes are held together by Hank's assumed invulnerability, and their harmony is shattered by the destruction his energies precipitate. In the final scene this energy is reconciled with nature, but the balance it achieves remains precarious. Like the raft that bears Huck and Jim towards the slave markets of Louisiana, the river floats logs and men down to the mill and its saws. Men are reconciled in an interval of domestic harmony, but the feminine nurturing principle remains beyond them. So does the possibility of work which might produce a creative rather than a destructive culture, and lead to more than a temporary and exclusive community.

CHAPTER 9

NETWORKS OF TIME

We have seen how Leslie Epstein's novel *Pinto and Sons* (1990) depicts both the extermination of a people and the closing of a frontier, literally as the mine explodes in the bowels of the earth. The closing frontier is both a fact of history and a metaphor of individual growth and development. As metaphor, it has been appropriate only since the renaissance destroyed the notion of a fixed identity and opened instead the infinite possibilities of individual experience and achievement. We dethroned God from His seat of universal power and returned Him instead to the role of eternal jester first allotted Him by the writer of the Yahwist Genesis. The new worlds offered scope for these new possibilities, but once there the immigrants quickly found their dreams enclosed by the wilderness and shackled by the cultural fetters they had brought with them from the old world. For although this culture taught them to see the new worlds as "a new earth and a new heaven," filled with sensuous delights of taste, scent, and colour, it did not teach them to value these worlds for themselves. Rather than building an economy on what was available, they introduced the plants and animals of the old world and engaged in an orgy of destruction which razed the forests that terrified them, displaced the plants that had delighted them, and exterminated the tribes that had first welcomed them (Turner, 1980; Watson, 1984; Rolls, 1969, 1981; Reynolds, 1982).

While the frontiers remained open, successive generations could escape the sites of destruction by moving out in the continuing search for a delusive freedom. The individual could still hope to find vacant land to subjugate to his will, to find a space to construct a society in accord with his own desires. Once the frontiers closed the land contradicted this hope of individual freedom implanted by the culture of expansion. Settler societies had to find a new cultural economy that would retain the ideal of freedom within the confined space that they now found themselves sharing with the rest of humankind. The domestic novel and the bildungsroman of the old world both reflected the patterns of a closed society rising to prosperity on the tide of wealth flowing from the new world. While this wealth created new possibilities for the individual, their fulfilment was still dependent on the exigencies of society. Behind this society's literary forms stands Shakespeare's tragic vision of a world which denies the great hopes it excites. Nevertheless, for these writers, from Goethe to Mann, hope remained more important than restraint. They did not seek with Shakespeare a return to a mediaeval unity based on the denial of the individual, but strove to keep alive within the adult prisonhouse a tiny glow from the clouds of glory they had trailed into childhood. This pattern culminated in Sartrean existentialism where the individual is all, but the paroxysm of nazism that elicited the existential response also marked the end of the expansionist phase of history that placed the human at the centre of all being. These new circumstances demand an ideology that will detach the ideal of freedom from its dependence on material expansion. Neither the mythology of the frontier nor the forms of the old world offer this detachment.

Although they have always been governed by the drive to expand, the people on the frontiers have had to contend with a material reality which has imposed its own ironic pattern on individual choice. The story of settlement is written with the lexicon of drought, fire, flood, and bankruptcy. The domestic novel of the family and the bildungsroman of individual maturation are both too cosmic and too narrow to accommodate the narrative of either the open or the closed frontier, but as the frontiers have closed writers have adapted them to confront the problem of environmental as well as social containment. Rather than confronting the violence of the frontier in the manner of McQueen or Kesey, these writers have recognized that once the frontier is closed, there is no place else to go. Rather than taking arms against the violence which has devastated the new world, and which in turn destroys the alternatives they try to construct, they go back to their own origins to discover the source of both the violence and the creativity to which they are heirs. Randolph Stow and Christopher Koch have both done this in their novels of wartime childhood in Australia, and in America's Pacific Northwest Ivan Doig and Molly Gloss have done the same in narratives which try to recover the essence of settlement from memories and journals.

In *This House of Sky*, Doig traces his own origins back to the moment before daybreak on his sixth birthday when, high on the Montana plains, his "mother's breathing wheezed more rapidly than ever, then quieted. And then stopped."

> The remembering begins out of that new silence. Through the time since, I reach back along my father's tellings and around the urgings which would have me face about and forget, to feel into these oldest shadows for the first sudden edge of it all. (p.3)

The book, part autobiography, part history, moves in both directions from this point. Forward through his own growth to adulthood and separation from the high country of his birth. Back to his father and grandfather and the other Scots who first came at the end of the nineteenth century to this Smith River Valley in Montana. They were lured by the long prospects of an empty country to be filled, driven, Doig tells us, by Scots mulishness and the deep Caledonian notions of raising sheep and grazing them on mountain grass which cost nothing. Nothing, that is, but the work of their lives, for by the time Doig's memories begin

> the doubt and defeat in the valley's history had tamped down into a single word. Anyone of Dad's generation always talked of a piece of land where some worn-out family had eventually lost to weather or market prices not as a farm of a ranch or even a homestead, but as a *place*. (p.22)

The countryside of his youth is already a history of the defeated hopes of families who have left behind only their name to mark a place in the atlas of memory. The frontier had in effect already been closed, for the empty land could not support the people who poured onto it. In the routine which his father now repeats, they had to force open a space for themselves, and even then few were able to hold on to it. The ethic that develops from their struggles is not one of domination but of survival. Doig's father

Charlie is a survivor, moving doggedly from one job to another, always honing the skills that make him a valued worker but never his own master. His grandmother is another. She escapes from a surly father, brings up her family and throws out her drunken husband so she can live alone, treats her son-in-law with suspicion and her grandson with gruff love but eventually moves in to make them a home. Like Charlie Doig, she succeeds by learning to accept fate, by making a world rather than attempting to conquer it.

These two very different people provide the major poles of the narrator's childhood and youth. The father teaches him the environment and the skills of living with it, the grandmother establishes a centre of domesticity within it. Behind both lies the memory of Ivan's mother, the frail girl who seems both a part of nature and its victim. Her death was for the narrator both the end of the dimly remembered unity of infancy and the beginning of conscious memory, as though everything afterwards has been just "Time Since." Her deathday on the mountain was also the day when his father's life had "begun to end there where hers did" (p.302). But the thirty-odd years that end Charlie's life create Ivan's, giving him first a childhood and a land, then, with his grandmother, a home, and finally passing on the responsibility of the father. The narrative does not end with Ivan accepting this responsibility for father and grandmother, but with him building his own past from the memories of their words and lives. These words tie him both to the land their work has made, and to the storms and tides that sweep over and around the land, taking us outside time and beyond all human control. The book opens and closes with these storms, with his mother's death and with his own near-drowning, the "scuff against death" when he had been "swirled out of deepest hazard" and linked by memory into all the past he shared with father and grandmother:

> I feel . . . as if the two of them too somehow stood up out of the slosh of death with me, the one giving his cocked grin of wryness at having survived one time more, the other muttering at the receding ocean and marching us all off into dry clothes.
>
> Then my father and my grandmother go, together, back else-where in memory, and I am left to think through the fortune of all we experienced together. And of how, now, my single outline meets the time-swept air that knew theirs. (p.314)

But if they are no longer inside time, the single outline he shares with them belongs in both time and place. It is the story of "the close of an unforgiving annal of settlement" that began in the 1860s when the first white settlers had trickled into the Smith River Valley in Montana. The annals begin with hopes raised by the land on days when

> the warm sage smell met the nose and the clear air lensed close the details of peaks two days' ride from there . . . Mountains stood up blue-and-white into the vigorous air. Closer slopes of timber offered the logs to hew homestead cabins from. Grouse nearly as large as hen turkeys whirred from their hiding places. And the expanse of it all: across a dozen miles and for almost forty along its length, the Smith River country lay open and still as a gray inland sea, held by buttes and long ridges at its northern and southern ends, and east and west by mountain ranges. (p.19)

But the land is treacherous, and does not fulfil its promises. It produces men like Charlie Doig, who learn to read its moods and the ways of the people and animals who live on it, and it rewards them with the skills needed to survive in it and the pride and independence that comes from knowing their own strength. But it does not fulfill the promise of economic independence with which it first drew them. The range belongs to the big ranchers, the men of money who employ Charlie to do their work for them. Even so, they often meet defeat at the hands of the land and its seasons, and are succeeded by still wealthier owners. Charlie and his mother-in-law are eventually able to make a space of domesticity, but the work which creates his bond with the land and its people never produces a society at home in it. The towns remain makeshift refuges, while the ranges remain as property to be exploited by others.

In *This House of Sky*, Doig's family and their friends belong to a culture which has been generated by the work of the three generations of white settlers in the magnificent but unforgiving mountain country of Montana. However, this culture still remains in conflict with the land. The people who own the land exploit both it and those who work it. The people who work it find only temporary dwelling places, and their children leave for the cities. In *Winter Brothers*, Doig goes further in his search for the origins of this ambiguous relation of people to a land which at once produces them and rejects them. He leaves the fortunes of his own family and country and follows instead those of a Boston yankee named James Gilchrist Swan who, like Doig himself, chose to be an edge-walker of the continent, a crosser of borders who became "a westcomer, and stayer" (p.5).

> Because, then, of this western pattern so stubbornly within my life I am interested in Swan as a westcomer, and stayer. Early, among the very earliest, in stepping the paths of impulse that pulls across America's girth of plains and over its continental summit and at last reluctantly nip off from the Pacific, Swan has gone before me through this matter of siting myself specifically *here: west*. (p.5)

Doig describes a winter he spent delving into the voluminous diaries in which Swan recorded his life in meticulous detail. With Swan as companion, he travels "back where we have never been" to ask the question, "how deeply alike and how different?" (p.11). In recording the journey he takes with Swan to the edge of the continent, he is recovering both the impulse that tugged Europeans across America and the meaning it takes as it comes to its end: in space, at the Pacific; in time, in the two generations between Swan's and his own. By taking him back, Swan provides the clue to how Doig has sited himself.

The generations of settlers invaded the land to use it, to graze and plough and fence it until it yielded them its wealth. Swan before them and Doig after come rather to learn from the land, to hear and record what it has to say to them. They are both writers who remain at a slight tangent to the rest of society. Unlike Kesey's loggers or Doig's own settlers, they are not concerned either to make a home or to impose themselves on the land, but to make themselves at home within it. Words furnish both the implements for their enterprise and its harvest. In his diaries, Swan creates himself from the people and land around him. As he reads the diaries, Doig recreates Swan in terms of his own, later, consciousness, and so grafts onto his specific settler heritage the tradition of the wanderers with whom he has chosen to throw in his lot. This tradition encompasses not just the lands of America, but the oceans which encompass and delimit them and which first bring Swan to the west.

The ocean was not just a barrier which protected America from Europe for so many thousands of years. The ocean produced

Europe's first definition of America. Voyagers from Brendan to Columbus gazed across the ocean and constructed mythical worlds before they encountered real ones. Columbus went in search of the east, and so when he came to the far side of the ocean he concluded that the countries he found were a part of Asia, and named them accordingly, appropriating the actual people to his fantasies. The far Atlantic then became the Spanish Main, pathway for wealth to flow from a new world to the old, and highway of opportunity for pirates and venturers from every port of Europe. For the Pilgrim Fathers, the ocean became the valley of the shadow of death, thus making a safe crossing providential and the landing place a promised land. As the promise, and the pilgrims, shifted west, the ocean behind became a barrier keeping them safe from the contaminations of Europe. Beyond this barrier a free people pursued the manifest destiny of conquest. For the companions of Ahab, however, even the sea was not a barrier, and they pursued the trail of conquest and destruction to the furthest stretches of the Pacific until they destroyed even themselves. Ishmael, the wanderer, is three times reborn—in the arms of Queequeg, in the sperm of the whale, and in the ocean itself. While his companions are destroyed by the ocean and the beast they seek to subjugate, Ishmael receives new life from one of the native people, from the whale, and from the ocean itself. In choosing the whaleroad to the west, and companioning himself with its first people, Swan takes the same path away from prosperity and toward the possession of himself he eventually finds on his expedition to the islands off the shores of Canada.

This reading is not, however, Swan's own, but Doig's recreation from the diaries which chronicle their author's constant attempts to give his life some material stability and success. Unlike autobiography, diaries present their author facing a future where everything is still possible. Autobiographies look back to the past their authors have already lived, and so construct them teleologically, shaping them to a known conclusion. Doig retells Swan's open narrative in the light of a destination he already knows in part, even if full knowledge waits on his further perusal of the diaries. We read the narrative with him in knowledge also of the later history of Swan's west, the knowledge that Port Townsend did not become its metropolis, that the Indians lost one way of life without being given the opportunity of another, and that the railways made great cities but left the wilderness marked but not subdued. With this knowledge, we read Swan's diaries not because of his hopes but because of the sources of those hopes in the understanding he gained of the land and people among whom he lived. By presenting the diaries in terms of his own recovery of them, Doig discovers in them the origin of a new America which, within the bounds of the ocean, discovers its country as a part of itself rather than as an object to be conquered. By reading a record of the opening of the frontier to the ocean backwards from the present of a closed frontier, Doig paradoxically discovers a new frontier of the inner life where the promise of the new world may at last be fulfilled. This hope depends on transcending the opposition between culture and nature which since the first settlement has driven men to impose their will on the land and so destroy both. This transcendence recovers a nurturing culture which produces individuals who see themselves as a part of nature as well as recognizing nature as a part of themselves. The objective reality of the land forms the basis of their own subjectivity.

Doig confronts the reality of the land at length in the trilogy of novels that begins chronologically with *Dancing at the Rascal Fair* (1987). These three novels take the McCaskill family at fifty-year intervals from the time in 1889 when they first come from Scotland to Montana. The first written, *English Creek* (1985), is a kind of new world bildungsroman which tells of how Jick McCaskill, grandson of two of the firstcomers, passes literally through rites of fire to come into his own inheritance as a son of the land. This means not only undertaking his share of adult labor—no problem for a boy raised among ranchers—but accepting responsibility for the land and for himself. The climax of the novel comes during the forest fire, when Jick accepts the work at the base camp and his father accepts the advice of his mentor and the sole responsibility for the consequent decision which puts at risk his career and the forest on whose care he has spent his life. Jick, retelling the moment forty-odd years later, recognizes its importance to the men immediately concerned:

> These years later, I wish I could have those next minutes
> back to makings. Could see again that slope battle, and our
> fire camp that the sacrifice of the slop had saved. Could
> know again the rise of realization, the brimming news of my

eyes, that the Flume Gulch fire steadily was quenching itself against my father's fireline, Stanley Meixell's fireline.

I couldn't speak. For some time after, even. My mouth and throat were as dry as if parched by the fire. But finally I managed:

"You knew the slope would go like that."

"I had the idea it might" was as much as Stanley would admit. "Superheated the way it was, from both the fire and the sun."

He looked drained but satisfied. I may have, too.

"So," Stanley said next. "We better get to work on goddam supper." (p.324)

This paragraph sums up the action, the work guided by skill, knowledge and courage which leads to the fire's extinction. The significance of the episode lies deeper. Jick comes to recognize this only later that night, as he lies in his sleeping bag thinking over the day's events.

Jick has known Stanley as a drunk and drifter, but he knows he is also one of the legendary rangers who first surveyed the forests for the nation. Stanley is about to explain that while he was still ranger he had given way to whisky and allowed his forest to burn. Jick's father Varick, also a ranger and Stanley's disciple and friend, had reported the dereliction of duty, leading to Stanley's dismissal and a lasting rift in the bond that had joined them. By taking Stanley's advice, Varick restores his sense of his own worth and the link between them, while accepting that both know that what Stanley has made himself by his indulgence cannot be undone. Each accepts responsibility for himself, for what he is and everything he has done. From this, Jick recognizes that his own brother, in sticking by his decision to work as a cowboy rather than follow the career his parents have chosen for him, is accepting the same responsibility.

> Up against a decision, my father had chosen the Two country over his friend, his mentor, Stanley.
>
> Up against a decision, my brother had chosen independence over my father.
>
> Rewrite my life into one of those other McCaskill versions and what would I have done in my father's place, or my brother's? Even yet I don't know. I do not know. It may be there is no knowing until a person is in so hard a place. (p.328)

At this earlier point in his life, Jick is conscious only of the rebuff he has received from Alec and of the burden of his sole knowledge of the state of his brother's affairs. Yet by intervening in these affairs with his vain request for him to come to his father's aid, Jick has already accepted a measure of responsibility. His moment of reflection marks his further passage into adulthood with the recognition that each such decision must be made alone, and that the individual is responsible for all their consequences. In *Ride with Me, Mariah Montana*, the final novel of the trilogy, Jick, now himself an old man and a widower, faces just such a decision with his daughter.

The novels of the trilogy belong particularly to the new world, however, because these consequences of decisions taken by generations of McCaskills are not merely individual or domestic. They shape not just the people but also the land which nurtures them. The trilogy culminates in Jick McCaskill's decision to leave his Montana ranch. It begins with Angus McCaskill's decision to stick with his friend Robert Burns Barclay in leaving Scotland to take up the new lands of America. By taking up these lands, they commit themselves to a destiny which will fit them to forms they could never have known in Scotland. Angus makes his choice quite deliberately as he watches the west coast of his homeland, "as handsome a coast as could be fashioned," and remembers

> each last inch of it everlastingly owned by those higher than Angus McCaskill and Rob Barclay. . . . Those whose names began with Lord. Those who had the banks and mills. Those who watched from their fat fields as the emigrant ships steamed past with us. (*Dancing at the Rascal Fair*, 1987, p. 8)

The high valleys of Montana offer freedom from the "men with white hands," but the freedom can be earned only by accepting the harsh geometry of the survey that allots each homesteader a rectangle of 160 acres, and by giving to it the work of "axe, hammer, adze, pick, shovel, pitchfork" and the "true tools" of "hope, muscle and time" until they earn what their dour neighbour calls "bragging rights to this country" (p.91).

The work of settlement separates the homesteaders from the old country and gives them into possession of the new, the valley they make their Scotch Heaven. Angus recognizes the separation when he watches "the erect American back of Rob as he took the news of his father's death into the house on Breed Butte" (p.128). He recognizes it in himself when he finds his wife, who from the first has found America too vast, is still "turning back like a compass needle towards Nethermuir and all its defeats." He explains to her: "everything I have is here now. Scotland is an old calendar to me" (p.218).

Doig indicates the separation from the homeland, the constitution of America as a home, in the speech patterns of the three novels. The first still has the rhythms of Scotland, and is freely interlarded with authentic and reconstituted gobbetts of Burns as Angus himself or the children he teaches put the substance of their lives into rhyme. The Scots burr remains even in the generation of *English Creek*, where Beth tells young Jick of his father's courtship:

> . . . I hadn't been around him and those other Scotch heaveners while I was away at college, and I'd lost the knack of listening to that burr of theirs. About the third time that night he said something I couldn't catch, I asked him: 'Do you always talk through your nose?' And then he put on a *real* burr and said back, 'Lass, it saves wearrr and tearrr on my lips. They'rre in prrrime condition, if you'rrre everrr currrrious.' (p.123)

Jick himself tells his tale in the pure demotic of the northwest, a master of the concrete detail that reduces the illusions of the abstract to the sense of experience. This quality appears particularly as he recalls his life in *Ride with Me, Mariah Montana*, in remarks that sum up the learning of his life: "As a rancher trying to make a living from this country I subscribe to the reminder that view is particularly hard to get your fork into" (p.108). Or the keen assessment of character: "He was a pale ordinary enough guy sitting behind the desk there, but he did his own killing" (p.91). Yet the same rhythms can dig deep into experience to discover the patterns that tie it together, as when nightfall above English Creek elicits his "private theory . . . that lulls of this sort are how a person heals from the other weather of this land, for the light calmly going takes with it the grievances that the Two is a country where the wind wears away at you on a daily basis, where drought is never far from happening, where the valley bottoms now in the perfect shirtsleeve of summer

dusk were thirty-five degrees below zero in the nights of
February" (p.115). The same language allows his recognition of
the changes that time has brought to the girl who took his brother
from him, that "the girl version of Leona had gone down its road
at full gallop" and that she now has her own "earned earth"
(p.223). The rancher's metaphors describe with the authoritative
evaluation of lived experience.

Not so the nervous excitability of Riley and Mariah, who
gulp down life and regurgitate it in the blunt words of a
generation that must make its meanings without the assistance
of either the land or tradition. So, pressed by Mariah to explain
what he is writing, he tells her bluntly:

> Mariah, ring off. Shoot whatever the fuck you want and
> they'll slap it on the page next to whatever the fuck I write
> and that'll be that. Simplissimo. (p.31)

Yet, when he sorts out the words into writing, he can also
penetrate to the underlying patterns, as in his description of the
failed attempt to transfer a grizzly:

> But, as the shotgunner still held the gun pointing toward
> the grizzly, these survivors, too, seemed as lifeless as the
> furred victim. (p.159)

These words do not come from his own experience, but from his
art as an observer. This art enables him to act as remembrancer
of those who have made the country, to such effect that the truth
he uncovers in his description of the rancher at first drives Jick
beside himself with rage. He feels as if he has been "stripped
naked, painted rainbow colours, and paraded across the state"
(p.200). With whatever cruelty, Riley is able to record not only
the tradition, but also its supplanting by the America it has made
possible.

In taking the land for themselves and their children, the first
settlers had also to accept responsibility for it if they were to
make it their home and not remain merely dwellers upon it, like
the Williamsons on their Double W, or Gobble Gobble You as
their neighbours christen it. These ranchers are the successors of
the men of money who own Scotland. The conflict with them
runs throughout the trilogy, as they treat the land merely as a

source of profit, exploiting it through overgrazing, using their bank to foreclose on their neighbours, eventually selling out to a corporation that tries to buy out the last of the McCaskills and replace his husbandry with the business of computers and animal units. In resisting the offer, Jick, last McCaskill in the Two Medicine country, keeps faith with the grandfather he never knew, as well as with his own parents.

This faith is expressed by Jick's mother Beth in her speech to the Fourth of July Independence Day picnic gathering at Gros Ventre, when she honours the work and memory of the pioneers, and particularly of the man who gave his name to English Creek. After recalling the history of the valleys, and the names of the families, "all but one"—the one that "ended up by holding the land, by outright buy or by lease from the First National Bank . . . after each and every one of those sales and foreclosures," she concludes by coming back to the figure of the man who started it all:

> . . . I think it could not be more right that we honour in this valley a man who savvied the land and its livelihood instead of merely coveting it. I think it could not be more right that tall Ben English in his black hat amid his green fields, coaxing a head of water to make itself into hay, is the one whose name this creek carries. (*English Creek*, p.162)

The work on the land produces a unity with the people and the shared culture which is expressed in the dance that concludes the day's celebrations, as recalled by Jick:

> Probably if you climbed the helmet spike of the Sedgwick House, the rhythm of those six squares of dancers would have come quivering up to you like spasms through a tuning fork. Figure within figure within figure, from my father's outlook over us, the kaleidoscope of six simultaneous dance patterns and inside each the hinged couple of the instant and comprising those couples' friends, neighbors, sons, wife with flashing throat. The Lord of the dance, leading us all. (p.212)

The dance integrates individual and family in a community created by their work in this new land but carrying with it rhythms and patterns from time immemorial.

The work which produces the community also generates a knowledge of the land that is both objective and subjective. Jick muses on this in *Ride with Me, Mariah Montana* (1990), where, just after learning of the unfulfilled love that cast its blight on the hopes of all four of his grandparents, he thinks back on the offer he has just received from "everloving goddam corporaiders" of WW, Incorporated: "some distant multibunch who saw you as a scrap of acreage they could make tax arithmetic out of" (pp.100–01). Recalling that a land analyst he has consulted has informed him that "this land and locale were best fitted to support Animal Units," he reflects that:

> ... the wisdom of the microchips amounted to pretty much the local knowledge I already possessed. That to make a go of the ranch, you had to hard-learn its daily elements. Pace your body through one piece of work after another, paying heed always to the living components—the sheep, the grass, the hay—but the gravitational wear on fences and sheds and roads and equipment also somehow attended to, so that you are able to reliably tell yourself at nightfall, that was as much of a day as I can do. Then you get up and do it again 364 tomorrows in a row. Sitting there seeing the ranch in its every detail, knowing every ounce of work it required, Jesus but how then I wished for fifteen years off my age. I'd have settled for five. Yet truth knows every way to nag. Even if I had seen that many calendars, would it do any good in terms of the ranch ultimately? Maybe people from now on are going to exist on bean sprouts and wear polyester all over themselves, and lamb and wool belong behind glass in a museum. Maybe what I have known all my life, which is ranching, simply does not register any more. (p.110).

The land and the ranch exist objectively, but they also exist in the subjective time constituted by the needs and desires of those who work them and those who use their products. The market that made the settlement of the valleys possible also broke the link between the consumer on the one hand and the producer and land on the other. Inevitably, it eventually replaces the producer's products, and so destroys also his links with the land. *Ride with Me, Mariah Montana* is the record of one man's attempts to keep these links alive, and through them to ensure the continuity of the work of three generations of his family. But, like his brother Alec, his children want responsibility for their own lives, and refuse to maintain continuity. Although Jick finds a solution that keeps his property out of the hands of the corporate raiders and at the same time restores links with the lives that preceded European settlement, he is unable to avoid the conclusion that the ranching he has known is obsolete. The land belongs to the corporations, and his children can find their independence only by moving on. As his ex-son-in-law, Riley Wright, puts it, "Montana is a great place to live, but it's no place to spend a life" (p.213).

The closed frontier, however, offers no further place to settle and make a home. Instead, people must find freedom in constant movement. As Jick, his daughter Mariah and her ex-husband Riley make their journey through Montana they discover themselves, the land, and the land's continuing power to heal. This healing, however, comes from contemplating the land in nature reservations, by talking with people who have made their living from it, or by moving through it, like the geriatric members of the Baloney Express delivering their used cars, or like Jick himself, coming to terms with his bereavement. But these successes depend on an independence wrested from the land, not on a continuing productive relationship with it. As Jick remarks at one stage, the signs of a rancher's success are his tonnage of vehicles, TVs, VCRs, his snow equipment and his video dish. The little party travel in the ultimate symbol of prosperity, leisure, and the new mobility, a recreational vehicle. Mariah and Riley both earn their economic independence by working as artists, the one using photographs and the other words to discover and record the truth of the country.

The truth they uncover is not the rural myth of progress from hard beginnings to independence and prosperity. The story is marred not only by parasites like Good Help Hebner, but by the failures that repeatedly strike at the toughest and most industrious. They are reminded of this when, in the carpark by the Yellowstone River, they meet the broke and barefoot man who has been robbed while he travels in search of work. He symbolizes the contemporary settler, the man who has not had a chance to make it. This "whispy-whiskered specimen of woe" recalls for Jick all those other families whose dreams had been destroyed by the Depression, when:

> . . . other pickups were on the road, passing through the
> Two Medicine country from the droughted-out farms of the
> High Line with the bitter farewell GOODBY OLD DRY
> painted across their boxboards, and families of the Depression
> crammed aboard with whatever last desperate possessions
> they had managed to hang on to. The human landslide set
> loose by auction hammers cracking down. (p.234)

The journey without a destination may be healing for those with
resources, but for those without it merely prolongs desperation.

Yet the trilogy does not finish on this note. Riley may light
off for California, whose name Jick and his fellows regard as the
American word for away, but for Riley it is the future: "There's
just more, well, more California than there is Montana to the
world any more" (p.214). Mariah may have rejected both the
ranch and marriage, but she has her role as photographer at
large. Like Riley with his words, she will be able to play the role
of King's Remembrancer, the figure from the tale in *Rascal Fair*
who keeps track of time so that "things can be fixed in mind
around here" (*Rascal Fair*, p.132). They can complete the work
of Angus McCaskill, described by his neighbour and rival in love
as a "man with poetry on his tongue and decent intonations in
his heart" (*Mariah Montana*, p.86). Angus wanted to rhyme his
life into meaning and celebration but failed to make a couplet
from his love. With words and pictures they can also penetrate
to the meaning of Jick's life, as Riley already has in his lament
for the ranchers, and use the time his gift of his farm buys for
them and their generation to find ways of bringing back into the
future the land which fashioned them and their restless
independence.

There is, however, a further paradox here. Jick's gift of his
land to the Nature Conservancy surprises, even shocks, his
neighbours because it endorses an environmental ethic that is
the product of the cities rather than of the generations of settlers.
Their ethic is that repeatedly expressed by Jick in his remarks
to the effect that he is just a rancher trying to make a living from
the land. By giving his land as a gift for conservation, and insisting
that it be used to support buffaloes, he is contradicting the work
three generations. Yet the gift also expresses the care for the land
which has also grown from that work, and which Maria and
Riley have learned both from their own upbringing and from

their travels. This care can no longer be expressed through traditional ranching, and is contradicted by the business of contemporary agriculture which reduces land to capital. These traditional practices, however, depended as much on the cities as do the new. Only the industrial markets enabled the original settlers to free themselves from the servitude that had bound their forebears in Scotland and elsewhere, and the technology of the cities has in turn freed their descendants from the drudgery that marked the lives of the firstcomers. The rural mythology, hostile to the cities, celebrated an illusory independence. Riley and Maria are able to use their words and pictures to build a truth from the mythology only because they are no longer a part of it. They come to understand the country from the inside, but they belong to the city. They are merely travellers in the countryside, for their work is with words, not directly with the land. If the ethic of the land that Jick finally discovers to them is to survive, writers and artists will have to show the cities how to restore the land to their own culture, and not merely portray it as a place of escape within a culture of consumption. The city is now the only frontier that remains open, but until it discovers its relationship to the land that sustains it, it will remain a frontier where exploitation produces only alienation.

CHAPTER 10

WITHDRAWAL FROM VIOLENCE: WRITING BY
AND ABOUT NATIVE AMERICANS

I

In Ivan Doig's *Dancing at the Rascal Fair*, Rob Barclay and Angus McCaskill have their photographs taken in Helena, Montana, on Hogmanay at the end of their year of leaving, 1889. They send it back home to "Let them in old Scotland see what Montanians are" (p.33). The official closing of the American frontier is still a year off, and the two Scots boys have become Americans, "Emigrants changed by the penstrokes of the Cumbrae Steamship Line and Castle Garden into immigrants. Survivors of the Atlantic's rites of water, pilgrims to Helena" (p.33). Yet the immediate object of their pilgrimage, Rob's Uncle Lucas, still eludes them. In Scotland, his annual postal gifts and his reports of the Great Maybe mine had beguiled them, leading to their decision to migrate to Montana. But when they find him, he proves to be a man with no hands. He had come to the new land in search of a fortune, which he tried to gouge directly out of the earth by mining. But like the miner entombed by a cave-in of his tunnel on Ballarat at the opening of Henry Handel Richardson's novel of migration to Australia, *The Fortunes of Richard Mahony*, Lucas's avarice had brought him destruction. He had failed to set his charges properly, and the earth took its vengeance by blowing off his hands. Unlike the Australian miner, however, he has survived to make his fortune, selling drinks and lending money to those who still have hands to work the land. Yet just as Henry Handel Richardson's trilogy shows the eventual destruction of those who initially find fortune on the goldfields, so Ivan Doig's shows how even the successful homesteaders are eventually forced from their lands. In neither country are the new settlers able to produce a sustaining relationship with the land. The older Barclay's loss of his hands acts as a metaphor for this failure to build a future.

The root of this failure is that the work of the newcomers, whether as miners or ranchers, destroys the wilderness they come to and the lives of the people they find there. Doig's novels preserve something of the stories of these earlier people in the words of the half-blood Indian survivor, Renee Toussaint, but they are unable to restore them to their land. Nor are they able to establish the newcomers in right of possession. As in Australia, they are defeated by wildfires and weather, corporations and banks. The best Angus's ultimate inheritor, Jick McCaskill, can do is bequeath his memories to his daughter and return his land to a wilderness that will preserve the memory of the earlier people. This wilderness however remains fenced off both from the lands about it that a remote corporation exploits for profit, and from the lives of the city-dwellers who provide the demand that drives this exploitation. With the original peoples driven from the land, the division of the modern culture from its source in the land remains unbridgeable.

The original settlement of the new world required not only the displacement of the people but also the extinction of their culture. In Latin America, the Conquistadores achieved their ends by applying the power and cunning of the renaissance prince. But while they displaced the indigenous leadership, they left in place some remnants of the native society and most of the natural environment. The settlers of English America on the other hand added to the ruthlessness of the renaissance the righteousness of the reformation. Driven by the will to advance themselves in the standing of God and their fellows, they suppressed all other passion and feeling in the achievement of their ambitions. The desires they so pent up found, however, an outlet in the physical destruction of dissidents who would corrupt their Eden, and the native vegetation, fauna, and people that obstructed its planting.

Richard Drinnan (1980) describes the sexual passion and violence that inflicted almost three centuries of rape, arson, and slaughter on the North American Indians. In *Beyond Geography*, Frederick Turner (1980) describes how this violence extended to the whole of the natural world as the settlers made the native peoples complicit in the destruction of their homelands:

> . . . in order for the scheme to work, the Indian hunters, trappers and dressers had to be made to want the imported items that the traders had to offer. Here again we encounter the clash between history and myth, with the whites, driven to enormous technological ingenuity, producing a vast array of seductive items for peoples of the globe whose spiritual contentments had kept their own technologies at comparatively primitive levels. Regarding this phenomenon, enacted everywhere whites invaded the wilderness, we know now that there has been no people on earth capable of resisting this seduction, for none has been able to see the hidden and devious byways that lead inevitably from the consumption of the new luxuries to the destruction of the myths that give life its meaning. From the acceptance of guns, powder, shot, flints, metal traps, woolen blankets, capes and metal cookware to deportation, the reservation, and cultural extermination is an unforeseeable way. All that is known is all that can be: and this is that these new luxuries make daily living easier, and myths or no, all humans have wanted some relief, some margin against the beloved lands. None have known how much margin would be too much. (p.279)

Once their link with the land was severed, the people sickened and their social structures died. Their own mythmakers attributed their sickness to the witchcraft that had brought whites to the land. For all the economic success they have achieved, the whites have not been able to destroy the break made at their first coming, and so have not been able to produce a culture in harmony with the land. Some of their writers have now turned to the first peoples to learn from them how to build the relationships which may repair the ills of modern society. At the same time, the native writers of America and elsewhere are endeavoring to recover from their own past the links that may give them back the wholeness denied to them by European cultures.

Although the European navigators and settlers around the Pacific compel our admiration for their courage and achievement, reading the records of the destruction they wrought can only fill us with sorrow, anger, and guilt. These records provide the substance of the stories told in America by Turner, in Australia by Eric Rolls. The realization of these costs of imperialism has led not only to a recognition of the need to respect the land, to develop sustainable forms of production, but also to a renewed interest in the native cultures and a readiness to listen to those who speak for them. At times this interest takes the form of a return to the cult of the noble savage and a romantic flight from the complexities of the modern world. Young people flee the cities to talk to the trees, and are found wearing headbands and beating drums deep in the woods. Newly aware of the environment, they demand new forms of agricultural and industrial production, which in turn require not just a different technology but a change in our attitudes to the land. In short, the survival of modern industrial society depends on a change in the culture bequeathed to us by the imperial venturers who laid its foundations. The search for alternatives to our culture of exploitation takes us back to the supposed simplicities of the peoples who came before us in the lands we have settled.

As anthropologists and others have gradually uncovered for us the mythological systems of these native peoples, they have shown that the apparent simplicities of their ways of life are sustained by complex cultures. These assign all their members a place in relation both to the land on which they depend and the time in which they exist. This relationship is the opposite of the way of seeing established by European cultures that subordinate time and place to individual will. Instead, in the native cultures of North America, Australia and the Pacific, individuals realize their potential only as they find their identity in a land that incarnates mythic time. Kim Stafford (1986) explains how the Indians of the Pacific Northwest named places for things that happened. Interestingly enough, Les A. Murray (1982) shows the same practice among the rural settlers in his "Buladelah-Taree Song Cycle," which amongst other things is trying to establish a similar mythic relationship between the new settlers and the land to that which had been enjoyed by its earliest inhabitants. By personalizing nature, both groups find their own place in nature. Similarly, Ronald and Catherine Berndt (1989) write of traditional Aboriginal mythology as presenting "a land that is resonant with sound and presence," that speaks unequivocally, underlining what people imply is its concern for the affairs of human beings."

The violence of white settlers societies arises from their culture of domination. The myths of the native peoples record many instances of violence arising from personal ambition or frustration. This violence is portrayed, however, as a disruption of societies that essentially depended on nurturing and regenerative relationships with the land. Among the native peoples today, violence is a product of their dispossession and exclusion. Nineteenth-century white writers, from Fenimore Cooper in America to Henry Kingsley and Rolf Boldrewood in Australia, romanticized the violence of this dispossession in novels that dramatized settlement as a conflict between barbarism and civilization. Their works, however, also established the myth of the Edenic wilderness. For Cooper, and later American nature writers from W.H. Hudson to John Muir, the coming of the settler has destroyed Eden. In Australia, writers at first saw settlement as fulfilling an Edenic potential. Later writers blame the failure of this dream on the land itself. Only with a novel like Katharine Susannah Prichard's *Coonardoo* do we find the blame for this failure put on the inability of the settlers to understand the land. Xavier Herbert is the first writer to portray fully the consequent violence. At the same time, in the portraits of Norman in his first novel and Prindy in his last, he suggests, as well as in explicit authorial comment, that the Aboriginal people hold the key to such understanding.

II

In America in the sixties, Margaret Craven's *I Heard the Owl Call My Name* (1967) brought together the two themes of Edenic wilderness and native harmony. The novel examines both the strength that holds together a community still in possession of its land and traditions, and the forces already undermining this strength. Yet, while the novel portrays the community from the inside, it does so through the eyes of a white man, the priest who gives himself to its service and is allowed to commune with it.

The priest is contrasted with the teacher, another white man sent by his authorities to bring to the village people what white society believes they need. But the teacher remains enclosed in his own culture, accepting the posting only so that he can receive the isolation pay that will allow him to spend a year in Greece, "studying the civilization he adored" (p.24). Implicitly, his failure to connect with his present dooms his plans to discover his cultural past. His is the colonial cringe for which culture is external, something that offers us a chance to escape from

ourselves for a time, not something to sustain us in society and
the natural world, as it is for both the priest and the Indians.
His first conversation with Mark, the priest, is only to complain
about his material circumstances and to declare himself an atheist.

> The vicar might as well know, right now that, as for himself,
> he was an atheist; he considered Christianity a calamity. He
> believed that any man who professed it must be incredibly
> naive.

The vicar's reply takes us to the heart of the book.

> There were two kinds of naivety, he said, quoting Schweitzer;
> one not even aware of the problems, and another which has
> knocked on all the doors of knowledge and knows man can
> explain little, and is still willing to follow his convictions
> into the unknown. (29)

The attitude of the vicar, and of the book, is that of Schweitzer.
Mark is prepared to listen and to learn, and so is admitted to
the community, the group of people who are in communion with
each other. Through them, he is able to enter into the wider
communion with the past and with the land that holds the past
that gives their culture its being.

Yet, like Schweitzer in Africa, Mark remains an outsider. The
village peoples are able to extend their communion to him, but
he is not able to extend his to them except through the
consolations he is able to bring from his Christian faith. These
are real, but they are offered as comfort to a dying community
rather than as strength for one renewed in the wider society that
is already intruding on its isolation. Mark works to support those
members of the community who recognize that its truth will
endure only if its younger members obtain an education in white
as well as Indian ways. The novel, however, ends with the potlatch
to Jim Wallace, Mark's Indian friend and spiritual heir, and then
with the vicar's own death and the return of his soul "to the
village that he had loved."

> Past the village flowed the river, like time, like life itself,
> waiting for the swimmer to come again on his way to the

climax of his adventurous life, and to the end for which he
had been made.

Wa Laum

(That is all)

(p.133)

Although on its own, this ending sounds like Wordsworthian
romanticism, the peace it brings has been achieved through the
whole action of the novel, which serves both to educate Mark
in the villagers' understanding of their environment and to
identify their empathy with the land with his own love for a God
he finds in human life without pretending to understand. It is
a mysticism of action rather than of contemplation. The basis of
the strength that Mark finds is the life of the people, which in
turn is concentrated in the two figures of Jim Wallace and his
bride, Keetah, who between them are left to carry on Mark's
work and to protect the village in a changing world. By confining
its action to a time when the village remains intact, if threatened,
the novel portrays this strength, but it leaves unanswered the
question of how it can survive either the incorporation of the
village in an alien economy or the dispersion of its people and
their separation from the source of their culture.

III

Farley Mowatt's writing conveys even more starkly the
strength of a people living in a culture of unity with their land,
and the terrible destruction of this culture by the intrusion of a
white economy and the indifference, or, worse, ignorant
benevolence of white authorities. In the documentary narrative
People of the Deer he travels to discover the last remnants of one
of the Inuit tribes of northern Canada. These tribes themselves
had been victims of the prejudice and savage hostility of the
Indian tribes bordering their territories. One of the earliest of the
Hudson Bay *bois-coureurs* describes the brutal massacre inflicted
by his Indian guides on a party of Inuits they casually
encountered. (MacLennan, 1969). The people Mowatt describes
are not, however, victims of sudden assault, but of starvation
brought about by the withdrawal of the fur trade for which they
have abandoned their traditional hunting. Without a trader from

whom to obtain supplies and bullets, and without stocks of the deer on which they formerly depended, they are left to die of cold and hunger. Even when Mowatt's reports lead to government intervention, the supplies made available lack the fat the Inuits need to supply body heat during the long winter, and so only prolong their agony.

Yet, for all the anger the author feels, the emphasis of the book is not on the destruction of the people but on the depth of their feelings for each other, for their past and for the land. Living at the very brink of existence and with the barest material support, they nevertheless possess an intricate culture that produces a rich capacity for love, friendship and courage. Mowatt does not construct an image of the noble savage, but of people with whom we can share a common humanity if we take the trouble to understand them. As in Shakespeare's *King Lear*, this humanity is not created but tested by the worst that man and nature can do.

There is, however, a vast difference between the world of Lear and the country inhabited by the people of the deer. Shakespeare offers a moral drama deliberately detached from any specific time or place, but dealing with the problems of order and chaos that confronted his own time. Mowatt's people are precisely located in the Canadian arctic, and are victims of two quite specific changes in western economic practice—the rise and fall of the fur trade—as well as of particular political policies and government practices. Rather than inhabiting a generalized mythic realm, their mythology explains their identity, places them in time and place, and gives them the means of survival in the land they inhabit. It fails not because of inherent weakness but because it is undermined by a European ideology that has flourished since Shakespeare. This places individual consciousness and choice at the centre of the mental universe but allows them to flourish only as they are incorporated in the global enterprise of exploiting the land to produce commodities for sale. When the market fails them, Mowatt's people quite literally perish.

In telling their story, Mowatt is not merely arousing our anger in the hope that we will persuade governments to take action to avert calamity. His book had this effect, although as he explains in a final chapter, the consequent actions saved the lives of the people at the cost of reducing them to penury and dependence. As importantly, the book is a call to its readers to realize what they have lost through the destruction of this particular people, and by realizing it, to preserve something of their wisdom. Nor need this realization be merely an act of piety, a remembrance of times past, for Mowatt presents a practical plan by which the people could be enabled to preserve their ancestral way of life as a living culture on the borders of the modern world. The book makes it clear that the preservation of this traditional culture would provide a source of strength for our own. Because this possibility still exists, at least at the time that he writes, his book is not a tragedy, although it deals with a tragic fate. Instead, his anger subsumes tragedy in hope.

This hope arising out of tragedy provides the narrative pattern of the book. Mowatt does not tell the history of all the Inuit peoples, but the story of his discovery of the Ihalmiut, the People of the Deer, an inland group of the Inuit. This discovery is presented both as a fulfilment of his own early and passionate interest in "all the animals that haunted the rolling prairies near my home in Saskatoon" (p.1), and as the answer to the sense of restlessness and futility that envelops him during and after the second world war. He fills the emptiness of his own soul with admiration for the People of the Deer and with anger at their fate. The reason he journeys to them is not primarily a wish to discover their identity, but a longing to recover a truth he can no longer find within his own culture.

Mowatt begins his narrative with an account of how, as a boy of fifteen, he went with his uncle to the Barrens that are their home. He makes this journey by a ramshackle railtrain, the Muskeg Express, which takes him away from civilization "out of the forests and within sight of the ice-filled waters of Hudson Bay" (p.4). It is not however these waters that later call him back, but his first sight of *la Foule*, the annual migration of the deer that stops the train in its tracks. "For the next hour we stayed there, and for an hour the half-mile-wide river of caribou flowed unhurriedly north in a phenomenal procession, so overwhelming in its magnitude that I could hardly credit my senses" (p.4). This sight remains a dormant memory during the author's engagement in the battles of the second world war and his postwar restlessness, until it is revived by the tales of an old frontiersman. The memory draws him once again on a journey to the Barrens and to his eventual encounter with the deer and their people. When, eventually, he earns the people's trust, they discover to

him their culture and the intricate laws and customs that bind
them to the land they share with the deer whose annual
migrations enable them to survive on the edge of the world.

Before he can come to this knowledge, however, Mowatt has
to prepare himself. First, he goes back to university studies; then
he travels back to the Barrens by way of Churchill, where he
hears tales of the land's hostility to careless humans; finally, he
spends a summer with Franz, the halfblood trapper who finally
introduces him to the People. Franz's story of the finding and
adoption of his own children, left to die of starvation and cold
after their parents' own lonely deaths, is a miniature of the whole
history of the Ihalmiut. Yet, to become possessed of this history,
Mowatt has to undertake yet another journey into the Barrens,
live with the People while they teach him sufficient of their
language, making him one of them, and pass through an
encounter with Kakumee, the shaman who has allowed the poison
of white ambitions to corrupt his magnificent powers and so
enter and destroy the ways of the People. The final stage of his
journey becomes a pilgrimage when he persuades his guide and
mentor, Ohoto, to take him even further into the Barrens, beyond
any country they have visited, to the lake and the country known
to Ohoto and his fellows only through their fathers' stories from
a time when it was a meeting place of all the Inuit people. This
journey takes Mowatt through a dead land, inhabited neither by
humans nor by deer, but filled with the bones of the dead and
the Inukok, the stone men built by the ancestors of the People,
the figures which open Mowatt to the full reality of the dwellers
of the Barrens:

> They stand immutable, contemptuous of the winter gales
> and of the passing years, imbued with an essential quality
> that belies their faceless forms and gives them more than
> a semblance of reality as men. . . . This is because they were
> built not to keep some memory green, nor to express the
> hidden passions of a sculptor's hands. The Inukok have being
> because they were created as the guardians of living men
> against a loneliness which is immeasurable. (p.200)

Only by experiencing this loneliness is Mowatt ready for the full
insight into the lives of the Ihalmiut as his mentor and guide,
Ohoto, gradually reveals to him the spiritual beliefs that guide

the people, his father's story and the past of his people. Yet, before he can tell this tale, Ohoto himself is forced to confront the spirits of the land, surviving only because Mowatt literally brings him to a rebirth, freeing him from the forces of death that were dragging him to join his ancestors. The narrative presents this event both literally as an account of the will to survive, and symbolically to suggest that the white man still holds the power to restore the way of life that he has destroyed.

Although Mowatt provides a detailed and deeply sympathetic account of the life of the Ihalmiut, his narrative belongs firmly within the western tradition. At one level it is, as I have already suggested, a modern tragedy. The corrupt shaman, Kakumee, has elements of Macbeth in his grasping for power by means that he knows must destroy him. But the people as a whole enact the tragedy of King Lear, who is embodied in the person of Ohoto, the man who has already lost one family to the forces of the nature he is again forced to confront, naked and alone in the furthest Barrens. Like Lear, he discovers here that love is stronger than the most destructive passions, but also like Lear this discovery comes too late to alter the fate of his people. Ohoto survives at the end of the narrative, but the final chapter and two forewords remind us how precarious his and his people's survival remains.

Although Ohoto's fate places him in the position of a Lear, the twentieth century does not allow any individual to bear the whole burden of the public and the private in the manner of Shakespearian tragedy. An atomized culture leaves individuals as objects rather than agents. Our interest in Ohoto is greater because he represents a much earlier culture when the individual could still be responsible for his people, but this culture has already lost its strength before Mowatt encounters its survivors. Ohoto is not exposed to the brute force of nature because of his own pride, but because his people have colluded with the whites to destroy the bond between society and nature. Their unforeseeing greed has destroyed the deer that supported the People. Just as Lear is no longer a man when he ceases to be a king, so the People no longer have any substantial being, any significant existence, when they cease to exercise their stewardship over the deer and become mere trappers for the white traders. When the whites abandon them, they are left alone to contend with the nature they have contemned.

Yet, despite its tragic elements, Mowatt presents this story not as tragedy but as pilgrim narrative. Like the first settlers, he goes into the wilderness in search of Eden. Like them also, he finds his Eden fallen, but with a wisdom going beyond theirs he attributes the fall not to the first inhabitants but to his own people. His Chapel Perilous is in ruins, but we have the power to restore it. His narrative thus functions as a morality for white society, convicting us of our sins and at the same time teaching us the reparations through which we can earn our own grail of wisdom.

By describing the destruction of a culture that had previously been linked with the land, Mowatt implicitly condemns the European cultures that have destroyed this bond in their own societies and thus deny it to others. He celebrates the past of a people who have this link, and asks us to join in preserving it for the future. Writers from the native peoples themselves, however, concentrate their attention on the individuals who have been cast adrift from their traditional cultures and are unable fully to function in any other. Their narratives are shaped by the efforts of these individuals to find their way back through the clash of cultures to the place of origin. The land is important to them not as the site of an Eden to be discovered in the future, but as an Eden from which they have been driven into exile. Their journey therefore is envisaged neither as a cleansing nor an escape, but as a return.

Although Mowatt's writing forced the Canadian government to take some responsibility for the physical condition of the Inuits, his book closes with a report of the failure of these schemes to confront the fundamental problems. He remains optimistic, using the example of Greenland to suggest how the People can be given access to the natural resources that will enable them to maintain their culture, and in fact integrate it with the culture of the wider community. Yet, although his book is an eloquent plea to consider the needs of the minority, it, like Margaret Craven's novel, is written from within the majority culture and responds to its needs. The writers value the native peoples not only for themselves, but because they continue to represent the independence and harmony with nature that the white settlers consistently sought in the new world and that the societies they developed continually denied. The difference is that writers of this generation recognize that the values of European culture as they have developed since the renaissance can only be fulfilled in the new world as the settlers learn to respect the indigeneous environment and its people.

IV

Native writing is a vexed question in all the nations of the Pacific. Native cultures go back for thousands of years before the arrival of the white settlers, and the "literature" that expresses these cultures is in the native languages and is usually part of an oral rather than a written tradition. Since white settlement, some of this work has been written down, either by anthropologists and folklorists relying on native informants or, more recently, by native writers concerned to tell their own tales. At the same time, as literacy has spread, native writers have used writing to extend the literature of their own languages into modern forms. This work, however, is either concerned with recording a past that is now gone or with addressing a particular audience within the present. In considering the interaction of imported cultures with the land and indigenous traditions, I am concerned with native writers who have used the English language to produce work that recovers their traditions as a part of the contemporary cultures of the Pacific.

Even this work, however, raises problems of definition and of audience. Although written in English, much native literature is addressed primarily to its own people, and many native writers argue that they are not interested in white reactions to it, and even that white readers and critics have no business to comment on it. But published literature requires an readership, and in all the countries of the Pacific these readers must include whites to provide a sufficient market to justify publication. Native literatures therefore must be defined by authorship rather than by audience.

Yet, Thomas King points out (King, 1990, p.x), defining native literature by the race of the author presents problems even in a single country, making "a rather large assumption . . . that the matter of race imparts to a Native writer a tribal understanding of the universe, access to a distinct culture, and a literary perspective that is unattainable by non-Natives." It also assumes, as he argues, a commonality between Natives raised in the city and in the country, those raised by whites and speaking English and those raised by their own people and possibly in native languages, between educated and uneducated, and between those still living in a tribal way and those who have long left this way. "We know that this is a romantic, mystical, and, in many instances, a self-serving notion that the sheer number of cultural groups in North America . . . and the varied conditions of the various tribes should immediately belie" (p.xi). His solution essentially is to accept as native all those writers who consider themselves so. This properly places emphasis on the cultural relationship between authors and their origins, between the particular work and the tradition from which it comes and which it makes new in contemporary culture. The whole of native writing thus becomes both a remaking of contemporary literature to incorporate the tradition displaced by imperialism and a recovery of that tradition in terms of contemporary circumstance.

The displacement of the native heritage has been both social and linguistic. After the native wars had destroyed the indigenous societies, the victors removed children from their parents and forbade them to speak their mother tongues. The white systems of education actively denied the validity of native ways and beliefs, continuing in the classroom with schoolbooks the war begun in the wilderness and the bush with firearms and poison. As Paula Gunn Allen writes in her introduction to *Spider Woman's Daughter* (1989),

> To use educational warfare effectively you have to have your enemy in captivity. Thus the Indian school system was developed to aid the military and "legal" establishment in processing the resigned, defeated young Natives who fell into its hands. Schools that were little more than concentration camps for young people were erected all over the West, Midwest, and even in the East . . .
>
> But Indian schools and mission schools are only special cases of the American school system in general. In these programs, from Head Start through graduate school, the young of this land are taught to view the world only through Protestant-derived, purist, Anglo-American eyes. The materials, values, cultural expression forms, models, and techniques, sciences, facts, and thinking processes taught are all cut from the Anglo-American model. Children who resist this intense, compulsory indoctrination are punished in a

> variety of ways: flunked out, forced out (or graduated illit-
> erate in a society that requires literacy as the price of dinner)
> shamed, coerced, beaten, put in tiny cells in late-spring and
> early fall heat or winter cold, denied, discounted, and thrown
> away, as though human beings were yesterday's leavings.
>   . . . The results of these methods . . . can be seen on
> every reservation and urban conclave . . . Native people
> suffer the ravages of despair brought on by too much shame,
> too much grief, and too much inexpressible and helpless
> fury. (p.15)

Allen's story has all too clear parallels in Australia, and, to a
lesser extent, New Zealand and the Pacific Islands. It repeats
methods refined by the English in their attempts to exterminate
the Celtic cultures of Scotland, Wales and Ireland. But unlike the
Celts, the native peoples of the Pacific had nowhere else to go.
The consequences of their repression are not merely mental and
cultural, but physical. As Allen points out, the life expectancy
of American Indians is still around forty-nine years, and their
lives are characterized by "alcoholism, fetal alcohol symptoms,
non-consensual sterilization of both men and women, an
appallingly high child and teen suicide rate, dismal employment
opportunities on and off reservation, and intense community and
intrapersonal conflicts." Yet, she concludes, "still we have great
hope" (p.17).

For the native peoples of America, as for those of Australia
and the islands, this hope comes from political action and the
cultural recovery that underpins it. In both political and cultural
terms, the critical move in this action has been the recovery of
power over language. In some cases this has been through the
restoration of the native languages as the medium of education,
in others by the assertion of dialect as a legitimate form of speech,
but in all cases it has expressed the demand that the native peoples
be allowed to speak for themselves rather than through some
sanctioned intermediary. The literature of the native peoples is
a part of this demand that we listen to the voices of the victims.
Writers in the native languages deliberately exclude Europeans
from their audience, asking only that we respect their
separateness. But the native writers who choose English as their
medium are making an even more radical demand of the colonists.
By choosing to speak in our language of their concerns they are

undermining the certainties that we have imposed on them through our command of this language. They are making it sing new songs, tell new tales. And to the extent that they incorporate their own names and idioms in this language, and force its grammar to expand to comprehend the terms on which they lead their lives, they are asserting their part in the ownership of a language that they are forcing to express a multitude rather than a singularity of cultures. This appears most clearly in the poetry collected by Andrea Lerner in her anthology of native American writing from the Pacific Northwest, where the open forms developed by modern European poetry to express the loss of certainty are used instead as a means of incorporating experience that lies outside both European sensibility and the security of mainstream living.

We see this extension of language in the simple poem that Victor Charlo, "parent, poet, philosopher, theologian and teacher," writes for his students at the Two Eagle River School:

> You say
> old days fold into one another
> and new days seem the same.
> Yet each moment shifts with the sun,
> nothing will be the same as this:
>
> when wind breathes the Flathead alive,
> you are the center this instant
> for all, you are the creation
> of the universe one more time.
>
> (Lerner, 1990, p.27)

The opening of the poem describes the fashionable boredom expressed by contemporary students anywhere. Its solution, that everything is always new and always complete in the individual person and the individual moment, is a variation of popular existentialism tempered by Zen. But the wind is specific to the Blackfeet, and so makes not just a specific person, but a member of a particular tribe at a particular time, the heir of the world—a total reversal of colonialism, which denied both specific and universal value to tribal experience.

This poem is simple, even conventional, in its expression, yet it still serves to open European forms to native American experience. Even more open is Dian Million's "The Highway,"

about travelling to Oregon, fishing, camping. Written in free verse,
it ends:

> we make camp
> and listen to the river
>
> I walk to the edge
> of every night thinking
>
> what if the river called
> and we were not there.

(p.132)

The first of these couplets has the essentialist simplicity of much
modern verse, distrustful of the grand gesture, safe only with
the concrete images of immediate experience. In the second
couplet the metaphor of the edge changes the sign of the river,
image of both time and nature, into a sign simultaneously
referring to both one of the alternating phases of all time, night
that follows day, and the darkness that marks the end of time,
the night that swallows all life, the brink of time where we always
are. Only the most daring of the contemporary Europeans—
Seamus Heaney, Vincent Buckley—will come with us to this point.
But the final couplet takes us beyond any contemporary
sensibility, back to the responsibility of the tribes before our
coming. Nature here is not the sublime other, not even a guarantee
of our existence, but the part of the world for which we are
responsible, the other part of the dialogue that alone creates
reality. The poet's contemplation of absolute loss between these
two lines is also an assertion of the absolute totality of being.
This totality is not, however, merely a vaguely numinous
aspiration, but exists as concrete reality in the tradition of the
native American people. Like Charlo, Million gives her words
authority by their appeal to the tradition from which she writes.

The stories collected in the American anthologies of native
writing do not portray the kind of idyllic past that Farley Mowatt
suggests in his account of the Inuits, nor do the editors dodge
the cruelty and violence that characterized Indian life, as indeed
it characterized renaissance Europe. But whereas Mowatt's form
compels him to portray the native people as innocents, an integral
part of the world of nature that we have destroyed, the writers
in these collections tell of people acting within an autonomous

culture according to their own norms and patterns. While warfare, with its accompaniments of brutality and courage, is central to these patterns, the writers present it neither as an example of tragic fate nor of moral breakdown, but as a part of the inevitable cycle of human life. This view places the stories closer to Homeric and other epic literature than to any of the classic or renaissance forms of European culture. The characters in the stories are neither Virgilian heroes following destiny, nor Shakespearian princes or Pilgrim Fathers trying to command the circumstances of their lives. Rather, they learn to command themselves in the face of hostile fortune.

The bonds which join people within a single tribe or nation exclude others from their fellowship, and so from claims to pity or compassion. When such pressures as the European invasion force tribes into each other's territory, war thus becomes inevitable, although the history of Indian resistance contains plentiful examples of tribes overcoming these barriers to unite against the greater enemy. But even in times of peace, the tribe's integrity depends ultimately on its ability to maintain its place and its lands against intruders. The warrior guarantees this integrity, and war thus becomes not a supreme contest for power but a spiritual testing of both women and men. Glory is the reward of victory, and defeat is the greatest dishonour. Yet, as Paula Gunn Allen writes, the native culture "necessarily entails comprehending death as one of the ways of coming to terms with the spiritual underpinnings of earth life" (p.30). Despite its brutalities, their warfare never partakes of the inhumanity and lust for destruction we find even in sympathetic accounts of the destruction wreaked on the native peoples by their white conquerors.

Paula Gunn Allen's collection shows both the part women themselves take as warriors fighting for their people and their role in maintaining societies that have otherwise been shattered by warfare with the whites whose superior powers allow them to play the part of the malevolent gods in earlier tales. In "Yellow Woman" Leslie Marmon Silko (b.1942) portrays a narrator confused when she finds herself playing the role of the Yellow Woman of her grandfather's stories. At the same time the man who takes her away seems to guarantee her continuing link to her land and her people. This strength drawn from their common past enables several of the women in these tales to resist the powers of the whites. E. Pauline Johnson (1861–1913) shows a woman turning back his deceit on the missionary who has robbed her of her people and her tongue in the name of Christianity only to deny her the right to the love she has won from his son. The missionary is destroyed by his own contradictions, but more often the whites use their power to achieve their aims at the cost of their integrity. In these stories power cloaks itself in philanthropy, particularly in the guise of the social worker. So Vicki L. Sears (b.1941), in "Grace," allows a brother and sister to be fostered into a native family that brings healing to the wounds inflicted by years of institutions only to remove them again when the death of the husband places the foster-mother, Grace, outside the official definition of nurture. In "The Warriors," Anna Lee Walters (b.1946) shows how alcoholism precipitated by the experience of modern warfare in Korea turns the hero-figure of childhood into a hobo who dies of exposure, leaving his nieces only with memories of the mythical legions of warriors with whom they shared the struggle to survive. Most grimly, Louise Erdrich in "American Horse" retells the story of the theft of the child, son of a deceased father, by the wicked witch, in this case a social worker abetted by a treacherous relative of the boy he captures. This relative has become a policeman, and travels in a car emblazoned with the picture of Red Tomahawk, the renegade Indian who butchered Sitting Bull. The story pits the instinctive love of the Indian family, driven to exist on the fringe of society, against the cold rationality and shallow sensuality of the white officials who snatch the boy into the control. The story ends as the boy is "astonished to hear a great rattling scream, and then another, rip out of him like pieces of his own body and whirl onto the sharp things all around him" (p.61). The sharp things represent the uncaring and destructive culture of white authority, and the scream is both a protest at the fate of the Indians and a symbol of the force that is tearing them, individually and collectively but physically, apart. Yet, while the force is destructive, the fact that it produces a scream of protest is also testimony that it generates its own countervailing force for survival.

V

The question of survival is at the heart of novels by Leslie Marmon Silko (b.1948) and James Welch (b.1940). Both novels deal with Indians who have land to live on, but have lost the culture that might join them to it.

We see this at the beginning of Welch's *Winter in the Blood* (1974), where the narrator is "Coming home to a mother and an old lady who was my grandmother. And the girl who was thought to be my wife. But she didn't count." Neither, he explains, does anyone. "I felt no hatred, no love, no guilt, no conscience, nothing but a distance that had grown through the years." This distance comes partly from the country, that "had created a distance as deep as it was empty," until "the people accepted and treated each other with distance." More importantly, it comes from within the narrator himself: "it came from within me. I was as distant from myself as a hawk from the moon" (p.2). The novel is about his attempts to come back from this distance, to recover the significance of the "Earthboy place" where he stops on the first page, although "no one by that name (or any other) had lived in it for twenty years . . . the Earthboys were gone." Their loss, their absence from everywhere except the graves within a rectangle of barbed wire, symbolizes his own loss. The failure to replace them is symbolized by the haying he helps with after his return to the emptiness of home.

Unlike the haying that Jick McCaskill helps with in *English Creek* (Doig, 1984), which celebrates the triumph of the communal spirit over personal discord, this haying is an exercise in power. Lame Bull, who has become "the property owner" by marrying the narrator's mother, is learning to enjoy the rights of proprietorship, but even within his enjoyment there is an element of disharmony:

> All day he grinned as he mowed through the fields of alfalfa and bluejoint. He grinned when the little tractor putted into the yard next to the granary. . . . He let his whiskers grow around his round face. Teresa complained about his sloppy habits, his rough face. She didn't like the way he teased the old lady, and she didn't like his habit of not emptying the dust and chaff in his pants cuffs. He grinned a silent challenge, and the summer nights came alive in the bedroom off the kitchen. Teresa must have liked his music.

> We brought in the first crop, Lame Bull mowing alfalfa,
> snakes, bluejoint, baby rabbits, tangles of barbed wire,
> sometimes changing sickles four times in a single day. Early
> next morning he would be down by the granary sharpening
> the chipped, battered sickles. He insisted on both cutting
> and baling the hay, so my only job was the monotonous one
> of raking it into strips for the baler.... He tinkered endlessly
> with the baler, setting the tension tighter so that the bales
> would be more compact, loosening it a turn when they began
> to break. Occasionally I would see the tractor idling, the
> regular puffs of black smoke popping from its stack, and
> Lame Bull's legs sticking out from the baler. He enjoyed
> being a proprietor and everything went smoothly until we
> hired Raymond Long Knife to help stack bales. (pp.23–4)

Raymond Long Knife "came from a long line of cowboys"
and "had become shrewd in the way dumb men are shrewd. He
had learned to give the illusion of work, even to the point of
sweating as soon as he put his gloves on, while doing very little"
(p.24). His employment terminates in a bout of fisticuffs, an
infection to Lame Bull's hand, and the end of his grinning: "he
had decided that it was improper for a property owner to grin
so much" (p.30). But Long Knife merely precipitates the crisis.
The indiscriminate baling of snakes, weeds and hay, the constant
trouble with the machinery, Lame Bull's assertion of his rights
as owner, show that he is just playing at farming. Both the style
of agriculture and the rights of proprietorship belong to an alien
culture. They continue the disruption first brought into his life
by the narrator's father, First Raise, whose skill with machinery
allowed him to enter the white male society that took him away
from his own family and into a companionship of alcohol that
to the narrator even then seemed false:

> I had another whisky with Lame Bull. I thought of the hours
> my father had put in here, joking with the white men, the
> farmers from out north, the cattlemen to the east, the men
> from the grain elevator—they were acquaintances; they had
> bought me beers on those occasions First Raise dragged me
> in. But they were foreign—somehow their lives seemed
> more orderly, they drank a lot but left early, and they would
> be back at work in the morning, while First Raise . . . (p.41;
> ellipsis in original.)

The ambiguity of First Raise's life made him both hero and disrupter to his sons. By sending the boys alone to bring in the cattle for the winter, he entrusted them with adult responsibility but also put them at risk, not from the natural world, but from the world of machinery to which he had given his own allegiance. The narrator's admired elder brother is killed in front of his eyes when he is struck by a car as he is bringing the cattle across the last obstacle before home. This death leaves the narrator adrift in the hostile world through which his brother had seemed to offer direction. Just as the road separates their home from the ranges, so the death of his brother sunders him from both his Indian past and the alien imperatives of contemporary American society. This disruption is symbolized both by his continuing lameness and by his refusal to take the opportunity of becoming the token Indian staff member in the hospital that offers treatment for his lameness. He is spiritually crippled, and needs the healing that can come only from his own people.

Yet none of his own people is immediately available to offer this healing. Teresa, his mother, provides a stable centre for the household, and preserves the land for her family, but her own strength is undermined by her dependence on the Catholic priest in the nearby town. This priest is an outsider, "a white man who refused to bury Indians in their own plots, who refused to set foot on the reservation" (p.59). He has nothing to offer the narrator, and resents Teresa offering him anything except disapproval. His mother's friends, Ferdinand Horn and his wife, gossips who refuse to become involved, merely reinforce his mother's disapproval. Within the household, Teresa's mother, daughter and wife of chiefs but mother of her only child by a white drifter, represents both the historic disruption of the tribes and a focus of present disharmony. She condemns the "wife" her grandson has brought home because she is Cree, not Blackfoot. Yet, blind as she is, isolated by age and debility on her rocking chair, she is able to confer on her grandson her own memories and the clues he needs to find himself, to heal the wounds of his own and his family's past. In search of this healing, he leaves home on a quest that takes him first through white bars and bedrooms in search of his wife, and then back to the hills, to the old Indian, Yellow Calf, who talks to the animals and knows the seasons as a part of himself, and through him to his spiritual source.

When he returns home after his quest, he finds that his grandmother is dead. Her death sends him on one last journey, to the graveyard and then again to Yellow Calf. As he digs the grave for the old lady, he remembers again and comes to terms with his brother's death. Then he realizes that Yellow Calf is his true grandfather, the man who kept Teresa's mother alive after the slaughter by the whites and her abandonment by the surviving Indians. Returning from the visit, he tries to rescue a calf drowning in the dam, and instead kills old Bird, the horse he was riding when the car struck his brother. This, followed by the burial of the grandmother, finishes his business with the past. Although he remains outside the family, now reduced to his mother and her new husband, he has learned his own place in history. The novel does not conclude with any hope for the future, but it does reach a peace with the past.

VI

This past is even more disruptive in Leslie Marmon Silko's *Ceremony* (1977), which is also a novel about healing. Tayo, the young Indian at its centre is, like Welch's narrator, doubly wounded, by the history of his people and by his own life. His own life however has been destroyed by his involvement in exactly the same kind of European warfare that in the previous century destroyed his own people. Also like Welch's character, Tayo is tormented by the thought that he has survived while his more worthy brother, or foster brother, dies. This thought drives Tayo too on a quest that leads from the bars and drifters of drab inland towns back to his own past. This past becomes, however, not merely his personal history, or even the history of his people, but the past of all people. His quest becomes a search for the ceremony that alone can defeat the witchery of evil and keep the world and its creatures alive. Tayo finally completes this ceremony, and thus for his time defeats witchery, at the site of the mine from which white men dug up the uranium ore for the first atomic bomb. Yet this bomb is not in itself the ultimate symbol of evil. The ultimate evil is the violence that has destroyed the Indians and their land, and that has finally produced the bomb and the wish to use it. Tayo is almost defeated at the point of completing his ceremony because his revulsion at this evil allows it to enter his own heart. He is literally saved by the earth itself, which has numbed his hands with cold and so causes him to falter at the very point of committing the act of violence that will destroy both him and his mission.

The ceremony that Tayo must complete is the continuation of a story that is itself as old as time. At the beginning of the book the interruption of the story, by the destruction of the tribes and their customs and by the implication of their own people in this destruction, specifically in the war, is bringing about the death of the world, symbolized socially by the aimless drift of the Indians, physically by the drought that is stifling natural life on the reservation. The novel at first portrays Indians as victims, suffering from the lies of the whites who have first driven them from their land, then refused them a place in white society, then involved them in the violence of the war but given them no home to return to. As the story develops, however, it locates the immediate source of evil in Eno, the Indian who has surrendered to the power of the whites even as he defies them, and now can live only through the death of others. In the story he becomes identified with the original witches, who use their power to choke the springs of life, and with the witch who first brought the story of the whites into the world, and thus created the principle of death. This principle, made concrete in nuclear devastation, unites all people in resistance. Tayo, child of white and Indian people, is able to transcend racial division even as he recovers the heritage of his Indian people. This heritage restores the sources of life, gives him the strength to resist the witchery embodied in Eno, and so prevents the story from coming to an end.

In refusing an ending, the author is rejecting a cultural principle that is central to European history, culture and literature. Whereas preliterate societies tend to think in terms of cycles, European culture is built on the concepts of purpose, conflict and resolution. The teachers of Europe—Greeks, Israelites and Romans—all have, as their founding legends, narratives of purpose. The wrath of Achilles interrupts the fated process of Troy's destruction, and the eventual fall of the city frees Odysseus to embark on a ten year's journey home. Abraham, and later Moses, reverse the process, leaving civilization to lead their people into a wilderness and found a nation. Virgil's Aeneas brings together both motives, repeating the voyage of Odysseus not to get home but in order to found a city destined to bring the peoples of the world under its imperial rule (*Aeneid* I, 5; VI, 851). The purposes of Moses and Aeneas inspire the religious and secular zeal that conquers the west for the white man and the Pax Americana. But to the original peoples on whom this rule is imposed it is a lie, a desolation of the natural rhythms that ceremony keeps alive to integrate the people and their land. In place of ceremonies that bring together inner and outer reality, placing us in a world mapped by the stars and mountains that surround us, imperial rule gives us private property, land surveys, and the straight lines of barbed wire fences:

> The lie. He cut into the wire as if cutting away at the lie inside himself. The liars had fooled everyone, white people and Indians alike; as long as people believed their lies, they would never be able to see what had been done to them or what they were doing to each other. He wiped the sweat off his face onto the sleeves of his jacket. He stood back and looked at the gaping cut in the wire. If the white people never looked beyond the lie, to see that theirs was a nation built on stolen land, then they would never be able to understand how they had been used by the witchery; they would never know that they were still being manipulated by those who knew how to stir the ingredients together: white thievery and injustice boiling up the anger and hatred that would finally destroy the world: the starving against the fat, the colored against the white. The destroyers had only to set it in motion, and sit back to count the casualties. But it was more than a body count; the lies devoured white heats, and for more than two hundred years white people had worked to till their emptiness; they tried to glut the hollowness with patriotic wars and with great technology and the wealth it brought. And always they had been fooling themselves, and knew it. (p.191)

Tayo has cut the wire fence to take back the cattle that the white rancher has stolen and impounded on land that formed part of the sacred mountain and has now been appropriated and enclosed. Tayo has been led to them through the ceremonies of old Betonie, the shaman, and a mysterious woman, who also possesses the powers of a shaman but who restores Tayo to himself through their lovemaking. Unity with her brings him back to unity with the land, and so with all peoples. He is no longer seeking merely personal healing, but now has a mission to renew the ceremony. The recovery of the cattle, a breed peculiarly adapted to the conditions of the reservation and so a promise of economic independence, is a necessary step to the completion of the ceremony. So, to, is his discovery that, while the whites may be agents of the witchery that is destroying his land, they share with him the predicament their lies have produced. They therefore need the ceremony as much as do the Indians.

The ceremony does not function in the novel as a mystical or spiritual escape from the exigencies of modern life, but as a practical restoration of mental and social health through the recovery of vision. At the beginning of the narrative, Tayo is destroying himself with alcohol rather than trying to piece together the fragments of his shattered self. Like his fellow veterans, he looks back to a time when, as a U.S. Marine, he was accepted everywhere by white society, and particularly by white women. They were able to forget they were Indians and fuck their way to self-respect. Now the war is finished, they are again cast to the margins, unhappy on the reservations, given nothing but veterans' compensation and the booze it will buy, and treated with contempt because they cannot make a place for themselves. Yet, as Tayo realizes, they bring this contempt on themselves because they turn their back on their own people and accept the values of the whites.

> They spent all their checks trying to get back the good times . . . trying to bring back that old feeling, that feeling they belonged to America the way they felt during the war. They blamed themselves for losing the new feeling; they never talked about it, but they blamed themselves just as they blamed themselves for losing the land the white people took. (pp.42–3)

But the divisions in Tayo go back before the war and beyond the physical dispossession of the native people. They go back to his mother, who admired white ways, tried to find admission to white society by sleeping with white men, and was finally destroyed by her own self-contempt. They go back to his aunt, who brings him up in her family but keeps him as an outsider because of his white father and his mother's shame. They go back to his admired foster brother, Rocky, who was brought up to succeed in white society and turned his back on the native ways Tayo respects. They go back to Tayo's uncle Josiah, who teaches him respect for the land but is himself unable to respect the Mexican woman he goes with, so that her passion brings death instead of renewal. "That night she danced he was already a dead man, a living dead man who sucked life from the living, desiring and hating it even as he took it" (p.85). When Rocky is killed in the war and Tayo returns, he finds himself heir to all these guilts and divisions. He overcomes them only by learning the story of each of them, by learning how to fit them into the continuing cycle of stories that continually renews the ceremony.

This story is, however, cyclical, not repetitive. As Tayo learns from old Betonie, the attempt of the old men to keep the ceremonies utterly unchanged is as sterile as their abandonment through surrender, like Rocky, to the authority of white culture or, like the other veterans and their whores, to its vices. Both forms of abandonment are a betrayal of the unity of land and people. Tayo's delusion that the corpse of the Japanese soldier is the body of his uncle Josiah, is in fact a recognition of the truth that Japanese and Indians are one, that, as Betonie explains, "Thirty thousand years ago they were not strangers" and that the divisions he saw are a part of "what the evil had done: you saw the witchery ranging as wide as this world" (p.124). Betonie draws the maps that give Tayo his place, and enables him to recover his cattle, and thus his land, and eventually survive the night on the pile of nuclear waste and so resist the force of witchery. His quest fits the old stories into new experience, and so renews the old ceremony.

Tayo takes his part in this ceremony as he fits together the stories. The book does the same by alternating his story with poems from mythic times. Many of the references in these poems remain outside the knowledge of any reader not steeped in Indian lore, but at the same time they admit us to their cyclic time. Both by their form and their presence they challenge our ideas of a purposive narrative leading to clear resolution. As Ts'eh explains to him before she leaves him, the forces of witchery, of white culture, want to bring his story to an end: "They want it to end here, the way all their stories end, encircling slowly to choke the life away. The violence of the struggle excites them, and the killing soothes them" (pp.231–32). As Tayo waits on the mountain, he is tempted to give them this ending, toward which the whole novel seems to have been leading. "He was certain his own sanity would be destroyed if he did not stop them and all the suffering and dying they caused" (p.252). Thus the witchery "almost ended the story according to its plan" (p.253). But Tayo fumbles, and so remains true to his earlier intuition, when

> He cried the relief he felt at finally seeing the pattern, the way all the stories fit together—the old stories, the war stories, their stories—to become the story that was still being told. He was not crazy; he had never been crazy. He had only seen and heard the world as it always was: no boundaries, only transitions through all distances and time. (p.246)

So he is able to return home and tell the old men what he has learned, to bring them the renewal the earth has given him. This, however, does not bring the book to a close. It finishes with another poem, fitting the book into the cycle of the witchery of darkness that "started it journey" and "has come back on itself" (p.261). The darkness is only "dead for now," but the book ends not with darkness or destruction, but with the single word, "Sunrise" (p.262). This is both a description of what the author has shown us, and her hope for our common future. The sun it invokes is one of the gods who, in the cycle of legends, has rescued his sons, the winds, from witchery, and has thus brought life back to earth. The sun itself stands for the natural cycle of life, of which death is a part, as opposed to the purposive culture that brings death as an end. But sunrise is also the start of a new day, a day we have never lived before. The cycle is renewed because it is always changing, and so always alive. In taking his story back to his people, Tayo shares with them the gift of new life his healing has brought to him. The book thus becomes itself an offering of new life to its readers. Its relation to its readers is that of the shamans to Tayo: it offers to correct our vision. The dominant culture is based on lies and destruction. By teaching us to see the native culture as both other and authentic, it offers us the opportunity to share a wholeness based on the cycle of nature that we all share. In rewriting this cycle to incorporate the experience of postwar America as seen from its margins, the book extends the culture of the western American Indians to apprehend a unity that embraces the whole of humankind without blurring the distinctions that make every experience of a culture unique.

Chapter 11

The Canadian Pacific: Sense of Time and Place in Writing from British Columbia

Although the literatures of the Pacific Northwest of America share a sense of place, Canadian writers seem to have a greater sense of the isolated individual and the precarious nature of human society than do their counterparts from below the border. While settlers in the United States look back to a time of expansion, the people in the stories from the Canadian Pacific tend to find themselves abandoned on the coast and in its mountains. Their lives and the worlds they create in response to the environment are contingent in a way the American settlements rarely seem to be. Their sense of isolation pushes them back from a city culture which seems irrelevant, but at the same time the native peoples seem aliens with nothing to offer the newcomers, who relegate them to the fringes where they become symbols of the degradation of the land.

The first Europeans to do business on Canada's Pacific coast came from the south or from the sea: from Spanish settlements in California, from Russian bases in Siberia or from English trading-posts in China. The English, coming at first in search of the Northwest passage to Asia, penetrated the hinterland through Puget Sound and along the Fraser and Columbia rivers, down which later came the trappers and agents from the east. The Hudson's Bay company established bases at Victoria on Vancouver Island and at Fort Vancouver on the Columbia, before treaties made in London and Washington D.C. forced them to withdraw to the present boundaries. British Columbia itself remained independent, joining the federation late and reluctantly, and only after the promise of a link to the east by way of the Canadian Pacific railway. Its people continued, however, to look out across the ocean to Asia, which continued to offer markets and provide migrants. They did not come to the new land to plant farms so much as to harvest the natural wealth of fisheries, mines, and forests. Even today, four-hundred year old Western Red Cedars go under the saw daily as lumber company executives boast that they will spend the next 45 years cutting the last of the old-growth forests. Although the province is now largely urbanised and comfortable, its literature continues to reflect this direct encounter between a nature which is both prolific and unforgiving and humans who are at once admiring and exploitative.

According to E.D. Blodgett, all Canadian literature is a writing of translation. Whereas the United States has expanded as new states have adhered to the original constitution, Canada has expanded only through a process of renegotiation which continues to this day. This need of Canadians to accommodate others combines with an uncertainty about their own tenure to produce a literature that emphasizes the isolation of people in the landscape. This gives rise to what Northrop Frye has called a garrison mentality (Frye, 1972), or what Atwood calls images of survival (Atwood, 1972). These images are crystalized in Ethel Wilson's work. In the affluent suburb of Vancouver, Ethel Wilson's comfortable investor enjoys a fine view of the mountains through his view window, but once the light fades the same window exposes him to the menace lurking in the darkness. In another story, a bride, taking the train into the mountains from the open prairies, reflects that "any suggestion of a town or even a dwelling was so improbable as to make one wonder, Will the curve of any small hill or valley here ever become home to people who will live here and die here—all so empty of life now?" When she notices a sign of life. "(Yet see, a hawk!)," the parenthesis that interrupts the flow of the narrative also sets nature apart from the human space of the train (Wiebe, p.2). This opposition of the safety of enclosure and the threatening freedom of natural space is typical in western movies like *Stagecoach*, where the boundary between the two is transgressed by arrows and bullets. Equally typically, however, the movie hero subdues the menace that emanates from outside. In Wilson's story, the safe space is invaded and destroyed by a failure of the technology that has intruded into nature.

Even when man becomes completely at home with nature, using it as an extension of himself, it remains implacable. In

Wilson's "From Flores," Captain Crabbe and his passengers are killed and those they sought to succour left distraught because one seaman, "a difficult wilful enjoying man of poor judgement," chooses to defy the storm rather than ride with it (Green and Sylvestre, 1967, pp.427–35). Unlike Captain Ahab, he lacks in his defiance the dignity of obsession, and is merely trivialised by self-will. Colin, the hero of her novel *On the Highest Hill* (1949), has the dignity of a man who has learned to be alone, to accept life or death as it is offered. The mountain, however, makes the final choice for death. Colin survives a blizzard crossing only to plunge to his death when the snow platform gives way beneath him just as he is about to leap to the path to safety (ibid., pp.421–27). The garrison he has established in his own physical capacity is destroyed by the element to which he entrusts it. His achievement is entirely in his acceptance.

I

The precarious nature of the European occupation of the Pacific Northwest provides the subject for George Bowering's *Burning Water*, in which George Vancouver's voyage in the *Discovery* from 1791 to 1795 becomes not only the occasion for a contest of wills between British and Spanish imperialism, but an illustration of the conflicting modes of European appropriation of an alien environment.

Bowering himself appears in the novel as its narrator, trying to reconstruct characters in a time remote from himself and his world. Significantly, he flies off to Trieste to undertake this task, removing his body "from the western edge of European America to the eastern tail of western Europe, that strip of seaman's coast that everyone at one time has seemed to desire" (p.10). A seaman's coast is presumably a useful place to try to get inside a seaman's mind, but more importantly a coast remote from America is the place to get inside the European desires that produced the Americas we know.

Bowering's novel is a projection of his own desire to know the past and the different desires of British and Yankees, Russians and Spaniards that came into play around Vancouver's ship. In particular, on shipboard he contrasts the scientific desires of Vancouver to get the new land exactly down on paper and of the naturalist, Menzies, to appropriate it physically, both by collecting a garden of specimens and by erotic adventures with its women. On the land, Spanish desire overcomes English rectitude when Vancouver allows himself to be bedded by the Spanish commandant in Nootka sound, Don Juan Bodega y Quadra. Quadra, born in Lima, describes himself as "officially a Spaniard" but actually an American: "My first sight of land and sky was American. I knew brown Americans all round me." His own desire is for companionship and the delicacies of civilized life, and although he carries out his duties faithfully he rebukes Vancouver for repeating in his nationalist zeal "the games you played in childhood" (p.28). At the end of the novel, these childish games destroy the ambitions of both Vancouver and Menzies as their rivalry leads them to destroy each other and the fruits of Menzies' collecting. The only information left to return to England is the precision of charts that map a coast leading nowhere. The outcome of the voyage has been to prove the northwest passage a myth.

Well, not entirely. At one time, as they sail farther into Howe's River, the ships pick up speed until

> *Discovery* seemed to be skimming on the tops of the small waves . . .
> Then he felt the bow of the *Discovery* go up, and the surge of power as the sails caught and the waters dropped below and behind them. . . . The sun shone white over the miles and miles of cumulus, and picked out the moisture shining on the sails of the two ships alone in all that fluffy sea, coursing eastwards effortlessly now, at home in the jet stream. (p.134)

The narrator for a moment gives the navigator his own twentieth-century experience of flying eastwards from his home in Vancouver to his refuge in Trieste. Vancouver and his men are for a moment elated at the dream projected back on them, but then

> they experienced another, less happy feeling, a regret for the long coniferous shoreline with no man-made spires and fences. In time this feeling of separation would pass, but for now they dreamed like men bewitched. (p.135)

Technology has granted the northwest passage of which Vancouver dreamed, but in doing so it has destroyed the shores he knew and the people who watched his journey along them. The nostalgia attributed to him here in reality belongs to the narrator and those he speaks for, the descendants of the European colonists who took themselves the shores that Vancouver had charted.

The suggestion that the whole voyage, and consequently the subsequent settlement, is misconceived, occurs repeatedly through Bowering's novel. The personality of George the Third, the king in whose name Vancouver sails, suggests that the whole thing is a ghastly mistake. The king, we are told, dismissed the paintings of Blake because he was the first Englishman for generations to recognize that everything worth representing can be represented by the human form, and some things are too terrible to represent (p.25). The king, in other words, is opposed to everything that Blake, Vancouver and their fellows of the enlightenment were determined to reveal. No wonder that, when Vancouver announced that their landing spot in Western Australia would be called "King George's Sound," his deputy remarked that he "had had occasion to hear that argued more than once" (p.81). The novel raises this question in regard to his navigators rather than about their royal commander. Their sailing date, the first of April, suggests to Vancouver that they are just "a ship of fools." Menzies' botanical collections make the ship look like a "floating island." When they try to adapt their customs to the new lands, cutting "from the native bushes a strange wood which they formed into antipodes of British musical instruments" they do not reproduce their homeland but rather convert the new land into Prospero's island, where "a twangle of a thousand instruments seemed to hum around his ears." But in these South Seas the voyagers are the Calibans, who in Tahiti permit the women to live on board so that "a lot of people got venereal diseases. Vancouver thought they were fools for it" (pp.82–83). The Indians who observe their coming to Nootka Sound, who suffer their insults, and whom they massacre, are similarly doubtful of the sense of the enterprise.

Vancouver's ambition is to transform the world by facts, to give it sound English names and to mark his charts with "Fathoms, leagues, rainfall, names, all facts." His ship "was a fact factory" (p.186). But this obsession with facts notes only the external and ignores the truth. Vancouver reveals his blindness to reality in his argument with Menzies over the significance of the Indians' totems. Language, he agrees, serves a useful purpose. "Learning a naked foreigner's tongue is the first step in creating some form of government." But art cannot serve power, and is therefore irrelevant to him: "carving and daubing of trees is not a useful pursuit in the affairs and government of men, and I will not waste my time upon them." When Menzies dares to suggest that they, too, may be a language, he replies that a

> language that is neither spoken or writ is a language neither heard nor read, and therefore a failure at the principal task of language, that is to communicate information from one person to another . . . (p.42)

Vancouver speaks with the voice of positivist technology. He cannot comprehend Menzies' alternative voice of science, that is ready to admit that there has been a failure of communication, but does not "leap to the conclusion . . . that the failure lies in the expression of the language." Although Menzies' science may serve imperialism, he himself remains outside it, accepting that "everything in nature has something to tell me" (pp.42–43).

This episode suggests that the enlightenment could have led to a different result from the imperialism it furthered. It may have lacked the barbarity of the renaissance, but its instruments followed rather the example of George the Third than of Blake or Menzies. They were determined to impose their patterns on the new lands rather than to learn from them. As Quadra comments, the Spaniards may "deposit their priests first upon the soil of new lands, while the British begin with their convicted prisoners" (p.138), but the end of their occupation is exploitation. The narrator sums it up:

> The Spanish gave the Indians wooden crosses.
> The Yankees gave them whiskey.
> The English gave them nothing. (p.191)

The consequence is not only the degradation of the native peoples and their lands, but the narrator's inability to find himself at home in either sphere. Except for their brief, magical flight, the fools of Vancouver's ship have yet to find fulfilment for the desires that drove them.

II

Daphne Marlatt, in her narrative sequence of poems, *Steveston*, deals with a community of people who themselves, in most cases, came to Vancouver from the Pacific and who, led by less ambitious dreams, both accept their environment and defy the social conditions it has engendered. They would not be at home anywhere else, but the irony of their lives is that they were an offence to their neighbours, first during the war because of their colour and later, in postwar affluence, because of their shabbiness. Their town has now been developed as a tourist venue.

The first edition of *Steveston* grouped together the photographs that capture from time the moments of its people. In the remaining pages the poem flows sequentially through time. In the second edition the two media alternate, so that the narrative flow is repeatedly checked by blocks of photographs showing people isolated in the shutter's instant. As the author comments, they have been cut off from the lives they have lived immediately beforehand, and which they resume immediately afterwards. The words, on the other hand, place these lives not only in their own sequence but in the complex events they help to form.

The first poem, "Imperial Cannery, 1913," focusses on a young woman standing by the cannery as she waits to join her mother when the shift begins:

> Standing inside the door (the river . . .) her shadow lies just inside the cannery floor, sun, pouring down outside, the river streaming slow, slow, by. Now she feels old enough
> [. . .]
> [. . .] waiting for work, the wheel that time is. Whose hands are standing still, here, empty. Whose friends also surround her,
> waiting, waiting all morning for the fish to come. Nothing moves
> but occasional strands of long hair the subtle wind is lifting, up off the river, the Fraser, mouth of the Fraser here where it
> debouches, into marsh, delta, swirling around & past those pilings of the cannery wharf they are standing on, muddy & pale grey teeming, invisible fish. . . (p.16)

Although time seems halted, it is not. The wind moves, the fish move, and the girl's thoughts move. For the moment she is caught in a single web with sun, wind and river, so that nature and human are one. This unity is, however, broken immediately the cannery starts, and she hears the harsh work inside and the noise of the boats beyond. Until she joins them,

> [. . .] she is in her
> element, dreaming of sails, her father's, or a friend's sail, at the
> Imperial which owns their boat, their net, their debt. But the
> Fraser gives of itself, incessantly, rich (so the dream goes)
> & wooden houses jammed on pilings, close together, leaning, with
> wooden walks and muddy alleys, laundry, & the dry marsh grass that
> stutters out of silt the dykes retain, from a flowing ever
> eroding & running river . . .
> [. . .]
> [. . .] barefoot on the dock in the wind, leaning
> into her threshold of work, machines, the wheel that keeps turning
> turning, out of its wooden sleeve, the blade with teeth marked:
> for marriage, for birth, for death.

The Fraser river becomes a metaphor for the richness of nature, while the marked blade becomes metaphor both for human work and for the cycle of destiny we inscribe through our work on our lives. The grubby township represents the hopes and disappointments of the settlers, who create a life for themselves despite the controls capital exercises over their work. For the moment, nature, culture and the individual are in a produced harmony. Yet the company has final control of this harmony, and eventually time brings the people to the war and the loss of their settlement. The young are forced to leave the tight community of their Japanese settler ancestors and find a place for themselves in a wider and less harmonious society. The fishing village of Steveston thus becomes a metonym for the history of this coast, which offers riches for the newcomers to build their homes, but leaves them subject to the control of capital which takes the riches of nature for itself and eventually uproots the people who have harvested its wealth.

III

Bowering and Marlatt both seek to recreate the past in order to understand the present. Robert Harlow and Jack Hodgins, by contrast, construct new histories in order to produce different futures. Their works move freely through all tenses as their multiple narrators face Margaret Atwood's challenge to free themselves from the bondage of history that makes them victims and become instead actors "for whom creative activity of all kinds is possible" (Atwood, 1972, p.38). Robert Harlow's *Scann* (1972) deals with the pioneers who fight the northern wilds of British Columbia to build a world to fit their desires, and the next generation who unsatisfactorily act out their desires in the built world they inherit. Jack Hodgins, in *Spit Delaney's Island* (1976), deals with Spit and other characters who try and fail to use Vancouver Island as a refuge from the changes of history, but in *The Invention of the World* (1972) he shows us people resolutely determined to break from this pattern and build their own world on the island. In his *Innocent Cities* (1990) a determined widow involves these worlds in a wider community that stretches across the Pacific to the Australian goldfields.

Scann opens firmly in the present as the editor of its twice-weekly newspaper looks at the special issue he has produced to celebrate the fiftieth anniversary of Linden, the town where Harlow has set his two previous novels. Linden is defined in the first paragraph by its population, its buildings, its industrial plants and the population supported by its natural gas boom. The aerial photograph shows everything important, "but no garbage, cracked cement, peeled paint or wear-and-tear." The photograph also shows the "great curve of the Linden river" that "flows from the east and runs south out of the picture." This river, that gives Linden its place, also suggests the time and space outside the picture that gives it its meaning. This meaning is not contained in the paper that Scann has edited. It belongs to the "wildness" he feels in everything he does, and which "terrorizes and fascinates him to observe it and to see what new embarrassment it will reveal." The aptly named Scann, the observer, sits inside

his skull watching his "animal out there acting," trying to trap
it back inside and pin it down in words. He recognizes that "this
separation of himself from his acts is a madness," but it is a
madness necessary to the writer. The actions he observes are not
only the enactment of his own lusts, but the pursuit of their
desires by those who have made the history whose externals he
has recorded in his papers. The chief action of the novel is the
action of his imagination by which he tracks down these other
actors so that he can record the truth of their histories that the
newspaper must omit.

Scann claims that no true writer is interested in beginnings
or endings. Like the river in the photograph, events wander
apparently at random in and out of his story. The story does,
however, focus on one particular tract of the river valley and one
particular episode in its history. The tract is the area above Linden
where Henry Auguste Linden, who gave his name to the town,
set his traps. The episode is the journey he makes through this
area with the town's real founder, Thrain, and the struggle
between them for Thrain's soul. Significantly, while we are told
all about Linden's Scotch-German origins, and about Thrain's
son and wives, Thrain himself remains only a surname. He barters
his soul for Linden's lands, and outlives Linden by some eighty
years, but the price of his bargain is that, despite the years and
the fortune and the wives, he remains virtually anonymous,
bearing a name that is no more than a detached signifier. Although
he survives the deadly winter through which he struggles with
Trapper Linden, the town bears Linden's name and, at the end
of the book, Thrain's death leaves Scann in possession of its story.
In this story, Linden returns to life as the expression of the strength
by which the wilderness was forced to yield to European desire.

The symbol of the wilderness—the wilderness that continues
to threaten the order imposed by society—is the wolverine,
carcajou, the antagonist who pits himself against Linden, asserting
by his actions his rights to the country that the trapper seeks to
flatten beneath his footsteps. The contest is not merely one for
occupation, but a struggle for power over the land. Carcajou
empties Linden's traps, and finally betrays him into his own
trap, only to be himself destroyed by Linden's ally, the porcupine.
But the porcupine and carcajou together entrap Linden's other
antagonist, Thrain, who seeks to gain power over the land not,
like Linden, to make it his home, but to exploit its wealth. When

the wolverine attacks the porcupine, the porcupine spines become implanted in its feet and jaw, so crippling it. Nevertheless, the wolverine is able to seize Thrain's arm in its jaws, which continue to cling long after the animal is dead. Even when Thrain chops off the body, the teeth hold on and the spines continue to work their way beneath his skin. This injury returns Thrain to Linden's power at the very moment that the trapper seems destroyed, and the two thenceforth survive only through their mutual dependence. Together, they suffer the pangs of hell until they are carried away in an icy river which, far from regenerating them, carries them both away towards death. Although Thrain escapes, through the agency of Linden, his soul has already perished. Nothing remains except wealth and his betrayal by the next generation, his own son and the half-breed son of Linden whom he has raised. The triangle of wolverine, Linden and Thrain represents the three stages of European relationships to the new world. The first stage is nature as savage, impenetrable and unyielding. The second is the stage of the woodsmen who penetrate the wilderness, are at home in it and use its products, but effectively leave it untouched. The men are changed by the wilderness, acquiring its savagery. Yet, despite themselves, they open the way to the exploitation brought in the third stage by men like Thrain, whose hotel, unlike Linden's various cabins, brings people to it to lay the foundations of a town. Thrain, after his victory over Linden, brings to the town its first aircraft, symbol of the technology that destroys the distances which had isolated the west and through which he had fought Linden.

But this aircraft also brings Thrain to another symbol of human penetration—the anachronistic slave plantation left by Zed Morton and now subject to the sexual-sadistic regime of his daughter Phillipa. Thrain destroys this regime as he had destroyed Linden, and takes Phillipa's daughter Anthea as his second wife, destined to be the mistress of his sons. Through the sons, this episode is linked also to Scann's wartime involvement with Thrain's son, Wing Commander David Thrain, D.S.O., D.F.C. This episode portrays the triumph of Canadian nationhood, its heroic participation in the international struggle for freedom, as black comedy. The forces that produced imperialism return to destroy the social and personal order at its heart. David Thrain's rule of the squadron is based on the same professions of freedom as Zed Morton's plantation, and his upright courage proves as

destructive as Morton's more blatant oppression. Both express
the paradox by which the imposition of power destroys its
objectives. Linden subjects Thrain to his will but loses his own
life and the woods he had made his home. Scann, writing about
the previous generation, contains them within the power of his
words, only to have old Thrain literally burn the words in the
last episode of the book. The narrator, who in turn contains Thrain
within the structure of the novel, still finds neither a beginning
nor an end to its events. The last sentences show us Scann at
the end of his three days of creation:

> He stands before Thrain's absolute quiet. The urge to dance
> is upon him—his animal maybe. Or it may be the result of
> a moment of new consciousness. Hardwon. He does not
> dance. Writer Novelist Scann goes carefully, husbanding that
> moment, through the door, tramples blue roses and walks
> with tenderness on his left foot, the one that put out the fire.
> (p.307)

Despite the Scann's efforts of imagination, Thrain retains his
secrets. The animal—the wilderness, his true nature—remains
outside and unconquered. Scann's putting out the fire may have
saved some of his script, but it may also have extinguished his
spirit. The tenderness of his foot is a reminder of how Linden
was crippled at the end of his life. In other words, or despite
the words, at the end of the novel everything is still to write.
The end of imperialism leaves us still with the task of making
the colony a home, or of keeping our desires alive within its
demands. Yet the novel also implies that it is only in the colony,
still hedged by wilderness, and not in the ordered homeland,
that we will learn to accommodate the animal within us that,
unaccommodated, drives humankind to the kin madnesses of
slave plantation or war machine. The mythical figure behind *Scann*
is Lear rather than Prospero.

V

In *The Invention of the World* Jack Hodgins, rather than sending
Lear back onto the blasted heath, summons Cuchulain once more
from the wilds. In the person of Donal Keneally he brings to the

forests of Vancouver Island the accumulated Celtic mythology of masculine strength, inspirational vision and the subjection of the peasantry. If in *Scann* the Canadian garrison has become a slave plantation, in Hodgins' novel it takes the equally characteristic North American form of a colony of believers united around a divinely appointed teacher and leader. The only sanction this leader claims is his own masculine strength, bolstered by the skills of the prestidigitator, but eventually his spurious claims to wisdom are bested by the women who endure and succeed him. The colony founded to embody the power of masculinity survives as a refuge maintained by a woman as a place of recovery for those damaged by the pressures of the world of men. Its leader, Maggie Kyle, draws her strength from the woods where she was raised and where she learned to free herself from both the violence of her parents and from the men she used to find her freedom.

The first of these men erupts onto the first pages of the novel as an embodiment of Cuchulain himself,

> dressed for work or play, it made no difference: a pair of low-crotched blue jeans hacked off above his boots and held up by wide elastic braces, a white T-shirt stretched over his thickened middle, and a shiny new aluminum hat sitting level on his head catching sunlight like a warrior's shield. He roared, "Blast you woman for your donkey nature!" and whipped off the hat to scratch around in his hair. (p.4)

This is Danny Holland, Maggie's first man and father of the boy she is to marry off this day. He is humiliating one woman, and is bent on humiliating Maggie later on. He continues to bluster in and out of the novel, until eventually Maggie is able to turn her back on him. Existing only in his maleness, he has no story of his own. He appears in Maggie's two weddings—her son's and her own—which frame the novel. In the first, he humiliates her until he forces her to acknowledge him, touching his chest and offering him the beer in the fridge. In the second, he leads the battle of the chainsaws and dominates the party until "the bride, who, sitting in a pile of debris, eyed him back with a vengeance" subdued him. She goes off instead with Wade Powers and his double, the man whom she has enabled to discover himself. With Wade, she returns to the House of Revelations and the record of its chronicler, Becker, whose narrative has shaped the events of the novel, and who has appeared in its pages in a preface that precedes even Danny Holland's eruption.

Between the two weddings, the narrative takes us through the events that give them their meaning. The first is the miraculous birth of Keneally, his travels in search of his true homeland, and the charm by which he breaks through the fearlessness of the Irish villagers and transports them to toil for him in his Canadian colony, building his House of Revelations. Keneally, with his colony of slaves and his three chained wives, finds the object of his search, the place for his colony, but finally is unable to subdue it to his will. Cuchulain has the power to dominate, but not to create (p.246). His house is given life only through the efforts of his wives, and later of Maggie. His settlement is denied life by the destruction on which it is built, so that his third wife, Lily, wonders when she arrives there, *"what have they done to it so that I feel as if I should keep my eyes always on the ground."* She realizes that part of the answer is that "they've cut down all the trees, anything that tempted you to look skywards." His power, built on the murder of his mother, and injured by his apparent murder of his first wife, is maintained only by his ability to keep his followers' eyes on the ground, and is irrevocably destroyed when they finally refuse. He dies deep in the earth, removed from the source of light and life. Only Lily and, later, Maggie keep life in the House of Revelations, just as it had been given life in the first place by the wife who came with him from Ireland, "the sprightly girl from Cahirciveen who'd . . . become a kind of goddess in his god-play" (p.119).

Keneally's tyranny parallels the means by which, as Julius Champney, another of the denizens of Eden, remembers, the British first established their authority on the island by hanging two uncomprehending Indians. The reference to this incident generalizes the story of Eden to make it a paradigm of the settlement. Just as Keneally built his colony on murder, the British founded their settlement on killing authorized by the laws they introduced. Just as he razed the timber, the settlers built streets on the plan "laid out for all time . . . by a man who'd never set foot on the island" (p.221). The colonists, pursuing their own dreams, "leapt over civilization, which would embarrass it, all the way from frontier town to Disneyland" (p.233), and in the process destroyed their dreams. But the House of Revelations remains as a sanctuary and destination for those injured souls who are still in search of a dream.

These searchers are all unable to escape the past. Julius Champney, refugee from the straight lines and killings of the prairies, likes neither the island nor its people but has nowhere else to go. Although he has travelled the world, the truth of place has eluded him. Even the great orange rock of Uluru turned out to be no more than a rock, and he now seeks meaning from time rather than place. He is obsessed by his attempts to hear the voices of the past, the last words of the Indians executed to make the colony safe for civilization: *"You could tell us, first, what we done."*

This obsession cuts him off from the present and so sours him that he is unable to endure any productive relationship with its people. Madmother Thomas, warped by her childhood in Keneally's colony, searches the island for the birthplace that will give her back a sane identity. Wade Powers, trying to escape his family's need for an achieving busyness, builds a fake past to trap the tourists. Strabo Becker, the chronicler, tries to recover the true past but is able only to construct a collage of cuttings and memories that hint at hidden facts but conceal the truth of responsibility. Lily, trying to recover the dreams of her husband, Keneally, becomes the last of the followers whose flesh he devours. Only Maggie and Wade, taking Becker with them to chronicle their travels, exorcise the past by returning to the land of its origins and the empty mountain before coming back to their own pilgrimage to Maggie's birthplace on the island and the discovery that they belong there and to each other.

Their reconciliation to life and the future, their escape from the past, is symbolized by the wedding ceremony, the "second growth," with which the novel finishes. The ceremony is celebrated in three parts: a Gargantuan country feast, a similarly Rabelaisian fight with chainsaws that finishes in the destruction of the hall and its furnishings, and a final hour of speeches, finishing when Maggie and Wade spread the warmth of their love to the assembled crowd. The love that achieves this reconciliation is neither sentimental nor idealistic, but grounded in the concrete realities of common experience, mutuality, and carnality. Yet, in leading to the fairy-tale ending of the lovers' departure for the enchanted castle, where, *if they're not dead nor gone they're alive still*, it contradicts the basic premise of imperialism that the new world will provide a new start. The fairy-tale denies change or linear progress, allowing only the recurring cycle of birth, death and renewal. Just as Keneally reincarnates Cuchulain, the history of his Revelations Colony of Truth repeats the cycles of Celtic or classical mythology. The Canadian setting changes the imagery but not the form. The devastation of the colonists, their destruction of the forests to reproduce their Celtic circle of houses around the well of truth, leads them as certainly as the children of Thebes to feed on their own flesh until finally their saviour is immolated beneath his own city. But from devastation comes renewal, as the new growth of the trees returns nature to the colony and allows the second growth of the colonists. Unlike the islanders, however, who believe in their ownership, Maggie and the new colonists remain sojourners, accepting both their past and their environment rather than demanding ownership of either.

VI

In *Innocent Cities,* Hodgins uses a similar fairy-tale pattern to contain the twin colonialisms of Vancouver Island's Victoria and the antipodean goldfields of Ballarat. The opening scene brings the reader to Victoria, B.C., when the "world was farther away . . . and we were only an infant city out on this edge of the continent by ourselves. Mountains, forests, sea." This primeval scene is however immediately obscured by the bustle of colonialism, the "arrival of ships bearing travellers from India, Chile, England, San Francisco—from every corner of the Empire and the vast new world" that "gave us the sense, occasionally, of living at the centre of things" (p.xi). As readers, however, we are not invited to identify with these newcomers, still alarmed by the natural environment, "the crashing waves and the giant coniferous trees and the wild green forest undergrowth" and "amazed that the monstrous elements of their adopted home had not yet been reorganized into tidy European gardens or reduced to familiar stretches of horizontal California desert" (p.xiii). Instead, the first-person plural invites us to identify with the older colonists, and particularly with Logan Sumner, who "had grown up here when the island was still a colony and the city not much more than a palisaded fortress of exaggerated dreams." Sumner accepts both the natural world of mountains and waves and cliffs and trees and the human settlement of private homes and public buildings, opium factories and spired churches, cows and loafers, gardens and cemetery. He belongs in this colonial world of history, but he is also a fairy-tale figure, a singer who hopes each morning that he may sing into being a newer world and a larger truth.

Logan Sumner plans to begin a new life with a new marriage. These hopes are, however, shadowed by the historical accident that leads him to a beach littered with wreckage from a recent shipwreck. The violence of nature, symbolized by "broken timber and painted words . . . boards . . . so brutally smashed [that] many of the words existed without any context, almost without any meaning" brings into question any attempt to make sense from existence (p.xvi). Then, in the first chapter of the narrative proper, his marriage is further shadowed by the arrival from across the same seas of the unexpected wicked stepmother—in this case, the unsuspected widow from Australia. History is embroiled in mythology.

History is concerned with facts, and mythology with truth, but the reliability of both forms of discourse is soon questioned in this narrative. Before Logan Sumner meets the widow, we see the tombstone which records his grief for his first wife, his curse of God, and his continual rewriting of the state of his own hopes and expectations. His first conversation with the widow identifies the unreliability in the colony of both the names and the records of the colonists. And the course of history in the novel allows this unreliability of words and the status they ascribe to people to unravel the lives of most of the characters.

Words are the spring that drives much of the action. James Horncastle is in court at the beginning of the novel because his words have, once again, offended his rival Samuel Hatch. Sumner Logan is diverted from his courtship when he is required to rescue his carpenter, Zachary Jack, from the gaol where he has been flung because his use of native words upsets the white citizenry. Most importantly, Kate Horncastle finds herself trapped in Australia by "a crowded, strangling jungle of words, of beautiful *names*," and flees to Vancouver in the belief that there she may be able again to live in "a world of ordinary *things* again, a world of regulations and laws that created some human order" (p.85). Yet she eventually finds herself imprisoned in

Canada by the same words she has used to destroy Horncastle's apparent marriage and make a place for herself. Canada itself is distinguished from Australia because of its reliance on the words it uses to bring to it the same distinctions that order English society, assigning people roles rather than allowing them to make their own as they can in the southern colonies. These assigned roles in turn are at the heart of the Reverend Mr. Trodd, the "small mean-mouthed little man" who uses the form rather than the spirit of words to destroy Norah Horncastle's claims to James and brands her an adultress. Finally, the whole calamity of abandoned and reclaimed marriages arises from interrupted and concealed communications.

Yet finally, *Innocent Cities* is about work rather than words. While words conceal truth from its characters, their work creates it, whether in the form of Zack's fantastic flying machine that actually succeeds in lifting into the air, of James Hardcastle's hotel that he sustains by his words until Kate reduces him to silence, or of the buildings Sumner Logan designs in his head and Zachary Jack builds with his hands. The novel comes closest to explaining the relationship between truth and reality when Sumner explains his buildings to Annie McConnell and Norah Hardcastle:

> In the world of architecture, . . . you would have a hard time trying to determine which are the false faces and which are the real. If we got to what we might think is the original— even that would be only a sort of facade, to convince the world of what we wish them to think. This elegant house must have elegant people living in it. This unpainted old-fashioned saloon must be for the hard-working man to drink in with his friends. This roadhouse stands for tradition and ties to the Old Country. To the designer, the *real* building remains in his head . . .
>
> "Which is to say," said Norah Hardcastle . . . "that you would have to keep stripping them away until you were looking right into the heart of our Maker." (p.289)

The clergyman and most of the citizens protect themselves from this heart with the words by which they construct their categories and their mythololgies. The builder finds it through the work by which he builds the history of the new worlds. Unlike *The Invention of the World*, this novel shows a way that the innocent cities of the new world can escape the cycles of mythology they bring with them and make a new start. Sumner Logan's most eloquent statement is the home he builds for himself, taking his model from the dwellings of the Indians and constructing it beneath "a great roof kept up by a structure of posts and beams carved from giant trees" (p.384). Behind this he leaves the barn built by his uncle and the small shed built by his carpenter from driftwood. Around it he designs a garden of plants from the new world, and within it he allows a marriage that provides freedom for both his wife and his daughters. His work has reproduced in the circumstances produced by the colonists the unity of culture and nature that had existed before they came.

VII

As colonial history begins with the intrusion of a foreign culture in an alien environment, the environment is necessarily a protagonist of historical fiction like the novels of Harlow and Hodgins. Another west coast writer, Audrey Thomas, is more concerned with human relationships in the present, with mothers and daughters, lovers, adolescents looking at adults or adults looking backward to their own adolescence and the decisions that have led them to where they now are. The environment in her stories is more a means of isolating people from their normal society so that they may confront their own inwardness. Her settings range from Greek islands to African tropics to Scottish dampness. Yet when she returns to Vancouver Island the setting becomes more than a device or a convenience, a place to examine the truth of people. "Breaking the Ice" (Thomas, 1986) employs the familiar metaphor to describe the early intimacies of a relationship that involves both the lovers and their daughters coming to know each other in the snowy setting of a holiday house over Christmas and New Year. The snow first isolates the woman from her past, and then generates a warm intimacy that enables the separate pasts of the lovers and their families to blend and enrich each other. The setting thus becomes a part of the action, creating the new situation as well as distancing the old. The characteristic concern of later twentieth century writing with the relationships and inwardness is thus matched to the equally characteristic attitude to the natural environment as a refuge from the distractions of urban life and as a place of healing for the wounds inflicted by modern living on our true, inward selves.

Daphne Marlatt, in *Ana Historic* (1988), brings these two modes together. The novel is concerned with the recovery of history, or more accurately with the recovery from history of the schoolteacher Mrs. Richards, who made history but was barely recorded in it. Yet the title of the book, *Ana Historic*, is a statement warning us that it both is and is not an historical work. Ana, written A-N-A on the cover, is at once the given name of its subject, Mrs. Richards, the prefix ana-, meaning alternatively reversion or progression, or the doubling of article and prefix as "an a-historic," a narrative that is not historic. The novel rewrites history to give Mrs. Richards her place, but it also undermines history by suggesting that the past can never be recovered: "once history's on-stage, histrionic as usual (all those wars, all those historic judgements), the a- historic hasn't a speaking part. what's imagination next to the weight of the (f)actual?" (p.139). By using imagination to go behind the stage of history, the narrator recovers her own past, or rather reconstitutes her childhood and her mother in her present. The a-historic (anhistoric) subject, Ana, thus becomes also the narrator, Anna, and the narrator's mother, Ina, to whom she addresses her story, but whose words and memories, like Ana's, also become part of the story, a multiple narrative that can never be contained in a single voice. These multiple voices, brought alive in the imagination, recover separate pasts of the three women, their companions and their town, and so rebuild the narrator's own place in the present. Just as in her earlier poem, *Steveston*, Marlatt recovered the lives behind the anonymous photographs, here she finds herself behind the anonymity of the past.

The novel begins by presenting life itself as an act of colonising. The opening sentences put together the words heard, felt, expressed not as a search for identity but as a way of finding the speaker's space.

> Who's There? she was whispering. knock knock. in the dark.
> only it wasn't dark had woken her to her solitude, conscious
> alone in the dark of his snoring more like snuffling dreaming
> elsewhere . . . she turned the clock so she could see its blue
> digital light like some invented mineral glowing, radium

> 4:23. it was the sound of her own voice had woken her, like an echo asking,
>> who's there?
>>> echoes from further back, her fear-defiant child voice carried still in her chest, stealing at night into the basement with the carving knife towards those wardrobes at the bottom of the staircase. wardrobes. wordrobes. warding off what? (p.9)

The broken sentences are reminiscent of the opening of Joyce's *Portrait of the Artist* . . . Marlatt, however, immediately locates her attempt to recover memory in the present, where the speaker's partner snores beside her. The sentences are broken not by the partial incomprehension of childhood but by the tentative nature of her recall. She makes it clear that this is not just the past seeping back through the disjointed words that have lodged in her memory, but a deliberate attempt to disjoint language so that the past can seep back through the spaces between the words. Even the absence of capitals to reinforce the beginnings of new sentences helps to chop through the confining logic that language imposes on experience. At the same time, however, the use of words, their careful arrangement on the page

an echo asking

> who's there?
>> echoes from further back

emphasizes the fact that she has nothing except words through which to recover her experience. The words force us to acknowledge the reality of presence by drawing attention to the way they create its illusion. The past is the colony they make real to us in its otherness.

Just as George Bowering showed how Vancouver's charts of the American coast converted the continent into the positivist concepts of the European enlightenment, or Jack Hodgins traced the ordering of Canadian society in the categories brought from Britain, so Daphne Marlatt shows language placing the child within its constructs of class and gender from the moment it ceases to be infant and starts to talk. The narrator, looking for the Lost Girl, the consciousness that exists as part of the mother and the universe before speech separates her from both, "you who is you or me. she. a part struck off from me. apart. separated" (p.11), can find her only in the interstices of her narrative. She exists only in memories of a "house on the side of a mountain on the edge of a suburb surrounded by . . . those woods the boys on the rest of the block claimed as theirs" (p.12). Within her world lies her own wood, the "old Wood . . . where they nestled in a womb, exchanging what if's. . ." This wood, her own, is, however, both defined and threatened by the other wood owned by the boys, by the threat of one of the "what if's": "what if the boys came down from their fort in the Green Wood with slingshots and air gun?" So even the centre of her privacy is defined from outside, leaving the Lost Girl to endure as the Heroine who "wanted something to do not something that might be done to them." She is defined as a tomboy, her identity "double masculine, as if the girl were completely erased" (p.13). The attempt to recover herself through words thus leads only to the erasure of self that the words perform. Instead of colonizing her past, the narrator becomes herself again colonized by the language she uses.

The rest of the novel can be described as an attempt to escape this colonization by rescuing another of its victims, the teacher who was omitted from the words of the history that she made. This decolonization however involves a second. By tracing Mrs. Richards' life in Canada, her separation from the British origins that continued to define her, the narrator is also able to separate herself from the gentility her own English mother imposed on her, and so recover the mother that she had lost in the mother's words.

> o the cultural labyrinth of our inheritance, mother to daughter
> to mother . . .
> —and i suppose that you see me as the monster hidden at
> the heart of it?
>   . . .
> the monstrous lie of it: the lure of absence. self-effacing.
> (p.24)

This monstrous lie is produced by the masculine history of colonization, the lie that imposes power on others. The lie appears in the novel in the attempts to pin the colony down in facts— about the timbers and their uses, about the inhabitants, about the condition of the roads—that play through the novel as a counterpoint to its acts of recovery. The power of fact is symbolized in the engineer who controls the donkey-engine dragging the logs from the forest:

> . . . *Think what this mastery over huge, heavy logs means . . .*

> history the story, Carter's and all the others', of dominance. mastery. the bold line of it. (p.25)

As we have seen, in Ken Kesey's *Sometimes a Great Notion*, this power runs out of control and destroys the men who would command it. Marlatt, by contrast, frees herself from power by freeing both her narrator and her subject from the masculine dominance to which colonialism subjected them.

The subject of the novel—or rather, the subject of the narrator's research—stands for the two other female subjects hidden in the book—the narrator and her mother. The narrator, Anne, tells her story to her (dead) mother—also a migrant—as a way of overcoming the separation that words first imposed on them. This separation is parallel to the separation of the two women from their mothers and their motherland by the fact of migration. But the Mrs. Richards of the novel presents the reader with a further problem. We are told that the narrator is reconstructing her from a journal in "the archives" (p.30), and a note to the text acknowledges assistance received from the Vancouver City Archives. This note says also that "this is a work of fiction; historical personages have been fictionalized to possible and / or purely imaginary lengths." It does not say whether Mrs. Richards is one of these historical personages. The narrator does, however, tell us that the people at the archives of the fiction "think her journal suspect . . . 'inauthentic,' fictional possibly, contrived later by a daughter who imagined (how ahistoric) her way into the unspoken word of her mother's girlhood" (p.30). Historian, narrator and novelist are thus confounded. The truth is what we construct from the past, just as the colony is what the colonists make from the environment they find waiting for them.

Ana Historic grows from the same kind of bustling colonial environment we found in Jack Hodgins' two historical novels. This time, however, we are on the other side of the Strait of Georgia, in the milltowns that will coalesce to become the metropolis of Vancouver. On her arrival at Hastings Mill, where she has been appointed schoolteacher, Ana sees

> the piles of lumber, the heavy smoke, the low sprawling sheds. So many men, so foreign-looking, dressed in such an outlandish assortment of clothes.

She learns that they come from all around the world, the cosmopolitan crowd that constitutes the colonial worlds:

> Some of them will be Kanakas from the Pacific Islands . . . Some of them will be natives, of course. And then there are always those roustabouts—Italians, Portuguese, Irish . . . who have drifted around the world to end up at this unlikely spot. Adventurers.... (p.15)

This is the crowd to whom Ana is to bring proper culture: "she would have spoken a proper English, the Queen's English, they said. After all this was *British* Columbia, 1873." But these cultural expectations are immediately contradicted by the cosmopolitan origins of the colony, its newness, and its setting.

> The day was frosty still in places where the sun, blocked by buildings, by the massive bulk of trees, of mountains even, had failed to penetrate. A subtle white sparkle, ethereal as powder. And everything else legible, easily read: the rawness of new wood, the brashness of cleared land, of hastily-built houses, outhouses, leantos. And beyond them, the endless green of the wood, a green so green it outgreened itself, hill after hill. When she turned she could see the mountains behind her hanging close, close and yet aloof. Beautiful, she thought, or perilous. But not pretty. . . she knew this was not Europe and Mary Shelley's monster would never speak his loneliness here. (pp.15–16)

The mountains are alien to a monster who is the frightening product of European culture and technology. They do not allow him a voice. In the Spanish film that the narrator recalls, however, the monster befriends and is protected by a lost girl. In the story of Ana, Ina and Anne, the lost girl learns to speak his name, "a man's name for man's fear of the wild, the uncontrolled. that's where *she* lives" (p.142). The woman whom men bring into their colony, into their lives, to tame the wild, is also the wildness that they fear. By learning this, Anne is able to control her own fear and her narrative, and to restore the mother whom the fears of men took from her and destroyed.

The novel therefore concludes as an act of decolonisation, freeing Ana from history, Ina from the death-in-life of electrotherapy, and Anne from the burden of subservience to the past and to marriage. The critical episode in gaining this freedom is not so much the narrative conclusion, that leaves both past and future open, as it is the narrator's participation with Ana in the parturition of the first white baby born on Burrard Inlet. This birth unites culture and nature in the lives of the mother, the midwife, and the observer who are brought together in the "women's work," the "mouth speaking flesh" that Ana "touches to make it tell her present in this other language so difficult to translate. the difference" (p.126). The acceptance of biological difference enables the women to transcend the social difference imposed on them by men. It enables Ana to make the choice between living her life as a sole woman or surrendering to marriage. It enables Anne to understand how solitude, separation from the bustle of life, destroyed the joyous, creative woman she remembered as her mother. It enables Anne to find independence in her own marriage.

The narrative does not however end there. We are not in fact told what happens to the narrator's marriage, and even Ana's apparent choice is left open. Moreover, just as in *Burning Water* the Indians framed the explorers' activities with their detached commentary, the events of *Ana Historic* take place under the silent scrutiny of Indians who frighten Ana when she goes for a walk in the woods, and who, in the person of the servant girl Harriet, watch without words as the first white baby is born on the inlet. Similarly, men continue their struggle for dominance, unaware of the women's knowledge that nevertheless gnaws at their security. The colonial culture may have broken from its origins, but the mountains and the woods still remain outside, a threat to its confidence.

CHAPTER 12

RECLAIMING THE LAND: NEW ZEALAND

A feature of New Zealand Maori writing is the authority it gives to strong women. Some writers, like Patricia Grace, themselves fulfil this role in their communities as well as in their writing. The narrator of Keri Hulme's *The Bone People* has chosen to withdraw from her community and use her strength to construct a self-sufficient life. By calling his novel *The Matriarch*, Witi Ihaemara places a strong woman at the centre of the work. The novel is about its narrator's search for an identity in the Maori culture. The matriarch becomes the author of this identity. Through her the power of the past flows to give meaning to the present.

Artemis, the matriarch, is not the subject of the novel, which is concerned with the way Tamatea, its male narrator, recovers his place in the past and in his family. The matriarch becomes, literally and figuratively, Tamatea's author. As he explains at the beginning, "After all, she was the one who turned my own life into fiction from fact" (p.1). Yet this beginning of the novel is not the beginning of his story. To find this beginning, Tamatea has to follow his uncle's promptings and trace his own memories back to when he can again become an observer watching and listening where the matriarch "was sitting with the child on the highest terrace of Ramaroa pa, the ancient hill fort above the village of Waituhui." In reconstructing her the narrator places himself within the whole cosmology and history of the Maori people. Or rather, the matriarch places him there in the words that also fit him to a destiny he cannot avoid.

> Ah, mokupuna, but your life began even before you were born in Waituhui. You may have taken your first breath here but, ara, you have eternity in you also. . .

> At your beginning was Te Kore, the Void. Within the
> Void, the Nothingness, there came Te Po, the Night. After
> a timeless time, Te Po began to change . . . (p.2)

The Maori creation myth that follows does not merely provide
cultural background for Tamatea's life. Rather, it begins the
institution of Maori myth and history in his life so that he becomes
their bearer. Just as the narrator's earlier remark has refused any
distinction the reader might want to make between fact and
fiction, so this passage overrides distinctions between myth and
history, communal and individual being. By incorporating in her
grandson the story of her people, the matriarch remakes the
people in him. The book thus becomes not just a cry for attention,
an explanation of a human situation or a response to history, but
a direct intervention in history. The story of the Maori people
is the story of how they are made from the void, come to the
Pacific and the land of Hawaiki and then Aotearoa, how the land
makes them and how they then struggle for the land. The
matriarch's story is this story, but it is also the story of her
European legacy, symbolized by the systems of parliaments and
courts, the operas of Verdi and the stones of Venice that are
lapped by waters that reach finally to the homes of the other
seafarers in Aotearoa and Hawaiki. In joining these legacies, the
book directly recovers the lands and seas that make its people.
The novel does for its people what the matriarch instructs Tamatea
he must do for himself:

> . . . because this is your land, you must know it like it knows
> itself, and you must love it even more than it loves itself.
> You must get to know its very boundaries, e mokupuna
> [grandchild], and every part of it because without this
> knowledge you are lost. Without it, you do not possess a
> land. You become a person without a homeland. You become
> a man who will never know aroha ki to iwi, love for your
> people and your land. If you do not know this love then
> you cannot fight. Someday, you may need to know so as
> to challenge any person who might wish to take this land
> from you. (p.95)

Although these words are immediately addressed to Tamatea,
in the economy of the novel they speak directly to the readers.
First to the Maoris, but then to any reader who hopes to be at

home in the new world, actually or sympathetically. To read the novel is to take some possession of the land in this way. Its writing simultaneously offers this possession and destroys the legitimacy of any other claim to ownership. At the same time, as the narrator reflects on the actual situation of his people, he laments the dispossession that leaves them alienated from both white society and each other, preventing their spiritual possession being realized in actuality, or perhaps even being recognized by those who could claim it. The novel's absorption in cosmology does not deny its realism about the present.

> . . . And gone, gone is the grandeur of the village. . . . You can tell it is a Maori place simply because of the look . . . of the defeated . . . (and I can still remember the sneer in the voice of a university lecturer in Auckland who took his geography class on a field trip of Otara, pointing out the typically Maori ghetto dweller in his typically Maori home, and his conclusion that 'No matter what opportunities one gives Maoris, one will always find them in homes like these.' My first reaction was to ask what was wrong with being brought up in a typically Maori home; my second was to say, in a loud voice, that 'What you are seeing is the result when one is an oppressor and the other is oppressed.' I didn't pass geography that year) . . . (p.105)

The incident shows not only the oppression suffered by all Maoris, but the alienation from the land suffered by the possessors as much as the dispossessed. The claims of the university discipline are destroyed by its evident failure to comprehend even its own terms. The narrator, on the other hand, can both see the village as it now is and remember when "it still retained its magic and its heart," when his grandmother told him that "'We had eternity in us'," when on a time the veil between day and night lifted and, with his grandmother, Tamatea descended into the otherworld where gods and men commune and he lived again the birth of time from the Void. His knowledge of this possibility keeps it alive in the land, offering escape from the misery and alienation that are otherwise the lot of his people.

This theme is central both to the mythological strand of this novel and to the story of the land wars that is woven through it. The author incorporates in his fiction a history of the Maori insurrection led by Te Kooti in 1868 and subsequent years, and the later parliamentary struggles in the same cause by Wi Pere. These two historical characters are kin to Tamatea through the matriarch, who is niece of one, granddaughter of the other, and thus connected back to Thomas Halbert, the wild Scot who was among the earliest white settlers of New Zealand. In educating Artemis in the ways of both Europeans and Maoris, Wi Pere trains her to continue the land struggle that she eventually bequeaths to Tamatea. The recovery of this past is the first step in his renewal of the struggle. The end of the struggle would not be the expulsion of the Europeans, but rather the realization of the alternative always possible in the history of the land wars, and actual in the time of Halbert, when European settlement left Maori dominance intact. In the twentieth century, this can only come as Maoris fully absorb the European heritage within their own tradition. Tamatea, university educated, married to a European and working in a European environment, has to restore the dominance of his Maori identity before he can give freedom to his own children or his people. To do this, he must come to terms with both the violence and the temporary triumphs of his people in the land wars, as well as the pain of their eventual defeat.

Apart from myth and history, there are at least two other threads to the narrative of this restoration. One is the story of the land marches and the political struggle in which the matriarch herself was involved. The other is Tamatea's personal struggle to find a place in his extended family. This prompts him in the first place to search back in his memory for his grandmother, but is also the major theme of the concluding section, where he finds himself in conflict first with his grandfather, who wants to bestow his mana on Toroa, an alleged half-brother, and then with the incarnation of the matriarch herself. His memories of the matriarch centre on a single episode during the land march of 1949, when Artemis confronted the elders of the opposing tribes and won her right to speak for her own people. This one episode is expanded and interwoven with each of the other strands of the narrative, becoming itself an instance of myth penetrating and subverting history. It links the earlier land wars, to which it is parallel, and the mythology, which it re-enacts.

The confrontation between the matriarch and the competing tribesmen shows her at the height of her powers. First she uses sheer strength of will to maintain her right to speak. But she quickly goes beyond this to confront the whole force of mana arrayed against her. She achieves victory only with the aid of Tamatea, who is still a child but is joined in her power. When she first rises to speak, she is overwhelmed by spirits, but his power repels them. At the welcoming feast, she summons a shower of spiders to entrap the old man who attempts to take Tamatea's mana from him. Finally, when she is excluded from the conference with the Prime Minister, she summons the whole power embodied in the Maori mythology to break down the doors. "The adze of our ancestors . . . the greenstone, announcing its name, *bade them to succumb*" (p.446). This mythical power is the same that the narrator has just told us he used himself, years later, to destroy Toroa's pretensions to the mana. Yet these victories, which link the present with the past, also divide it. Ihaku, Tamatea's grandfather, is likened to the historic Rakaihikuroa who plotted the death of the twin heirs of his rival, but the vengeance that overtook him, like that Tamatea threatens on his rival, perpetuates the cycle of violence. The myth that links Tamatea to the land also links the family to the violence and bloodshed that has cost it the land.

The final section of Witi Ihaemara's novel brings out the implicit contradictions. Until this point, the matriarch has been presented as the champion of the people and their rights to the land that constitutes their being. Tamatea is similarly presented as the rightful successor to her role. The worrying opposition they meet, from her husband or his mother, and even from his father, seems to be the product either of jealousy or of individual weakness. But the last section, "Succession," complicates these easy oppositions. To start with, the matriarch's victory at the land rights meeting, the inter-tribal hui, is a demand for submission, something quite different from communal recognition of her power. In asserting his right to succession, Tamatea is forced to make the same demand, to the consternation of his father and the uneasy assent of his mother. The demand in turn divides the family that he claims the right to head. Then, after his grandfather's death, he is forced to acknowledge that it is through him that he derives some of his most important mana, that which descends from Hine te Ariki, daughter of the taniwha, the spirit that led the Maoris from Hawaiki. When, after his grandfather's soul returns to Hawaiki, Tamatea is forced to confront the final contradiction that he has inherited from the matriarch. This is symbolized by her European name, Artemis, the earth mother. This has seemed until this point to symbolize the European and Maori traditions that she brings in unity to the soil of Aotearoa. When he visits Venice, however, this unity proves deadly, and Tamatea is literally rescued from the matriarch's fatal embrace only by the joint power of his mother and the taniwha. Even this power however is ambiguous, for the taniwha, having broken through the spider webs that symbolize the deadly power of the myth, then drags his mother away from him and back to New Zealand. The novel ends with him resolving to return home, but still alone on the foreign soil of Venice. There is no guarantee that on his return he will possess either his own land or the other tradition Artemis tried to bring to it. The strength of the myth has been shown to be as much in death as in life. The reader, with Tamatea, has yet again to endure the twelve changings of the night without any certainty that this time they will lead to the coming of Te Ao Marama, the World of Light. The only certainty the novel offers is that this World exists and provides the hope for our daily existence. Myth may enlighten the tasks of living, but life must still be lived.

The two closing paragraphs of the novel open it to the future and to Tamatea's mother, Tiama, who has been largely disregarded in the narrative. She was not the matriarch's choice for her son's wife, and throughout her life and beyond the two women have been rivals for Tamatea's allegiance. Artemis virtually seduced the boy, using the sexuality that the narrator comments "permeated all aspects of Maori life." The first woman was created from mud and earth by the god Tane. She had a daughter, "whom Tane married. This was the first incest." The daughter becomes Death, who crushed the demi-god Maui between her thighs, "and thus death and destruction were brought permanently into the world." The female reproductive organs consequently became known as "the house of misfortune and disaster. . . . Woman was therefore non-sacred and proscribed" (p.23). But Artemis, named after the European goddess of birth and destruction, makes no distinction between male and female sexuality. As she instructs Tamatea after seducing him,

> In sex is power. . . . Knowing when to give pleasure and
> when to take, to be ruthless, are lessons that you must learn.
> . . . But most of all, you must know when and how to overrule
> the passions of your body . . . (p.369)

Her speaking at the Wellington marae in defiance of her hosts and of tradition is of the same effect as her taking Tamatea to herself and away from his mother and grandfather. By these actions she takes the power of the Maori into herself, but at the same time introduces conflict and division into the people and her own family. Tamatea is able to take this power for himself only when he finally wrestles with her memory and turns his back on her to follow his mother home. He goes on this journey with his wife, herself from outside the clan and the people. The book thus ends with the hope that the divisions will be healed without diminishing the power passed on from the matriarch.

II

The narrative of *The Bone People* begins with a description of Kerewin waking in the tower where she works through art and science to interpret and integrate the culture and nature she has collected in books, artifacts and found objects. She sustains her life by fishing. It thus appears that she has made a completely self-contained world that allows its solitary human dweller to produce her life in harmony with culture and nature and, through her art, to provide a future for others. But this self-sufficiency proves to be an illusion. Simon's arrival proves that neither he, Kerewin nor Joe, Simon's adopted father, can live alone. For Joe, Simon represents the future he has denied himself, but instead the violence he has chosen precipitates Simon into Kerewin's world, bringing with him the struggle for power and dominance from which she has withdrawn. Simon forces her to accept responsibility for its violence. In a last desperate effort to avoid responsibility, she destroys her tower and retreats into the wasteland. Only here, in the wilderness, can she finally accept that she is not alone. The bone-people, the bones of her ancestors which remain in the land, restore her to the community without which her culture has been barren. Only through her acceptance of the history that contains her people, and her acceptance of Simon and Joe as her present, is she able to find a way of recovering the links between culture and environment, between land and people.

The opening pages of *The Bone People* introduce the reader to a world where place and people have both been disjoined from the words, the culture, that alone can make sense of them. The first passage, entitled "The End at the Beginning" is set out in the form of free verse, the first three stanzas beginning "He walks down the street . . .," "He walks down the street . . .," and "She walks down the street. . . ." The fourth stanza proclaims the theme of the book, but attains its full meaning only when we have read the rest of the novel.

> They were nothing more than people, by themselves. Even paired, any pairing, they would have been nothing more than people by themselves. But all together, they have become the heart and muscles and mind of something perilous and new, something strange and growing and great.
>
> Together, all together, they are the instruments of change. (p.2)

The rest of the book shows how they come together and change, but it also shows how the change is outside both their intent and their control.

The next two sections further add to our confusion. Both start with the Biblical words, "IN THE BEGINNING." The first goes on, "it was darkness, and more fear, and a howling wind across the sea." We later learn that this is a shipwreck interpreted through the inchoate mind of a child, but even after reading the whole book it remains impossible to identify precisely the actions to which his words refer. The Biblical connotations are clearer, conflating "In the beginning God created the heaven and the earth" with "In the beginning was the word." This novel makes literal the perception that the word is god, that the world of our knowledge begins with the fact of our perception through language. It also, however, casts ironic doubt on this perception by placing it in the mind of a boy who refuses to use language. His refusal to speak forces Joe and Kerewin to listen, and so leads them out into the language that restores them to a place in the culture of the community from which, in different ways, they have cut themselves off. Before they can find this place, however, they have to plumb the depths of despair and violence within themselves. Only then are they ready to give themselves to the healing power of the land.

This irony continues into the third sequence, the perception of the boys' foster-parents that opens with the words "IN THE BEGINNING, it was a tension . . ." This tension precedes the death of the wife and their son, but inaugurates the father's possession of the lost boy, Simon P. Gillayley—or rather, the boy's adoption and possession of his father. In reading this, we need to remember that Polynesian adoption customs operate both ways, with parents as much adoptees as children. We are in no danger of forgetting that western culture imposes on this tradition the concept of parental ownership of the child. This concept, violating natural relationships far more than adoption does, produces the subsequent violence with which the characters deny their own deepest reality.

Before we encounter this denial, however, the author leads us through a more conventional narrative that apparently introduces us to the real people who are to be the novel's protagonists. We first meet Kerewin in the tower she has built to keep the world at bay. In this tower, where she makes her own art, she has assembled a library and selection of artifacts that represent the world's cultural tradition. Her tower is a symbol of fulfilment, but, with its European echoes of "The Lady of Shallott" and, further back, Rapunzel, it is also the symbol of a sexuality that imprisons. The experience it represents is sterile because it is not connected with the lives of others. By contrast, the boy Simon, whose mute state suggests innocence, is in fact the vehicle of experience. He penetrates her mental as well as her physical barriers and thus opens the way for his father, Joe, to invade her life.

Simon's arrival in the tower announces the novel's delayed opening. It encourages expectations of a conventional plot where the child brings both man and woman to realize that they need each other to complete themselves. The remainder of the book, however, disappoints such expectations by showing that the two destroy each other and the child. As the opening has warned us, the two separately are only people. Only "Together, all together" do they become "instruments of change" (p.2). The element that brings them together, overcoming the opposition of individual and culture, is the place—in this case, not the land alone, but the littoral, the undefinable boundary of solid land and ever-changing ocean from which comes Simon P. Gillayley, the boy who refuses to speak. His silence represents a land and people who will speak to the newcomers only on terms that transcend the divisions of race and language that both black and white cultures impose on them. His silence is the language of the bone people, the people who have possessed the land with their lives, and whose language we can learn only by the intimacy of silence.

III

In *Symmes Hole* the New Zealand novelist Ian Wedde writes for the forgotten people, the white first-footers who sailed beyond their law to join their blood with the Maoris in establishing a community that belonged to both black and white, to the islands of New Zealand and to the sea that surrounded them and gave them their highways and their livelihood. To tell their story, Wedde rewrites the story of Moby Dick. He embeds the historical original of the white whale, Mocha Dick, in the history of the western colonisation of New Zealand and the Pacific, transforming it from a symbol of unconquerable nature, the measure of our hubris, to an image of the savagery within humanity that drives our struggle to conquer and subdue. In his pseudonymous introduction he identifies whaling as the prototype of the systems of market capitalism, and the white whale as the submerged rumour that "haunts and infects those plying the market grids . . . a 'rising damp beneath the retirement home of academic record' . . ." (Wedde, 1986, p.9). In this novel, however, the whalemen themselves inherit the spirit of Mocha Dick, building in New Zealand their own paradise as an escape from the grid that capitalism casts across the globe. Like Witi Ihaemara in *The Matriarch*, Wedde attempts to recapture the past for a people whom received history has submerged just as the ocean submerges the great whale. The past of this people is not the mythic precolonial time of *The Matriarch*, but the anarchic period when the whalers preceded the missionaries, governors and land companies that reduced the land to their measure. Wedde's heroes are mariners who, like Ahab, fling their dare in the teeth of nature, but who at the same time learn to read nature until they can find their place within it. Far from being corrupted by the islands, they accept the violence they find there and in themselves, and join with the natives to build a commonwealth that, in contrast to the pandemonic state Melville finds in the Encantadas, creates the freedom that imperialism denies.

Wedde's story, with its two protagonists striving a century apart to find their way home, reaches back to the earliest legends of western imperial imperialism. The *Iliad*, precursor of Troy's fall, is a tragedy of human pretension. Its successor, *The Odyssey*, chronicles the heavy fate of men who defied the gods, but celebrates the ability of the hero who obeys their behests to overcome both nature and alien humanity. Odysseus has triumphed at Troy; he returns home to cleanse Ithaca of the intruders who have usurped his power. His voyage, as we have noted, provided the model for the legendary foundation of the Roman Empire by Aeneas and of the Portuguese Empire by Vasco da Gama. For Wedde, however, the voyage becomes a comic interplay of drunken blundering and providential accident. Like Odysseus and Ahab, his characters begin their voyages amid chaos and bloodshed, which they continue to spread around them.

The only consistent viewpoint offered in the novel comes from the shadowy Doctor Long Ghost, also known as John Troy. Troy is the man, part charlatan, part savant, totally detached and amoral, who shared Herman Melville's sojourn in Tahiti. In Wedde's novel, he is credited with Melville's metamorphosis from the carefree Harry the Reefer to the serious novelist. When Melville is rescued from the shore of Typee, John Troy, Doctor Long Ghost, himself a fugitive, extends to him the recognition as a free spirit that separates him irrevocably from the other crewmen. By accepting this recognition, Melville becomes complicit in the Doctor's cultivation among the crew of the anarchic spirit of revolt that is to lead the two of them to the calaboose, but which frees them from bondage either to authority or to circumstance (pp.171–76). This freedom, however, carries its own obligations. Doctor Ghost "incorrupt like a sore cleaned by maggots" (p.181), disappears to the California gold fields. Melville is forced by the Doctor's knowledge of him to "go back, . . . to construct and plant the slow bomb that will fumigate the quarantine hulk of his nation's consciousness" (p.161). John Troy forces him to reproduce in the history of the Pacific the tale of the fallen city. In the time of the novel, the unnamed fugitive tries to reconstruct the history of the fall as he flees through the city's ruins.

The novel is constructed as a classical triptych. In the first part, John or James "Worser" Heberley finds his way from the oppression of nineteenth-century England to New Zealand and a remote settlement of Maoris and white seamen. Simultaneously, the fugitive, after escaping from a literary reception, wanders the streets and harbour of Wellington, New Zealand's capital city. His wanderings start with him vomiting the food of the reception over the statue of Richard Seddon, New Zealand Premier at the turn of the century and author of the policies of social security at home and imperial participation abroad that gave its society its contemporary characteristics. The fugitive's vomiting forth of pretension and illusion parallels Heberley's rejection of England and choice of a home and a future among the outcasts who constitute the "new people" of the islands. But while Heberley earns his right to "a house . . . a woman . . . fish just offshore" (p.58), the fugitive finds his home only a temporary refuge where he takes refuge from responsibility by fainting. His unconsciousness contrasts with Heberley, who has learned the seaman's lesson, always to know where he is and who he is. This comes to Heberley first as a navigation lesson as he takes the ship in heavy weather through the narrow and treacherous strait that leads to Te Awaiti, where he makes his home. The navigator's choice of where—where to reef the sails, where to hold the helm straight for the point and where to swing it, where to commit the ship to the currents and where to commit himself to a home— depends on the prior knowledge of who he is, whom he has been made by the combination of the circumstances he has been thrown into like the ship into the strait, and the choices he has made in their midst.

Heberley is born into the poverty of early nineteenth-century Britain and, at the age of eleven, apprenticed to a brutal master. He starts to take charge of his life when he first attempts to run away, and eventually succeeds in becoming an itinerant seaman, shipping from London to Newfoundland and the West Indies, and eventually becoming involved in Pacific whaling and coastal shipping from Sydney. Two further decisive moments in his life are his rescue and acceptance by Australian Aborigines, and his subsequent decision to ship for New Zealand with Captain Guard, who completes his education in navigation and offers him the prospects of making his own life in New Zealand. This life offers him an escape from the tyrannies of sea captains and the deracinated existence of a seaman. The freedom it promises, however, comes at a price. He has to build his own house, and he obtains his woman only by accepting the authority of her father, and with him the cultural imperatives of Maori life, including the savagery and cannibalism that for Europeans had been the marks of their exclusion from humanity. On board the whaling ship, the massacres of Maoris had been as much a part of his life, and just as bloody, as the massacre of whales (pp.61–67). Heberley recoils when he realizes that Guard's vision means making his life among these "cannibals" (p.60). Yet, as he later recalls, his perspective is changed by the sight of the magnificent Maori war fleet returning from its bloodthirsty expedition. The sight of the boats, a flotilla united by human purpose, brings back to him the whole of his own life not now as a sequence of events suffered, but as a pattern over which he has command:

> Down-channel in the grey distance the flotilla crawled across the still surface of the water. The usual haphazard strike of paddles had given way to a rhythmic plunge and flash along both sides of the great canoes . . . in the high feather-tassled prow of each leading canoe stood a man who held up his weapon and yelled the stroke, and Worser could hear the low rhythmic choral grunt of the rowers. From the rabble of lesser canoes in the wake of the great ones there began to be heard the wailing of women's voices. . . . As the canoes came to the beach Worser could see they were decorated with severed heads and hands . . .
>
> And he stood there at the back of its all. . . . Only a bit under a fortnight since the whaling had begun, not more than three weeks since his house had been built, a month since he'd got his name—a month of probational tenure in the place. And he stood there, slack-jawed. Because through all his life with more in it than most men would even dream of—his own crawling about on the surface of the water with no more purpose than a waterbug has on the meniscus above trout—through ice and fire, the three-hundred and sixty degrees of a horizon's meaningless compass points at whose centre he was stalled in a magnetic eternity, the close surf-loud loom of Pacific reefs and islands, dock-whores of Santiago-de-Cuba stripped smooth of cunt-hair, the lanced men dragging blood through the white sand . . . whistle and clout and his neck and tongue going stiff under Chilton's rope-end, his fingers sticking to ice on the yards off Newfoundland, old Slobberchops lying in his own aniseed piss under the sad light of the galley-lamp . . . the level look in old Swindle's eyes as he paid out short dollars . . .
>
> . . . through the moments whose joy he understood least—smell of squab pie again, yes, the girl's dark narrow

back under peppery thatch . . . nights he'd sat with a bit
of biscuit with junk beef on it . . .
        . . . through his entire life up till *this* moment, he had
never felt on the outside of his own life, of where his life
was. (pp.218–9)

The price he pays for this control is the reversal of all his values.
Instead of the cannibals being objects of fear and contempt, he
accepts their war fleet as a symbol of communal purpose and
their leaders as the authorities in his life.

This reversal is consistent throughout the novel. Its account
of whaling, although drawing on independent sources, is to a
great extent a re-imagining of Herman Melville's *Moby Dick*. While
the details are the same, the effect is one of horror rather than
admiration. Melville portrays the whale as man's antagonist,
alternatively terrifying and benign, who provides the measure
of man's physical and spiritual quality. Moby Dick himself is the
rogue whale, the spirit of evil that drives Ahab to madness. Wedde
reverses this. He portrays whaling as bloody massacre,
characterized by "raw, shark-torn corpses," the "stink of
fuel . . . across the filthy deck" as "oil black smoke streams through
the rigging lit by the furnace amidships." During the flensing,
instead of the regenerative "whitest and daintiest of fragrant
spermacetti" (Melville, p.333), we find Captain Swindle "blowing
arpeggios through a silver flute" and "turning slightly away from
the infernal scene" as "sharks to starboard smack and worry at
the third cadaver" like "dogs snarling as they lapped blood in
the Smithfield gutters" (Wedde, p.63). His memory of this scene
leads Heberley directly to the massacre of the Maoris, which
similarly closes as "sharks came into the bay" (p.67). Just as the
white settlers wiped out the Maoris who were in their way, so
"between 1827 and 1840" the whalers almost exterminate the
Southern Right whales from their nurseries around Cook Strait:
"Because the whalers would kill the calves first, and then get the
mother when she came to help" (p.113). The quality of compassion
that brings the whales undone provides the measure of human
callousness. The whaling industry in its turn provides the basis
for the capitalism that eventually surfaces in twentieth-century
Wellington in the form of a McDonald's restaurant. The smooth,
homogeneous surface of the multinational purveyor of junk food
masks the horrors of exploitation on which it is built. But Wedde's

Mocha Dick also cruises in the consciousness below this surface, threatening once more to reverse its apparent order.

But, while the whaling industry is depicted as a destroyer controlled by the greed of capitalists in distant Boston and Sydney, the whalers themselves wade through the blood they shed to earn a precarious independence on the shores where they establish their anarchic colonies. In another reversal, Wedde portrays these colonies, based on blood shed by cannibals and whalers alike, as allowing more humanity than modern Wellington, built on the systematic colonisation of Wakefield and his colleagues. Wellington is a modern manifestation of Symme's Hole, the hollow in the earth where Symme dreamed of establishing the ultimate capitalist utopia. To further his dream, he financed Wilkes' expedition to the Pacific. Wilkes failed to find the Hole, perpetuating his name only in the barren Antarctic waste of Wilkes Land, but his expedition, in the mind of Wedde's fugitive, marks the final parcelling up of the Pacific for western capitalism. It finished the work of Wakefield and Cook, who, in another reversal of mythology, Wedde portrays as the man who brought the natives not healing and nutrition but lilies that brought slow paralysis and death. The description of their effects originated the myth of the islands as lands of lotus-eaters ripe for colonial discipline.

Wedde himself accepts the myth of the lotus-eaters when he imagines Melville's decision to leave the island paradise of *Typee* and confront his fate on American soil. The whites may infect paradise with their diseases (p.185), but the islands are equally dangerous to them. Fayaway's island of "orange blossom and sweet coconut balm" is also permeated by the "cloying sickish odour of pooepooe, faecal breath of the night breeze of the middens and latrine groves." The fecundity of the island to which he abandons himself is identified as the source of a magic rooted in female sexuality and leading to a fear of absorption in the other: the "fermentation of humid vegetable mould, the sexual sorcery of night-scented flowers, great white moths with glowing eyes and voluptuously furred antennae crouched over the trembling lips, sucking and sucking. And around him in the dark, the breathing of the household—that tender, intimate unconscious abandonment to the air they all shared . . ." (p.162). Wedde, or his fugitive, speculates that Melville's fear of losing himself in this paradise leads to a "fear of impotence" that gives his writings a "promiscuous flippancy" (p.163). This fear of a sexuality identified with the islands of the south seas however also permeates the novel. Its nineteenth-century characters produce themselves in the rigours of combat, establishing their homes on shore only as place of refuge and relief. Women are the prizes they earn and the celebrants of their victories as they return from their cannibal raids or whaling expeditions. The twentieth century fugitive similarly finds his way home only to reject it, and set out on further wild journey of orgiastic penetration.

The heroes of the novel continually reverse the accepted history of colonisation. Heberley and his companions were the "new men" despised by Edward Gibbon Wakefield, hallowed progenitor of organized settlement in Australia and New Zealand, as "savages," people who "have become rotten before they are ripe" (p.233). Yet they are the men who, because they know where they are, make it possible for the colonisers to find the land they crave. Heberley acts as pilot for Wakefield's brother, the Colonel, whom he discovers to be an aristocratic ninny, "building an imaginary city" in the new land before he knows who he is himself (p.192–94). Because he has escaped the oppressive conventions and mendacities of civilization and knows who he is, Heberley recognizes the Colonel's total incomprehension of the Maori people whose right to the land he believes he is buying. He also realizes that he and his like have no place in Wakefield's dream city, which will reproduce the old world they have escaped from. The rights of property will be respected, children will again be thrashed for the theft of a few plums from the tree, and the new people will be "made thieves and poachers all over again" (p.234 and passim).

The epitome of this old world remade in the new is Edward Wakefield's son Jerningham, the gentlemanly arsonist who sets a whole mountainside forest ablaze just to see what it looks like (p.79). Yet it is Jerningham, not Heberley, whose name is commemorated on contemporary maps of New Zealand. The reversal of the established order attempted by the new men has been defeated, and the novelist can do no more than recall the brief period of its success. Only the spirit of Mocha Dick continues to cruise beneath the surface of our consciousness, reminding us of the bloody basis of present prosperity, and threatening once more to overthrow the order culture has imposed on nature. In the final section of the novel, Wedde's fugitive escapes both marriage and Wellington to try to recover the spirit of nature in a return to the land with his former hippie mistress, but although their journey conjures up the past of Melville and Heberley it leads to no future. The book ends with the image of an "old man's big skull ghosted back to a bony yellow mask" where "one stroke-smitten eyelid hands in a perpetual wink" (p.322). The secret discovered by the "new men" remains hidden in a past destroyed by the ravages of capitalism. It cannot be recovered either by historical research or by romantic escapism.

The element missing from Wedde's rewriting of colonial history is the concept of nurture. It is a book about men, about their predatory exploitation of the seas and their exploitative use of women on land. Its nineteenth-century heroes earn their freedom, but they remain alienated from the land. They prove themselves in an ocean which is portrayed not as a source of life but as a place of bloody conflict which tests the combatants' fitness to live. The killing fields of the ocean are not just a part of life, but the place where the living are most fully themselves. The nurturing paradise offered by the islands in its midst seduces masculinity from its proper purpose. Melville must "quit paradise," rejecting Faraway and her feminine sexual sorcery and returning to his homeland to carry on an imaginative combat under "orders every bit as lonely as those opened by Wilkes, by Ahab"—that is, by the navigators. Those who remain remote from the rigours of conflict, the merchants who enjoy its benefits from afar, and the systematic colonists who try to tame the land, are shown as sterile agents of a capitalism whose only monument is the barren wasteland of the twentieth-century city from which there is no longer an escape. Its twentieth-century victim, who tries to flee it and find himself in the past and the land, lacks productive ways of relating to either. He remains nameless, while the future of colonialism remains still to be discovered.

CHAPTER 13

AUSTRALIA: THE VIOLATED CONTINENT

I

English-speaking settlers arrived in Australia and New Zealand over the same period as their fellows occupied Pacific North America. In both the United States and Canada, however, this settlement followed a long history of Spanish settlement and exploration and a century or more of fur-trading. The movement to the Pacific coast was either an extension of the westward trek or a continuation of coastal invasions. Even in New Zealand, the first settlements were trading posts in a complex network of whaling, sealing and trading that encompassed the Pacific and involved the newcomers in relationships with social structures they could identify with their own. The first settlement in Sydney Cove, New South Wales, however, was isolated both geographically and historically, and brought its inhabitants into direct contact with a society they could not comprehend and whose people had occupied their lands longer than any other people on earth. The settlers were trapped between an ocean that Cook alone had crossed and a completely unknown interior. When they turned their backs on the ocean to explore the interior, they found a desert. Ever since, they have clung to the shores, but have feared to look beyond them. The beach rather than the desert has become a central feature of Australian life. Only on this margin between alien land and alien sea do Australians feel comfortable with themselves. They still have to come to terms both with their place and their past.

William Dampier, the first Englishman to sight Australia, found its people the "miserablest people in the world," but on his second visit responded favorably to the environment of their native land. In his *Voyage* he mentions trees and shrubs that

253

were "sweet-scented . . . and had at this Time either Blossoms or Berries . . . And these generally smelt very sweet and fragrant . . . There were also beside some Plants, Herbs, and tall Flowers, some very small Flowers, growing on the Ground, that were sweet and beautiful, and for the most part unlike any I had seen elsewhere." (Dampier, 1981, p.108) In this garden he found also a variety of birds, "all singing with a great Variety of fine shrill Notes," but few animals. The natives he encountered were, however, less pleasing to eyes trained to classical styles of beauty. Instead, he encountered a party led by a chief in war paints, "not for Beauty or Ornament, one would think, but as some wild Indian Warriors are said to do, he seem'd thereby to design the looking more Terrible; this his Painting adding very much to his natural Deformity; for they all of them have the most unpleasant Looks and the worst Features of any People that ever I saw, tho' I have seen great variety of Savages" (p.122). The "poor Creatures" offered no material culture to compensate for their lack of physical attraction, for Dampier saw no signs of houses or cultivation, nor any artifacts apart from their spears. As the land offered no prospects of profit, after some three weeks of exploration Dampier "resolved to leave this Coast, and accordingly. . . set sail towards Timor" (p.125). Despite its favorable description of the landscape, this first formal English attempt at exploring Australia, or New Holland as it was then known, thus added nothing to the accounts of Dutch seamen. It did however establish it as a *terra nullius*, an empty land that, while it offered no opportunities for European enrichment, threatened no serious resistance to European encroachment.

Captain James Cook painted a similar picture when, a century later, he reached the east coast of Australia. He described the nakedness of the inhabitants, the "mean small hovels" in which they lived, and their lack of any knowledge of metals. However, he also described their features as "far from being disagreeable" and their voices as "soft and tunable," and noted that even in their primitive canoes they seemed to have visited "the most Distant Islands which lay upon the Coast." The land they inhabited was not, he claimed, the "barren and Miserable Country that Dampier and others have described the western side to be," but an "Extensive Country" where "it can never be doubted but what most sorts of Grain, Fruites, Roots &ca of every kind would flourish here once they are brought hither, planted and cultivated by the hand of Industry . . . " Far from being "the most wretched people upon Earth" the natives "in reality . . . are far more happier than we Europeans; being wholly unacquainted not only with the superfluous but the necessary Conveniences so much sought after in Europe, they are happy in not knowing the use of them." These remarks about both the land and its people reflect Cook's sanguine outlook but they are all qualified by his observation that "We are to Consider that we see this Country in the pure state of Nature." Its Edenic state is offered for our contemplation as an object lesson, not as an object that should be left untouched by our "Industry." Rather, Cook implies that the fertility of the land could enable a judicious European settlement to obtain for itself the Edenic tranquility the natives enjoy without labour (Cook, 1969, pp.83–85.)

Cook's remarks helped to form the opinions that led the British government to establish there a colony to accommodate the convicts that the newly independent American states now declined to receive. But there was a deep flaw in the ideology that guided this foundation. On the one hand, the new country offered the space for men to grow into the kind of freedom enjoyed by the Aborigines. On the other, convicts had to learn the discipline and subordination enjoined on them as members of the lower orders of society. As a Select Committee of the House of Commons was to observe, reformation was to begin as convicts were "domiciled in a family . . . and forced into habits of industry and regularity." By experience, they would learn something of family, until on the expiration of settlement they could receive a grant of sufficient land to maintain themselves as independent yeomen farmers (Clark, 1957, pp.116–20). This ideal of settlement directly contradicted both the ideal of the noble savage and the reality of the Aboriginal economy of hunting and gathering. The destruction of this economy led directly to the devastation of Aboriginal society and of the environment which had supported it.

While this devastation may have been inevitable, it was not unintended. Sir Joseph Banks' advice on the new settlement included among its advantages the fact that "there would be little Probability of any Opposition form the Natives," who were not only few in number but "naked, treacherous, and armed with Lances, but extremely cowardly" and "constantly retired from our People when they made the least Appearance of

Resistance" (Clark, 1957, p.61). They could, in other words, be displaced without difficulty. The displacement began even when Governor Arthur Phillip, on his first entrance to Sydney Harbour, admiringly named Manly Beach in honour of their fine stature. This linguistic gesture simultaneously appropriates the land and its people to European modes of thought. When the Aborigines failed to live up to the role these modes assigned them, responding to the invasion of their lands and the theft of their goods by spearing the intruders, Phillip responded by authorizing the first punitive expeditions. These served to legitimize the assaults and massacres that continued over the next century and a half. Most settlers and governors viewed the Aborigines as vermin to be displaced as soon as possible in favor of sheep and cattle and their human minders. For the Aborigines, the coming of the whites was disastrous. The violence of their dispossession remains to haunt white Australians to the present day, leaving them uneasy in their possession of a land that remains alien.

This unease continues to be expressed in a language that has been unable fully to accommodate to antipodean reality. Australians are brought up as linguistic schizophrenics, able to respond equally to images of May as spring and as autumn, marking the heat of Christmas with cards of snow and holly, and changing Easter's northern mythology of renewal from a celebration of the returning sun to thanksgiving for its imminent decline and the prospect of reviving rain. The original connotations of Manly Beach have been superseded by images of sun, surf, and concrete, but the name continues as a reminder of the values it displaced and of the history our hedonism seeks to escape. In the Bicentenary year, 1988, the Aboriginal writers Colin Johnson and Kath Walker deliberately sought to reverse this process of linguistic obliteration by discarding their European names and rewriting themselves in the language of their country as Mudrooroo Narogin and Oodgeroo Noonuccal. These names deliberately recall the place and the people whose stories they inscribe in the English language.

Johnson's first novel, *Wild Cat Falling*, used the form of the conventional social realist novel to tell the story of a teenager whose black identity compounds his rebellious nature to trap him in a cycle of delinquency and punishment. The novel ends with his return to the country and, implicitly, his native heritage.

It remains within the tradition of protest literature, and so serves as a challenge to white conscience, but not to white consciousness. This further challenge becomes explicit in his second novel, *Long Live Sandawara*, which rewrites both the treacherous native and the rebellious teenager of white mythology as heroes of Aboriginal liberation. While the violence of the novel eventually dissipates its own energies, it is important as Johnson's first attempt to imagine an alternative to the historic subordination of Aboriginal society.

The opening scene of *Sandawara* is very like the saloon scenes in the work of James Welch or Leslie Marmon Silko. Johnson, as he was then known, opens his novel with the sentences:

> A heavy white cop fist had smashed Tom in the jaw for dumb insolence; but that was yesterday and today his dole cheque has arrived to ease the pain. He sits at the bar, finishes a beer and orders another from a scowling barmaid. Beside him sits a thick-set girl, quite light-skinned but with the beetling brows, heavy cheeks and big-breasted body of the lubra. (p.1)

The absence of hope, the emptiness filled only by violence, booze, and the vague promise of sex, are the same qualities found by Tayo in *Ceremony* or by the narrator of *Winter in the Blood* as they try to escape from the quests imposed on them.

The story of these three novels is also similar. In each, the central character is caught in a world of violence and dissipation, and each finds an older man whose words restore continuity with tradition and provide a centre or purpose for his life. But whereas the characters in *Ceremony* and *Winter in the Blood* use violence as a means of avoiding their sense of guilt for the death of a brother, and can find salvation only by breaking from the cycle of violence and degradation, Johnson's characters find salvation in violence. In all books the characters have the sense that, in stealing from the white man they are merely taking back some rent for the land he has stolen from them, but Silko in particular presents violence as part of the Indians' condition as victims. Tayo wins his final victory by resisting the "witchery" the whites have implicated in the land, by refusing to answer it with his own violence. More ambiguously, the narrator of *Winter in the Blood*, returning home and accepting his grandmother's death and the loss of the horse that has tied him to his brother's death, accepts that his own place is on the land rather than wandering through the bars. In *Sandawara*, however, Johnson presents violence as the logical response to the violence by which the Aborigines, the Nyoongas, have themselves been displaced. The old man who gives Alan back his tradition links him back also to a history of resistance and war. Alan's own attempted assault on the bank therefore logically extends the casual demand that whites should pay for their occupation to a war of liberation to take back what they once owned. The book is therefore more highly political than its American counterparts. Like the work of Witi Ihaemara or Keri Hulme, it is not merely an expression of the contemporary situation, or even a response to it, but a sustained attempt to imagine an alternative.

Part of the novel's honesty is its recognition that the alternative it imagines is impossible. Noorak, the old man who gives Alan his past and the story of Sandawara's revolt, lacks the strength to do any more than pass on this legacy. Sandawara himself remains an isolated hero. He leads his band of guerrillas by the power of his individual charisma as shaman and warrior, and so remains a figure of individual courage rather than of collective resistance or rebirth. Adam Shoemaker has argued (Shoemaker 1989) that this weakness in the historic hero comes from Johnson's reliance on a limited number of sources, mainly Ion Idriess's 1952 fictional account of the police hunt for the actual Sandamara. But, by the slight change of the name of this character to Sandawara, Johnson indicates that he is not interested in the facts of history so much as in re-imagining them. By changing the perspective while sticking to the main outline of Idriess's story, Johnson converts the Aboriginal rebel from a courageous but brutal outlaw to a fully human hero. Sandawara's achievements in an earlier generation inspire Alan to emulate him in the present through an act of collective rather than individual resistance. His followers are not the primitive brutes of white fantasy, but vagrants trying to clutch elements of dignity from the brutal urban society that has displaced the integrated culture of their forebears. Noonak gives Alan the strength that enables him to give both love and purpose to his group of outcasts, a sanctuary from the alcohol and drugs, casual sex and violence, that otherwise destroy them. But Alan's rebellion itself depends on violence. Despite his overt politics, his appeal to his followers is personal, like Sandawara's, whose name he takes with his role. His ambitions are thwarted when his followers are blown away in the storm of police fire that brings the inevitable end. The novel's success is in imagining, through Alan, both an alternative form of the past and a possible future. Its failure is its inability to envisage possible action towards this future.

Yet this failure must be qualified. The novel ends neither with the police bullets that fell Alan's band of "kids who didn't even know how to use their guns" (p.159), nor with those that finally stop the earlier Sandawara. His last words before he "falls back into freedom" are "'Brothers, the white man can never take what I have'" (p.166). Immediately after these words, the narrative tells of the later Sandawara ducking back into the bank and seizing his loot. He then goes back to Sandawara's last witness, Noonak, the "old Jacky Jacky taken far from his country to languish in a white man's prison, then ejected, old and broken, to live as best he could, bereft of land, hope and people" (p.169). With the money he has taken from the bank, he takes Noonak back to his land, where he will receive his initiation at the old man's hands. This journey back to the land thus both restores Noonak's past and from it gives Alan a future. Like Silko in the conclusion of *Ceremony*, Johnson suggests that only the land itself can give its people the power to resist the witchery, the violence, in which the white man has implicated it.

In his later novel, *Doctor Wooreddy's Prescription for Enduring the Ending of the World*, Johnson sidesteps the problem of effective action in the present by setting his story entirely in the past. Again, he relies mainly on white sources for his history, remaking one of the central stories of white Australian mythology to fashion it as a story of Aboriginal pride and tragedy. Like Witi Ihaemara, Johnson, by recreating the Aborigines' struggle for their land, is making their claim to it legitimate. Again like Ihaemara, Johnson starts this process by his choice of language. As the language of the Tasmanians has been lost, Johnson effects his change by capturing the English language for his purposes, making the Aborigines the insiders and the whites, the *num* or ghosts, the outsiders, the intruders who come from the sea to destroy the land and its people. In telling the story of this intrusion and of the resistance to it, Johnson both recreates the alternatives which existed and integrates these possibilities in contemporary Aboriginal tradition. The book thus assists also to bring into being the Aboriginal people who have succeeded to the dissipated tribes. Thus, although unlike *Sandawara* it is not about particular political actions, it is itself a political action.

The central Aboriginal characters, Wooreddy and the woman Trugernanna, whose violent rape is one of the first consequences Wooreddy sees of arrival of the whites and who later becomes his wife, become accomplices of William Augustus Robinson in his self-chosen "friendly" mission to save the Tasmanian Aborigines from the whites and, more particularly, from themselves and their heathen ways. The practical effect of his mission is to destroy the remnants of the tribes that have survived white settlement, to remove any possibility that an Aboriginal society might have continued to exist in those parts of the island unsuitable for white settlement, and to condemn the wretched survivors to misery and lingering death at the settlement of Wybalenna on Flinders Island. In the final part of the book, Robinson takes Wooreddy and Trugernanna with him to Victoria to assist him in his new role as "Chief Protector" of the mainland Aborigines, and again leads them to disaster. The novel ends with the hanging of one of Robinson's proteges, Ummarrah, and the death of Wooreddy off Flinders Island. "Robinson gave a cry of horror and vomited as Ummarrah gave a last convulsive kick and went limp," but he recovers sufficiently to take his other charges to the boat that was to remove them to their homeland. As the Aborigines are settled amidships, "Robinson left the ship and the disagreeable episode came to an end for him" (p.206). Although the author has earlier allowed him a few moments of self-doubt, he is able to set aside the fate he has, despite his genuine compassion, brought on the Aborigines and is, like even the worst of the other settlers, free to enjoy the profits of destruction. He may have failed to bring his charges to either an earthly or a heavenly paradise, but his own rewards are certain.

Despite its grim history and this grim conclusion, however, the novel is one of hope. Robinson's travels with the Aborigines through the harsh west coast country of Tasmania give him some understanding of the tough resilience of the Aborigines and the harmonious relationship they had created with the land. More importantly, Johnson shows both the effective resistance of some of the Tasmanians, before disease strikes them down, and the persistence with which his companions are able to subordinate Robinson's purposes to their own, making him for a time their agent rather than their leader. When, in the final section, Wooreddy and Trugernanna join the Port Phillip natives in walkabout, they discover a unity of religion and tradition that transcends divisions of geography and language. During their travels, while Trugernanna accomplishes a delayed revenge on the sailor who had first raped her and so precipitated her subsequent fate, Wooreddy has a vision that finally unites the divisions of earth and sea, of good and evil, into a unity that encompasses the whole of creation. When he rejoins his fellows, the whole party exchange dances and songs amongst themselves, renewing tradition at the very moment of its extinction. Johnson's novel is a further moment in this cycle of renewal. In its last lines, as Shoemaker observes, the world comes ablaze with the colours of the Aboriginal flag:

> The yellow setting sun broke through the black clouds to streak rays of light upon the beach. It coloured the sea red. . . . Suddenly a spark of light shot up from the beach and flashed through the dark sky towards the evening star. As it did so, the clouds closed again and the world vanished. (p.207)

Wooreddy's world has died with him, but its values live on in the memory and in the imagination that can continue to enlighten the present.

II

The violence with which they displaced the native peoples continues to haunt the imagination of white Tasmanian writers. Most recently, Cassandra Pybus, in *Community of Thieves*, has woven the story of Robinson, Wooreddy and Truganini (the more common spelling) into the story of her own forebears who succeeded to Aboriginal lands in Oyster Bay and Bruny Island. Like Johnson, she recognizes distinctions among the whites in their attitudes and conduct towards the Aborigines, and she explicitly acknowledges the possibility that the encounter between the two cultures need not have led to the destruction of the earlier society. However, while she acknowledges that the settlers were prisoners of their own assumptions, she insists that, without

judging our forebears, the present generation has inherited the
guilt and has the power to make reparation. She points to the
obduracy of Tasmanian legislators toward land rights, and the
oblivion in which the Van Diemen's Land Company still tries
to shroud the massacres its servants committed in order to ensure
its possession of the lands that profit its British shareholders to
this day. Her narrative places Robinson rather than the natives
near its centre, and so emphasizes the tragedy of blind good
intentions rather the starker tragedy of the destruction of a culture.
She shows further how hopes of cultural adaptation by natives
who tried to obtain land to support themselves as farmers were
thwarted by white prejudice and lack of good faith, and how the
memory of the few who succeeded has been obliterated by those
who find it easier to believe that a whole race perished as the
cost of inevitable progress. She shares with Johnson the
understanding that the first step towards reparation is the
readiness to imagine both the past and the alternatives it offered,
but she insists also that for whites this must be based on a
willingness to look unflinchingly at the stark facts that remain
not only as a barrier between whites and blacks, but between
whites and the land. The point of origin of her narrative is her
own love of the country and her childhood memories of the
beauty and security of the estate her forebears had created by
the displacement of the blacks.

While Pybus places the dispossession of the Aborigines at
the heart of her own ambiguous feelings towards the land, Patrick
White sees the mode of dispossession as the key to the alienation
of the settlers from their land. In *Fringe of Leaves*, this alienation
is evident from the first in Mrs. Merivale's genteel distaste both
for the land from which her husband makes his living as a
surveyor and for the ordinary inhabitants of the city the settlers
have built. Mrs. Merivale has ventured into the interior only
once, and still recalls with exaggerated horror such moments as
her encounter with a lizard. She now views the world only from
the safe enclosure of a carriage. Similarly, we first meet Austin
Roxburgh in the safety of the ship's cabin from which he refuses
to go either on shore or on deck. He is at ease only with the
sonorities of Virgil, whose stoicism of words contradicts
Roxburgh's habitual valetudinarism. His nature makes him
uncomfortable with people and places, so that he prefers to keep
to his room on land or his cabin on the ship. As he sets out on

the return voyage, he admits that the whole voyage to Australia has been a mistake. He acknowledges the fertility of Van Diemen's Land, but judges that there was "never an emptier, more hostile country" than the Colony of New South Wales (p.68). He eventually perishes when, cast by the forces of nature onto a hostile shore, he attempts to play the Virgilian role of English gentleman and is speared by the savages he would conciliate.

In contrast to these timid reclusives, his wife, Ellen, strides boldly into the outdoors, whether at her childhood home in Cornwall, in Van Diemen's Land or on the ship, or after they are marooned on the northern coast of Australia. Even Roxburgh admits that she differs from him in her judgement of the new land, but attributes this to her "fanciful, or 'romantic,' streak." She feels alienated in the face of his education and respectability, apologizing that she will "only ever know what my instinct tells me" (p.35). This instinct, however, enables her to see truly. She responds with hostility to the ugly spectacles of convictism, but with an openness to the country itself. When her husband condemns the land and its flowers as "more strange than beautiful," she withholds judgement; "I haven't made up my mind . . . Whether beautiful, or only strange, I doubt I shall ever forget the flowers" (pp.33–34).

A country girl who has been bathed in the Celtic mystery of St. Hya's well, Ellen's alienation is not from the country but from her husband's genteel and detached enlightenment, and from the inhumanity the same system generates through his philistine but practical brother, Garnett. Yet Garnett also represents the sensuality her nature craves and the aggression necessary to impose the veneer of European civilization on a hostile land. His homestead, the ironically named "Dulcet," is a symbol of imposed order, enclosed by symbols of the power that maintains it:

> The hedge was of thickset clipped box; the cypresses had been trimmed too, as well as decapitated, which gave the precincts a military, if not a penal air. (p.85)

This "rigid discipline" prevents the visitor judging the house solely on its promise of comfort after the long journey. The Roxburgh's stay there is marked by a hollow similitude of English country life, as well as the tale of the cruel disposal of its former proprietor, Garnett Roxburgh's first wife, the shooting of the mare that displeases him and the setting aside of the convict girl he has impregnated, and of course his rape of Ellen. Yet his rape occurs in response to a "sensuality buried inside her" that "had risen to the surface and wrestled with his more overt lust" (p.140).

Her rape by Garnett makes her aware of her own nature, and by extension of the brutal nature of a colonization that both redeems and degrades the civilization from which it springs. English settlement in Australia regains the vitality that Garnett and Ellen both retain but which those who still belong at Home, like Austin, have lost. If, however, this vigor is to lead to anything other than brutality, it must be brought into communion with the land. Garnett is incapable of such communion. Ellen's subsequent precipitation beyond the coastal fringe of leaves, into an interior beyond the laws of the System, brings her to communion with the land in the form of the Aborigines who have possessed it and the escaped convict, Jack Chance, whose labours are giving it to its new masters. These encounters enable her to return to civilization without again losing the deepest self that her marriage to Austin had denied. The ancient land quite specifically heals the ills of the culture that is being imposed on it. The process of healing is, however, limited to Ellen, the initiate, and leaves society itself unaffected in its divisions of gentility and brutality.

III

The convicts and Aborigines who eventually give Ellen Roxburgh the freedom of the land haunt Christopher Koch's novels as symbols of the continuing alienation of the settler society from the land it has colonized. This land is remote, an island off the mainland, looking south only to greater emptiness. This emptiness and remoteness that both contains and sustains forms the centre of Koch's first novel, *The Boys in the Island*:

> Tasmania is an island of hills, a fragment separated from the parent continent by a wide stretch of ocean. It is different from the hot Australian mainland; it has a different weather and a different soul, knowing as it does the sharp breath of the south, facing the Antarctic. No wars, no horrors, no

> disturbances have ever reached the island: no horrors at all,
> since the last convict transport made the long run from
> England, when the island's dreaded name was Van Diemen's
> Land, in that bad, smelly old century of rum and the lash.
> (p.8)

The denial of horror is the reminder of the horrors by which the
colony was founded, which cannot be expunged from the country
by a mere change of name, any more than can the memory of
the first people on the island. Their presence is also implicit in
any reflection on the recent origins of white settlement:

> The island's people have not been there long: not two
> centuries. The dark, stone-age people the colonists found
> when they came there have all been wiped out; they are a
> lost race. But they are still a reproachful memory in the
> island's silence . . . the places of the bush seem to wait; they
> wait, the dead-quiet eucalyptus gullies, the damp bracken
> hollows, the dark-haired groves of she-oaks whose grey bark
> is like the mummified flesh of that race; and a single road-
> side mailbox, far out of sight of its house, can look forlorn
> as a lost child. Forlorn, all marks of men, in the lonely places
> of the island which still doesn't quite belong to them, nor
> they to it. (pp.8–9)

Even the city, the outpost of alien culture that both contains and
sustains the lives of Francis Cullen and the mates of his childhood,
cannot quite forget the land that surrounds it.

> The country's yellow grass reaches stray fingers into the
> suburbs; and standing in almost any street, you can glance
> up and see the near rusty-green and farther dream-blue
> ranges, their tree-serrated tops poignant against the sky: a
> reminder of farness. (p.9)

The novel is an account both of the intensity given to the years
of boyhood by this farness, and of Francis's attempts to escape
its confinement and fulfill the dreams it has implanted in him.
These dreams are, however, for something that cannot be found
in ordinary life. He neglects his schooling, escapes instead into
a love affair with Heather, the girl he meets at the Greendale
Hop Carnival, the communal celebration of the fertility that
settlement has realized in the land. The carnival sweeps the

youngsters away in its conviviality, but the intensity of their
affair comes from the awareness it brings to both of them that
it marks the end of their youth, that they can never again know
this happiness and innocence. Just as European carnival is
followed by Lent, the land's past overshadows their youthful
happiness with its suspicions and hostility. The crazy aunt stalks
the lovers and prevents their intimacy, the brutal father destroys
any possibility of joy within his family. Francis has an intimation
of the end of the affair when he goes off "to another week of
school, leaving her forlorn in the prison of the country yard"
(p.90). The affair comes to its end when she chooses to remain
in the prison, to follow her mother by marrying Donny, her
father's companion and fellow.

Thwarted in love, Francis escapes to the mainland and
dissipation, but finds neither brings the satisfaction it promises.
Eventually his dreams are brought to an end by the commonplace
mechanical carnage of a car crash. The novel ends with his
reflection on the impossibility of the dream; *"When you grow up
there's nowhere it can happen"* (p.198). The end of childhood is like
the end of colonialism: an acceptance of defeat. Tasmania is both
the same as anywhere else, and the only place he can find himself.

In his fourth novel, *The Doubleman,* Koch returns both to
Tasmania and to the theme of dreams and their fulfilment that
is central to colonialism. This time, however, the quest takes the
narrator, Richard Miller, not merely to the mainland, but to the
other world of magic. Like Patrick White's Ellen Gluyas who
bathed in St. Hya's Well, Richard wants to escape from his
material environment into the mysteries that come from the
immemorial time of the human race. His retreat into these
mysteries however disqualifies him from living in the present.

In this novel Koch, through his narrator, again insists on the
separateness of Tasmania: "Politically, it is part of the
Commonwealth of Australia; physically, it is not" (p.23). Yet, for
all its remoteness, it remains ineradicably British, a colonial
outpost that clings to its origins in order to deny its strangeness.

> Our seasons were the seasons of English storybooks, and of
> the films we saw on Saturday nights, brought from the
> northern hemisphere. Our great-grandfathers had put
> together a lost, unknown home in landscapes that made it
> all perfectly natural: Georgian houses with classical porticoes;

> hopfields and orchards; chimney pots rising on gentle
> hillslopes, in the subtle, muted lights of East Anglia . . .
> Norman and Gothic churches had appeared; discreet brothels;
> banks; Salvation Army hostels. . . . We were living, when
> I grew up, in the half-light of that Empire the ultimate end
> of whose bridge of boats was Hobart.
>
> And it was all strange. The island was unalterably
> strange in the end, hanging like a shield above Antarctica.

Richard Miller himself is a stranger in this world. In his childhood
he is set aside from others by an attack of polio, or infantile
paralysis, that leaves him lame. He is divided within himself by
his knowledge that he is not really an English Miller, but the
descendant of Lutheran Germans who prudently changed their
name in the First World War. Nor can he hide from the colony's
origins. He knows that he does not live in "dry, Time-flattened
Australia," but in the "other island" which had been

> Van Diemen's Land. It was a name that had rung and chimed
> in Cockney and Irish songs of hate; the name of a British
> penal colony that had once been synonymous with fear
> throughout the Anglo Saxon world. At the place called Hell's
> Gates, on the savage west coast, a penal settlement so terrible
> had been created that convicts had murdered each other to
> secure the release of hanging, or had fled without hope into
> the icy rain-forest to leave their bones there, and sometimes
> turn cannibal. Van Diemen's Land had also removed a whole
> race: the few aboriginals the colonists had found when they
> came, and whose last remnants, deported to a smaller island
> in Bass Strait, had pined away, staring across the water to
> their lost home. (pp.23–25)

These contradictions of Tasmania's history are repeated in
Richard's own schooldays among the Christian Brothers of St
Augustine's, the school that in its attempt to implant in the south
land the practices of Christian virtue succeeds only in repeating
the brutalities of convictism. After a particularly vicious episode,
the narrator reflects on the strangeness of his "familiar situation":

> Down below, our native town, our small, gimcrack colonial
> city, on the edge of the Southern Ocean; up here, this
> magisterial, medieval world of cloisters, Latin and the strap.
> We lived in two dimensions, I saw; and 'Panis Angelicus'

> woke a pleasure in me that hardly seemed my own . . . the
> hymn was anciently beautiful; the whole stern book of
> Europe was in it. (p.34)

This beauty comes from a past that lies outside time, quite different from the history that haunts Richard in Tasmania. Even before he recognizes the strangeness of his native land, Richard has accepted himself as a changeling, set aside by the terrifying onslaught of the polio that released him from death but left him permanently marked. His awareness of a beauty outside daily experience drives his attempts to escape from the present into the other worlds of fantasy, music, and magic. These worlds offer the promise of escape from the cruelties that have accompanied the European invasion, or the dullness that enshrouds the lives of those who attempt to deny their past. The enchantment he seeks, however, proves illusive, the product of Duessa, the deceiver, or the Queen of Faery who offers mortals brief joy at the cost of eternal damnation.

Richard's search for other worlds is also an attempt to reconcile Europe and Australia, to bring to an alien land the natural religion that had once joined it with its Aboriginal inhabitants, and which lives still in the folklore of Europe. Under the influence of Broderick, the "man in the lane" who seems to live apart from the material world, he glimpses this magic in old books, in the occult, and most grandly in the music made by his wild cousin, Brian Brady, and Broderick's protege Darcy Burr. Eventually, these two take Richard's European wife Katrin to give shape to his dreams through their incarnation as the musical trio, Tam Lin and the Rhymers. However, Richard's search for a way of living in this world without sacrificing the joy it promises for the pain it brings ends in disaster. The Duessa returns and, in alliance with Darcy, the reincarnation of Broderick the enchanter, attempts to take Richard back from Katrin, but is herself raped and murdered by another of her victims.

Like Francis Cullen in *The Boys in the Island*, Richard Miller has to learn to distinguish enchantment from truth. The successive figures he encounters in his youth—the figures of faery he adds to his toy theatre; Broderick, who introduces him to the dark world of Eleusinian mystery; Deidre, the Duessa or Queen of Faery who more literally seduces him in his first love affair; Brian Brady, the young Tam Lin who escapes from Brother

Kinsella into the land of faery, the world of music, and never finds his way back to his "ain country"—prove to be enchanters who begin an "enslavement to the past" that holds him into adulthood. The epigraphs to the early chapters, taken from mediaeval balladry and governed by the figure of Spenser's Duessa in the epigraph to the first section, point to the falsity of their promises. We are given a hint of the contrast between this seductive land of faery and true spirituality by the narrator's encounter with the Franciscan who briefly visits his school. The Franciscan also advises the boys "to try and withdraw your heart from the love of visible things, and to turn to the invisible." This Richard and Brian do, but they ignore the second part of the Franciscan's warning. "Sensuality, however full of innocent delight to you now, has its dangers" (p.38). Neglecting this warning, the boys follow the path of sensuality to the invisible world, and find themselves enchanted instead of enlightened.

For a time at the end of his schooldays Richard seems to make the world his own when he overcomes his physical handicap to follow his cousin Brian Brady on a tough bike ride from Hobart across the hills to the sea, where "his agony ended."

> Clearing the brow of a final rise, we'd come out of the hills and the enclosing gum forests, their metal-green ramparts left behind; we coasted downhill, freewheeling, in a long, splendid arc of relief, where my leg need pump no more. At the bottom, we were out on a white, straight road that ran above the beaches near Swansea, in open, moor-like, tussock country of she-oaks and tea tree, with no human signs except phone wires, and the dry-stone walls along the paddocks, built by the pioneers. The rain was over, and these sweet, pale spaces lifted my heart. (p.57)

For a moment, nature and humans are at one, with the accomplishment of the labour of old pioneers and modern technicians enabling us to forget the cruelties of the past in contemplation of a scene of achieved harmony. This, however, is the scene the Duessa is about to enter, and Richard is once again led astray. Only after years on a false track does he finally escape when he accepts responsibility for his own life and gives his wife, Katrin, another European enchantress, responsibility for hers. As the novel ends, the Duessa is dead and Katrin and Richard are free to sustain each other through love rather than magic. This love can, in turn, sustain the father and child Katrin has brought with her from the refugee camps of postwar Europe.

This resolution is practically dictated by the mythological form Koch has chosen for the novel. The power of the faery world that the book evokes is of necessity destructive, leaving damnation or escape as the only alternatives possible for those who become involved with it. The path that Richard takes from the clean Tasmanian hills and beaches leads to a deracinated urban world whose magic takes the form of pop music, drugs and casual sex. Far from taking him away from human cruelty, his quest takes him further into its meshes. Yet the ending, when he breaks free from his enchantment as he witnesses its agents destroy themselves, does not resolve the problems that first drove him on the quest. Unlike Francis Cullen, who returns to Tasmania and school at the end of *The Boys in the Island*, Richard is still living and working in Sydney, the city that is the antithesis to the countryside that permeated the city of his youth. And the countryside of Tasmania remains defiled by its convict past, by the acts of terror that imposed European culture on it. Richard's attempt to resolve the conflict of land and culture by going back to the culture's mythological origins has failed, but the failure emphasizes the urgency of his quest. The loss of magic at the end of the novel leaves him more alone than at the beginning. There, he was sustained by a family who gave him a past, and a city alive to both the cruelty and the beauty of its surrounding country. Now, in a city that turns its back on its hinterland and pullulates mindlessly on the shores of its beautiful harbour, even in marriage he is alone. The family he has married comprises three people whose past has been taken from them by the horrors of twentieth-century Europe. These horrors, which repeated on a vastly greater scale the cruelties of Van Diemen's Land, were also the product of an attempt to return to a mythological past. The destruction at the end of the novel empties the double world of magic of its glamour, but it leaves the source of its power.

For a moment, when his Duessa first left him, Richard had felt at one with his island: "Nothing stood between me and those fathoms: up here on my barrow, I'd become the centre of a vast process of transfiguration" (p.124). The Duessa leads him again out of this world into its double, the world of magic, but her destruction does not give him back this sense of the singleness of man and nature. He is left only with the alienation that gave the past its power to enslave. As he gazes at the moon in the last sentences of the novel, he knows that there is no double world for him to enter, but he is still to learn to live in this one. Bound to the earth of Australia, his imagination remains firmly European.

Richard Miller's failure to discover in European mythology a way to expiate the crimes of the past and achieve unity with his native earth is due to a contradiction in his own perception of the myth. The beauty of the Tasmanian landscape has been marred by the masculine brutality of its conquerors. Broderick and Darcy, the gatekeepers of the occult world Miller enters, are male. But the seducers, the agents of evil, are female, incarnations of the ancient earth goddess Artemis in her various manifestations as Hecate or the Queen of Elfland, the inarticulate girl Denise or the mature Deidre Dillon. Even Katrin becomes for a time one of their servants. Although Deidre's death frees Katrin and Richard from her enchantment, it also leaves them separated from the powers of nature that she incarnated, and which represent the only alternative the novel envisages to the alienation produced by the masculine aggression of colonialism. The novel's suppression of the feminine is rooted in the same fear that is implicit in the ways that European man, through the ages of imperialism and industrialism, has used technology to suppress the natural world rather than to learn to live more fully within it.

IV

In Tasmania the European dream reaches its furthest point, historically and geographically. The cruelties of the cultural imposition and the failure of the settlers' hopes are however common to the Australian experience. They provide the theme for the epic novels of settlement. As we have seen, the "Proem" to Henry Handel Richardson's *The Fortunes of Richard Mahony* tells of the revenge the land takes on those who, pursuing their dream "of vast wealth got without exertion," and, trying to tame the soil, become its prisoners.

> It was like a form of revenge taken on them, for their loveless schemes of robbing and fleeing; a revenge contrived by the

ancient, barbaric country they had so lightly invaded. Now,
she held them captive . . . lying stretched like some primeval
monster in the sun, her breasts freely bared, she watched,
with a malignant eye, the efforts made by these puny mortals
to tear their lips away. (p.11)

Richardson writes of the gold-miners who raped the green earth.
Her protagonist, Richard Mahony, keeps himself fastidiously apart
from the crudities of gold digging and money-grubbing, taking
his profit instead by genteel investment, only to be struck down
at the height of his prosperity and literally held captive in an
asylum for the insane.

The central figure in Brian Penton's *Landtakers* is a young
Englishman who similarly thinks he can make his profits while
holding aloof from the brutality he sees all around him on his
arrival in the convict colony of Moreton Bay. He is ingenuous
but not innocent, for his ambition of restoring the fortunes of his
family's Devonshire retreat depends on him learning to excel his
rivals in their brutality, and so excludes him forever from the
ancestral gentility he continues to believe he craves. The novel
ends with him, blinded and dependent, dreaming of his youth
but held captive by "new mirages" that will wring "a few more
years of living and struggling out of him." He is surrounded not
by the old scents of the "garden at Owerbury" but by the sound
of the new land, "the sound of the wind in the she-oaks" (p.360).
Yet the European name of these Australian trees reminds us that
an imported culture still holds our perceptions of this most ancient
of lands in its thrall.

Xavier Herbert's novel of the Northern Territory, *Capricornia*,
begins with the most savage irony of any account of western
settlement of the Pacific rim:

Although that northern part of the Continent of Australia
which is called Capricornia was pioneered long after the
southern parts, its unofficial early history was even more
bloody than that of the others . . .
    The first white settlement in Capricornia was that of
Treachery Bay—afterwards called New Westminster—which
was set up on what was perhaps the most fertile and pleasant
part of the coast and on the bones of half the Karrapillua
Tribe. (p.1)

The condemnation of native resistance embodied in the first name, Treachery Bay, and the later euphemism of New Westminster, symbolizing both imperial ambition and democratic pretension, are a metonym for both colonialism in general and the fictitious history of it that the novel will provide. Yet the land that the whites seize so violently takes its revenge on them. The violence of the seasons destroys their material ambitions, and no fewer than 21 of the novel's characters meet violent ends, as the result of their own brutality, because they surrender to the alcohol that is the universal solace, or because of their sentimental delusions that they can find a sanctuary from the savagery around them. The only hope the novel offers is through Norman, more accurately "No-name," the abandoned half-caste child of one of the less responsible white adventurers. But both his father and his foster-father become, like the characters in Richardson's and Penton's novels, captives of the land they try to tame. They try to conceal Norman's true origins, which then return to make him doubly an outcast and drive him to the final act of betrayal of his own lover and her daughter. The land itself mocks all dreams.

V

The epic of settlement is a form of the quest narrative that originates in western culture with the stories of Odysseus, Abraham, and Moses. Christopher Koch is unusual in his explicit use of the mythology of faery to frame his quests. His characters seek a destination beyond this world that will nevertheless link the colonial present with its furthest ancestral past. The epic of settlement, in contrast, seeks to recover in this world the Eden from which we were driven in the past. The failure of this quest leaves the seeker captive in a land that simultaneously holds and alienates him. David Malouf's novel of settlement, *Harland's Half Acre*, shows how this initial failure leaves the descendants of the settlers shut off equally from their cultural origins and their environment.

Malouf presents his chronicle as the deliberate reconstruction of experience by a variety of observers whose chief text is not their own memories, but the work of a painter, Frank Harland. The novel begins, not with recollection, but with an act of naming that simultaneously renders the land familiar and foreign.

> Named like so much else in Australia for a place on the far
> side of the globe that its finders meant to honour and were
> piously homesick for, Killarney bears no resemblance to its
> Irish original. (p.3)

Like Doig's first comers in Scotch Heaven, Malouf's Irish settlers,
members of a different segment of the Celtic diaspora, want to
reproduce their past in the new land. But, after this opening
paragraph, Malouf makes no attempt to chronicle their settlement.
In what is perhaps a typically Australian gesture, he starts instead
with the family already in decline, the hopes and pretensions of
the founders already declining into ruin or indifference. In place
of either a virgin landscape or the dreams they sought to impose
on it, he describes the land's present tatterdemalion appearance:

> It is lush country but of the green, sub-tropical kind, with
> sawmills in untidy paddocks, peak-roofed weatherboard
> farms, and on the skyline of low hills, bunyah pines, hoop
> pines and Scotch firs of forbidding blackness. Tin roofs flare
> out of an acre of stumps. Iron windmills churn. On all sides
> in the wet months there is the flash of water. These are the
> so-called lakes. Rising abruptly around fence-posts to turn
> good pasture for a time into a chain of weed-choked lily-
> ponds, they are remnants of a sea that feeds one of the great
> river-systems of the continent—fugitive, not always visible
> above ground, but attracting at all times of the year a variety
> of water-fowl and real enough to have had, when the native
> peoples were here, an equally poetic name that no-one has
> bothered to record. (p.3)

Malouf's settlers are mere transients. Their occupation of the land
is haphazard and precarious, threatened by a nature they have
not bothered to learn. The settlers have even forgotten the names
of the past, and with them the understanding of the land that
they themselves lack. Yet the land is still lush, and it does support
its inhabitants. The land is the given, not the object, and the
novel is in essence a record of how it makes these transients its
own, rather than of how they establish themselves in the land.
Malouf starts his story a generation after the pioneering struggles,
which are understood in retrospect through the perceptions of
the children, just as the reality of the land itself is eventually
revealed through the perceptions of the painter.

Malouf disposes of the actual process of settlement in a couple of paragraphs, beginning with the blunt statement that "Harlands are brought up on the story of how they first won and then lost the land." His story effectively starts from this fact of their failure. In retrospect, he tells us of the overland trek that brought the first three Harland brothers to an area that immediately reminded them of home, that is, of "a place they had never laid eyes on but whose lakes and greenness were original in their minds." Their first coming into their future is thus in effect their coming into their past, and they take possession with a ruthlessness that matches the bloody dispossession of their Irish ancestors: "One brief bloody encounter established the white man's power and it was soon made official with white man's Law." Yet the new land gives them no more permanence than the old, and the paragraph in which they come into possession concludes by noting that "Within a generation the Harlands had squandered most of what they owned and were reduced to day-laboring for others; or, like young Clem Harland, to grubbing a livelihood from odd patches of what was once a princely estate" (p.3).

Although the novel is about the life of Frank Harland, his father Clem represents the mystery of the land that he spends his life trying to unlock. Clem is introduced to us as already a failure, "a dreamy, fresh-faced youth, not keen on hard work . . . He was full of notions, all cloudily unreal" (pp.3–4) The talk in which he shapes these cloudy notions is his reality. The author explains, "He made himself up out of it. He made the world out of it. His cloudy speculations, the odd questions he put, the tales he told of experiences that had come to him at different times and places, were flesh and spirit to him because they touched on what he was most deeply moved by, the mystery of *himself*" (p.5). Clem's apparent helplessness nevertheless attracts a wife who attempts to refine and toughen him to the actuality of things, but after bearing him two children she dies, victim of her reality when she is poisoned by a rosethorn in the garden she has cultivated. Then Clem marries for a second time, this time to a waif, and Frank is banished to relatives while she bears a further three boys. When she dies, a victim of the same Spanish flu that across the Pacific decimates the settlers of Ivan Doig's Scotch Heaven in *English Creek*, Frank returns to share the rest of his childhood with his four brothers and their loving but helpless father in the cocoon-like warmth of their one room shack.

In this shack, each boy in turn moves up through the bed hierarchy and out into the wider world, but in another sense none of them leaves it. The older brother drops out into a criminal life, the next brother to Frank becomes in his turn a housekeeper for the others in Brisbane, where he recreates the kind of warm sanctuary they had known as boys. Their house is a typical Queensland dwelling, raised high on stilts to catch the breeze. Underneath, the stilts and vines enclose a mysterious space of darkness, and here their nephew eventually hangs himself. This death shatters their illusions of security, just as their father's amiable nullity, his possessive warmth, had never completely hidden the menaces of the physical world outside the reality he tried to construct with his words. The initial assault of settlement, the quick dispossession of the natives, cannot be so easily expiated, not even in the city built to keep the settlers safe from the land and their past. So, at the end of the novel, Frank Harland returns to the bush, this time neither as a settler seeking to dominate it nor as a sojourner trying to keep it at bay, but as a painter trying to discover its inward structures, to allow its patterns to construct his life and his work. Only thus, on his canvas, does he enter into possession of his modest half acre.

VI

In *Harland's Half Acre* the Aborigines represent a lost presence, a way of possessing the land that white occupation destroyed, and which can be recovered in some measure only by means of art. Thea Astley, in *It's Raining at Mango*, more explicitly identifies the massacre of the Aborigines as the fact that permanently alienates the whites from a land that they nevertheless come to love. She had already dealt with this issue in *A Kindness Cup*, where the schoolteacher returns to a small Queensland town for its "Back to Taws" week, the occasion that brings back former residents to recall the past and the small town values that have made this nation great. Tom Dorahy interrupts the sentimental self-congratulation by insisting on going back to taws in the colloquial sense. He insists on delving into details of Aboriginal massacre that men who are now the town's leading citizens had led twenty years before. Predictably, his efforts are rebuffed, not least by the white farmer whose efforts to protect the Aborigines and the land had eventually driven him into exile. At the end of their celebration, the townsfolk turn on the teacher and his companion, the unwanted emissaries of their silenced conscience, with the same savagery as they had turned on the natives. Then, as the singer's voice "soars and falls in nostalgic untruth . . . The hate-pack is gone. . . . Full-throatedly, the audience joins in the singing and roars chorus after chorus." The novel closes with the sentence that is also the town's epitaph: "It has almost forgotten the victims already" (p.154).

A Kindness Cup gives a sharp picture of the vicious evil that underlies the apparent sociability of the country town. Its satire is, however, directed at the hypocrisy of the townsfolk rather than at the basis of their society. The massacre is not so much a basis of their prosperity as an inevitable outcome of their narrowness, the hardness of their hearts which shuts them off from life and is the one unforgivable sin against the holy ghost. In her later novel, *It's Raining at Mango*, the settlement of the country is itself shown to depend on this sin. The opening paragraph sets the problem:

> Even at the end of things she is still looking for a reason as she had been at the beginning, puzzling in a muddleheaded way while she watches that fool of a Reever, legs dangling from fifty feet up where he has lashed himself for the third day into the crown of a celerywood tree. (p.13)

We quickly learn that we are in the 1980s watching a confrontation in a North Queensland rainforest between conservationists and developers. It is only as the novel develops that we learn that the eyes through which we are observing belong to Connie Laffey. Connie is also her parents and her grandparents back to her great-grandfather Cornelius Laffey, who established the beginning of things in 1861 by travelling from Canada to North Queensland with his small Columbian press. Connie's past includes those who endure in their relation to the land and its people, including Cornelius's wife Jessica Olive, his son George and grandson Will. It also includes those who, finding the country unendurable, flee. Cornelius leaves his family and escapes south. His daughter Nadine gives herself to the handsome drifting bushman and then to a brothel which floats with her out to sea in a cyclone. Connie's American husband simply returns home. Reever, the last of the family, combines its two traits. He lives in sympathy with the land, but can find no place in it, and at the end of the novel sets off north with the great-grandson of the Aboriginal the Laffeys had befriended in the last century. His departure returns the novel to both its narrative and its chronological beginning. Reever leaves for the "nothingness . . . the heat, the mangroves, the flies . . . the mainland natives" that had confronted Cornelius at the beginning. His departure leaves Connie with Cornelius' bewilderment, and her own.

The source of this bewilderment is the savagery with which the settlers treat the land and its people. Cornelius begins his experience as a newspaperman by witnessing the ugliness and desolation of a settlement founded on greed and abandoned by the further drive for wealth. Later, with his infant son George, he witnesses both the massacre of Aborigines by incoming miners and the grisly remains of earlier massacres. George continues to be haunted by the memory of a partly decayed hand still beckoning out of the soil. In adulthood, returning from his own attempts to escape to sea, George sets out to create his own paradise against this memory. His mother senses only failure from the attempt to tame "this dangerously new country":

> Her pursed lips wanted to scorn the romanticising of settler drudgery, the sort of rubbish that those southern jingoistic papers printed, mush doggerel by scribblers who'd barely come to terms with the day-to-day and failed to understand the tension between landscape and flesh. Only men would write it. A woman wouldn't waste the time, couldn't find the time to waste.
>   . . . She saw an unending line of women working on bare brown plains, by cow-bails, at wood coppers, at clotheslines strung between gums, at meat-safes damping down the sacking covers, sweeping tamped earthy floors, tacking bits of cretonne on fruit-box dressing tables, on and on and on, thanklessly, and making sure dinner was ready on time. (p.72)

By itemising the drudgery Jessica Olive contradicts the image of paradise even as George is pursuing it. In search of his dream,

> he waved creator hands and established for her a low-veranda'd sprawl of a homestead farther down the slope,

> with a giant bamboo windbreak; he waved his hands again
> and fruit trees shoved up laden, close to his house walls,
> and the paddocks greened into a summer pasture for
> prodigious milkers. (pp.73–4)

George never realizes his dream. The physical labour he puts out
of his mind but has to expend as the price of its achievement
strikes him down with a heart attack. His children, who are
brought up by a feckless uncle, come to share his dream, but in
their attempts to possess the land become alienated from society.
Will seeks support and human comfort from the latest wave of
settlers, the hippies who seem to share his green dreams, but
they too want only to use the land for their own purposes. The
desire for intimacy that he has satisfied by living in solitude with
the land destroys him when he tries to extend it to another human
being. The opposition that Jessica Olive set up between masculine
romanticism and feminine practicality can be overcome neither
by abandoning society for nature, as Will attempts, nor by
exploiting nature for the self, as the hippies attempt.

Both the drudgery of the women and the romanticism of the
men are rooted in the alien culture they are trying to impose on
the land. For women, the cost is their own destruction, but in
men the dream breeds aggression. George is content to use his
imagination to build his paradise, but the miners who preceded
him used picks to tear at the land and guns to massacre its
inhabitants. The killing continues down to the present, when
Will is forced to watch helplessly while drunken loggers assault
his Aboriginal companions outside the country pub. This assault
is silently condoned by the publican and policeman, just as the
local member of parliament encourages the assault by bulldozer
on the rainforests where the novel begins and ends.

It's Raining in Mango is not written as an epic of settlement,
but as a discontinuous narrative framed by the two scenes of
Reever in the rainforest. The form corresponds to the experience
of its protagonists, whose lives, far from being grand narratives
of meaning, are merely occasional vivid moments of passion or
terror linked by long intervals of drudgery and puzzlement. While
the country takes possession of them, they do not take possession
of it. It continues to mock their dreams, their attempts to make
sense of it in terms of an imported culture. The fragments of
their lives therefore serve as an apt metonym for the continuing

attempts of Europeans to settle ourselves in this country. No longer European, we are still learning to be Australian, to live within the country rather than destroying it in our attempts to turn it into our own particular form of paradise.

The novel, however, goes further in deconstructing the logic of colonialism. Its action is based on the oppositions of masculine and feminine, native and settler, nature and culture. Yet none of these modes of action is conclusive. Will, in trying to live with nature, denies his own sexuality, but the hippies who use this weakness to destroy him contradict their own ethos of tolerance. Reever, setting off for the north with Billy Mumbler, holds out the promise of a reconciliation of culture and nature, but his own childless and workless state suggests that he can do no more than repeat Cornelius's history as a sympathetic but powerless sojourner. The novel finally suggests the irrelevance of the binary oppositions that western culture tries to impose on the lands it subjugates.

PART THREE

LOST EDENS

Chapter 14

Living with Darkness:
Native Peoples of the Pacific

To the first European seamen and traders who came to the Pacific, the islands seemed to offer a paradise of sensual pleasure and wealth. To the first missionaries, however, they seemed places of darkness, characterized by cannibalism and pagan sexuality. In separating the islanders from their traditions, the missionaries imposed a moral code that contained vice and justified greed, but merely suppressed desire. The darkness was moved within, emerging only in the periodic chiliastic and revolutionary outbreaks that served to justify continued suppression. The subsistence economies that had supported traditional structures of authority were destroyed, while the dependent economies that succeeded required bureaucratic regulation but could support no culture that could restore the connections between people and either their past or their environment. The coming of political independence merely transferred responsibility for their state to the people of the islands, but did nothing to restore the fragmentary nature of their lives. As a consequence, we find the literature of the islands continually plumbing and gauging the inner and outer darkness they find in them.

I

Ian Wedde and Witi Ihaemara have both written novels that through imagined pasts restore New Zealanders to their status as Pacific Islanders. Those in the littoral states do not have this option. In the Pacific Northwest of America and in Australia, the emigrant culture is preoccupied with its struggle with the land, and the native cultures with resistance. Yet the ocean offers a challenge, whether as, for Mudrooroo Narogin's Doctor Wooreddy it is a source of evil or for Daphne Marlatt's cannery folk, of livelihood. The people of the littoral can however venture among these islands only as aliens. For Thea Astley, writing as an Australian about the Pacific, whites are doubly outsiders— as expatriates coming from the outside, and as colonists forcing outside patterns on the people who belong in the islands.

Her first excursion into the Pacific, in *A Boatload of Homefolk* (1968), presents Australians in one of their common guises, as tourists, but also in one of their less common roles as colonialists. The Pacific island is a means of revealing the intruders to themselves by isolating them from their usual context, and its natives serve largely as a background for the consequent action. In three events, however, the island and its people are decisive in determining this action. The priest, Father Lane, effectively terminates his career by his aborted attempt to seduce Johnny Terope, the slender native boy who "knew too much of the needs of older people, and would with pressure grant these" (p.18). Johnny in turn stalks the elderly tourist, Kitty Trumper of Condamine, to the summit of Mt. Tongoa, the volcano where she seeks absolution and communion by bathing in the warm waters of its lagoon. When she turns back to the jungle where Johnny lurks, he destroys her in his act of robbery by declining to add rape to his crime, uttering instead the words that kill her: "Oh, no! You very ugly laydee" (p.211). Finally, the Pacific itself erupts in a hurricane that destroys the frail buildings within which the whites keep to themselves. The only structures that survive are the mission chapel and the gaol. The white attempts to penetrate the island's skin lead to their own destruction, but the physical bases of colonial rule remain intact. Within this structure, the natives can find no autonomy. Johnny Terope's twin acts of betrayal leave him still confined by the European definitions of his reality.

These definitions are themselves challenged in Astley's next fictional excursion to the Pacific, *Beachmasters* (1985). This is set on the island of Kristi, where the local mixed-blood leader Tommy Narota leads a futile rebellion against the successor state to the Anglo-French dominion over the island group of which it is a part. Although the places and events are fictitious, they bear a close resemblance to the historical events of the 1980 rebellion of Jimmy Stevens against the new state of Vanuatu (Crocombe,

1982). The name of the island where the federal capital is located, Trinitas, is a reminder of Quiros' quest for a land where he might establish a kingdom of heaven. The fictitious island of Kristi corresponds with the island of Santo, or Espiritu Santo, where Stevens led his rebellion. The island was so named by Quiros, who believed he had found the Austrialia del Espiritu Santo of his quest. The explorer is recalled in the novel by the hut where the old planter, Lorimer, lives above "Quiros' tatty camp at the Bay of the Two Saints, the New Jerusalem" (p.42). Not far from this hut, Tommy Narota has found his own promised land in Vanape, where he has cleared the jungle and "begun his own strange cult in the gardens of Vinape, a cult that drew its bits and pieces from half-absorbed Christian ideology and island myth" (p.98). Astley's novel reminds us that the struggle to make the islands a home for the spirit still continues. Although its action is about one episode in the ending of colonialism, its focus is not so much on this external contest for power over the islanders as on the struggles of the islanders, brown and white, for power over themselves.

In the chronological time of the novel, this struggle is waged by Tommy Narota, son of a brown-skinned woman and

> one of those island knockabouts that Europe spewed out in the Pacific, a big bugger of a man, bearded ginger, with pale Anglo-Saxon skin and blue eyes, his appetite for sun and women, liquor and the sea, making him a force all those years ago, *longta'im bifor*, when he traded and peered for landfall along the black sand coasts. (p.3)

Malcolm Orwin, as he was known, represents the same kind of colonialism that Becke deals with in his yarns of the South Seas. He exploits both the country and the women. Yet he is also one of the people Wedde describes, throwing his lot totally in with his new country. He does not share the beliefs of the islanders, but he is prepared to drink kava with them and mix their songs and magic with his own. He is the head of a household where Tommy and his mother are at home. However, although Tommy "had thrown white, as they said in those parts," after "he watched his papa cough himself to extinction, saw his mama waste from the lack of the big blusterer," he discovers the truths of colonialism. He found himself

light-skinned enough to show promise, but too dark, of
course, to get anywhere on the island with a long memory
of planter picnics and drinks on verandahs and the cocktail
gabble of the ruling classes.

The two worlds did not touch, could not touch, except
through feelers of resentment and envy. (p.5)

Tommy stills the resentment by working until he can acquire his
own wealth and land. When he returns to his father's plantation
and finds "nothing to return to," the house and fences and
memories of his childhood in ruins, he weeps and takes the first
of his wives to his own house in Vinape, where he establishes
a community of his own.

Although he had thrown white, a darker tug decided
him. . . . He flung himself into custom and as the years
floated in and out of the floating islands and he took other
wives to his house in Vinape, he felt in the black marrow
of his bones that here was home. Others joined his community and the village lived with their gardens and the sound
of the river in the gorge . . . children clustered, grew . . .
Tommy Narota plumped out with the spirit comfort of
Vinape, bearded, benign, a *yeremanu* [headman] in his own
village. (p.10)

This narrative of the achievement of paradise comes at the
start of the novel's chronological time, suggesting a dialectical
solution to the colonial clash of cultures. Tommy has created
something new. But the chapter of his history is shadowed by
its placing as the memories that comfort him in the Mataso town
gaol where he has been locked up for seven years "on the grounds
of treason and inciting to rebellion against the state" (p.3). That
fact in turn is shadowed by a prologue that warns us that the
island of Kristi is like one of the fish in its waters, which is "able
to look in opposite directions at the same time" (p.1). The prologue
further warns us that there are more than two of these opposite
directions. Among the natives there are *man bush* and *man soltwata*,
and among the Europeans there are British and French and
Australians, planters and traders, missionaries and government
men. These different people variously share three different
tongues, so that while "The eyes move two ways. The voice moves
three." Whatever happens, there are three ways of saying it, yet

it is all contained in a single unity of nature and the humans it contains. "And therein, in that unity of land with man, lies the trouble." For other men do not leave Tommy alone with his community. He becomes the victim rather than the agent of the aborted revolution contrived by French colons and Yankee entrepreneurs who exploit his charismatic attraction and the violence of his love for the island (pp.99–100), which he dreams of as a kingdom

> wiped clean of colonial settlers, unless they, too, were prepared to swing on the lianas of custom. Then, oh then, the whole *aeland* would assert the pride of its myths. (p.10)

But this dream of Narota is rooted in the past, and is doomed to failure. In a world where global politics and economics are intertwined, the great powers cannot allow a small community to revert to the kind of autonomous existence Narota's dream would require. But neither are the people of the islands or elsewhere prepared to forgo the goods and technology available through the global economy, which Narota himself had used to establish his community. Independence can come only through the kind of alliance with external power that destroys the pride of the myths, and with them Narota's hopes of a community based on tolerance and customary land rights. The environment that produces the "unity of land with man" also links man with the necessities of the wider world, and thereby produces the contradictions that destroy unity.

Although Narota's rebellion precipitates the action of the novel, he is not its focus. His history is merely one of several that are presented in retrospect to explain how the characters become involved in the action that reveals their relationship to the land, and thus any future they may have on the island.

These characters fall into three groups. There are those who, like Bonser, mechanic and gun-runner, are merely exploiters seeking their individual gain. Bonser is descended from a blackbirder who sailed with "the monster captain of the *Carl* which was trucking flesh to Australia." He then carved his own plantation from the jungle, setting it off with a road "with marker-posts at every beating along its ten-mile length. . . . Resentment saturated every acre." We are told that "the viciousness of the genes seeped through two generations . . . emerging refined as

greed or duplicity or carelessness." Bonser supports the rebellion
for purely mercenary ends, and involves the boy, Gavi Salway,
to cover his own tracks. He is a bully, a drunkard and an adulterer,
who remains untouched by the beauty of the islands whose mana
rejects him, although he does not realize this (pp.42–44). Yet, like
Louis Becke's Bully Hayes, he is the kind of person who could
not exist outside this rough, still frontier society. He represents
the "necessary brutality of colonialism" that the British governors,
unlike the French, prefer to ignore, to conceal behind imperial
ceremony and ignorance. Yet both French and British
administrators play essentially the same role as Bonser,
manipulating the natives in the interests of their own careers and
power. The difference is that, unlike Bonser, who enjoys the fleshly
comforts of the natives, the officials regard them with contempt,
and so remain outsiders.

The second group comprises the planters who consciously
try to make the islands their own. These may acquiesce in the
necessity of brutality, but their attitude tends rather to the
paternal. They include the Duchards, who intrigue with Narota,
Planter Salway, Gavi's grandfather, who came to the islands as
a clerk and became captivated by them, and Lorimer, the
wanderer who eventually comes to rest in a hut overlooking
Two Saints Bay, "under great vaults of sky and chancels of
unending forest." For Salway, Lorimer is the "complete and total
conqueror . . . with poetry and silence and enough food to extend
the varied patterns of his days" (p.134). By reducing his material
needs he seems to have reconciled nature and culture in his life,
and by the giving of himself in friendship he seems to reconcile
the conflicts of religion and race that otherwise divide the island.
His diary expresses the sense of a discovered wholeness:

> Despite the indifference of nature all about me and the
> terrifying threat of its power of—what can I call it?—con-
> tinuance—I can only sit back gape-mouthed in these early
> mornings. Words aren't enough. The softness of it all, the
> draped clouds on the great ranges to the north and west and
> the Pic thrusting like a needle with the sun coming up,
> stretching the grey into blue as it comes. . .
>   I am making a bamboo flute for Arim like the one he
> gave me . . . (p.155)

The gift of the flute, product of human skill that produces beauty from the air, is a symbol both of art and of human mutuality. Lorimer has made his paradise in the Pacific. Yet these pages of his diary come to life only after he has been brutally and casually murdered by those he had befriended and admired. The rebellion, produced by the same forces that brought Lorimer to the Bay of the Two Saints, invades the sanctuary he thought he had found there. The island rejects him and the other planters who try to make there a home for an imported culture.

Finally, there are those who give themselves to the island and its people. These include the doctor, the priests and the headmaster. Yet, losing themselves in the service of others, they still try to impose their ideals and so remain outsiders. Only those who "allow the island to devour them" become a part of it. Pere Leyroud comes close to this. He recognizes Tommy Narota as a "soul Brother" (p.98), and comes to realize that the "striving or yearning of all men towards the godhead boiled down to a set of time-strained parallels and the Satan figure of his own dark places was the stone *lesevsev* which blocked the way to life" (p.94). Yet his loyalty to his god leads him to fail Gavi in his moment of need, when Leyroud is unable to accept that his life of giving has been, like that of the colons, a life of taking: "He had removed their gods and replaced with his own" (p.93). He is therefore unable to convey to the boy his understanding that, beneath the differences, all is the same. The only characters who succeed in establishing this identity are those who give themselves completely to the island—Madame Guichet, abandoned on its shores by a lugger captain, and Chloe, mistress of the Dancing Bears. Because they ask for nothing, they are able to give to others without diminishing those they give to.

The events of the rebellion are presented through the eyes of these outsiders who are judged by their responses. As outsiders, however, the events do not change them, except in their relations to the island. But Salway's grandson, Gavi, is involved in a different way. His discovery that he is in fact of mixed blood precipitates a rebellion, a division, in his own consciousness. His further discovery that his mother is both a niece of Tommy Narota and half-sister of his father makes him not only an islander but a victim. Worse, he is a victim of the man he admires and who gives him his place in society, his own grandfather. Salway, the planter who has brought his grandson up to respect the island

and all its people, is revealed as the white man who uses the islander for his comfort and abandons her at his convenience. Salway represents the colonialism that seeks to make the islands its home and their people his family, only to be forced by its own necessities to betray its ideals. The division of their allegiance between Europe and the Pacific produces offspring whose union can only be incestuous. Gavi, product of this union, is forced to choose his identity, to take sides and accept responsibility for shaping events rather than merely responding to them. The consequence is that he brings about the death of Lorimer and the expulsion from the island of himself and his family. Gavi's act of rebellion destroys the work to which his grandfather had given fifty years, and his destiny proves to be with his inherited culture rather than with the blood of the natives it has exploited. Yet he cannot deny his responsibility for that either, and his last act before leaving the island is to acknowledge the gaoled Narota as his uncle. The implication is that with maturity he may be able to build from his experience a place with room for both sides of his inheritance.

Astley's novel thus takes us through the transition to the postcolonial Pacific, but shows that independence neither frees Europeans from their guilt nor restores the islanders to their paradise. The history that bound each to the other continues to hold them together, and the shift in political power merely strips away the authority that had hidden the issue of responsibility. The beauty of the islands remains only a promise until we have learned to understand its necessities, which go as far beyond the pragmatism of the Bonsers as they mock the romanticism of a Lorimer or a Narota.

II

For Albert Wendt, the Pacific, or rather Samoa, is home. He writes as an insider, but for his islanders, as for the whites, the Pacific is a Paradise lost. The whites who came to the Pacific destroyed the Eden they found, but they left behind them another dream, the dream of the *papalagi* way, the European way of life, that makes it impossible for the islanders either to return to the old or to restore a new Pacific way. While the old ways are destroyed by white intrusions and local greed, the new way is made impossible by the survival of old structures of power, and particularly the dominance and masculine values of the big man, after the decay of the traditions that had supported them. So, in Wendt's stories, the chief repeatedly becomes the agent of destruction. Yet the new men who flee to Apia or New Zealand to escape his authority find that they have lost both family and community. Their education simultaneously frees them from tradition and alienates them from their land and people.

In Wendt's first novel, *Sons for the Return Home* (1973), the idealism and passion of youth transcend the racial divide to produce the harmony of love. The young Samoan, taken by his parents to New Zealand to get the education that will enable him to succeed at home, falls in love with a *papalagi* girl. Their love, however, founders on the rock of culture when the girl aborts her child rather than risk marriage apparently founded on the accident of pregnancy. This act contradicts the basis of their love. They had overcome the cultural division by accepting their feelings as the product of their common human nature. The girl becomes pregnant when she forgets to take her pills when they go on a holiday into the mountains of New Zealand, yet, as she makes clear when she regrets his wasted seed floating away on a river, it is also a consequence of yielding to her deepest needs. Her fear that their love alone is not strong enough to accept its consequences is a denial of its basis, and inevitably destroys it, leaving the boy alone to return to Samoa and fulfil his parents' ambitions for him. In the village, however, he finds he has become alien, an outsider there as in New Zealand. The parents who have sacrificed themselves and their sons for this return home find that the sons no longer have a home. On the plane back to New Zealand, the son accepts his isolation: "He had nothing to regret: nothing to look forward to. . . . He was alive: at a new beginning. He was free of his dead." He identifies himself with the legendary hero Maui, who, falling in love with the goddess of death, lost his quest for immortality as the goddess crossed her legs on him. "He imagined Maui to have been happy in his death" (p.217). The lesson of the island culture is that the only freedom is death.

Wendt's second novel, *Pouliuli*, or the darkness (1977), starts from the point reached by the son at the end of the first. At its opening Osovae Faleasa, a *matai*, or chief, realizes that the apparent success of his life is completely empty. Instead of

accepting his power over the community, which expresses the
strength that flows to him from the community, he wants to be
himself, to be free. Escaping into the refuge of an assumed
madness, he observes the true feelings of his family and
manipulates the politics of the clan to replace self-seekers with
the only son he can trust. His madness and his politics force him
to take with his friend Lemigau Laaumatua a journey into their
joint past and the memories of loss, emptiness, and darkness that
continue to haunt them. The memories include failed love affairs,
village conflicts, the visit of the missionaries and the tensions
between Osivae and his father. Central to them is the episode
of the old man whom the boys took care of when he wandered
into their village. The man is a prophet, tormented by a perfect
memory that threatens to trap him in the past it makes present
to him. He keeps fear at bay with his constructions of stone
circles, each with a single stone at their centre, the image of a
contained and secure world. Faleausa steals this centre stone,
making it impossible to complete the circle. When he recalls this
act of betrayal that drove the man away, he remembers that it
was on the eve of the outbreak of the first world war that was
to break the circle of the world order.

Faleasa's companion Lemigao is a cripple and a fatherless
man, unwanted by his family, who is forced to make a place for
himself with his fists and his wits. He resembles Maui, for, as
he tells his wife, "he had always wanted to make Death his wife"
(p.79). His joke proves a disastrous prophecy, for his pride
destroys both his marriage and the son through whom he tries
to live his ambition. But Faleasa is similarly possessed with death.
He resents both his father and his mother, and makes an alliance
with Lemigao against the rest of the village. When, in his old
age, he uses this alliance to free himself from obligation and
control the village beyond his own death, he destroys himself.
At the end of the novel, he has become like the old madman
trying to complete his circle of stones. Faleasa completes the circle
of his days as he becomes truly mad, standing on the topmost
step of the church like a figure by Edvard Munch, "his arms
outstretched to the dazzling sky, his mouth fixed in a soundless
scream" (p.144). The last words are given to Laamatua:

> It's all vanity, isn't it" You wanted to be free in the last years
> of your life but that too was vanity . . .

> Sleep on, my friend, while the world dreams of
> terror . . . (p.145)

The disruption of culture from nature, of the individual from the village in the village of Malaelua becomes an image of the twentieth century.

The narrative of Faleasa's betrayal of the old man is set beside the story of the legendary hero Pili, who brought to humankind the gifts of fire, the fishing net and the war club. Faleasa finds in such stories "lucid glimpses of the past and the present, and of the darkness that was the future . . . the essence of pre-papalagi beliefs about the cosmos and man's place in it" (p.94). Pili earns his place on earth by confronting his divine father and winning back his mother from him. His companions in his exploits are Insatiable Appetite, Strong Flight, and "Pouliuli": Darkness. Laamatua offers Faleasa the first two of these, but he will not accept the gift the old man offers him of the third, and so is swallowed by it without achieving wisdom. The divide between our century and the past is too great to be bridged by legends or prophecies.

Albert Wendt's major work, *Leaves of the Banyan Tree* (1980), offers a history for this divided consciousness over the five generations from the coming of the white man to Samoa until the present. Like Faleasa or the son in the first novel, the central figure in this novel is also a hero of the legendary past. Pepe, the hero of the central section of the novel, earlier published separately in *Flying Fox in a Freedom Tree* (1974), takes for himself the name of the village's founder, Pepese. By this choice of "that irresponsible, deranged hero of Sapepe's pre- Christian and cannibalistic past" (p.242), as his father Tauilopepe considers him, Pepe repudiates his father's religion and the code of "God, money and success" it stands for. At the end of the section of the novel he dominates, Pepe stoically accepts death on his own terms, rejecting the comforts of any religion. The preceding section of the novel tells of the struggle for his soul, the following of the struggle for his legacy. In the end, both Pepe's loyalty to the past and Tauilopepe's adulation of material progress succumb to a new force stronger than either of them: to a man whose only loyalty is to himself and the darkness within.

The conflicts between the characters are carried out in terms of the separate narratives they tell and by which they are controlled. The novel opens with Tauilopepe's mother, Masina, conducting the family prayers that provide the narrative framework of her life. A devout Christian, her fundamentalist religion provides the standards by which Tauilopepe judges others. This religion causes him to reject the traditional narratives of his father and grandfather, and the conduct of his son, Pepe. Tauilopepe, however, follows a different narrative for his own life. While his mother is praying, his mind wanders to the profits he will earn from his copra crop, and then to the debts he already owes to Malo, the storekeeper, and to the "bitter thought of all that money disappearing into the steel drawer in Malo's store" (p.3). This leads to the alternative narrative by which he asserts his authority in the village to destroy the newcomer, Malo. He blends this with his mother's religion by having himself made deacon and preaching his inaugural sermon on the theme of "God, money and success." To achieve these ends, however, he has both to use Malo's wife and invoke the authority of the senior *matai*, his father's comrade Toasa. But, although Toasa is forced to support Tauilopepe for the sake of the survival of Sapepe, he follows the different narrative that comes from traditional lore. Pepe, watching how his father's ambition sets him aside from the village, chooses to follow Toasa, and so destroys Tauilopepe's narrative at the very moment of its fulfilment.

The central part of the novel tells Pepe's story from the time he arrives in Apia to go to school in accordance with his father's directions until his death in hospital from tuberculosis. In his manner of death, and in the story he leaves behind, Pepe follows the example of Robert Louis Stevenson, the white chronicler of Samoan life. In his life, however, he chooses rather to act out the role, to follow the narrative, of Pepese, the legendary founder of Sapepe who built his life on his own strength, not on his position. Pepese, son of Tane the father of humankind, "challenged all the gods and won" (p.198). Similarly, Pepe challenges his father. He is expelled from school, organizes theft and arson, is gaoled, succeeds in business, abandons his religion, marries a Catholic, in every way contradicts his father's practices and hopes. By living an instinctual life, he restores the harmony of man and his environment that Toasa had taught him about in his stories of the gods, and which is contradicted by the sterility of both the missionary church and the materiality of his father's ambition.

When his friends meet a village girl with "the gift of peace, of healing people's fears" their community is complete, and they feel whole again. But wholeness cannot last. The traditional past reaches into the present in the form of the girl's husband, and death strikes her, her lover, and his comrade, Pepe's friend Tagata. The letter Tagata leaves tells their story:

> *The papalagi and his world has turned us and people like your rich but unhappy father and all the modern Samoans into cartoons of themselves, funny crying ridiculous shadows on the picture screen. Nevermind, we tried to be true to ourselves . . .* (p.226)

The only legacy he leaves is "1001 laughs." In a world where the traditional culture has been shattered by the material ambitions introduced by the whites, the only alternative to greed is laughter. Pepe lives his life to the end by this creed, but after his death his father seeks to rewrite his story.

The final part of the book shows how this narrative of Tauilopepe's is destroyed by a more powerful narrative. Tauilopepe tries to conceal the truth of his son's life by building a new church in his memory, and has his first heart attack trying to shift one of the boulders of its foundations. At the same time, he takes over Pepe's son, Lalolagi, bringing him up to despise his father and live the life he had dreamed of for Pepe. But the triumphant end to this narrative, when Lalolagi is to return to Sapepe with his New Zealand education and prove himself the true heir by succeeding to Tauilopepe's power over the villagers, is thwarted by the arrival of a pretender, Galupo, who claims to be the son Tauilopepe engendered on Malo's wife, and so the heir to both families. Galupo controls the villagers by his knowledge of their inmost stories, while keeping himself aloof by the stories that show only his ability to create his own being. These narratives divide all people into Other Worlders, who live by illusion, and himself, who lives without either existence or inner reality. His origins remain as mysterious at the end of the novel as at his first appearance, and we cannot tell whether any of his stories have any more substantial basis than their utility. Yet he suborns the professional establishment of Apia and defeats the scheming of Tauilopepe to gain complete possession of Tauilopepe's legacy and complete power over his people. In his person the single linear logic of individualistic capitalism triumphs over the narratives of both ambition and heroism.

These narratives are important because they fill the gap between the aspiration the characters have for unity with nature and their perception of the social world that determines their lives. Nature is both fecund and destructive. It is represented by the storm that sweeps the village as Tauilopepe impregnates Malo's wife, and by the power of greed and passion that takes him to her loins. The same power is manifest in the hurricane that, in the final part of the book, destroys Tauilopepe's plantations and ambitions and delivers him into the power of Galupo. But it is also represented by the lava plains that Tagata has reached, where life has been stripped to its elements yet still survives in the plants that grow "through the small cracks in the—lava, like funny stories breaking through your stony mind" (p.208). It is represented in the ancient banyan tree that Tauilopepe leaves when he destroys the rest of the jungle to make his plantation, which links the village and its people with the past, and which is nearing its death at the end of the novel.

While Pepe is the central figure of the novel, within whom its conflicts are played out and who achieves his own transcendence of division, its most active character is his father, Tauilopepe, the matai who is heir to the traditions of Sapepe but who betrays them in his quest for power and wealth. His belief in progress cuts him off from the past and the land that his forebears had tended. He deliberately rejects the history of his family, from the great-grandfather who had been "the only matai who had resisted missionary penetration into Sapepe, and who had died in the last pre-Christian battle" (p.63). In rejecting this history he rejects its values:

> A history of birth and sudden brutal death . . . whole generations bursting into the world only to die swiftly, forgotten in the profusion of the unchanging bush. The people of earlier generations had superstitiously believed that the land had an identity, that it was to be revered and loved for what it was. His father had been one of those men without vision or education; men who were also ignorantly lazy. (p.14)

The condemnation of the past as ignorant and superstitious comes from the Christianity that Tauilopepe accepts as an ideology of progress. The new religion, however, provides no relation with the land nor means of facing the darkness of death. He is left with only his bush knife, symbol of masculine aggression, with which "to defeat that dread feeling of inadequacy which over the years had become as real as the flesh on his bones" (p.14).

Tauilopepe believes he loves his clan and family, but love for him means control. Apart from his mother, the only person close to him that he cannot destroy "by being who and what he was" is his second wife, Teuila, who

> came to realize that what he called love was not a giving of himself but a taking and shaping in his own image of everything within his reach. This was the reason . . . why an honest and admirable son like Pepe had devoted his whole short life to rebelling against Tauilopepe and what he represented. (pp.234–35)

Pepe, refusing to allow Tauilopepe to shape him, chooses Toasa instead as his mentor. The old matai, friend of Tauilopepe's father, teaches him the traditions of the village and gives him the strength to choose laughter to confront the darkness in his own being.

While Tauilopepe seeks wealth and power, Toasa tries to keep together the village and its traditions. Like Tagata, he has climbed to the lava plains, where he has conversed with eagles and the aitu, the ghosts of lost gods. For him the bush is sanctified by the past.

> To Toasa, the bush had always been a mystery—impersonal and aloof yet always there watching, like the sea. His ancestors had taken from it, after appeasing it with prayer and ritual, only what they needed; had cleared only small areas for food gardens. They had learnt through the centuries to live with the mystery and the gods in the mystery. They believed that the gods and the land and the bush and the sea and all other living creatures were indivisibly part of that perpetual cycle of birth, life, death, and rebirth. (p.62)

The land gave its people status, and disputes over ownership often led to war, but the bush remained until the papalagi came and outlawed it. "They bought land, bush-free land . . . with guns, cheap goods, and lies." This is why Toasa helps Tualapila obtain and clear the land for his plantation, although to him "the past had no meaning." Toasa recognizes that the "world he was

trying to prop up would sooner or later collapse completely."
Tauilopepe represents the future, and Toasa helps him because
he is the son of his friend and because he may still influence him
to maintain some continuity with the past. His battle with
Tauilopepe for Pepe's soul is a battle for this continuity.

The coming of the whites has however irreparably broken
the bond with the past and the land. Tauilopepe wins his battle
for the village, but loses Pepe to the darkness that calls to him
from the bush and from Vaipe, the slum of Apia "that churchgoers
call the dark world of sin and all-things" (p.186). This world is
an outland, beyond the power of both tradition and the law, but
its apparent freedom is transitory, inevitably destroyed by
eruptions from the world of order it affects to disdain. Tagata,
the flying-fox whom Pepe follows into this darkness, hangs
himself on his freedom tree, and Pepe dies of the disease he has
chosen with his way of life. His son becomes a creature of
Tauilopepe, denying his own father, only to be destroyed in his
turn by the usurper. The strength of the bush cannot be recovered
by Tauilopepe's wealth and power nor replaced by the darkness
within that claims Pepe's allegiance. The only victor is Galupo,
the nihilist who cannot be divided from his self because he accepts
no inner reality, no true self formed by allegiance to others or
to the land.

Yet despite the darkness, Wendt's work is not nihilistic. He
is deeply pessimistic about the possibility of healing the divisions
inflicted on the individual and society by the colonialism, but
the desire for unity and transcendence persists. Even Galupo is
forced to offer hope and dignity to his people in order to achieve
his purposes. Although its leaves may be dying, the banyan tree
is still alive at the end of the novel. There is a hope that the
people will yet learn to listen to the narrative of its leaves, and
so repair their own lives.

III

Albert Wendt's novels are studies in destruction. In these
modern tragedies individuals are destroyed, not because of some
fatal flaw in their constitution, but because they are brought up
to believe in authority and just reward in an age controlled by
impersonal forces of markets and bureaucracy. His contemporary,

Epeli Hau'ofa, finds in the same postcolonial circumstances a comedy of pretension and misapprehension. It would be tempting to attribute this difference to the difference in their nationality. Wendt comes from Western Samoa, one of the successor states of a nation divided by imperialism and wracked by economic problems. Epeli is a Tongan, from a group of islands that maintained at least nominal independence and a continuing ruling family. In fact both writers have been nomads. Wendt was educated in New Zealand, has worked in Fiji, and is now a professor in Auckland. Hau'ofa grew up in New Guinea, holds a doctorate in anthropology from the Australian National University, and now teaches at the University of the South Pacific in Fiji. Although they both write about specific places, they themselves represent an emerging Pacific consciousness.

The difference in Epeli Hau'ofa's work, I believe, is not due to his nationality so much as to his stance. His stories are not in the main about chiefs but about the lives of ordinary people. The narrative is supplemented by the sardonic comments of Manu, the cynical local observer who, we are told, is the only teller of the big truths of his country. Manu is the insider who, because he understands his fellows, rejects their ambitions and formal values as mere delusions:

> 'Religion and Education Destroy Original Wisdom' cry the letters on the back of Manu's shirt. 'Over-influenced' says the front of the same garment. The wearer of the said shirts is one of the best known characters in Tiko; and although His Excellency is the most famous, Manu runs a very close second. As for telling it like it is, Manu is the only teller of big truths in the realm. This is not to suggest that our country comprises a nation of liars as some unmitigated foreigners seem to think, far from it. Truth comes in portions, some large, some small, but never whole . . . (Hau'ofa, 1983, p.7)

The people of Tiko, the Tikongs, are the objects of local and international authority, but they stubbornly persist in leading their own lives. The fragmentary nature of their truth represents not only their economy in its use for authority, but also the fragmented nature of perception in a divided world. Because Manu stands slightly askew to the world, he can recognize the limits it places on the truth.

Like Manu, the people of Tikong reverse the expectations the world tries to impose on them. Their religion demands such energetic observance from them on Sundays that they are obliged to devote the rest of the weak to sloth and the other vices that flow from it. Religion itself is, like patriotism or education, a means to material gain. So they are unable to understand Tavita Poto when, returning home with many degrees, he idles his time away instead of obeying the injunction to "Go forth and serve the Government and the Church with all your strength, with all your heart, and with all your mind," ensuring that "The Almighty and His Excellency will . . . make you the Minister for Money, and we, your humble Family, will become rich!" (p.47). In refusing to use his talents to this end, Tevita Polo in fact demonstrates that he is a true man of the Tikongs, even if his fellow citizens consider him a hypocrite, a rich man pretending to be poor and trying to introduce foreign ideas, like democracy, into Tiko. Tevita Polo follows the first law of the Tikongs, which is to follow inclination rather than duty. By leaving the country alone, except for his genuflections toward democracy, he follows the ideals of Manu, who recognizes that "Tiko cannot be developed . . . unless the ancient gods are killed." Therefore he works "to keep the ancient gods alive and slay the new ones" (p.18).

This rule merely perplexes the "Doctor of Philosophy recently graduated from Australia," a parodic self-portrait of the author.

> The good Doctor works on Research for Development. He is a portly man going to pot a mite too soon for his age; and he looks an oddity with an ever-present pipe protruding from his bushy, beefy face. The Doctor is an Expert, although he has never discovered what he is an expert of. It doesn't matter; in the balmy isles of Tiko, as long as one is Most Educated, one is Elite, and a Wise Man to boot. (p.18)

Experts from abroad make Tiko and the Tikongs the object of their plans, sometimes, like Sharky Lowe in the story where the Doctor makes his appearance, enriching themselves in the process, and at other times making fools of themselves or merely ensuring a comfortable billet for their old age. Lowe's reputation as "an expert native handler" connects the new economic colonialism with the old imperialism. On the other hand, local experts like the Doctor or Tevita Polo, remain locked into the traditional culture. Having returned home with the benefits of education in a foreign culture, they are expected to employ their learning to enrich their families. In all cases the methods and goals of the expertise remain foreign to the purposes of the Tikongs. Cattle provided by foreign aid are slaughtered to make feasts, fishing boats operate at a loss because their crews return to land for sex before their catch has filled the holds at sea. Tevita's talk of democracy is regarded as irrelevant by the taxi driver who himself is about to leave for New Zealand. The foreign learning and expertise remains locked in the culture of a global economy that can establish no connections with a culture centred on the family and aspiring to a life of material ease and sensual satisfaction.

The stories, however, reveal also the dark side of life in Tiko. The title of the story "The Glorious Pacific Way" parodies a popular slogan of Pacific politicians, but traces the way that an international aid bureaucracy dominated by such slogans corrupts the simple interest of a native enthusiast in his own past and turns him instead into "a first-rate, expert beggar" (p.93). On the other hand, in the opening story, "The Seventh and Other Days," we see how the lowly worker is able to exploit the vanity engendered in his superiors by the foreign experts whom he looks to for approval. Others are not so fortunate. The story "Blessed Are the Meek" shows the ease with which the poor, subject to the sanctions but without the protection of the traditional culture, are exploited by their fellows. Its hero, Puku Leka, is described as "a good man and a noble example of what a Tikong should be."

> He knows his standing in the community and pays proper respect to his earthly betters; he is patient, long suffering, and devoid of personal ambition; he carries the burden for his family, church, village, and country without complaint and without much expectation of earthly reward. He and countless others of his kind are essential for the continued stability of the realm of Tiko. And although he is a tall man he walks short, for his spirit is humbled and his back permanently bent. (p.74)

Colonialism and its aftermath have displaced Puku Leka and his fellows from their culture, but they remain outside the concerns or the ken of the international experts. Despite the fishing and gardening that continues to nourish many of its inhabitants, the

Tiko of Epeli Hau'ofa's stories is now fully incorporated in a global economy but his characters remain outside its culture. The source of their wealth is elsewhere, so work loses its meaning. For the new bureaucrats, it is a means of manipulating outside structures to provide goods for the office-holder's family. For the remaining gardeners and fishermen, the surviving activities of the subsistence economy become a form of leisure. Only those at the bottom of the structure are deprived and humbled as they continue to carry out the essential tasks that maintain it.

Unlike Albert Wendt, Epeli Hau'ofa is not concerned with recovering continuity with a traditional culture. Rather, he is concerned with the failure of an international economic culture to translate itself into the ways of Tiko, and the failure of traditional values to function in the face of an international economy. Most of the characters in his stories manage to live satisfactorily in the gap between reality and ideology, but the warnings of Manu and the example of Puku Leka remind us of the price paid for this alienation of culture from the economy.

IV

Much of the writing from the Melanesian nations of Papua New Guinea and Solomon Islands has come from former students at the University of Papua New Guinea, where it was nurtured by Ulli Beir. As in many of the Polynesian states, this writing at first took the form of poetry dealing with personal feelings, the retelling in English of traditional tales and songs, or autobiography. The poetry claims the language of colonialism to express a traditional lore and sensibility. The prose narratives of autobiography and the fiction that develops from it directly confront the colonists by making a place for their characters between the clash of colonial and traditional cultures. They become directly political as this place constitutes the basis for building the new nations.

John Saunana, in *The Alternative* (1980), dramatizes the struggle for independence in the Solomon Islands through ten years in the life of Maduru Buru, a promising student who progresses from the mission school of his village to expulsion from Prince Edward Secondary School, the institution established in the capital by the British government to educate the future leaders of the country. He matures over this time through a series of conflicts, mainly with institutionalized racism but also with the conservative villagers of his home. These conflicts give him the strength to stand alone and to give a lead to his fellows in their struggles towards independence. The novel closes as he accepts nomination to stand for election to the new parliament.

Maduro's conflicts with his villagers arise from his jejune attempts to teach them the new ways he has learned from white schooling. His conflicts with authority occur when he is forced to demand recognition as a person rather than allow white authority to use him to satisfy its own ambitions. The first of these conflicts occurs when he is required to shame himself by playing the Virgin Mary in a Christmas pageant. The critical episode comes when he leads a school rebellion against a teacher who neglects his duties and belittles his students. The rebellion is successful, but Maduro is expelled and consequently is unable to get a job in a town still controlled by whites. He becomes involved in a riot and is imprisoned, but on his release leads another successful rebellion, this time against rules that prevent the natives drinking in the European section of the hotel. This success consolidates him as a black leader, and his nomination to parliament is presented to him by the native teacher who had covertly supported his rebellion at the school.

The dialogue in Saunana's novel is stilted, except when it is in the local pidgin, and we learn little of the inner motivation of the characters. The conflicts do, however, expose both the seductive power of the European image of effortless wealth, and the essential contradiction of the colonial system that offers the image. Like black slavery in America or convictism in Australia, the system depends on the assumption that authority is right and its subjects wrong. Any questioning of authority therefore becomes a challenge that must be put down to preserve the system. The act of questioning in itself is evidence of the inferiority and evil intent of the subject. This contradiction is most starkly evident in the practice of education and the law. Teachers assume the benevolence of the system and so the inferiority of the students, who can acquire merit only by total acquiescence. The students are not being taught to understand the native society, but to acquire the ability to manipulate the religious and social systems by which the colonists control it. Their education thus simultaneously devalues the students' families and traditions and ensures that independence will make little change to the system of control.

It is not entirely a coincidence that when John Saunana became Minister of Education and Training in an independent Solomon Islands government he promoted the development of a new curriculum in local schools. The hero of his novel, however, fails to finish his studies and is instead sentenced by a black magistrate to six months in prison with hard labour. As the magistrate explains to his friend the hotel manager, it is not good for the Europeans to lose in court, as it "degrades your social status." The use of the second person indicates both his distance from the Europeans and the chosen subservience to them that dictates his efforts to ingratiate:

> I've been trying for ages to get rid of some of these lius [idlers] about the place. . . I'm appalled by the way these kanakas constantly make fools of themselves. Let's face it, Cliff, they are a damned nuisance to us all. (p.96)

The magistrate's corruption, begun with education and concluded with bribery, is complete. He has accepted the values of the colonists. The man he sentences, however, continues to challenge the system by refusing to accept the valuations it places on him.

V

The Australian novelist Trevor Shearston explores the imposition of colonialism and its values on Papua (British New Guinea) around the turn of the century. His novel *Sticks that Kill* (1983) juxtaposes events in Papua with the emergence to the south of an Australian commonwealth that may assume responsibility for the colony. The public events of the novel correspond closely with the history of the colony from 1901 to 1906, and include several multiple shootings and one massacre of the natives, as well as a major journey of exploration.

The Australian characters are simultaneously trying to escape from British control and to establish their own colonial values, which they fondly imagine will be free of British condescension. Both Australians and British officials are however locked into the same logic of a colonial society where action powered by individual ambition is directed and constrained by the official ideology. The novel is concerned with the variations of this ideology and their consequences. It commences, like Xavier Herbert's *Capricornia*, with the arrival from the south of two newcomers in a frontier colony. Unlike the novel of settlement, which traces the careers of its characters in their new environment, Shearston concentrates on the interaction of actions and values. At the centre of the story is the most adaptive of the newcomers, John Rhys, an Australian clerk whose position gives him little power but a view from inside the establishment. Rhys, a sociable young man, is determined to get to know the colony both intellectually and physically. He affronts convention by accepting the native constable as a friend, learning the native language, and taking a native mistress. On the other hand, his companion, Leslie Tyson, who has already been a judge on the Queensland goldfields, comes to an established position of power. As the colony's judge, and later as acting administrator, he is directly involved and forced to take sides in the power struggles of the colony. He affronts the missionaries by placing a value on native traditions and inviting them to stage a "durbar" to show off their dancing, but he imposes the law ruthlessly and learns to take pleasure in killing. He shares with the British an interest in native custom, but the natives remain for him totally alien, objects of spectacle or use, not beings sharing a reciprocal humanity. Yet he rejects the rigid distinctions the British make among the whites, together with their inflexible concepts of morality. When Rhys jeopardizes social convention by acknowledging his black concubine, Tyson uses his knowledge of the darker side of the British interest in anthropology to protect the younger man. This action however arouses the hostility of the guilty as well as the enmity of the upholders of public morality, and so brings about Tyson's eventual destruction. The novel ends with Tyson dead, the Australian officials and miners discomfited, and the British again firmly in control with their policy of protectionism. Only their continuing alienation from both protected and protectors suggests the fragile nature of their victory.

The official policy of the colony avoids confronting the conflict of interests at the heart of the colony by seeking to reconcile protection of the natives with the economic development of natural resources. The British emphasize protection, the Australians exploitation. While the Australians despise British paternalism, their own general attitude to the natives, which Shearston shows continues the practices of the Australian frontier, exposes the avarice behind their own professed democracy. For Judge Tyson as much as for Police Commissioner Rorke, the law is a means to development and consequently to profit. The British on the other hand justify their rule through an ideology that reduces the natives to dependency. As the Lieutenant-Governor, Lambert, explains:

> Your Papuan is a child . . . We have a mandate to protect him. No-one would be happier than I if we could encourage the sorts of schemes [the planters believe] we should have, *and* protect the Papuan from the consequences of them. . . (p.44)

This ideology of separation ignores the material inequalities that determine the relationships between Europeans and Papuans. The missionaries go with gifts, the miners and planters with firearms. Both groups are backed by the power of the colonial government. These material factors ensure that the relationship of Europeans to natives cannot be one of partnership, let alone of subordination.

The two groups of colonists, British and Australian, are ranged along a continuum of exploitation that runs from idealism to materialism. Roughly speaking, the British believe in conversion and control, the Australians in fucking and shooting. Within these there are further distinctions between missionaries and officials and between officials and miners. Some of these ideological differences are expressed in the early argument that Lambert tries to soothe to the conclusion of his official ideology. This argument commences when the British magistrate, Fabian, expresses his delight in native customs. The Australian policeman, Rorke, repudiates this view as easy sentiment, wanting "to see the whole place turned into a nigger zoo" (p.43). The blacks, he argues, are savages who threaten white lives, and who are dying out anyway. Their interests are irrelevant. For Fabian, these ideas will guarantee extinction "as surely as flour and arsenic" did in Queensland. But Rorke exposes the flaw in Fabian's own protective ideology when he hints at the suppressed sexuality behind his interest in photographing native tattoos, "Especially the little girls" (p.45).

The law administered by Lambert, Tyson and Rorke is an attempt to impose order on these contradictions. The miners see through its pretensions, just "Lotsa long words an' no bloody common sense." They also reject with contempt its attempt to place any restraints on exploitation by taking account of the interests of the natives: "Only one law in this country, yer honour—the coon is right" (p.98). The Scots missionary Lockhart takes the same attitude from the opposite point of view: "Legally! . . . The word stinks o' death!" (p.173). But he sees further to the historic contradiction behind Tyson's ambition to use the law to open up the country and enable the colony to "pay its way":

> Aye, bring your arsenic and flour and Winchesters and we'll have another Queensland. Tell me, when the 'compass of the law as ye see it' finally reached 'em, did y'r blacks count their blessings at bein' slaughtered wi'in it instead of wi'out? Y'r Anglo-Saxon's a strange animal . . . He's born wi' the belief that men such as those yonder on the beach have been holdin' the land in trust for him through all their genera- tions till he arrives t' wipe them away and claim his birth- right. It's a tale familiar tae a Scot as well . . . but I know, and I'm ashamed, that Scots have hunted down y'r blacks wi' the worst o' 'em. (p.173)

Lockhart's words accurately trace the origins of colonialism to the dispossession of the European peasants that changed the relationship of nature and culture by breaking the link between ownership and working of the land. His recognition, however, offers no solace to the natives being dispossessed by the latest generation of capital. He himself continues to impose his religious authority on the natives until the latest tribe of prospective converts turns on him, killing and eating the missionary and his followers. Tyson attempts to redress this failure of religion with the full weight of the armed law and so precipitates a massacre that denies the ideologies of protection and justice alike. His consequent suicide leaves the British protectors in control, but the sullen crowd of miners who place the Australian flag over his coffin provide an assurance that the protectorate in its turn will yield to naked exploitation.

Ironically, the most sympathetic characters in the novel are Lockhart and Tyson, the two most responsible for the destruction of the native culture. Both follow their conscience despite their self-doubt. Lockhart's belief that he has come to give, not to take, marks his inability to acknowledge that the natives have anything to offer him other than obedience. His refusal to accept that they might receive him with anything other than gratitude brings about his eventual death, and his arrogant disregard for his colleagues leads to the symbolic destruction of his life's work when they self-righteously burn the manuscript of his autobiography. Tyson's belief in the necessity of the law is marked by a similar blindness to the actual consequences of his behaviour, but leaves him untainted by the hypocrisy and self- seeking of his accusers. Even the observer, John Rhys, whom Tyson has saved from the wrath of the self-righteous, allows his verbal scruples to deny the judge his friendship in a moment of need. Tyson can claim no such indulgence for himself when he accepts the logic of colonial law and refuses to extend his tolerance to the blacks. Like Lockhart, he is destroyed by the same inflexibility of principle that he applies to the destruction of others.

Lockhart and Tyson are sympathetic because they accept the consequences that their fellows try to deny. Tyson recognizes that the rigidities of a law that protects the rights of the invader necessarily lead to the kind of slaughter that the other officials try to conceal behind standing orders or pretences of protection. Lockhart accepts martyrdom as the price of an evangelism his colleagues use as a way of imposing their codes of personal conduct on a whole community. Neither ideology allows any place for reciprocal relations or mutual feeling between the races they bring together. The inequality of the people produces a rigidity of law and feeling that allows escape only into orgies of sex or killing. The tension is manifest in Rhys, who from his first arrival in the colony is confronted by partly naked black women and crude jokes about sex, yet is simultaneously enjoined to keep apart from them. As he sums up his alternatives to a companion, "What am I supposed to do? Flog it every night till it falls off? Or get so shickered I can't find it, like every other bastard in this town?" (p.181) The vehemence with which he is condemned when he refuses to accept these alternatives exposes the guilt of those who conceal or repress their own sexuality. Tyson's role in protecting him from the consequences of his actions enhances their righteous indignation. This affront to their dignity in turn powers the horror with which they turn on Tyson when he surrenders to his own lust to kill.

Looking back from the end of colonialism to its beginnings, Shearston's narrative exposes not merely its injustice but also the way that the repression imposed by law and religion directs on the objects of rule the violence it seeks to curb in them. Yet it shows also how the land and its people change those who come to rule them. Although, as the colony takes possession of the colonists, they come to embody the savagery they fear, at the same time the desire aroused by the natural environment changes from mere greed or admiration and becomes love. The surly miner, Skinner, takes refuge from misanthropy to plant a garden. Lanyon laboriously cultivates trees in the barren streets and brings his wife and her child back to their home in the town where he leaves administration and starts a business. Tyson is overwhelmed by the majesty of the mountains in the country his expedition opens for development. Most of all, Rhys is repeatedly overcome by the sheer beauty that nature combines with its violence in the new land. His attempt to accept his black mistress with love rather than mere lust, and his acceptance of the friendship and guidance of the native constable, mark his acceptance of a bond to the land and its people. When, at the close of the novel, he prepares to return south, Lanyon invites him to acknowledge his surrender to the land through the secular communion of getting drunk together. "He pointed with a thumb towards the darkening she-oaks and waited for Rhys to move" (p.592). His movement, we know, will eventually bring him back to Papua. We know also, however, that he will never be at one with the land, because the alienated nature of colonial administration separates him from the land and the people that draw him to them. For those of Rhys's successors who have remained in Papua New Guinea, the equality conferred by political independence has now opened the possibility of work that can produce the unity of culture and nature that colonial law simultaneously proclaimed and denied.

VI

Vincent Eri's novel *The Crocodile* (1970), published before Papua New Guinea became independent, shows the impact of colonialism shown from the perspective of Hoiri Sevese, a young native who grows up in the Papuan village of Moveave, one of the missionary objects of James Chalmers, historical original of the Lockhart who figures in Shearston's novel. The village is set in an environment of fertility and wonder, where the "harsh rustle of the sago palms contrasted sharply with the slow gentle swaying of the coconut palms" and the "dust clouds twisted and turned, forming weird and wonderful shapes." It is, however, divided from its surroundings by a bamboo fence five feet tall that "had been erected on the orders of the Government officers who said that pigs must be kept away from the village." It is further divided within itself by the two missions, Catholic and Protestant, each with its own school, and each separating the villagers from the traditional past and the magic that might have accounted to Hoiri for the death of his mother. This death has further divided him within himself, for his father, a deacon in the London Missionary Society Church, has entrusted his care to a Catholic aunt who insists he transfer to the Catholic school. His new school is on "the windward side of the village, outside the fence . . . a lone building." The single schoolroom is dominated by three portraits: King George VI, Archbishop De Boismenu of Yule Island and St. Therese, patron saint of the school. They symbolize the foreign allegiance of the school, which imparts an education that proves useful for getting on with the white men, but serves no other purpose in Hoiri's life. The novel traces the way he and the other villagers make sense of the divided experience forced on them (pp.1–3).

The novel is loosely organized around three major episodes in Hoiri's life after he leaves school: an expedition by sea-going canoes to Port Moresby, Hoiri's marriage, and the three war years he spends as a carrier for the Australian army. The visit to Port Moresby provides a confusing vision of the plenty the white man apparently has at his disposal. His marriage provides the great satisfaction of a son, but is tragically broken when Hoiri's wife is seized by a crocodile while he is up the river on an excursion with the district officer. The war extends his knowledge of the whites, and brings him into contact with Australian and black American soldiers who accept him as an equal. His experience is, however, dominated by the authorities of the administration, particularly of ANGAU (Australian New Guinea Administration Unit), who are determined to keep the natives in their place and who at the end of the war steal the money he has earned by selling his carvings and reward him instead with five sticks of tobacco. "Five miserable sticks—just to blacken my lungs: then they send a doctor along with his wire ropes plugged in his ears to hear my breathing—." The man standing behind him underlines the significance of the payment as a symbol of colonial servility:

> That's a fault of our fathers and their fathers before them . . . Tobacco and sugar, two of the white man's most powerful bits of magic. . . . Get used to smoking and drinking tea and you'll slave for the rest of your working life for the white man. (p.170)

Hoiri returns to his village to use the last of his money to provide a funeral feast for his father, killed by pneumonia as a result of carrying for the white man. Hoiri's attempt to get compensation brings further humiliation when the administration officer rejects with contempt the ornate mission printing he proudly uses to sign his receipt for the miserable fourteen pounds he has been granted.

Leaving the administration office in confusion, Hoiri has a sudden vision of the wife he lost to the crocodile now alive and walking in front of him in the crowd. When the woman, instead of recognizing him, screams in fright, he believes she is removed from him by the magicians whose power the missions have put out of his reach. In his confusion, only his new bankbook and the thought of his son give him any hope of a future that may restore sense to his life:

> He felt cold in his heart and incredibly lonely. His life seemed a confused mess. . . . In a flash he saw in front of his eyes all the wasted years of carrying the white man's cargo. He knew that the white man, with all his wisdom and power, could not help him get his wife back. He did not see the policeman striding up to him and he was only vaguely aware of the hot rusty grip of the handcuffs around his wrists. As he started walking, he felt the square shape of the bank book in his pocket. "Maybe this money will send Sevese to the white man's school, maybe he will grow up to understand the things that baffle me," he thought numbly, as he was led back to the office he had wished never again to see. (p.178)

The book that opened with the symbols of division closes with the office, symbol of power and exclusion. Hoiri is still outside

the fence, where, like the school he had attended, he is allowed
only land littered with the discards of others: "food wrappings,
human and animal excreta and pieces of paper" (p.2). Hoiri is
lost between the gardens of his past, now neglected and
overgrown, and the incomprehensible world of the future that
offers wealth at the cost of dignity.

VII

Papua New Guinea is distinguished from the Polynesian
nations of the Pacific by its size and by the multitude of its
languages and tribes. Many of these tribes inhabit inaccessible
valleys, and until colonisation lived in ignorance of any others
except their immediate neighbours. Eri's novel shows how the
war took natives out of their villages and into distant parts, where
they learned a speech through which they came to know strangers
who shared a common predicament as colonial subjects. This
commonality provided one of the bases for the national culture
which preceded and accompanied independence. This culture,
however, remains incomplete, a product of the cities and of
education that continues to be in conflict with traditional
allegiances and regional loyalties. Because the political and
intellectual elites are largely the first generation to be educated
and urbanized, they remain torn between village and nation. In
the earliest modern fiction from Papua New Guinea, writers like
John Kasaipwalova and Russell Soaba take the violence and
cultural fragmentation of the cities as their theme. The three short
novels collected by Mike Greicus (1976) allow us to follow the
process of fragmentation from its inception.

Benjamin Umba's *The Fires of Dawn* (Greicus, 1976) shows
the tragic effect of the coming of missionaries to an area previously
isolated from white influence. The villagers exact bloody
vengeance on the family whose son has absconded to the mission,
which they blame for a recent wave of deaths, but are in their
turn ruthlessly cut down by the whites. August Kituai takes a
village already penetrated by white influence but still largely
living in its traditional ways. The money economy weakens these
both by offering the young men alternative opportunities in the
city and by imposing on all the villagers the need to pay taxes.
In "The Flight of the Villager," Kituai shows how one boy uses

the possibility of flight to the city to escape from the consequences of defying tradition by impregnating one of the village girls. Finally, Jim Baital, in *Tali*, traces the whole cycle from the villager seeking work in the city to his son taking a bride back to the village, where she finds life enclosing and intolerable. Tali, the son, one of the bright scholars on whom the future of the nation depends, has been educated outside his traditions but fails to find any alternative cultural structure to accommodate his desires. He is unable to accept the disciplines of a traditional marriage, but is equally unable to give himself to a marriage based on the reciprocity of romantic love. Consequently, both his heroism in the army and his attempt to return to his family's origins prove destructive to himself and his wife. Unlike his father, who has been content to be a house boy, the son can find no half-way house in the new society.

Tali's inability to partner a woman becomes a symptom of the inability of the New Guinea people to find a relationship to the land that has taken the place of their villages as the basis of their identity. His father explains his life as a series of

> journeys through this rapidly maturing young woman, New Guinea, with her seductive flesh and beautiful black body, her towns . . . the body that had robbed these two brothers of their birthright, their togetherness, their closeness, and everything that was given to them by the beloved Mother Nature. The towns . . . that had torn them apart from their parents, friends, and home. (p.103)

New Guinea is not the nature of its countryside but the allure of its towns. Tali, brought up in the town, is disinherited from his family and his own nature. Yet a return to the village is impossible. Tali's attempt to do so destroys his marriage. Only by finding a way of living with the new seductress, the town, can the new nation restore its wholeness.

The conflict between the traditional culture that nurtures unity between humans and nature and an urban culture that separates the individual from both nature and society reaches a tragic resolution in Russell Soaba's *Maiba* (1979/1985). The action of this novel takes place in a village on the margin of the national culture, yet its events constitute a microcosm of the larger history of the nation. The village here is presented through the feminine image of Maiba, who resists the masculine forces of seduction and rape that come from the city. Evil is defeated, however, only by bringing the power of Christianity to support the traditional values of the village, and the novel closes not in triumphal celebration but with "the gritting noise of his teeth" that marks the passing of the last legitimate chief of the village.

The novel opens with images of unity as "Maiba steps out of the ring of her fallen garments and walks down the yellowish sandy beach of Tubuga Bay to the edge of the sea water" (p.1). In shedding the old clothes she feels she is breaking with her past, "shedding her former skin for a new one" (p.19). The past includes her brief, failed time in the city; the future is a return to the security of family and village. The images of life in the village reinforce the idea of a productive unity of humans and their environment. Maiba, an orphan, has been taken in to her uncle's household and works together with her cousin Siril and his family to cultivate their fields. Their work and play weave together fields, jungle and ocean to provide a nurturing environment for the family. In the village the orator keeps their traditions alive with his nightly recitals, and the church supplies a moral and spiritual framework through its weekly services.

Yet this apparent unity of humans and nature, the old and the new, is disturbed by ominous signs of violence. Doboro Thomas, the orator who supposedly upholds tradition, also usurps the tradition of chiefly authority. Maiba's mother died at her birth, and for the first four years of her life she was paralysed from the buttocks down. The aunt who takes her in constantly taunts her, yet undermines the solidarity of the family by her own mendacity and adultery. Maiba believes she is ugly and rejected by her fellow villagers. With the other students, she walks to and from school in an idyllic world:

> enjoying the odor of the bush, or alternatively walking home along the coastal road which offered them the beauty of the sea at low tide, the reefs, the long stretches of yellowish beaches, golden sunsets behind purplish swaying palms, and rocks and exciting cliff faces on which the sea birds perched or under which the gentle waves—the long voyagers returning from oceans afar—reached the land with prolonged gurgles and tired sighs. (p.3)

Yet the students themselves roughly destroy this harmony as they jeer at Maiba for her appearance, and "the high school boys teased her even to the point of encouraging and finally forcing a primary school boy of Maiba's age to seize her roughly, push her onto the sharp rocky earth and attempt to make love to her." Her first admirer hangs himself, leaving his body to be found by children walking to school as "the half past seven morning sun cast its glory over the calm ocean" (p.4). The harmony of nature becomes mere indifference to human plight. Similarly, when Maiba emerges naked into the night from the ocean where she has cleansed her past, two men assault her and are only prevented from raping her when Siril attacks them and drives them away. Through the early part of the novel, Siril acts as Maiba's protector, the guarantor, with his uncle, of the security of the family and its ways. He and Maiba are complementary. She recognizes in him the source of the physical energy that performs their work, "the driving force behind all her labours." Maiba supplies the mental energy. She "did not depend on Siril to read a thick text book though Siril had felt the drive to do his reading while watching Maiba do so" (p.56). Yet when they leave the village on university scholarships this joint energy fails. They are expelled and return home, and Siril's mother has to abandon her dream that one day she will have a son who will drive her in a big car to see the sights of the town. Her material ambitions and circumscribed vision leave a vacuum at the centre of the family where maternal strength is needed to complement the physical strength of her husband and son. Maiba tries to supply this want, but as an outsider lacks the authority.

Maiba's discovery of her foster mother's adultery curses her with knowledge of the treachery that is poisoning her family. She imagines herself a creator who holds in her hands a lump of earth that has become a paradise, a sacred garden. The people she has ordered to walk on this island are

> to feel free within their own consciences and to be sure they are understood by the other creatures around them, to avoid complications and above all to be true to themselves, for there lay in the labyrinths of the island . . . what the world attempts to define . . . as nothing other than complete human happiness—only Maiba had regretted not having thoroughly explained all this beforehand . . . she had forgotten to arm them with consciences. (p.60)

Her dream is both a vision of the prelapsarian Eden that the island offers her family and village as their habitation, and a realization of her powerlessness to prevent its destruction.

Siril expresses a similar power of vision in the traditional dance in which he celebrates the gift of food (p.35), and more ominously in the drumming and singing with which he leads the dancers in the village square. While the centre of Maiba's vision is Eden, Siril sings of the threat to it. His song, in English words to the traditional beat and rhythm, actually invokes this threat in "a quest over an ancient promise left undone." The island of which he sings is still open to the winds and rivers and sea, but they have become "soul-forgotten." In the absence of divine sanction, nature is only a process of death.

> There are no gods, no historical premonitions, nor proud morning stars,
> For the island, as it sails also the oceans without philosophical or metaphysical scars.
> The island's rainbowish reefs wear smiles of flowers under calm waters,
> Where fish meets clam and dances out an aquatic love charm
> And the octopus spreads its fingers: seeing, feeling, feeding
> And responding to the music of the dancing fish, or clam, and . . . turning
> For the sea rages. All creatures die in the surge
> Of a weighty, grating tide . . . (pp.67–68)

This nihilistic vision, which robs nature of its beauty and its sustaining power, leads to the apocalyptic conclusion to the novel.

From the moment of his song, Siril, who has been the protective power of the family, is seduced to become an agent of destruction. The village orator, Doboro Thomas, has through treachery seized economic power, represented by the village, and used his wealth to pay armed thugs who terrorize the village in a ghastly parody of rebellion. Their deeds lead to the rape of an innocent schoolgirl and the murder of Maiba's foster father, Mr. Wawaya. Although he retains the strength to confront them before he dies, and to combine with Maiba and the pastor to disarm them, the former order is not restored. Maiba keeps Siril from his father, pronouncing on his actions the sentence that "For as long as you live . . . you will never know how it feels to have a father, to have a family, to have a household which you can call your own." But the villagers themselves, once the thugs are disarmed, lose their earlier passion for revenge and accept Doboro Thomas back as one of their number.

> No confessions are necessary from the old orator. He has done nothing seriously wrong to his fellow villagers. He is their leader. Every word that he utters is deeply respected. (p.112)

The only difference is that, at the death of Wayawa, his son, the true heir of the old chief, returns and takes charge of the family. This son has successfully completed his studies, and thus combines both tradition and education to offer a true centre of authority. The novel however merely hints at this possibility. For the present, the secular rebellion of Doboro Thomas has destroyed the sacred traditions of harmony with the land and community among the humans. Like the nation of Papua New Guinea, the village of Makawana has still to construct an identity that will support its people in the modern world.

CHAPTER 15

ASIA IN THE PACIFIC

Long before Europeans reached the Pacific, people from Asia had been travelling across its waters and along its shores. The Australian Aborigines arrived in their present lands at least 40,000, possibly 60,000, years ago, since when they have produced the longest continuous culture in the world. The Americas were settled by successive migrations of people moving by land routes from Asia, whose aboriginal cultures peoples retain cognate myths and legends. Settlement of the islands of the Pacific, probably by boat people from Asia, starting about ten centuries ago, continued until around 1200 AD (Spate, 1988, pp.1–30). Later, Chinese, Malaysian, Indian, and Arab traders and fishers were active in the western Pacific and, in their search for trepang, came as far as Australia (Clark, 1962, pp.5–9). Similarly, Japanese sailors worked the waters off North America. (Batman, 1985, pp.146–48). The advent of European imperialism brought major cultural and demographic changes to the Pacific. Portuguese, Spanish, Dutch, British, French, German, and American officials, merchants and missionaries imposed European control on Asian cultures in China, Japan, Southeast Asia, the Philippines, and Indonesia. A Chinese and Indian diaspora occurred as Chinese merchants recruited labour for the goldfields of California and Australia; Indians were sent to Australia as camel-drivers and to Fiji as labourers. Japanese went as labourers to Hawaii and western Canada, and pearlers to northern Australia. In the twentieth century, trade, war, and education have led to a further mixing of people around the Pacific. As English has become the second or even first language of Pacific peoples, distinct varieties of English have developed. At the same time, America in particular has become a goal for the aspirations of the educated classes. From the descendants of the first generations of migrants and from the new migrants to English-speaking countries, and from writers remaining in Asia but writing in English, have come new English literatures that are predominantly urban and cosmopolitan in their sensibility. While they may look back to a foreign country or a peasant hinterland for their origins, their immediate problems are those of making a home in the modern city.

I

The writing of Indian Fiji is the least urban of these literatures of the diaspora. This is probably because these writers are themselves only one generation from the land, and because the land itself is the central issue of Fijian politics. The writers' people made Fiji their home by working its land, but they remain forbidden to own it, and thus are doomed to perpetual alienation in their own country. Yet, although the writing tells the story of this dispossession, which culminated in the military coups of 1987, it brings to it an urban and liberal perspective. The schisms of the new land cannot be healed by an appeal to the pasts that divide its peoples, but only by the construction of a new culture that integrates both in the global and urban culture that is the irrevocable legacy of imperialism.

The Indians of Fiji are a people doubly dispossessed. First, their forebears were forced, by poverty and trickery, to leave their homeland and work in strange lands as indentured labourers. Most were illiterate, and had no understanding of the *girmit*, or agreement, by which they traded away their liberty. Second, the ownership of the land they came to work was reserved in perpetuity for the indigenous people, so the future could hold no hope of possession for them or their descendants. Their promised land, where work would unite them with nature, lay in the past. Like the epic hero Rama and his bride Sita, a cruel fate has exiled them from their kingdom. As a consequence, their writing expresses a particular kind of restless search for stability.

In Roger Pillai's stories (1980) the restlessness appears in a series of marriages that fall apart, love affairs that never begin, couples held in bondage by poverty or separated by prejudice, images of despair. The central story, "The Celebration," is about a husband whose determination to celebrate Christmas with a traditional feast destroys everyone's happiness. In the one story in the collection based on Fijian legend, "The Bride of Dakuwaqa," an unhappy affair is brought to an end when the shark-god returns to claim his bride. The devil of Muni Deo is the corpse of Muni, "a big, brawny, headstrong lad" who is found hanging from a tamarind tree after his marriage has been destroyed by village gossip and casual police brutality. Only once in these stories does Laxmi, the Indian goddess of good fortune, briefly visit this island where the people of exile still cling to sufficient hope to celebrate her festival.

The "'Fantasy Eaters" who provide the title of Subramani's collection (1988) similarly grope their way through nightmare and disaster in search of a happiness that most often proves to be a delusion, a fantasy. The opening story, "Sauna,'" is set in a village established when, "After indenture, a group of men and women scratched a little clearing from which the present squalid huts sprang up." The story is about the final breakdown of Dhanpat, who after a life of "splendid reassurance" is now "old, exhausted and bereft."

> Now, sitting in front of the temple, he saw how the protective armor had gradually disintegrated. The tenuous bond that existed among the disparate items of his daily life was breaking. More than ever he felt the pointlessness of daily rituals of toil and rest, prayer and persistence. (p.7)

The cultural framework that gives meaning and purpose to daily life has never taken root in the village, and so age reveals his life as meaningless. His internal collapse is matched by images of breakdown in the external world, where there is looting and stone-throwing, and fields of sugar cane that supply the villagers their subsistence are burned at night. In despair, Dhanpat sets his own hut on fire. The story ends with the bleak remark that "Dhanpat was taken away for observation. And the chief took possession of his land" (p.9). Neither work, family, friendship nor religion has enabled him to leave any trace of his life.

The novella *Gone Bush* in the same collection develops this theme at greater length through the life of the villager who escapes to education, security, and the city. By external standards Anandi is a success, accepted into the cosmopolitan political and academic establishment of the capital, Suva, and eventually being elected to parliament himself. But the education that lifts him out of the village where there were "no landmarks . . . nothing to hold anyone's feelings or imagination, only the faceless hills and bush," where "All that was wonderful was elsewhere or in books," does not bring him the wonders the books promised. He remains "wedged between Mewa Lal's [his father's] self-ease and Grandfather's heroic fantasies" with "something of Mother's great capacity for unhappiness" (p.98). Mother, father and grandfather represent three modes of adaptation to an imperialism that denies the authenticity of their own experience. They take refuge in narratives of heroism, subservience, and persecution, none of which restores power over their conditions. The narrator follows the path of escape through education, only to find that education, and even the semblance of power it leads to, is only another form of displacement. The schooling provided by cruelly inflexible Brahmins and Englishmen locked into their respective pasts is incapable of giving the students an understanding of their present. His tertiary studies give him status and position, but when he seeks the Hindu ideal of harmony with self and the world through family he is defeated by the distance his studies have taken him from his origins. The first marriage, begun with a full Hindu ceremony which Anandi interrupts by fainting untimely, is destroyed by Anandi's inability to give himself fully to it. The second is destroyed by the bride's inability to escape from her rebellion against custom, and by the incapacity of her parents to accept anything outside Hinduism's complete but closed circle of possibility. Shanta is unable to forget her earlier marriage to a Moslem, her family are unable to forgive it. Alone, the couple are unable to sustain a relationship.

The story of Anandi's childhood, education and marriages is sandwiched between two shorter episodes. The first, "Artists of the Sea," is an enigmatic tale of a holiday Anandi takes with a friend, the doctor who has tended him during a breakdown that caused him to suffer "another round of that creeping sense of annihilation" (p.77). As the two travel around the island they mix with tourists, talk of their marriages and contemplate the border of land and sea. The mood is given by the quotation from Byron

> *Man marks the earth with ruin—his control*
> *Stops with the shore.*

The two friends try to unravel each other's minds as they reflect on their wives, on the doctor's father, an illiterate peasant who abandoned his farm and took up fishing and was taken by the sea, on their lack of control over their own lives. The doctor says he has taken up sailing. They hover on the edge of a homosexual affair, and visit the shack where the doctor was brought up, which is now inhabited by a magnificent and deadly falcon, driven from its hills by greed rather than the bushfires. Finally, the doctor disappears from Anandi's life, leaving one last glimpse of him with his Australian wife, whose face is caught in a mixture of "fear and desperation" (p.87). There is no attempt to give a unity to the disparate images that develop the conflict of past and present, land and sea suggested on the opening page:

> I saw you staring at the waves again. How intensely you could feel the sea. Yet you seemed to me someone from a landlocked culture whose people were riders of horses. You were the romantic hero of a dimly-remembered Hindi novel. An atavistic reminder in a broken world. Always close to me, like a friend from childhood. (p.77)

The doctor, the friend who belongs to the land but stares with fascination at the sea where everything began, stands for the Indians of Fiji, a people transported across the sea from the land where they belong, marking the earth with their ruin but trying to escape back across the sea to a dimly remembered past.

The final section of the novel repeats this dilemma in the present. It starts with a party of the deracinated of city society, and closes with Anandi, now a member of parliament, coming upon Mansa Ram, a friend of his childhood. Together, they look at an album of photographs of the old village and its people, and its new concrete identity. Among them is the photograph of a young girl standing by the beach, the daughter of the village union leader who had opened the boys' eyes to the wonders of books and the possibilities of life. Anandi had been half in love with "the laughing face of the girl in the photograph. . . . She was my helpmate, my ideal love" (p.104). Now he realizes Mansa Ram, the ugly boy who "hated school, didn't care for reading and writing" and "swaggered aimlessly for adventure" before running off to the city, has married her. The prize Anandi had sought by striving through marriage, education and politics seems to have gone to the boy who merely took what life had to offer. Yet Mansa Ram has found only a personal solution. His contentment does not subdue the sea or restore the ruins with which man has marked the land.

Near the beginning of Subramani's novella he feels "rested and happy" as he awakes after thinking of the falcon, "the lonely executioner in the abandoned house" (p.87). Its ability to endure provides comfort. The story ends, however, amid images of impending disaster, of "charred stone and concrete and smoking trees . . . soldiers amok in the market place . . . blood on the footpaths" (p.134).

In Satendra Nandan's autobiographical *The Wounded Sea* (1991) the nightmares have become a part of Fijian history. The author was a minister of the government deposed by the army in 1987. His book opens with an account of his later escape from the island and its "landscape of ruins," and closes with a detailed account of his experience of the coup. In between, his story of his family and his life up to that time acts as a prism which reveals the elements of his people's history and their relationship to Fiji.

Even more than the characters in Subramani's stories, the members of Satendra Nandan's family are locked into their Indian origins. These origins confuse past and present, myth and reality. Baba, the narrator's grandfather, confused his identity from the first. Sent to register the new baby, he forgot the name the boy's mother had chosen and instead named him after a friend in the Indian village of his childhood. So, instead of having the royal name of Ashok Kumar, he became Beckaroo, the worthless one. Yet from the same grandfather he learns the stories of the *Ramayana* and so identifies with Ram in his time of exile in the forest. These tales are mixed with shrewd observations on local politics and petty prejudices against the Moslem community that no facts can refute.

> ". . . And they killed Gandhi" . . .
>
> Father shouted, "Gandhi was killed by a mad Hindu. . ."
>
> "*Arre*, son of an ass, how long will you believe radio and noospaper" This is *kaliyug*—the age of evil. And the truth will never be known." . . .

> ... Baba's prejudices were part of his being ... he had
> carried in his holdall from his obscure village in India his
> heritage and multicoloured obscenities. This island was the
> last place to change his subterranean thinking: an archipelago,
> surrounded by more than a cannibal ocean. (p.17)

His family remain as much a part of this archipelago as he. Father
may shout at Baba, but he can also refuse to accept Gandhi's
death, just as he believes in Rama's continuing existence (p.21).
He pours the first offering of his yaqona, or kava, to the Fijian
spirit of the place, which in its turn give the eggs for the yaqona
and everything else he needs, but he remains apart. Nandi airport
joins him to Air India and the posters of Hindu deities, and
yaqona and conversation with Birbal, the pundit from India, join
the shining silver birds of the airport to the Ramayana and the
great Hindu sages who first mooted the idea of aircraft. Father's
job at the airport, whose name itself recalls the bull of Shiva,
gives him the money to pay fees to send the narrator to school.
This, however, proves as confusing and disorienting as the family.

The language of education is English, which both empowers
and alienates. The narrator is first taught English by Birbal, his
father's yaqona comrade and the pundit who lights the flame for
both grandfather's and father's funerals. He "had come to us
from India via Suva. He knew no English—which, naturally, he
was appointed to teach. Fortunately, he never taught, except when
the inspector came from Suva" (p.40). He manipulates the
inspector with yaqona, flattery and deception, and intimidates
the class with the sound of the conchshell and the swish of his
tamarind stick. Yet, with the help of a gift of eggs, the author
becomes his favourite, monitor and informant, and, when he
pursues his education overseas, Birbal continues to mediate
between him and his family. He is the eternal babu, the power
that a crippled India nevertheless continues to wield in a
decayed British Empire. He keeps the past alive without being
able to empower it in the present. At the same time, his use of
the trappings of imperialism, the flapping Union Jack and the
class standing on their desks to sing "God Save the King,"
undermines the authority of the institution he unconsciously
parodies. But before opposition can take shape in the actual
circumstances of the island, the people must free themselves from
the past and learn to accept the "surrounding cannibal sea." The

false authority of English as a means of power grounded in the experience of others must be displaced by its use as a vehicle of universal values in which they can share.

Mr. Joyce, the English teacher the narrator meets when his father gains him admission to the high school, helps him to this use by giving him a gift at the time beyond his understanding, the power to see the universal in the particular. Mr. Joyce taught English, read Wordsworth, lines that remain for the narrator "littering my life, illuminating as sunlight after a storm on the landscape of little ruins." Mr. Joyce himself was dismissed for "teaching too many Western ideas to Indian children," but the narrator, after walking through many ruins, still remembers his reading from Hopkins:

> Margaret, are you grieving
> Over Golden Grove unleaving? (p.35)

Hopkins generalizes from Margaret's grief to "the blight man was born for." Satendra Nandan by implication generalizes from the plight of Fiji to the continuing plight of colonized peoples. The message Hopkins brings to his experience of Fiji is that the legacy of the Ramayana need not separate. Like all great poetry, it carries universal values that provide a basis for particular resistance. The grandfather who taught him to identify with Ram in the forests also taught him to see elephants even in Fiji where there were none (p.18). He did not, however, warn him of the jackals who arrived on the day of the colonels and, in the name of a fictitious past, denied all Fijians the opportunity to fashion their values into a community.

Satendra Nandan points to the linguistic bases of community both by his narration of the process of education in English and by his identification of the opportunity lost when the new nation kept the name of the old colony, itself an invention of imperialism. The name denies legitimacy to the Fijian Indians just when, after almost a hundred years, they have become "integral to the Fiji landscape" and "acquired some conception of what it is to be an islander." The story of Nandan's family and education shows the difficulty and complexity of the process by which "people whose ancestors lived on a subcontinent and whose way of life was shaped by great rivers and greater mountains" learned to "accept the nature of islands, surrounded by vast oceans." It shows also the continuing gaps between the people of the island. The family's cow, Lali, links Oceanic and Indian symbolism. It represents the nurturing and sacred elements of Hinduism, while it bears the name of the great gong that summons people to gatherings or gives them tidings of birth and death. Yet the cow disappears, and is found lying in a canefield, speared in the belly by unknown assailants. Grandfather identifies them as *Rakshasas*, the demons who assailed Rama in the forest. The Rakshasas are the destroyers, those who are neither prepared to share their wealth with others nor to allow others the enjoyment of their own goods. They exercise power not through the subtle forms of language but through shapechanging and violence. They represent not the destruction that can lead to renewal, but the violence that, by denying community, makes regeneration impossible.

The succeeding sections of *The Wounded Sea* show how the narrator's life, through a variety of friendships and loves, becomes intimately woven into the life of the island, even as he also learns to trust himself to the ocean that joins it to the rest of the world. The English language he learns and uses is a symbol of this ocean. In the final section of the book, however, his trust is destroyed. A government elected to represent all the people is deposed; the language of understanding is replaced, as in colonial times, by the bureaucratic language that assigns everyone a place in a predetermined order. If the central image of the first section is the wounded cow, the image of this part is, as in *The Odyssey*, the dying dog. When the narrator and his wife return to their flat after he has been released from detention, "our dog Snazzy came running, wagging her tail. . . Strangely, it was at that moment that I felt a pain in my heart. How could one explain to a dog a week-long national tragedy?" (p.167). But the dog, a symbol of total trust, becomes also image of the international betrayal of the Fijian people.

> Almost eighteen months later, I met the diplomat to whom we had entrusted the care of Snazzy when we left Fiji on December 3. He told me how Snazzy had died with a huge worm coiled around her heart. We had left some worm-destroying tablets with him, but it seems he never gave them to her. (p.168)

Because the relationship of dogs to people transcends particular cultures, even if it remains specific to them, this betrayal serves here as a symbol of the indifference that thwarts attempts to build new communities from the shards of imperialism.

Satendra Nandan's book remains as a record of the destruction of one of these potential communities. By denying the legitimacy of the experience of a part of this community, the beneficiaries of the military coup have excised a part of the common history of the island. By creating a myth of their own past, the colonels and the chiefs try to justify the oppression of women endemic to the traditional societies of the Pacific, as well as imperial oppression on the basis of racial categories, and industrial oppression on the basis of class. Their government rests on a lie which must be corrected before any of their people can have a future. Satendra Nandan's book, however, also provides a basis for a future by recording what had already been achieved as a culture adapted to its changed environment. The peoples of Fiji will not find their Eden by attempting to return to either of their separate pasts, but only by recognizing these as the constituents of a common present.

II

Philippines literature in English is the product of a culture formed from a mixture of indigenous and imported traditions and a society riven by class divisions between rich and poor. It contrasts with the writings of the Fijian Indians, who are similarly divided by class but who are at the same time separated by law and tradition from the other major part of the society in which they live. Philippines history has seen successive waves of invasion from the Asian mainland, Indonesia, Spain, and America, and its culture has been variously shaped by the different experiences of rural and urban poverty, by different languages, and by differential access to education and power. Alone among Asian nations the majority of its people are Catholics, but Hindu influences subsist within a Christianity which overlays earlier pagan beliefs and practices. Power is in the hands of an upper bourgeoisie or aristocracy who pride themselves on their Spanish affiliation, are allied to multinational capital, and rest their own authority on the feudal control they have imposed on a native peasantry and enforced with modern systems of law. The writer who works in English thus finds himself, like the narrator of Sionil Jose's novel *Tree* (1978), a cultural commuter endlessly trying to interpret one reality in terms of another. In explaining himself, the narrator provides a metaphor for the life of a nation that is politically independent, economically tied, and culturally confused:

> I am a commuter, not between the city and the village, although I do this quite frequently; not between the inane idealism of the classroom and the stifling reality beyond it, which I must do for survival and self-respect. I am a commuter between what I am now and what I was and would like to be and it is this commuting at lightning speed . . . that has done havoc to me. My doctor flings at me cliches like "alienation," "guilt feelings," and all the urban jargon that have cluttered and at the same time compartmentalized our genteel, middle class mores, but what ails me are not these. I can understand fully my longing to go back, to "return to the womb"—even the deathwish that hounds me when I find it so difficult and enervating to rationalize a middle-aged life that has been built on a rubble of compromise and procrastination. It is this commuting, the tension and knowledge of its permanence, its rampage upon my consciousness that must be borne, suffered and vanquished, if I am to survive in this arid plateau called living. (p.1)

The "inane idealism" represents modern liberal nationalism, the "stifling reality" the corruption and despotism with which it must contend, the village the source of tradition that simultaneously binds and gives strength to the present, while the city is both the focus of national aspirations and the point where the state is integrated into global networks of power and dependence. Jose's novel itself plugs into these networks, communicating the plight of his people to anyone who chooses to read his words. At the same time, its narrator delves deep back into his village past to discover the factors that have produced this plight.

The stories in Nick Joaquin's *Tropical Gothic* (1972) portray the Philippines, particularly Manila and its hinterland, as a seducer, its mixture of cultures and hopes beguiling its people into a world of mirrors which paralyzes action. In contrast, F.

Sionil Jose identifies the causes of the country's dilemmas as political. His sequence of novels about the town and people of Rosales traces the origins of the political impasse and explores the alternative forms of action that promise escape to a just future.

In the first of the "Rosales" novels, *The Pretenders* (1962), written earlier but chronologically later than *Tree*, Jose had already shown how these factors entrap the individual in a situation that allows alternatives but no escape. Its central character, Antonio Samson, has with his sister's assistance escaped from the village to America, where he becomes Tony and completes a doctorate that gives him prospects of bringing help, or at least understanding, to his people. Instead, on his return he marries into a wealthy family and finds himself completely within their power. His marriage forces him to leave the university where it had been his ambition to teach and work instead for his father-in-law, Don Manuel. Manuel believes that everyone can be bought, and that only the family matters. He realizes that Tony's price is self-respect, but this proves to be the only thing he cannot give him. Caught between the family and his ideals, Tony tries to choose both, but finds himself forced into continual compromise. He finds that his wife has aborted the child with whom she was pregnant when they returned from America, and then that she is sleeping with other men. He refuses to acknowledge his father, an unrepentant revolutionary who is serving a life sentence for striking the landlord. He even fails to carry out his last wish and reclaim the body to be buried next to his wife. He tries to salvage his respect by delving into the history of his grandfather, the leader who had brought his people to Rosales and established them in their village, but realizes he has betrayed this memory when he refuses to acknowledge his own son by a village girl. Finally, he is forced to recognize that the job he does for the family firm is meaningless, a mere gloss on corruption, and that even the journalist friend he looks to as a model of integrity is in Don Manuel's pay. Recognizing that he is powerless to use either his wealth or his education, or even to pass his ideals on to a child, he walks under a train.

Tony's death destroys his wife by revealing the emptiness of the life she has been living. Its meaning is recognized only by Lawrence Bitfogel, the college friend who comes too late to Manila to renew with Tony the ideals they had nourished together in their cold college lodgings. Bitfogel is feted by Tony's friends and relatives, but finds they deny the fact of his death, just as they deny the true nature of their society. They flaunt their wealth yet live their lives in fear even of the "youngsters with outlandish uniforms" who come to their help in a highway emergency. Bitfogel sees in these young people the same quality he had found in Antonio Samson, "who had gone to the United States and to its fountainhead of wisdom, if not of courage," and he sees how this quality has been destroyed.

> They were destroyed because they were bribed—and because they were destroyed, the country and the beneficent change they would have brought were lost—lost, and the future which once seemed evocative and real when it was but an academic subject to be tossed around in a crowded room on Maple Street, had been aborted in the dank bowels of the earth. (p.187)

These words serve as Tony's epitaph, but they fail to show the power of the bribe. The country is so corrupted by the wealth that lies in a few hands that there is simply no alternative. The university where Tony hoped to teach is controlled by the same men who run the family and its business. He could not have gone to America if he had known of his son. Writing does not provide a sufficient income to support a family, and the wealth he enjoys from his father-in-law comes at the cost of furthering the family's interests at the expense of the country. He is literally emasculated: denied power and progeny, suicide is his only resort.

The distortion of human values we encounter in *The Pretenders* appears in *Tree* in the image of a legless man dead in the bamboo shack where the narrator has gone to view him as a prodigy. The man had lost his legs in an accident at the rice mill which he had worked, and had since been maintained on a pension grudgingly given by its owner, the narrator's father Espiridion, "more as a result of a court order, I think, than sympathy" (p.46). His spirited daughter, Martina, is forced to labour for Espiridion to buy the medicines her father needs: "he had not been feeling well for weeks, but, in spite of this, had sent his daughter to work for us, and this was what Martina had done, knowing that her place was at home" (p.50). The medicine she brings inevitably comes too late. The narrator watches from the "small middle of the house":

In a while, she came out slowly and in that instant, I should have known from the dumb despair on her face, I should have stayed with her and understood her ways, why she came to the house swiftly and disappeared just as fast when she had done her work, how hurriedly she ate her meals— like a hog—the first days she was with us, the hunger in her belly that could not be easily appeased. Most of all, I should have understood how steadfastly, how proudly she took care of that cripple inside, how he, too, had sought to live by sending his only child to work for us, making believe that what was given to him by father was not charity, when all of us—but not the two of them—knew it was theirs by right. . .

        . . .

        I remember having peeped briefly into that darkened room at the legless figure there lying still and stiff, its eyes staring blankly at the gathering dusk . . . And this feeling came to me, freeing me from all other thoughts, this feeling of dread that I had intruded into a misshapen world that I had somehow helped to shape, and that, if I did not flee it, it would entrap and destroy me. . . I ran and ran—away from the macabre shadows that trailed me, away from Martina and her dead father, into the comforting brightness of our home . . . (p.51)

The history of the man on whose life is built the "comforting brightness" of the narrator's home, the pride of his daughter, and the unbridgeable gap of comprehension between the two worlds that nevertheless produce each other, epitomize the theme of the novel.

Tree comprises a series of episodes from the narrator's protected childhood in a barrio, or neighbourhood, of the town of Rosales. His reminiscences bring back at first the memory of an ageless setting outside his house beneath the balete tree that provided shelter for village gatherings and festivities, standing "guardian over the land and our lives, immemorial like our griefs" (p.2). But the first family scene he remembers is the gathering to mourn his grandfather, and successive episodes extend his acquaintance with grief and death as he gradually comes to comprehend the fissures hidden by the traditional order within whose security he grows. This order is sustained by his father's patriarchal authority, supported by callous beatings of those who displease him. His authority is not enough, however, to save the life of the man who defies the greater landlord, Don Vicente, and to restore to the peasants the land he has stolen from them. Nor can it protect them from the ravages of debt and drought, or comprehend the growing demands for independence and dignity that drive the younger generation to death in the forests with the timber getters, the Huk rebels, or the army. At the end of the book the narrator recognizes the tree that had seemed the guarantor of the old order as being, like his well-meaning father and the whole order of landlords, a parasite that has outlived the time when it might have given strength to the peasantry. Now it brings nothing but death:

> In the beginning, it sprang from the earth as vines coiled around a sapling. The vines strangled the young tree they had embraced. They multiplied, fattened and grew, became a sturdy trunk, the branches spread out to catch the sun. And beneath this tree, nothing grows! (p.135)

However, although these are the last words of the book, they do not cancel the narrator's belief that, even if he and his order who still bring death to their countrymen have "died long ago," truth is still "justice at work" (p.133). The novel describes the corruption of one class and the destruction of another, but it also celebrates those who, against whatever odds, defy circumstance to work for their own truths.

In the central novel of the sequence, *Mass* (1983), Jose shows just how great these odds are. He builds the novel around the character of Jose, or Pepe, Samson, illegitimate son of the Antonio Samson of *The Pretenders*. Like his father, Pepe has been brought up in poverty in the village of Cabugawan, where his mother and aunt toil and scrimp to give him the education that will enable him to follow his father's escape path. Jose, however, does not want the burden of gratitude or of expectations imposed on him by others. His escape from the village to Manila is also an escape from his family, and he quickly travels even further, from the shabby sanctuary of his aunt's apartment on the outskirts of poverty to its desperate heart in the squatters' slum of Tondo. His discovery of his father's identity only makes him more determined to avoid ideals, to live only to maintain his self-respect and live "simply, honestly, irrevocably and perhaps resolutely, a bastard." The stigma of his birth has, like an invisible tattoo, been "unerring in the devastation of my inner self." It has kept him apart, made him different from others, so he feels no loyalty to anyone other than himself. The only power he has is the power to choose to be what he wishes. In the barrio, he is no bastard, but "Pepe, the scholar, the loyal comrade" who can choose to be "Archbishop, or . . . the czar of crime of the Barrio" (p.2). He is determined to accept life on the terms it has been given to him, to live it for its enjoyment:

> . . . I like being here, transfixed on this plain, this vast limbo without rim called living. I like being here, feeling the wind and the sun upon my skin, the fullness of my stomach, the electric surge of an orgasm—now that I know it—course through me. (p.1)

Life does not, however, allow him this simple enjoyment. He discovers that, while his abilities give him the power of choice, circumstances determine the price to be paid for the choice, the kind of person it will make him.

As Pepe circles downward in place, he spirals about morally, searching for the escape from circumstance that will lead to purely being. His education, stumbling as it has been, offers a path itself and opens the others it had shown to his father: power through politics or revolution, wealth through marriage. Manila offers others. As politics and education move him upward through society, so he dives down through the lower depths of drug-pushing, prostitution and sexual perversion. Eventually the two paths converge on the army inquisition where he is tortured and the gaol where he undergoes the final humiliation of rape. In a final irony, in the torture chamber the "electric surge of orgasm" becomes the unbearable pain of the electric charge that is applied to his genitals and for a time renders him impotent. His recovery from this is effected only by the knowledge the girl he has loved has gained by taking the final plunge from the edge of the precipice of poverty into the abyss of prostitution. He has, however, to find his own escape from the corruption of poverty by accepting the responsibility for violence. By confronting the final tempter, the man who seduces even the revolution, condemning the poor to suffering and their champions to death in order to maintain his own sensuous enjoyment of power, Pepe makes his own choice. He shoots the seducer and returns to his home village on his way to join the revolution in the mountains.

Pepe's experience is rather like Dove's in Nelson Algren's novel of New Orleans in the Depression: *A Walk on the Wildside* (1956). Unlike Dove, he has an education that enables him to understand the causes of poverty and to choose some paths out. Similarly, his failure to find a way through any of these paths is reminiscent of the failure of hope in John Dos Passos's *Manhattan Transfer* (1925) and other realist urban fiction of the time. Jose's novel is however more political than the former, and its politics more grounded in an individual morality than the latter. Even in their most harrowing depictions of poverty and violence, the American novels retain a belief in the American dream. Poverty is cruel because it is an affront to the natural rights of man that should have space to flourish in the new world. Violence is an evil outcome of a poverty that reduces life to its lowest denominator. Sionil Jose however writes from an older culture that condemns poverty because it denies inner freedom.

Jose Samson's apparent hedonism is in fact a deeply moral statement of his determination to be himself even in a limbo created by others. His use of the term limbo comes from the religious perception of a world cut off from the grace of God, just as the ambivalent name of the novel, *Mass*, stands both for the religious ceremony by which Father Jess (or Padre Jesus) brings grace to the depths of the barrio, and for the mass of people who live there and who can only be set free by their own efforts to transcend their condition and recover the common humanity it denies them. As they organize the people of the barrio, Jose and Father Jess help them to recover this vision of the possible. Their efforts are thwarted, however, by the power of money expressed through the brutality of the police. Father Jess, like the lover Jose is forced to reject, remains a member of the ruling class. He can always return to the safety of their protected enclaves. Jose learns from them who he is, but he has to make his own choice of where he will be. He chooses to be with his own people, the people of the barrios and the villages they have come from. His apparent hedonism is rooted in a deep sense of self that will allow him to deny neither his origins nor the attachments formed simply by living. Revolution is not an intellectual game, but the only way out of limbo.

Sionil Jose's narrative is of course not history but fiction. As each volume in the series proclaims on a preliminary page, "All the events and characters . . . are real only in the reader's

imagination." It could therefore be argued that the Philippines
are a much gentler society than they portray, that the ruling
classes are not so corrupt nor the police so brutal, that the failure
of scholarship, organisation, or love to offer a way out is merely
contingent, that there are alternatives to revolution, that revolution
is itself merely another imposition of power. Jose himself is
unforgiving in his portrayal of the deceptions of the
revolutionaries, and particularly of those who claim to speak in
the name of the people, just as he is unillusioned in his depiction
of the conditions of the slums that destroy attempts at human
solidarity or compassion. Yet finally he shows that, while
circumstances may allow for the kind of charitable amelioration
practised by Father Jess or the purposive organisation carried
out by Pepe or the Brotherhood, these leave the logic of the
system untouched. The poor can only be freed by revolution,
and unless those in power concede it the revolution must be
violent. Although the poor may repeatedly betray or destroy
their own efforts, for them as for Pepe, there is finally only one
choice.

Pepe's choice depends on his having come to understand
that the sensual freedom he craves can only be realized within
a free community. He has to envisage this community in his
mind, recognizing both its limitations and its exclusions, before
he can leave for the mountains to join those who are fighting
to bring it into existence. He is helped to envisage it through his
reading, his studies and his discussions with colleagues in the
Brotherhood, but these provide only an intellectual framework.
This framework attains imaginative fulness only through his work
as an organizer in the barrio and among the students. From this
he gains an understanding of possibility, but also learns to
recognize his roots in the experience of the peasants working on
the land. When the bus takes him back to his village, "to the
plains of Rosales spread to our right, and beyond, the mountain
of Balungao, greenish blue in the distance," he is filled again
with the images of a past where the land nurtured its people:
"the edible snails, the string of green papayas I brought back and
Mother reproaching me for being away all day without her
knowing. I had lain under the trees in the foothills, listening to
the wind in the grass, the murmur of the water above the shallows,
to my heart" (p.156). This is the sentimental memory of a youth
when the world seemed in harmony with the self and its desires,

but it is also an image of the possible future that the revolution must fulfil if it is not to lead to another betrayal of mere power and ideology.

Jose is aware of the way that poverty and oppression distort both individual and communal life in the villages as well as in the urban barrios. In *Mass*, Pepe angrily rejects the remark of his aristocratic lover, Betsy, that even if the villagers are poor, "they and the village have a certain integrity." He remembers instead "the unending violence, the latent viciousness under the gloss of neighborliness that everyone seemed to exude." This realism does not, however, destroy the possibility of a community based on different values. Just as he refuses to accept any romanticism of the poor, so he refuses to accept that there is anything natural about their condition or behaviour. Both are the product of a particular system that denies them the opportunity to realize their humanity. "There is nothing romantic about poverty. It is totally, absolutely degrading" (p.146).

This observation identifies the central dilemma of revolution. Only the poor can free themselves, yet their values are so degraded by the present system that they no longer have the basis for constructing a better society. The other two novels of the Rosales sequence confront the dilemma directly by dealing with the attempts of the peasants to produce new values through the actual work of constructing a new society. In both novels, the first step is to restore to the peasants' ownership of the land from which they have built their economy, and whose theft is the central fact of their deprivation and exclusion from enjoyment of their own products. These movements, different in time and ideology, both challenge the dominant ideology of Philippines society, that some are born to rule and some to lifelong servitude. As the landlord Don Vicente explains it to his rebellious son Luis near the beginning of *My Brother, My Executioner* (1988):

> there are those who are destined to rule, to hold power, not because it is in their blood but because they are created to rule, to manipulate, in the same way that there are men destined to work to be slaves, to be patronized, to be cared for like children. (p.12)

Or, as he puts it more benevolently later in the same conversation, "there are no oppressors, no oppressed. There are only people who seize opportunities to make their lives better" (p.15). And, with the same insight as Pepe Samson, he adds that the "worst enemies of the poor are their own kind."

The action of this novel centres on the conflict between Luis and Victor, sons of the village woman Nena, who also appears in the novels in *Mass* as an old woman, serving as housekeeper to Father Jess at his mission in the slums of Manila. In the earlier novel we learn that as a young woman she had worked as a servant in the household of Don Vicente, the great landowner of Rosales. When she became pregnant by him he dismissed her, sending her back to the village and poverty. Having no other heir, however, after thirteen years he snatches Luis back from her and adopts him as his heir. Luis moves to the city, receives an education, becomes a writer and editor and eventually, after his father's death, landlord of Rosales. Meanwhile, his younger half-brother escapes to the hills where he becomes a leader in the Huk insurgency. The conflict between village and city, poverty and wealth, is thus both represented by the two brothers and internalized within Luis, who can free himself from neither part of his inheritance. As editor, he tries and fails to expose the conspiracy of silence between army and landlords to conceal the destruction of his mother's village and its people, obliterating even their memory in a mass grave levelled by the straight lines of the plough. He betrays his mother by accepting her desertion by his father, destroys his lover by projecting on her his anger at himself, and pains his wife by neglect. His life is a deception, a failed attempt to recover the unity of self and nature he remembers from childhood, before his father snatched him away into comforts he is too weak to abandon:

> I am home. I am home. This is the place honored in the mind and sanctified in the heart. Although he had been away, the sounds and smells were always with him—the aroma of newly harvested grain, the grass fresh with dew, the mooing cattle, the young herder's call for his water buffalos, the cackle of hens, the rustling of bamboo in the wind and most of all, the tones of his language, for there was in Ilokano the aura and the mystery of things left unsaid. There was the past, too, that did not have to be relived, which must be escaped because it spelled perdition and all the bog and swamp of his muddied beginning. How was it then, how were the hours, the moments in the river, in

> the water-lilied ditches, the taste of newly harvested rice?
> Bring back the strum of guitars, the children's eager voices—
> all the happiness that ended on a night like this! (p.21)

His failure to recover this unity of being makes his life a deception. His only moments of truth are occasionally in his poetry, where he recognizes his despair, his refusal to surrender his will to his father, and his final acceptance of death at the hands of his brother's men.

Even his memory of his past, however, contains its own contradiction in his refusal to remember the reasons that compelled both brothers to escape. The land he remembers is a made land, the product of human labour, but the labourers are denied enjoyment of its wealth and, eventually, even refused a place in it. Luis knows this, but refuses to accept its consequences, preferring to live with his comforts. His attempts as landlord to alleviate poverty are too little, too late. His brother's revolutionary logic is inexorable, and Luis is destroyed with his possessions. Yet the final voice in the novel, before Luis and his wife face their personal truth, is not given to the revolutionaries but to the army captain who is waging war against them. Like the Huks, he accepts the necessity of violence, but not of a solution imposed by violence. The Huks, he argues, will be destroyed, but pressure on the government can force it to change. Only thus can revolution escape what Luis condemns as the "meaninglessness of violence" (p.181). For Luis and Victor, however, there is only violence and death.

The final novel of the sequence, *Po-on* (1984), takes us back to the origins of the conflict in the times of Spanish control and its later supersession by the Americans. Both powers are equally contemptuous of the natives and ruthless in their suppression of any opposition, but whereas the Spanish are content to subject them to colonial authority the Americans cloak their imperialism in the ideology of progress and paternalism. Paradoxically, both powers contribute to revolutionary zeal, the Spaniards by their teaching of one God for all men, and the Americans by the example of their democratic constitution. The central character, Istak, is educated by his parish priest in Spanish and Latin, theology and science. When his father strikes and kills the new priest who has dismissed Istak as acolyte, destroyed his ambition of himself becoming a priest, and banished his people from their ancestral lands, Istak leads them on an exodus to find new lands where they may be free. During the dangerous times of their exodus and their successful settlement in a promised land, he acts as leader, priest, and teacher. In the second part of the novel, however, their peace is threatened by the Americans, and Istak goes as delegate to guide the republican army and president in its flight towards his ancestral home. The soldiers will not accept his assistance, but he joins them anyway and is killed in a doomed defence of the mountain passway. In this journey and final stand he experiences the truth of his wife's recognition that for the poor there is no flight from their fate (p.155), but also the truth in the words of Mabini, the revolutionary writer who has taken refuge with his people and who sends him on his final journey:

> We lose now, but we will fight again, each one of us, until
> they tire, until they are bloodied and wearied, until we are
> free and justice triumphs. (p.161)

On their own, these words are nothing but hollow rhetoric. The novel gives them truth by embodying them first in the experience of Istak and his little band as they join their strength to each other in their journey to a promised land, and then in Istak's more personal pilgrimage of return, during which he survives only as he trusts himself to his countrymen.

Po-on is about the beginnings of a nation that has still not finally emerged. This new nation is brought into being not by its leaders, who are carried away by vanity and divided by pride, but by the people who overcome their hostilities as they learn to trust. This trust is strengthened by their common revulsion at the atrocities committed by the invading forces, but it rests ultimately on their collective possession of the land. This is not the sense of ownership by the land of the hunters and gatherers, for the peasants themselves destroy the forests for their farms and drive the older peoples back into their mountain fastnesses. Nor is their ownership exercised through an artificial collective that in fact divides people from their land. Although the families support each other, each is directly responsible for its own plot. In Rosales, the promised land of *Po-on*, the ownership is not literal, but is made possible only by a benevolent landlord. But the peasants' use of the land is not simply exploitative. Unlike the landlords, they use it not merely as an asset but as a resource to be nurtured and to nurture.

III

Despite its divisions, the Philippines has a single culture, and Fiji has two cultures artificially kept apart. As a consequence, both Fijian Indian and Philippines literatures differ from writing in English produced around the Pacific by authors whose work expresses the experience of particular Asian components of multicultural societies.

Multiculturalism is itself a term with contrasting and conflicting meanings. On the one hand, it can be a form of separatism, giving groups of people the opportunity to maintain and preserve different traditions within the one society. On the other, it can look to a single culture that recognizes and respects its individual components, acknowledging their different origins and identities but promoting a dynamic interplay between them. The second of these views prevails in the work of English language writing from Asian communities in North America and Australia; Singapore writers, on the other hand, work within an official ideology that tends to a bland version of the former.

The stories in Gopal Baratham's *People Make You Cry* (1988) show Singapore as a cosmopolitan society in which people, detached from each other and their past, shop around as cultural consumers, searching for the religious, erotic, or familial satisfactions to compensate for the lack of community. The most poignant story in the collection, "Dutch Courage," is a lament both for a failed imperialism and for the loss of the common purpose that united people of all races in wartime resistance. Its central image is not the fortified compound but the orphanage where Father Noonan cares for the "bastards of the village girls who had gone to the city to find work, the younger daughters of large families abandoned as babies, the orphans of farmers killed by the security forces of the guerillas" (p.101). The children represent the failure of community, yet paradoxically they also suggest the hope for the future that the story's central character clings to in the image of his own mixed race child that is his last thought as he dies in an ambush.

In *O Singapore! Stories in Celebration* (1989) Catherine Lim reveals the tensions hidden beneath the official pronouncements. These stories are set in a thoroughly urban world where a benevolent government provides detailed prescriptions for a good life ruled by rationality and Confucian order. The story that concludes the volume, "'Write, Right, Rite'; or How Catherine Lim Tries to Offer Only the Best on the Altar of Good Singapore Writing,'" subverts this order by celebrating the human comedy of the writer simultaneously honoured for her contribution to the island-state's cultural renown and dogged by the official demands that her work portray the Singapore of official doctrine. Other stories glory in the human ingenuity that discovers ways of subverting orthodoxy in the interests of desire. The vehicle of subversion is, more often than not, language, which by re-establishing its connection to the baser forms of biological materiality undermines the abstract idealizations of official propaganda. Thus, in the modern fairy tale, the young man defeats the Wise Man and wins his princess with the question: "What local food in Singapore presents a biological puzzle to tourists?" Although the "Wise Man's knowledge of biology, like his knowledge of history and folklore was extensive . . . somehow he had never connected it with food or tourists." He concedes, and the young man wins with his triumphant shout: "Fish ball soup!" (p.106) With schoolboy delight, his language makes the unexpected connection and wins him his bride. His answers to the successive questions have restored the carnal bases and delights of human conduct that the public language excludes. Like the other stories, the fairy tale, by restoring the private, helps to provide power over the realm of the public.

Singapore's bland ideology is not, however, so much a cause as a result of the dislocation of public from private, which is a consequence of a deeper rupture in cultural traditions. This rupture forms the subject of Lee Lok Liang's "Dumb, Dumb, by a Bee Stung" (1981). At one level, this is the story of the funeral of a wealthy Chinese merchant, how it brings together the wealthy and powerful, and how they negotiate a fix between the demands of tradition and authority about the route of the funeral procession. The story's focus is, however, changed by the presence among the onlookers of a filthy hunchback urchin. He is first attracted by the music, to which he listens entranced. The rich man's funeral brings an unaccustomed richness to his life. But any sentimentality is displaced by his actions in pinching the ample bottom of the wife of the chief mourner and provoking her to let fly a vile fart. The way the mourners ignore the stench could be taken as a metaphor of their business and politics. But the true metaphor is at the close the story, when, while the businessmen sip tea and imagine themselves the eight wise fairies of Chinese legend, the hunchback writhes in the pain of stinging bees provoked by a stray shot from the other urchins who have been stoning him. He is the dumb object of their chant, the dumb one by a bee stung. His deformity, his pain, and his isolation are the consequences of a culture detached from its origins and now kept alive only in the externals of empty ritual. The paper bridge over the drain that replaces the bridge the funeral procession should cross over a cleansing river symbolizes the distance the culture has been removed from the physical environment that once gave it meaning. The disregarded urchin signifies the inhuman consequences of a culture that is no longer attached to the concerns of its participants, and which therefore can no longer sustain any kind of community. The powerful people in the story, comfortable in an international network of money and prestige, are at home neither in their own country nor with themselves. They rob even death of its meaning.

IV

Asian writing from Australia and North America is, like the writings of the native peoples in these countries, the product of cultures of the oppressed. The stories that Mena Abdullah wrote with Ray Mathews in *Time of the Peacock* (1965) express one of the most benign forms of this suppression. Set in a small country town, they give voice to one of Australia's neglected communities, the Indians who originally came to this country in the nineteenth century as hawkers and rural labourers. The family in Abdullah's stories is relatively prosperous but remains isolated from the local community. Its affairs are seen mainly through the eyes of the child whose enrolment at school necessarily involves her with the wider society. In the story "Grandfather Tiger" the visionary tiger symbolizes both the security of the family compound and the strength the child, Joti, must take from it to her school. The story ends with the bridging of the division as Joti brings home a schoolfriend. The tiger, his role finished, disappears. His memory, however, remains as a symbol of admixture without loss.

Abdullah's work comes from a community secure in itself. Brian Castro, however, writes from a community that, because of its proportionately greater numbers, has in both Australia and North America generated intense fear and loathing from the white majority. In eastern Australia and in California from the time of the goldrushes onwards Chinese miners and laborers were regarded as a threat to wages and working conditions, to morals and to health (Markus, 1979). Brian Castro, himself born in Hong Kong and part of a more recent migration to Australia, identifies the problem as a clash of cultures that carry different definitions of the self. His most recent novel, *Double-Wolf* (1991), is entirely European in orientation, using Freud's case-study of the wolfman to make identity itself the problem. Raising the question of what would happen to Freud's theories if the wolfman's story were itself a deliberate fiction, he examines the identity of a narrator displaced from childhood security by revolution, war, and migration. His earlier novel, *Birds of Passage* (1983), deals with similar issues through the person of a contemporary Australian-born Chinese, with the superbly multiethnic name of Seamus O'Young, who can establish his contemporary identity only by reconstructing the experience of Lo Yun Shan, the forerunner who migrated from China to Australia at the end of the last century.

The two stories in the novel move in opposite directions. Seamus, the contemporary narrator, has been born an orphan, and even his name is a fiction, an Anglicisation, or Celticisation, of what he believes was the Chinese original, Sham Oh Yung, but there are no records to prove it. He is officially an ABC, an Australian-born Chinese, the "first three letters of the alphabet . . . a classification which straddled two cultures"(p.8). His identity is only his name, his passport, and the journal of Lo Yun Shan which he discovers in fragments beneath a mirror, and which he finds, as he deciphers an interlined translation, speaks with his own tongues and accents. Otherwise, he belongs nowhere, at home in Chinatown but separated from it by language, set apart in the orphanage and at school by his racial features and the problem of his blue eyes. Lo Yun Shan, on the other hand, starts with a clear identity. His name comes from the Big Mist Mountain, his father is an important man who "wears a long gown and received taxes from the villagers, Shan is educated by the monks, a schoolteacher, and his father's proxies. This identity of family and person is however steadily destroyed, first by opium and then by migration and its consequences.

Trains and toilets play a major role in Seamus' world. Several times he opens doors or peers through peepholes to gaze at ladies in the privacy of the toilet. Similarly, trains provide not merely means of changing location, but an enclosed space from which the traveller gazes like a voyeur at a passing world going unconcerned about its business. But the train is also the place for meetings that may or may not have consequences. In one episode, when Seamus has escaped from Australia to travel in Europe, a man who briefly enters his compartment introduces himself as "Barthes, Roland" (p.71). This follows a conversation with a woman artist who has entered the compartment and discourses with him on the subject of painting, of recording "the process or references of which the subject is part" (p.69).

> "A body describes itself by its lines of tension," she went on, "by its wanting to become invisible, not exhibitory. It should never be conscious that it is being seen: that is its attraction." (p.69)

This is the condition of the world beyond the train, of the women Seamus peers at in toilets, and of the relationship between Seamus and Fatima after they marry. It is also the condition that Shan finds himself in when he enters Australia and with his fellow countrymen is reduced to the category of "Celestial" or "John Chinaman" (p.77). But this is also the ultimate state of alienation or non-being from which Seamus and Shan alike struggle to escape. It is the state of two-dimensional art of which Barthes writes in "The World as Object":

> Now, all art which has only two dimensions, that of the work and that of the spectator, can create only a platitude, since it is no more than the capture of a shopwindow spectacle by a painter-voyeur. Depth is born only at the moment the spectacle itself slowly turns its shadow toward man and begins to look at him. (1983, p.73)

Reciprocally, the migrant, the newcomer, the outsider, the alien can only create an identity, become a member of the new society, when society learns to see him looking.

Language, however, is the obstacle that prevents our looking at the world or its people. It divides people from each other, people who speak Chinese from those who speak English, generating the fears and repressions that lead to the brutal attacks on the Chinese miners. For one moment, Shan and the revolutionary idealist Clancy are able to transcend these differences in a silence when "Centuries of human history had sparked one small covenant in the souls of two men for a brief moment." The moment does not last, however: "The wind prevented the spark from catching" (p.117). Instead, the two meet in the homicidal fury that leads to Clancy's death and the end of Shan's time in Australia. Similarly, Seamus follows the track of his ancestor to the site of this encounter, where the two men meet in a time-warp that transcends history, only to lose will and voice and surrender to the care of women. The women restore him to his senses but not to communication, and at the end of the book he ambiguously appears to escape from all language into death, or into a wordless love, which may be the same thing. Australia finally gives Shan both fortune and a child, but neither he nor his descendant is able to find the language that will enable him to live in its land.

V

Brian Castro deals with migrants who never belong. Joy Kogawa fills her novel *Obasan* with the voices of the Issei and the Nissei, the first and second generations of Canadian Japanese who made Canada their home and then, during the second world war, were denied their citizenship, their homes and their existence as human beings. The Issei, the Japanese-born, are grateful that they have been allowed to survive, and want to leave the past at peace. "This country is the best. There is food. There is medicine. There is pension money. Gratitude. Gratitude." The Sansei, the members of the third generation to which the narrator, Naomi Nakane belongs, are concerned with the present and its problems. "Life is so short . . . the past so long. Shouldn't we turn the page and move on?" (p.41) But the second generation are "visually bilingual" (p.47). Aunt Emily, at home in both cultures, refuses to accept the acquiescence of the one or the deracination of the other. Her anger at her rejection by her native country continues to burn, and, recognizing that "The past is the future" she forces the narrator to share it. The novel is a record of how her uncle's death brings her back to a realization of her aunt's life, of the loss they had lived with and the strength that had sustained them, and through this to a recognition of her own loss.

These themes are conveyed through a series of visual images in the opening parts of the novel. The first is the memory of Isamu, her uncle sitting like Chief Sitting Bull at the edge of the prairie that is the closest he can again come to the sea that had been his element (p.2). The likeness to the Indian chief signifies both the common racial origins, a commonality stretching back far beyond white occupation, and the commonality of exile. Exile and hope are both signified by the second of these images, the photograph of the family in the new land, formally dressed and proudly displaying the first Canadian grandson. Finally, the snapshot of Uncle and Father as young men is an image of the achievement their subsequent fate denies:

> One snapshot I remember showed Uncle and Father as young men standing full front beside each other, their toes pointing outwards like Charlie Chaplin's. In the background were pine trees and the side view of Uncle's beautiful house. One of Uncle's hands rested on the hull of an exquisitely detailed craft. It wasn't a fishing boat or an ordinary yacht, but a sleek boat designed by Father, made over many years and many winter evenings. A work of art. (p.21)

The picture brings together the artifacts, the country, and the people in a unity produced by work. In the next paragraph this unity is broken by the RCMP officer who admires the boat as he confiscates it in the first act of the family's exile.

The novel is an attempt to make sense of the history of exile, harmony and renewed disruption conveyed by these images. It starts with the death of the narrator's uncle, which brings her back to comfort her aunt in the prairie town that had been the final point of their exile. Her uncle, Isamu, and Ayoko, the Obasan or aunt of the title, had been the still points in her childhood, and returning to her aunt's house, where nothing has been wasted and every stored object is "a link in her lifeline . . . her blood and bones" (p.15), forces her to go back through this childhood and its great disruption. These memories take her first to the house that is the extension of the photograph of the two men with the boat, a place holding the achieved security of family and childhood, a place of art, music, comfort and love. Beyond the house is the adult world of death, where prying old men threaten the secret places and dying chickens teach us our own guilt. Within the house, these threats are kept in their place by a culture of order and support. The outbreak of war, however, breaks the safe boundaries, bringing into the house the fear, racial hatred, and callous bureaucracy that destroys the family and scatters the wider community of which it is part. The people who think of themselves as Canadian Japanese find that they are merely Japanese, a hated enemy to be driven out of homes and province, and even out of the Canadian nation.

While the war is the occasion for this disruption, its causes lie deeper in the psychology of colonialism. The white Canadians, lacking confidence in their own possession of the land, fear anyone different who claims to share it with them. They derive their identity not from a shared present but from a foreign past. Thus, as Aunt Emily observes, when they drive out their Canadian Japanese they maim themselves. The Alberta farmer who exploits their labour without recognizing their humanity by so much as a neighbourly visit to the shack he allots them remains an alien in his own land. On the other hand, Rough Lock Bill, who saves Naomi from drowning and shares with her the stories of the Indians, enlarges both of them.

While their neighbours drive them out, the land itself makes them welcome in their first place of exile as they come to know it and learn how it can support them.

> Beyond the natural stone steps at the back of our yard is the path Uncle makes by which we enter the moist forest and the glade that is speared alive with fiddlehead stems. "Warabi," Uncle call them. He shows us which ones we are to pick. We carry metal syrup tins, Uncle, Obasan, Stephen, and I, as we forage through the woods in the green light . . . (p.139)

The common activity unites people and place. Even this consolation is denied them, however, as they are once again uprooted and driven across the mountains to hard labour on the prairies. The children eventually escape, but Uncle and Obasan survive only as she finds and fills her house with her past, and he escapes to the hilltop where the prairie seems to fade into his ancestral sea.

Aunt Emily struggles valiantly against this oppression, and forces her words on Naomi to ensure that the memory does not die, but her words are inadequate. They are powerless against the bureaucratic prose of power, the sentences carefully constructed to place human reality in safe categories, excluding the possibility of contact with lived experience. "The status of Mrs. Nakane has been carefully reviewed and it has been decided that she has retained her Canadian citizenship and therefore would be readmissible to Canada. However, the child is a national of Canada and as such is inadmissible. . . . It is assumed that Mrs. Nakane would not desire to come forward alone . . ." (p.213) The grammar carefully excludes any agency, and thus any human responsibility. The arbitrary categories of national and non-national are imposed on life, beyond the challenge of any words that try to express experience. Uncle and Obasan find only in silence the strength they need to give the children a future.

At the end of the novel, however, words break through both official indifference and protective silence. Naomi is finally given her grandmother's letter, written from Japan where the war had trapped her with Naomi's mother, and describing the horrors of the Nagasaki bombing which had finally destroyed them both. The greater horrors of destruction subsume the lesser horrors of slow death through exile and hardship. Yet, in the context of the novel, both arise from the same causes—the inability of people to accept each other, the fear of difference, the failure of a culture to unite people with their lands, the rejection of language in which the truth can be told. Ironically, however, the novel's strength and the tolerance that can arise from community gives grounds for hope that new societies like Canada have within their diversity the resource to show the world a way forward beyond division. Joy Kogawa has given voice to those whose silence kept alive this hope through the depths of their misery.

VI

In the twentieth century as in the sixteenth the favoured goal of the migrant is America, and now the United States of America, the true land of the Golden Mountain, the only country in the world where the people "saw the idea of Liberty so real that they made a statue of it" (Kingston, 1981). Even if the actual statue was given by the French, its ideal continues to flourish among those who are excluded, and who try every kind of legal and illegal trickery to come under its protection. Maxine Hong Kingston's first two books describe both the lengths to which Chinese migrants have gone to reach their destination and the conditions they have endured after their arrival. Their hopes, however, remain alive, even if they are expressed in rather less lofty terms than the Declaration of Independence: "The Gold Mountain was indeed free: no manners, no traditions, no wives" (p.62). This freedom, which excludes women and children, proves illusory even for the men, who find themselves tied to new forms of drudgery or bound to addictions of opium or gambling. Only those who accept their responsibilities for wives or families have a chance of realizing their dreams, either by returning with their savings to China or by bringing their families to America. In both cases, however, they remain torn between the dreams of the new world and the certainties of the old. Kingston's novels try to solve the twin problems of why the men from the narrator's ancestral village continually leave home in search of the Golden Mountain, and how they and their descendants become American.

Although Kingston writes of the generation of migrants who arrived in this century, and with the clash and contrast between the cultures of their homeland and their destination, her books start from the viewpoint of their American children, the "half-ghost Chinese." This is the generation represented by the two girls in the final chapter of *Woman Warrior* (1977). One, the narrator, has her tongue cut by her mother so that she may talk more freely, but then covers all her schoolwork in an opaque layer of black to hide its perceptions from everybody else. The other girl reads aloud the words of others, but refuses to speak any of her own. They are persecuted equally by the ghosts, the white people, who make them afraid to talk, and by their own people, the Chinese who refuse to reveal their secrets. The book closes with the story of T'sai Yen, the poetess kidnapped by barbarians who make her both warrior and concubine. The barbarians terrify their enemies with the death sounds of their weapons, but from these they also make music of cold perfection. T'sai Yen learns to make this music herself, and takes it back to her people. *Woman Warrior* and *Chinese Men* perform the reverse function. They translate the often harsh music of Chinese tradition into an English that gives the parents' voice back to the children, and so frees them to sing in the tongue that has become their own.

This translation of the experience of the earlier generation shows the price paid to obtain the treasure of the Golden Mountain. The cost falls particularly on the women, both those left at home and those brought out to help the men. These are the true heroes, the warriors, of her books. But the perspective of the children's generation also enables her to see the illusions within the American ideal, the way in which its professions of liberty make it at once the most sentimental, the most ruthless, and the most parochial of societies. Because this generation of American-Chinese want nothing more nor less than to be Americans but are at the same time seen as different by their fellow-citizens they are able to see America from both inside and out. Like the nisei in *Obasan*, they are perceptually bilingual. It is thus appropriate that the final story in *China Men* takes one of them back to east Asia for a tour of duty with the US Navy during the Vietnam war. His inability to enter into the lives of the Asians he encounters reveals his distance from them. He has become American, but by implication America can have no place in Asia until it learns the validity of his experience.

In both *The Woman Warrior* and *China Men* the essence of this experience is the change from a communal, rural culture in China to an individualistic, urban culture in America. The land of China was filled with hostile spirits, and its people constrained by the harsh necessities of a subsistence economy. Both tradition and social structure, however, ensured security and stability in this environment, albeit frequently at the cost of the individual. When, however, this tradition is separated from the context that generated it and translated to urban America, it loses its faculty of mediating between people and environment. The patriarchal family at the centre of the tradition becomes an isolated enclave, separating its members from the wider society rather than opening them to it. Father, who had been an honoured scholar in his village, is cheated of the product of his labour and becomes an angry drudge and tyrant. Mother, who had similarly earned a place of respect in her village as a doctor, shares his drudgery, but also becomes the strength that maintains the family as an island of security in a world populated by threatening white ghosts that tradition cannot contain.

Brave Orchid, the narrator's mother, is the hero of these cultural upheavals. She is the woman warrior of the stories that the Chinese parents stuff their American children's heads with before they can leave, "like the suitcases they jam-pack with homemade underwear" (p.82). These stories are filled with impossible combat against ghosts, the ghosts who contest the land of China with its human inhabitants, and the Europeans, the ghosts who walk the streets of America and threaten their Chinese neighbours. The woman warrior of legend is trained as a literal warrior who successfully leads armies into combat and overthrows a corrupt dynasty. Although she disguises herself as a man, she does not succeed by becoming like a man, but by combining in herself the strength of both men and women. The women who wage lonely battles in the stories of life in China and in San Francisco have to wage their battles within the space allowed for women. Some, like the one who, whether as a result of love or of rape is left uncertain, bears a child long after her husband has left for America is destroyed by the villagers. Brave Orchid wins her battles, becomes a doctor, brings healing to the villagers, until she is sent for by her husband and joins him in America, where she bears six children while maintaining the work of his laundry. Her stories keep alive for her and her children the China where she fought and won for herself a position that brought into unity modern science and a traditional culture. They in no way soften the harshness of this culture, with the rigidity and intolerance that manifest themselves in such practices as slavery and infanticide, but they relate this harshness to the conditions of survival in a subsistence economy. Further, despite its narrowness, they reveal the culture as based on reason and permeable to new ideas. When Brave Orchid returns as a doctor to her village, she is borne in a sedan chair and welcomed with garlands and cymbals. When, in a later period, the Communist "barefoot doctors" arrive, they "wear a blue plainness dotted with one red Mao button" (p.73). To each age its symbols, but the one honoured by Brave Orchid is the one that brings the past into the future. Yet the Communists, too, write their manuals on how to combat ghosts. It is in America that rationalism shatters unity, and even the Chinese migrants come to prey on each other (p.10). But Brave Orchid is generous enough to attribute this to the failures of the Chinese character. The reader may see it as the consequence of a culture that has failed to put down its roots in the new country. Brave Orchid's stories provide the soil from which the new generation may yet draw sustenance.

The Chinese people in these two novels maintain their lives in the face of the enormous racial prejudice endemic in American and other European Pacific societies until late in the twentieth century. Her most recent novel. *Tripmaster Monkey: His Fake Book* (1989) is set at a time when these prejudices seemed to be dying, the 1960s, and takes as its protagonist Wittman Ah Sing, a Chinese American whose manhood has almost been destroyed by prejudice at school but who sees himself as nothing less than an American, citizen of a country whose destiny is to fulfill the dream of all traditions. As "Tripmaster" he conducts this dream as a kind of psychedelic trip, but as Monkey, the venturesome trickster who in Chinese legend finds his way to the Golden Mountain of the west in India, he extends his journey to an America where everything is still possible. The vehicle of both dreams is a vast drama production that interweaves the whole of Chinese legend and history with the stories of Europe's westward expansion. The drama creates a new America that exists both within the mind and as a potential inherent in historical America. Its content is based on the Chinese novel of *Monkey* (Wu, 1942), but the protagonist's search for eternal life takes him through Californian existentialism rather than the Buddhist paths to enlightenment.

Unlike Kingston's two earlier novels, *Tripmaster Monkey* occupies an inner world constituted by words that signify no clear place in the outer world. Certainly, the action is said to take place in San Francisco, and the opening scene, like later journeys and performances, is precisely located. But, whereas the characters and events of *China Men* and *Warrior Women* are conditioned by historical and geographic necessity, those of *Tripmaster Monkey*, like those of *Monkey*, seem to occupy purely mythic space. The party at its centre apparently takes place in Oakland, and certainly belongs to the sixties, but its importance is psychedelic. The two chapters of the novel that are devoted to it tell the story of people on a drug trip, a film made from a pack of cards, the perpetual doubling of characters in a comic book, several readings of a possibly apocryphal film, an earlier trip to the islands of the Pacific, and the play of Monkey and the Havoc Monster. The only contingent events are the fight between Wittman and his host and Wittman's marriage, and even these are qualified as possibly transient states of consciousness. The events, like the whole novel, are not about history as it happens, but about history at the ultimate point where it emerges into consciousness, whether by the multiplication of people or by the multiplication of the psychic states of the one person. Both are embodiments of the "multitudinous ways of being human" (p.103). Yet finally, these ways remain abstract, unrealizable because they are conceived only in the words of artists whose work is words but who refuse to "work for money" (p.17), and whose only contact with the land is the Golden Gate Park, sanctuary of con-men and drop-outs. The man of power may pose, but Wittman and his friends do not win. Despite his dismissal, he remains essentially an employee of the toy department of a society where commerce has replaced productive work.

VII

The European invasion of the Pacific was inspired by the vision of a new Eden that was destroyed by the innate vice of the invaders. The Asian extension across the Pacific was produced by much more mundane motives, but its freedom from ideology has allowed a greater variety of human potential. As yet, this is still to be realized. Frank Chin's work shows how great the problem remains of recognizing the descendants of Asians as part of the American dream. Amy Tan shows the difficulty of comprehending the ostensible success of the migrants with the pain of their origins. Writers like Tim O'Brien show the opposite problem, the difficulty Caucasian Americans have in shedding their cultural blinkers in order to understand what they are doing in carrying the American dream across to the other side of the Pacific. Yet this interaction of America and Asia across the Pacific is simply the final stage of the historical process that began with Columbus. The European culture that has unified the globe has yet to learn to enter into mutual relationships with the lands it has subdued. Asian cultures maintain continuity at the cost of community. The native cultures that retain their connection with the land have been marginalized. The work of writers from these three traditions offers us the possibility of bringing them together to realize the human potential they jointly contain. The alternative is ecological and human disaster, for there is no going back to their separate truths.

BIBLIOGRAPHY

General

Amirthanayagam and Harrex, 1981. Guy Amirthanayagam and S.C. Harrex (eds.). *Only Connect: Literary Perspectives East and West*. Adelaide and Honolulu: Centre for Research in the New Literatures in English/East-West Centre, 1981.

Ashcroft, Griffiths and Tiffin, 1989. Bill Ashcroft, Gareth Griffiths and Helen Tiffin. *The Empire Writes Back*. London/New York: Routledge, 1989.

Bakhtin, 1981. M.M. Bakhtin. *The Dialogue Imagination: Four Essays*, trans. Caryl Emerson and Michael Holquist. Austin: University of Texas Press, 1981.

——, 1984. M.M. Bakhtin. *Rabelais and His World*, trans. Helene Iswolsky. Bloomington: Indiana University Press, 1984. [1965]

Barsh, 1990. Russell Barsh. "Indigenous People, Racism and the Environment." Melbourne: *Meanjin*, vol. 49, no. 4, Summer 1990, 723–30.

Barthes, 1983. Roland Barthes. *Barthes: Selected Writings*. Edited and with an introduction by Susan Sontag. London: Fontana/Collins, 1983. [New York: Hill and Wang, 1982].

Batman, 1985. Batman, Richard. *The Outer Coast*. San Diego/New York/London: Harcourt Brace Jovanovich, 1985. The European discovery and settlement of California and the Pacific west coast of North America.

Berman, 1982. Marshall Berman. *All that Is Solid Melts into Air*. New York: Simon & Schuster, 1982.

Berndt, 1989. Ronald M. and Catherine H. Berndt. *The Speaking Land: Myth and Story in Aboriginal Australia*. Ringwood, Vic.: Penguin Australia, 1989.

Carroll, 1892. John Carroll, ed. *Intruders in the Bush: The Australian Quest for Identity*. Melbourne/New York: OUP, 1982

Carter, 1989. Paul Carter, *The Road to Botany Bay: An Essay in Spatial History*. Ringwood, Vic.: Penguin Australia, London/Boston: Faber and Faber, 1987

Coetzee, 1988. J.M. Coetzee, *White Writing: On the Culture of Letters in South Africa*. New Haven, Conn: Yale University Press, 1988.

Columbus, Christopher.
————, 1892. Paul Leicester Ford, ed. *Writings of Christopher Columbus.* New York: Webster, 1892.
————, 1960. *The Journal of Christopher Columbus.* Trans. Cecil Jane, revised and annotated by L.A. Vigneras with an Appendix by R.A. Skelton. London: Anthony Blond and the Orion Press, 1960. Contains "The Journal of Christopher Columbus," from the abstract by Bartolomé de las Casas [1558], and "The Letter of Christopher Columbus describing the results of his first voyage" [1493].
————, 1987. *The Log of Christopher Columbus.* Trans. Robert H. Fuson. Camden, Maine: International Marine Publishing, 1987; references to paperback edition, 1992.
————, 1989. *The* Diario *of Christopher Columbus's First Voyage to America 1492–1493.* Transcribed and translated into English with notes and a concordance of the Spanish, by Oliver Dunn and James E. Kelley, Jr. Norman and London: University of Oklahoma Press, 1989.
————, 1990. *To America and Around the World: The Logs of Christopher Columbus and Ferdinand Magellan.* Boston: Branden Publishing Company, 1990. Contents include *The Journal of the first Voyage of Christopher Columbus,* translated by Clements S. Marham for the Hakluyt Society, 1893.
Dampier, 1699. William Dampier. *A Voyage to New Holland*: the English voyage of discovery to the South Seas in 1699. Edited with an introduction by James Spencer. Gloucester, UK: Sutton, 1981.
Davis, 1984. David Brion Davis. *Slavery and Human Progress.* New York and Oxford: OUP, 1984.
————, 1990. "Slaves in Islam": review of Bernard Lewis, *Race and Slavery in the Middle East: An Historical Enquiry,* OUP, in *NYRB,* 11 Oct 90, pp.35–39.
Derrida, 1976. Jacques Derrida. *Of Grammatology.* Trans. Gayatri Chakravorty Spivak. Baltimore: John Hopkins University Press, 1976.
————, 1978. *Writing and Difference.* Trans. Alan Bass. Chicago: University of Chicago Press, 1978.
————, 1987. "The Laws of Reflection: in admiration," in Jacques Derrida and Mustapha Tlili, eds. *For Nelson Mandela.* New York: Seaver Books, 1987.
Diffie, 1977. Bailie W. Diffie and George D. Winius. *Foundations of the Portuguese Empire, 1415–1580.* Minneapolis: University of Minnesota Press, 1977.
Dodge, 1976. Ernest S. Dodge. *Islands and Empires: Western Impact on the Pacific and East Asia.* Minneapolis: University of Minnesota Press: 1976.

Drinnan, 1980. Richard Drinnon. *Facing West: The Metaphysics of Indian-hating and Empire-building.* Minneapolis: University of Minnesota Press, 1980. A history of white attitudes toward the native inhabitants of North America.

Everson, 1976. William Everson. *Archetype West: The Pacific Coast as a Literary Region.* Berkeley: Oyez, 1976.

Fang, 1990. Fang Lizhi. "The Chinese Amnesia." *NYRB,* 27 Sep. 1990.

Fiedler, 1960. Leslie A. Fiedler. *Love and Death in the American Novel.* New York: Criterion Books, 1960.

———, 1977. *A Fiedler Reader.* New York: Stein and Day, 1977. Includes "Come Back to the Raft Ag'in, Huck Honey," first published in *Partisan Review,* and "The Novel in America," from *Love and Death in the American Novel.*

Franklin, 1979. Wayne Franklin. *Discoverers, Explorers and Settlers: The Diligent Writers of North America.* Chicago: University of Chicago Press, 1979.

Furber, 1976. Holden Furber. *Rival Empires of Trade in the Orient, 1600–1800.* Minneapolis: University of Minnesota Press, 1976.

Genovese, 1976. Eugene D. Genovese. *Roll, Jordan, Roll: The World the Slaves Made.* New York: Random House, Vintage Books edition, 1976.

Greenblatt, 1991. Stephen Greenblatt. *Marvellous Possessions: The Wonder of the New World.* Chicago and Oxford: University of Chicago Press/OUP, 1991. Discusses *inter alia* the function of literacy in supporting the Europeans' conviction of their own superiority, and of perceptions of the marvellous as complementing the doctrine of *terra nullius* to justify European possession of the Americas.

Hakluyt, 1589. Richard Hakluyt. *The Principall Navigations, Voiages, Traffiques & Discoveries of the English Nation. . . .* Facsimile edition, Cambridge, UK, for the Hakluyt Society, London, and the Peabody Museum, Salem. Two volumes.

———, 1927. *The Principall Voyages Traffiques & Discoveries of the English Nation made by sea or overland to the remote and farthest distant quarters of the earth at any time within the compass of these 1600 years,* second edition [1589–1600]. London and Toronto: Dent; New York, Dutton, 1927, Ten volumes. The Virginia voyages are contained in volume 6, and references are to this volume unless otherwise indicated.

Hartz, 1964. Louis Hartz. *The Founding of New Societies.* New York, 1964.

Jones, 1964. Howard Mumford Jones. *O Strange New World: American Culture: The Formative Years.* New York: Viking Press, 1967 [1952, 1954, 1964].

Kay, 1967. F. George Kay. *The Shameful Trade.* South Brunswick and New York: A.S. Barnes, 1967. A narrative history of negro slavery.

Killam, 1969. G.D. Killam. *The Novels of Chinua Achebe.* New York: Africana Publishing Corporation, 1969.

Leys, 1990. Simon Leys, "The Art of Interpreting Nonexistent Inscriptions Written in Invisible Ink on a Blank Page." *NYRB*, 11 Oct. 1990. (Review of Laszlo Ladany, *The Communist Party of China and Marxism, 1929–1985: A Self-Portrait.* Hoover Institution Press.) McDermott, 1966.

McDermott, 1965. John J. McDermott. "The American Angle of Vision." Two parts. *Crosscurrents,* Spring and and Fall, 1965.

Markus, 1975. Andrew Markus. *Fear and Hatred: Purifying Australia and California 1850–1901.* Sydney: Hale Iremonger, 1979.

Marx, 1930. Karl Marx. *Capital.* Vol. 1, translated by Eden and Cedar Paul. London: Dent, 1930.

———, 1959. Karl Marx and Friedrich Engels. *Basic Writings on Politics and Philosophy.* Various translators, edited by Lewis S. Feuer. New York: Doubleday: 1959.

Marx, 1964. Leo Marx. *The Machine in the Garden: Technology and the Pastoral Ideal in America.* New York: OUP, 1964.

Matthews, 1962. John Pengwerne Matthews. *Tradition in Exile: A Comparative Study of Social Influences on the Development of Australian and Canadian Poetry in the Nineteenth Century.* Toronto: University of Toronto Press, 1963.

Naipaul, 1969. V.S. Naipaul. *The Loss of El Dorado.* Harmondsworth: Penguin Books, 1969.

———, 1988. *The Enigma of Arrival.* New York: Vintage, 1988.

Phillips, 1958. A.A. Phillips. *The Australian Tradition: Studies in a Colonial Culture.* Melbourne: Cheshire, 1958.

Piedra, 1989. Jose Piedra. "The Game of Critical Arrival," *Diacritics,* Spring 1989, 34–61.

Quinn, 1973. David B. and Alison M. Quinn, eds. *Virginia Voyages* from Hakluyt. *London: Oxford University Press,* 1973.

Rhys, 1968. Jean Rhys. *Wide Sargasso Sea.* Harmondsworth: Penguin, 1968 [1966].

Ricoeur, 1981. Paul Ricoeur. *Hermenuetics and the Human Sciences: Essays on Language, Action and Interpretation.* Edited, translated and introduced by John B. Thompson. Cambridge: CUP; Paris, Edition de la Maison des Sciences de l'Homme, 1981.

Smith, 1986. *European Vision and the South Pacific.* Second edition. Sydney: Harper & Row, no date (1985?)

Spate, 1983. O.H.K. Spate. *Monopolists and Freebooters (The Pacific Since Magellan;* vol. 2). Canberra: ANU Press, 1983.

———, 1988. *Paradise Found and Lost (The Pacific Since Magellan;* vol. 3. London: Routledge, 1988.

Thompson, 1981. *See* Ricoeur, 1981.

Tiffin, H., 1982. Helen Tiffin. "The Metaphor of Anancy in Caribbean Literature." In Robert Sellick (ed.). *Myth and Metaphor*. Adelaide: Centre for Research in the New Literatures in English, 1982.

Todorov, 1984. Tzvetan Todorov. *The Conquest of America: The Question of the Other*. Translated by Richard Howard. New York: Harper, 1984.

Turner, 1947. Frederick Jackson Turner. *The Frontier in American History*. New York, 1947.

Turner, 1980. Frederick Turner. *Beyond Geography: The Western Spirit Against the Wilderness*. New York: Viking Press, 1980.

Wieland, 1988. James Wieland. *The Ensphering Mind*. Washington, D.C.: Three Continents Press, 1988.

Renaissance fiction:

Camoens. Luis de Camoens. *The Lusiads*. Harmondsworth: Penguin.

Cervantes. Miguel de Cervantes, *The Adventures of Don Quixote*, trans. Michael Cohen. Harmondsworth: Penguin.

Anthologies:

Allen, 1989. Paula Gunn Allen, ed. *Spider Woman's Daughters: Traditional Tales and Contemporary Writing by Native American Women*. New York: Fawcett Columbine, 1989.

Beier, 1973. Ulli Beier (ed.) *Black Writing from New Guinea*. St. Lucia: University of Queensland Press, 1973.

——, 1980. Ulli Beier (ed.). *Voices of Independence: Black Writing from Papua New Guinea*. St. Lucia: University of Queensland Press, 1980.

Bowering, 1984. George Bowering, ed. *The Contemporary Canadian Poem Anthology*. Toronto: Coach House Press, 1984.

Brink and Coetzee, 1986. Andre Brink and J.M. Coetzee. *A Land Apart: A South African Reader*. London: Faber, 1986.

Brown and Bennett, 1982. Russell Brown and Donna Bennett, eds. *An Anthology of Canadian Literature in English*. Toronto: OUP, 1982.

Chinweizu, 1988. Chinweizu, ed. *Voices from Twentieth-Century Africa: Griots and Towncriers*. London: Faber and Faber, 1988.

Davis, 1990. Jack Davis, Stephen Muecke, Mudrooroo Narogin, Adam Shoemaker (eds.). *Paperbark: A Collection of Black Australian Writings*. St. Lucia: UQP, 1990.

Goodwin and Lawson, 1990. Ken Goodwin and Alan Lawson, eds. *The Macmillan Anthology of Australian Literature*. Melbourne: Macmillan, 1990.

King, 1990. Thomas King, ed. *All My Relations: An Anthology of Contemporary Canadian Native Fiction*. Toronto: McClelland & Stewart, 1990.

Kramer, 1985. Leonie Kramer. *My Country: Australian Poetry and Short Stories, Two Hundred Years.* Two volumes. Sydney: Landsdowne Press, 1985.

Kramer and Mitchell, 1985. Leonie Kramer and Adrian Mitchell, eds. *Oxford Anthology of Australian Literature.* Melbourne: OUP, 1985.

Lerner, 1990. Andrea Lerner, ed. *Dancing on the Rim of the World: An Anthology of Contemporary Northwest Native American Writing.* Tucson, Arizona: Sun Tracks and The University of Arizona Press, 1990.

Malan, 1988. Robin Malan, ed. *Ourselves in Southern Africa: An Anthology of Southern African Writing.* New York: St. Martin's Press, 1988.

Rothenberg, 1968. *Technicians of the Sacred: A Range of Poetries from Africa, America, Asia and Oceania.* New York: Doubleday, 1968.

———, 1972. *Shaking the Pumpkin: traditional poetry of the North American Indians.* New York, Doubleday, 1972.

Wendt, 1980. Albert Wendt. *Lali: A Pacific Anthology.* Auckland: Longman Paul, 1980.

Wong, 1989. Diane Yen-Mei Wong, chief editor for the Asian Women United of California. *Making Waves: An Anthology of Writings by and about Asian American Women.* Boston: Beacon Press, 1989.

Africa: Fiction

Achebe, 1959. Chinua Achebe. *Things Fall Apart.* New York: Obolensky, 1959.

———, 1987. *Anthills of the Savannah.* London: Heinemann, 1987.

Achebe and Innes, 1985. Achebe, Chinua and C.L. Innes (eds.). *African Short Stories.* London: Heinemann, 1985.

Brink, 1976. Andre Brink. *An Instant in the Wind.* London: Fontana, 1983 [1976].

———, 1988. *States of Emergency.* London: Faber, 1988.

Brink and Coetzee, 1986. Andre Brink and J.M. Coetzee. *A Land Apart: A South African Reader.* London: Faber, 1986.

Coetzee, 1980. J.M. Coetzee. *Waiting for the Barbarians.* London: Secker & Warburg, 1980.

———, 1983. *Life & Times of Michael K.* London, Secker & Warburg, 1983.

Conrad, 1942. Joseph Conrad. *A Conrad Argosy.* New York: Doubleday, Doran, 1942.

Fagunwa, 1982. D.O. Fagunwa. *Forest of a Thousand Demons.* Trans. Wole Soyinka. New York: Random House, 1982.

Ike, 1970. Vincent Chukwuemenka Ike. *The Naked Gods.* London: Harvll Press, 1970.

Malan, 1988. Robin Malan (ed.). *Ourselves in Southern Africa: An Anthology of Southern African Writing.* New York: St. Martin's Press, 1988.

Matshoba, 1979. Mtutuzeli Matshoba. *Call Me Not a Man.* Harlow, England: Longman, 1979.

Mutwa, 1969. Credo Vusumazulu Mutwa. *My People.* London: Anthony Blond, 1969. Compiled from *Indaba, My Children* and *Africa is My Witness.*

Schreiner, 1890. Olive Schreiner. *The Story of an African Farm.* New York: A.L. Burt Company, no date. (1890?) By Ralph Iron (Olive Schreiner). With a preface by the author, signed R. Iron.

———, 1968. *Olive Schreiner: A Selection.* Edited by Uys Krige. Cape Town: OUP, 1968.

———, 1973. *A Track to the Water's Edge: The Olive Schreiner Reader.* Edited by Howard Thurman. New York: Harper and Row, 1973.

Soyinka, 1972. Wole Soyinka. *The Man Died: Prison Notes.* New York: Farrar, Straus and Giroux, 1972.

———, 1981. *Ake: The Years of Childhood.* New York: Random House, 1981.

Tutuola, 1953. Amos Tutuola. *The Palm-Wine Drunkard.* New York: Grove Press, 1953.

———, 1967. *Ajaiyi and His Inherited Poverty.* London: Faber, 1967.

———, 1987. *Pauper, Brawler and Slanderer.* London: Faber, 1987.

Asia Pacific

Abdullah, 1965. Mena Abdullah, with Ray Matthew. *The Time of the Peacock.* Sydney: Collins/Angus & Robertson, 1992 (Forthcoming). [1965].

Baratham, 1988. Gopal Baratham. *People Make You.* Singapore: Times Books International, 1988.

Castro, 1983. Brian Castro. *Birds of Passage* Sydney: Allen & Unwin, 1984 [1983].

Chin, 1991. Frank Chin. *Donald Duk.* Minneapolis: Coffee House Press, 1991.

Joaquin, 1972. Nick Joaquin. *Tropical Gothic.* St. Lucia, Q.: University of Queensland Press, 1972.

Jose, 1962. F. Sionil Jose. *The Pretenders.* Manila: Solidaridad, 1962. (References to sixth edition, 1987.)

———, 1978. *Tree.* Manila: Solidaridad, 1978, 1988.

———, 1979. *My Brother, My Executioner.* Manila: Solidaridad, 1988. [1979]

———, 1983. *Mass.* Manila: Solidaridad, 1983. [First edition in Dutch: 1982].

———, 1984. *Po-on.* Manila: Solidaridad, 1984, 1987.

Kingston, 1975. Maxine Hong Kingston. *The Woman Warrior.* London: Picador/Pan Books, 1981 [1975].

———, 1977. *China Men.* London: Picador/Pan Books, 1981. [1977]

————, 1989. *Tripmaster Monkey*. London: Picador/Pan Books, 1989.

Kogawa, 1981. Joy Kokagawa. *Obasan*. Markham, Ontario: Penguin, 1983 [1981].

Lee Kok Liang, 1981. Lee Kok Liang. "Dumb, Dumb, by a Bee Stung." In Amirthanayagam and Harrex, 1981, pp. 227–38.

Lim, 1989. Catherine Lim. *O Singapore; Stories in Celebration*. Singapore: Times Books International, 1989.

Morales, 1989. Alfredo T. Morales (ed.). *F. Sionil José and His Fiction: The Filipino's Journey to Justice and Nationhood*. Quezon City: Vera-Reyes, 1989.

Sharrad, 1981. "The Third Alternative: Nick Joaquin's Vision." In Amirthanayagam and Harrex, 1981.

Tan, 1989. Amy Tan. *The Joy Luck Club*. New York: Ballantine, 1990 [1989].

————, 1991. *The Kitchen God's Wife*. London: Harper/Collins, 1991.

Wu, 1942. Wu Ch'eng-en. *Monkey*. Translated by Arthur Waley. London: Allen & Unwin, 1979 [1942].

Australia

Astley, 1974. Thea Astley. *A Kindness Cup*. Melbourne: Nelson, 1974.

————, 1987. *It's Raining in Mango*. Ringwood: Penguin, 1989 [1987]. (see also Bibliography: Pacific)

Baynton, 1980. Barbara Baynton. *Barbara Baynton* (Portable Australian Authors), edited by Sally Krimmer and Alan Lawson. St. Lucia, Queensland: UQP, 1980. Includes *Bush Studies* (1902) and *Human Toll* (1907).

Berndt, 1989. Ronald M. and Catherine H. Berndt. *The Speaking Land: Myth and Story in Aboriginal Australia*. Ringwood: Penguin Books, 1989.

Castro, 1983. Brian Castro. *Birds of Passage*. Sydney: Allen & Unwin, 1984. [1983]

————, 1991. *Double-Wolf*. Sydney, Allen & Unwin, 1991.

Clark, 1962. C.M.H. (Manning) Clark. *A History of Australia*. Vol. I. Melbourne: MUP, 1962.

————, 1968–87. Vols. II–VI.

Clarke, 1874. Marcus Clarke. *For the Term of His Natural Life*. Melbourne 1884. Available in *Marcus Clarke* (Portable Australian Authors), edited by Michael Wilding. St. Lucia, Queensland: UQP, 1976. Original serial version, Melbourne 1870–72, available as *His Natural Life*, edited by Stephen Murray-Smith. Ringwood, Vic.: Penguin, 1970.

Critchett, 1990. Jan Critchett. *A "Distant Field of Murder": Western District Frontiers, 1834–38*. Melbourne: MUP, 1990.

Davis, 1990. Jack Davis, Stephen Muecke, Mudrooroo Narogin, Adam Shoemaker (eds.). *Paperbark: A Collection of Black Australian writings.* St. Lucia: UQP, 1990.

Franklin, 1936. Miles Franklin. *All That Swagger.* Sydney: Angus & Robertson, 1936.

———, 1980. *My Brilliant Career.* Sydney: Angus & Robertson, 1980 [1901].

Hall, 1983. Rodney Hall. *Just Relations.* New York: Viking, 1983 [1982].

Herbert, 1938. Xavier Herbert, *Capricornia.* Sydney: Angus & Robertson, 1938.

———, 1975. *Poor Fellow My Country.* Sydney: Collins, 1975.

Hodge and Mishra, 1990. Bob Hodge and Vijay Mishra. *Dark Side of the Dream: Australian Literature and the Postcolonial Mind.* Sydney: Allen & Unwin, 1990.

Janson, 1990. Susan Janson and Stuart Macintyre (eds.). *Through White Eyes.* Sydney: Allen & Unwin, 1990.

Johnson, 1965. Colin Johnson. (Mudrooroo Narogin). *Wild Cat Falling.* Sydney: Angus & Robertson, 1965.

———, 1979. *Long Live Sandawara.* South Yarra: Hyland House, 1979.

———, 1983. *Doctor Wooreddy's Prescription for Enduring the Ending of the World.* South Yarra: Hyland House, 1987.

Koch, 1974. Christopher Koch. *The Boys in the Island.* Revised edition. Sydney: Angus & Robertson, 1974 [1958].

———, 1985. *The Doubleman.* London: Chatto & Windus, 1985.

Lawson, 1972. Henry Lawson. *Henry Lawson: Short Stories and Sketches 1888–1922,* edited by Colin Roderick. Sydney: Angus & Robertson, 1972.

Lindsay, 1982. Jack Lindsay. *Life Rarely Tells.* Ringwood, Vic.: Penguin, 1982. Contains *Life Rarely Tells, The Roaring Twenties* and *Fanrolico and After.* Published separately, London: Bodley Head, 1958–62.

Lines, 1991. William J. Lines. *Taming the Great South Land: A History of the Conquest of Nature in Australia.* Sydney: Allen & Unwin, 1991.

McLaren, 1989. John McLaren. *Australian Literature: An Historical Introduction.* Melbourne: Longman Cheshire, 1989.

McQueen, 1989. James McQueen. *Hook's Mountain.* Ringwood, Vic.: Penguin Australia, 1989 [1982].

Malouf, 1978. David Malouf. *An Imaginary Life.* London: Chatto & Windus, 1978.

———, 1984. *Harland's Half Acre.* Harmondsworth: Penguin, 1984.

Matthews, 1987. Brian Matthews. *Louisa.* Melbourne: McPhee Gribble, 1987.

Penton, 1934. Brian Penton. *The Landtakers.* Sydney: Angus & Robertson, 1963 [1934].

Porter, 1963. *The Watcher on the Cast-Iron Balcony: An Australian Autobiography.* London: Faber, 1963.

Prichard, 1929. Katharine Susannah Prichard. *Coonardoo: The Well in the Shadow*. London: Cape, 1929.

————, 1956. *Working Bullocks*. Sydney: Angus & Robertson, 1956 [1926].

Pybus, 1991. Cassandra Pybus. *Community of Thieves*. Port Melbourne, Vic.: Heinemann, 1991.

Reynolds, 1982. Henry Reynolds. *The Other Side of the Frontier*. Townsville, Q: History Department, James Cook University of North Queensland, 1981.

————, 1987. *Frontier: Aborigines, Settlers and the Land*. Sydney: Allen & Unwin, 1987.

————, 1990. *With the White People*. Ringwood: Penguin, 1990.

Richardson, 1930. Henry Handel Richardson (pseud. of Ethel Florence Richardson). *The Fortunes of Richard Mahony*. London: Heinemann, 1930 [1917, 1925, 1929].

Robson, 1963. Lloyd Robson. "The Historical Basis for *The Term of His Natural Life*." *Australian Literary Studies*, vol. 1, no. 2, December 1963, 104–121.

Rolls, 1984. Eric Rolls. *They All Ran Wild*. Sydney: Angus & Robertson, 1984 [1969].

————, 1984b. *A Million Wild Acres*. Ringwood, Vic.: Penguin, 1984 [1981].

Shoemaker, 1989. Adam Shoemaker. *Black Words White Page: Aboriginal Literature 1929–1988*. St Lucia: UQP, 1989.

Stow, 1968. Randolph Stow. *The Merry-go-Round in the Sea*. Harmondsworth: Penguin, 1968 [1965].

Tennant, 1954. Kylie Tennant. *The Battlers*. London: Macmillan, 1954.

————, 1986. *The Missing Heir* (autobiography). South Melbourne: Macmillan, 1986.

Ward, 1958. Russell Ward. *The Australian Legend*. Melbourne: OUP, 1958.

Watson, 1984. Don Watson. *Caledonia Australis: Scottish Highlanders on the Frontier of Australia*. Sydney: Collins, 1984.

White, 1976. Patrick White. *A Fringe of Leaves*. London: Cape, 1976.

Wilde, 1988. W.H. Wilde. *Courage a Grace: A Biography of Dame Mary Gilmore*. Carlton, Vic.: MUP, 1988.

Canada

Atwood, 1972. Margaret Atwood. *Survival: A Thematic Guide to Canadian Literature*. Toronto: Anansi, 1979 [1972].

Birney, 1966. Earle Birney. *Selected Poems, 1940–66*. Toronto: McClelland & Stewart, 1966.

Bowering, 1980. George Bowering. *Burning Water*. Toronto: General Publishing, 1983 [1980].

Craven, 1974. Margaret Craven. *I Heard the Owl Call My Name*. London: Pan Books, 1974 [1967].

Frye, 1972. Northrop Frye. *The Bush Garden: Essays on the Canadian Imagination*. Toronto: Anansi, 1972. (?)

Green and Sylvestre, 1967. H. Gordon Green and Guy Sylvestre. *A Century of Canadian Literature*. Toronto: Ryerson Press, 1967.

Grove, 1957. Frederick P. Grove. *Over Prairie Trails*. Toronto: McClelland & Stewart, 1957.

———, 1961. *The Master of the Mill*. Toronto: McClelland & Stewart, 1961.

———, 1966. *Settlers of the Marsh*. Toronto: McClelland & Stewart, 1966.

Harlow, 1972. Robert Harlow. *Scann*. Toronto: McClelland & Stewart, 1977 [1972].

Hodgins, 1977. *The Invention of the World*. Toronto, 1978 [1977].

———, 1990. *Innocent Cities*. Toronto: McClelland & Stewart/St. Lucia: UQP, 1990.

King, 1990. Thomas King, ed. *All My Relations: An Anthology of Contemporary Canadian Native Fiction*. Toronto: McClelland & Stewart, 1990.

Klinck and Watters, 1966. Carl Klinck and Reginald Watters (eds.). *Canadian Anthology*, revised edition. Toronto: Gage, 1966.

Leacock, 1922. Stephen Leacock. *Sunshine Sketches of a Little Town*. New York: Dodd, Mead, 1922 [1912].

MacLennan, 1961. Hugh MacLennan. *Seven Rivers of Canada*. Toronto: Macmillan, 1961.

Marlatt, 1972. *Steveston*. Vancouver: Talonbooks, 1972. Photographs by Robert Minden.

———, 1984. *Steveston*. Second edition. Edmonton: Longspoon Press, 1984.

———, 1988. *Ana Historic*. Toronto: Coach House Press, 1988.

Mowatt, 1980. Farley Mowatt. *People of the Deer*. Toronto: McClelland & Stewart/Bantam, 1980 [1975].

Pratt, 1940. E.J. Pratt. *Brebeuf and His Brethren*. Toronto: Macmillan, 1940.

———, 1989. *Complete Poems*. Toronto: University of Toronto Press, 1989.

Skvorecky, 1985. Josef Skvorecky. *The Engineer of Human Souls*, translated by Paul Wilson. London: Chatto & Windus/The Hogarth Press, 1985.

Thomas, 1988. Audrey Thomas. *Goodbye, Harold, Good Luck*. Markham, Ontario: Penguin, 1988.

Welch, 1974. James Welch. *Winter in the Blood*. New York: Penguin, 1986 [1974].

Wiebe, 1972. Rudy Wiebe (ed.). *Stories from Western Canada*. Toronto: Macmillan of Canada, 1972.

New Zealand

Belich, 1988. James Bellich. *The New Zealand Wars and the Victorian Interpretation of Racial Conflict.* Auckland: Penguin, 1988.

Davin, 1981. Dan Davin. *Selected Stories.* Wellington/London: Victoria University Press/Robert Hale, 1981.

Evans, 1990. Patrick Evans. *The Penguin History of New Zealand Literature.* Auckland: Penguin, 1990.

Gee, 1983. Maurice Gee, *Sole Survivor.* London and Boston: Faber, 1983.

———, 1986. Maurice Gee, *Collected Stories.* Auckland: Penguin NZ, 1986.

Hulme, Keri. *The Bone People.* Wellington: Spiral, 1983.

Ihimaera, Witi. *The Matriarch.* Auckland: Pan Books, 1988 [1986].

Morrieson, 1976. Ronald Hugh Morrieson. *The Scarecrow.* Auckland: Heinemann, 1976.

Sinclair, 1988. Keith Sinclair. *A History of New Zealand.* Revised edition, Auckland: Penguin, 1988.

Sturm, 1991. Terry Sturm (ed.). *The Oxford History of New Zealand Literature in English.* Auckland: OUP, 1991.

Wedde, 1986. Ian Wedde. *Symmes Hole.* London and Boston: Faber, 1986/ Auckland: Penguin, 1986.

Pacific

Astley, 1968. Thea Astley. *A Boat Load of Home Folk.* Ringwood, Vic.: 1983 [1968].

———, 1985. *Beachmasters.* New York: Penguin, 1988.

Baital, 1976. Jim Baital. *Tali.* In Mike Greicus (ed.), *Three Short Novels from Papua New Guinea.* Auckland: Longman Paul, 1976.

Becke, undated. A. Grove Day, ed. *South Sea Supercargo.* Brisbane: Jacaranda; Honolulu: University of Hawaii Press, undated. Selected stories of Louis Becke, with introduction by the editor.

Crocombe, 1982. Ron Crocombe and Ahmed Ali (eds.) *Politics in Melanesia.* Suva: Institute of Pacific Studies, University of the South Pacific, 1982.

Daws, 1980. Gavan Daws. *A Dream of Islands: Voyages of Discovery in the South Seas.* Brisbane: Jacaranda; New York: Norton, 1980.

Dodge, 1976. Ernest S. Dodge. *Islands and Empires: Western Impact on the Pacific and East Asia.* Minneapolis: University of Minnesota Press; Oxford: OUP, 1976.

Eri, 1970. Vincent Eri. *The Crocodile.* Milton, Q.: Jacaranda, 1970.

Hau'ofa, 1983. Epeli Hau'ofa. *Tales of the Tikongs.* Auckland: Penguin, 1988 [1983].

Kelley, 1966. Celsus Kelley, trans. and ed. *La Austrialia del Espiritu Santo: the journal of Fray Martin de Munilla O.F.M. and other documents relating to the voyage of Pedro Fernandez de Quiros to the South Sea (1605–1606) and the Franciscan Missionary Plan (1617–1627).* Two volumes. Cambridge, UK: at the University Press for the Hakluyt Society, 1966.

Kituai, 1976. August Kituai. *The Flight of a Villager.* In Mike Greicus (ed.), *Three Short Novels from Papua New Guinea.* Auckland: Longman Paul, 1976.

Melville, 1960. *The Shorter Novels of Herman Melville,* introduced by Raymond Weaver. New York: Premier Books, Fawcett World Library, 1960. [1928]

———, 1961. *Moby Dick, or the White Whale.* New York: New American Library, 1961 [1851].

Mishra, 1978. Vijay Mishra. "Indo-Indian Fiction and the Girmit Ideology." In Tiffin, C., ed., 1978.

———, 1990. "Little India." Melbourne: *Meanjin,* vol. 49, no.4, summer 1990, 607–18.

Nandan, 1978. Satendra Nandan. "Beyond Colonialism: The Artist as Healer." In Tiffin, C. (ed.), 1978.

———, 1990. "Nandi." Melbourne: *Meanjin,* vol. 49, no.4, summer 1990, 619–633.

———, 1991. *The Wounded Sea.* Sydney: Simon & Schuster/New Endeavour Press, 1991.

Pillai, 1980. Raymond Pillai. *The Celebration: Collection of Short Stories.* Suva: Mana Publications and the South Pacific Creative Arts Society, 1980.

Sargeant, 1982. "The Problem of Language and Urban Culture in Contemporary New Guinea Literature in English." Footscray, Vic.: Humanities Department, Footscray Institute of Technology (now Victoria University of Technology). Unpublished paper, 1982.

Saunana, 1980. John Saunana. *The Alternative.* Honiara: USP Solomon Islands Centre/Institute of Pacific Studies, 1980.

Shearston, 1978. Trevor Shearston. *Sticks That Kill.* St. Lucia: University of Queensland Press, 1983.

———, 1979. *Something in the Blood.* (Short stories.) St. Lucia: University of Queensland Press, 1979.

Soaba, 1973. Russell Soaba. "Natives Under the Sun." In Beier, ed., 1973.

———, 1978. *Wanpis.* Port Moresby: Institute of Papua New Guinea Studies, 1977.

———, 1979. *Maiba: A Papuan Novel.* Washington, DC: Three Continents Press, 1979, 1985.

Stanbury, 1977. David Stanbury, ed. *A Narrative of the Voyage of H.M.S. Beagle*: being passages of the *Narrative* written by Captain Fitzroy, R.N., together with extracts from his logs, reports and letters; additional material from the diary and letters of Charles Darwin, notes from Midshipman King and letters from Second Lieutenant Barthlomew Sulivan. London: the Folio Society, 1977.

Stevenson, 1979. *The Strange Case of Dr Jekyll and Mr Hyde and Other Stories*. Harmondsworth: Penguin, 1979. Contains introduction and preface by Jenni Calder, as well as *The Beach of Falesa* [1892] and *The Ebb-Tide* [1893].

Subramani, 1978. Subramani. "Images of Fiji in Literature." In Tiffin, C. (ed.), 1978.

————, 1988. Subramani. *The Fantasy Eaters: Stories from Fiji*. Washington, D.C.: Three Continents Press, 1988.

Tiffin, C., 1978. Chris Tiffin (ed.). *South Pacific Images*. Brisbane: South Pacific Association for Commonwealth Literature and Language Studies, 1978.

Umba, 1976. Benjamin Umba. *The Fires of Dawn*. In Mike Greicus (ed.), *Three Short Novels from Papua New Guinea*. Auckland: Longman Paul, 1976.

Wendt, 1973. *Sons for the Return Home*. Auckland: Penguin, 1987. [1973].

————, 1974. *Flying Fox in a Freedom Tree*. Auckland: Longman Paul, 1974. Short stories and novella.

————, 1977. *Pouliuli*. Auckland: 1987 [1977].

————, 1979. *Leaves of the Banyan Tree*. Harmondsworth: Penguin, 1981. [1979]

————, 1986. *The Birth and Death of the Miracle Man*. Harmondsworth: Penguin: Viking, 1986.

USA

Allen, 1989. Paula Gunn Allen, ed. *Spider Woman's Daughters: Traditional Tales and Contemporary Writing by Native American Women*. New York: Fawcett Columbine, 1989.

Doig, 1980. Ivan Doig. *Winter Brothers: A Season at the Edge of America*. Orlando, Florida: Harcourt Brace Jovanovich, 1980.

————, 1984. *English Creek*. New York NY: Penguin, 1985 [1984].

————, 1987a. *This House of Sky: Landscapes of a Western Mind*. New York: HBJ, 1987.

————, 1987b. *Dancing at the Rascal Fair*. New York: Atheneum, 1987.

————, 1990. *Ride with Me, Mariah Montana*. New York: Atheneum, 1990.

Epstein, 1990. Leslie Epstein. *Pinto and Sons*. Boston: Houghton Mifflin, 1990.

Faulkner, 1955. William Faulkner. *Big Woods*. New York: Random House, 1955. Contains "The Bear," "The Old People," "A Bear Hunt," "Race at Morning," together with untitled prelude, interludes and postlude.

Glass, 1989. Molly Glass. *The Jump-off Creek*. Boston: Houghton Mifflin, 1989.

Ives, 1986. Rich Ives (ed.). *From Timberline to Tidepool: Contemporary Fiction from the Northwest.* Seattle/Missoula: Owl Creek Press, 1986.

Kesey, 1984. Ken Kesey. *Sometimes a Great Notion.* New York: Penguin, 1977 [1964].

Leopold, 1966. Aldo Leopold. *A Sand County Almanac: With Essays on Conservation from Round River.* New York: Ballantine, 1970. "Examine each question in terms of what is ethically and esthetically right, as well as what is economically expedient. A thing is right when it tends to preserve the integrity, stability and beauty of the biotic community. It is wrong when it does otherwise."

Maclean, 1976. Norman Maclean. *A River Runs through It and Other Stories.* Chicago/London: University of Chicago Press, 1986.

Rothenberg, 1972. *Shaking the Pumpkin: Traditional Poetry of the North American Indians.* New York, Doubleday, 1972

Silko, 1977. Leslie Marmon Silko. *Ceremony.* New York: Penguin, 1986 [1977].

Stafford, 1986. *Having Everything Right: Essays of Place.* Lewiston, Idaho: Confluence Press, 1986.

Wyatt, 1986. David Wyatt. *The Fall into Eden: Landscape and Imagination in California.* Cambridge: CUP, 1986.

Writings of the Native Peoples of America

Allen, 1989. Paula Gunn Allen, ed. *Spider Woman's Daughters: Traditional Tales and Contemporary Writing by Native American Women.* New York: Fawcett Columbine, 1989.

King, 1990. Thomas King, ed. *All My Relations: An Anthology of Contemporary Canadian Native Fiction.* Toronto: McClelland & Stewart, 1990.

Lerner, 1990. Andrea Lerner, ed. Dancing on the Rim of the *World: An Anthology of Contemporary Northwest Native American Writing.* Tucson, Arizona: Sun Tracks and The University of Arizona Press, 1990.

Rothenberg, 1968. *Technicians of the Sacred: a Range of Poetries from Africa, America, Asia and Oceania.* New York: Doubleday, 1968.

————, 1972. *Shaking the Pumpkin: Traditional Poetry of the North American Indians.* New York, Doubleday, 1972.

Silko, 1977. Leslie Marmon Silko. *Ceremony.* New York: Penguin, 1986 [1977].

Welch, 1974. James Welch. *Winter in the Blood.* New York: Penguin, 1986 [1974].

INDEX

Abdullah, Mena 343
Aborigines *see* Native peoples of Australia
Abraham 204, 273
Absalom Absalom! 40
Achebe, Chinua 106–109
Achilles 37, 204
Adam and Eve 54
Adventures of Don Quixote, The 14,
Aeneas/*The Aeneid* 70, 204, 205, 245
Africa *see also* South Africa 3, 9, 10, 19, 24–29, 32, 37, 91, 93–113, 139, 186, 227
African Americans 42–44
African slaves 4
Africans *see* Native peoples of Africa
Afrikaners 5
A.I.F. (Australian Imperial Forces) 52
Ake: The Years of Childhood 108,
Albany, Western Australia 123
Alcatraz 49
Alexander the Great 26
Algiers 20
Algren, Nelson 335
Allen, Paula Gunn 194, 195, 198
Alternative, The 302
American dream, the 37, 50, 75
"American Horse" 199
Americans 10, 44, 46, 48, 51, 57
Americans, native *see* Native peoples of America
Americas, the *see also* names of individual states, Americans, New England, New France,
New Spain, North America, United States of America xiii, 3, 4, 9–11, 15–21, 23–29, 46, 48, 49, 93, 95, 121, 155, 168, 170, 283, 303, 319, 328
Ana Historic 228, 231, 233
Anglo-Saxon poetry 83
Antarctica 139
Anthills of the Savannah 108
Anzacs 5
Apia 291, 294, 295, 298
Apollo xii
Appalachians 77
Arabs 15, 19, 319
Aragon 12, 15, 27
Arthur, King of Britain 18, 33, 70
"Artists of the Sea" 322
Ashcroft, W. 9
Asia *see also* individual countries xiii, 3, 9, 12, 15, 18, 25, 27–29, 32, 37, 91, 93–113, 139, 186, 227
Astley, Thea 276, 284
Astley, William (Prince Warung) 58, 60
"At Even" 80
"At the Cedars" 75
Atlantic Ocean 77, 169
Atwood, Margaret 210, 217
Auckland 299
Auschwitz 29
Austen, Jane xiv
Australia *see also* Native peoples of Australia 49, 51–71, 73, 78, 79, 87, 88, 93, 122, 123, 139, 140, 165, 182, 184, 185, 195, 225, 226, 253–282, 286, 303–305, 319, 343, 344, 346

Australian Aborigines *see* Native peoples of Australia
Australian National University 299
Australian New Guinea Administration Unit 310
La Austrialia del Espiritu Santo: The Journal of Fray Martin de Munilla O.F.M. and other documents relating to the Voyage of Pedro Fernandez de Quiros to The South Seas (1605–1606) and the Franciscan Missionary Plan (1617–1629) 117, 285,
Aztec Empire 3, 25, 27

Ballarat 181, 221
Banks, Sir Joseph 58, 255
Baratham, Gopal 341
Barlowe, Arthur 20,21
Barrens, the 190
Barthes, Roland 345
Basques xv
Bass Strait 267
Batman, Richard 319
Baynton, Barbara 63, 64
"Beach at Falesa" 129
Beachmasters 284
Beagle (boat) 120, 124
"Bear, The" 40, 43
Becke, Louis 132–134, 285, 288,
Beijing 6
Beir, Ulli 302
Belgium 98, 99
Benito Cereno 126
Bennett, Donna 82, 85, 86
Berndt, Ronald M., and Catherine H. 184
Beyond Geography: The Western Spirit Against the Wilderness 181
Big Woods 41, 44
Birds of Paradise 344
Black Americans *see* African Americans

Black Death, the xiii, 3
Blake, William 213
"Blessed are the Meek" 301
Blodgett, E.D. 210
Boatload of Homefolk, A 284
Boers 96
Boldrewood, Rolf (Thomas Browne) 185
Bone People, The 235, 241–244
Borneo 139
Boston 49
Botany Bay 55
Bougainville 120
Bowering, George 211, 217, 229
Boys in the Island, The 264, 268, 270
Brazil 139
"Breaking the Ice" 227
Brendon, Saint 169
"Bridegroom, The" 111
Brink, André 101, 103, 104, 111
Brisbane 67, 276
Britain *see* England
British Columbia *see* Canada
Brown, Russell 82, 85, 86
Browne, Thomas *see* Rolf Boldrewood
Bruny Island 261
Brussells 98,99
Brutus 33
Buckley, Vincent 197
"Buladelah-Taree Song Cycle" 184
Bulletin, the (Sydney) 132
Bushman 96

Cabot, John and Sebastian 19
Caliban 213
California 47, 48, 50, 124, 130, 178, 209, 224, 245, 319, 344, 353
Calvin, John 15
Camoens, Louis Vazde 3, 10, 11, 15, 25, 26, 106, 115, 116, 119
Campbell, Wilfred 80
Canada 73–91, 169, 187–193, 209– 234, 253, 277, 346–349

Canadian Magazine 78
Canadian Pacific Railway 85, 209
Cape of Good Hope 26
Capricornia 65, 272, 305
Caribbean 3
Carlile, Captain 20, 21
Carolinas 24
Carter, Paul 55
Cartier, Jacques 16
Castile 12, 15, 27
Castro, Brian 344
Catalonians xv
Cathay 10
Cebu 116
"Celebration, The" 320
Celtic culture xv, 195, 221, 224,
    263, 274, 344
Ceremony 203, 257, 259,
Cervantes, Miquel de 14
Ceuta 3, 10
Chalmers, James 309
Charlo, Victor 196, 197
Chaucer, Geoffrey 15
Chile 224
Chin, Frank 354
China/Chinese 10, 67, 25, 46, 47,
    70, 74, 85, 209, 319, 342, 344,
    346–354
China Men 351–353
Chinweizu 95
"Chosen Vessel, The" 63
Christ 3, 13, 27
Christendom 24, 27
Christians/Christianity 3, 11, 15,
    18, 20, 21, 24, 25, 27 34, 115, 117,
    130, 142, 186, 199, 267, 292, 293,
    299, 328
Churchill 190
Cipango *see* Japan
Civil War (U.S.) 112
Clark, C. Manning 52, 255, 256,
    319
Clarke, Marcus 58, 59, 60, 61
Clemens, Samuel *see* "Mark
    Twain"

"Collier, the Blackbirder" 134
Colombia 16
Colony of New South Wales 263
Columbia River 209
Columbus, Christopher 3, 10–13,
    15, 16, 19, 23, 27, 31, 122, 169,
    354
Columbus, Ferdinand 19
Commonwealth of Australia 266
Communist Party, the 9, 89, 352
Community of Thieves 261, 262
Conrad, Joseph 90, 93, 88, 99, 101,
    104, 106
Cook, Captain James 58, 120, 253,
    254, 255
Coonardoo 65, 185
Cooper, James Fenimore 36,37,
    185
Cornwall 263
Cortes, Hernando 4, 14
Couveur, Jessie (Tasma) 58, 60, 61
Craven, Margaret 185, 192
Crocodile, The 309, 367
Crocombe, Ronald 284
Crusades 3
Cuba 12
Cuchulain 221
Czechoslovakia 75, 89

Dampier, William 253, 254, 258
Dancing at the Rascal Fair 170, 178,
    181
Dante, Alighieri 15
Darwin, Charles 100, 120–124
Davis, David Brion 25
Daws, Gaven 115, 127
"Dead Loss, A" 133
Declaration of Independence
    (U.S.) 34, 35, 36, 51, 62
"Delta Autumn" 43
Denmark 20
Depression, the 177, 335
Derrida, Jacques 6, 30, 53, 101–103
Dickens, Charles 74
Diffie, Baillie W. 25

Dionysius vii
Discovery (boat) 211
Doctor Jekyll and Mr. Hyde *see* *Strange Case of Doctor Jekyll and Mr. Hyde, The*
Doctor Wooreddy's Prescription for Enduring the Ending of the World 259, 284
Dodge, Ernest S. 116, 117,
Doig, Ivan 165, 168, 170–173, 181, 182, 200, 274, 275,
Dos Passos, John 74 335
Dostoevsky, Fedor 74
"Double Buggy at Lahey's Creek, A" 63
Double Wolf 344
Doubleman, The 266
Drake, Sir Francis 4, 17,18, 19
Dream of Islands: Voyages of Discovery in the South Seas 115
Drinnan, Richard 181
"Drover's Wife, The" 57, 63
"Dumb, Dumb by a Bee Stung" 342

"Ebb-Tide" 130
Eden xi, 16, 37, 46,48, 74, 79, 93, 95, 106, 142, 143, 144, 181, 185, 192, 220, 273, 290, 316, 328, 354
Egypt 26
El Dorado 16, 17
Electrical Experience, The 73
Empire Writes Back, The 9
Engineer of Human Souls, The 88
England *see also* Scotland and Wales 3, 15, 16, 17, 19, 20, 22 23, 27, 28, 31, 34, 52, 55, 59, 73, 77, 79, 122, 195, 209, 211, 224, 286, 288, 304, 305, 306, 319, 346
English Creek 170, 173, 209, 275
Enlightenment, Age of 54
Epstein, Leslie 48, 49, 163
Erdrich, Louise 199
Eri, Vincent 309

Espanola *see* Hispaniola
Europe/Europeans *see also* names of countries xiii, xv, 3, 9–11, 14–16, 18, 20, 23–26, 28, 29, 32–36, 42, 55, 71, 74, 80, 88, 91, 94, 98, 100, 139, 168, 169, 193, 270, 286, 307
Eve *see* Adam and Eve

Fall into Eden: Landscape and Imagination in California 47
Fang Lizhi 7
Faulkner, William 37–46, 140
Ferdinand and Isabella (Spanish Sovereigns) 11, 15
Fiedler, Leslie A. 28, 35, 69
Fiji 299, 319, 320–328, 341
Fires at Dawn, The 312
Fitzgerald, F. Scott 90
Fitzroy, Captain Robert 120–124
Flight of the Villager, The 312
Flinders Island 260
Flying Fox in a Freedom Tree 293–298
Ford, Paul Leicester 13
Fort Vancouver 209
Fortunes of Richard Mahony, The 64, 181, 271
France/the French *see also* New France 16, 20, 23, 37, 70, 91, 286, 319
Franciscans 117
Franklin, Benjamin 35
Franklin, Miles 97
Fraser River 209, 216
Freud, Sigmund vii, 344
Fringe of Leaves, A 262
Frobisher, Martin 19
"From Flores" 211
Frye, Northrop 75, 210
Fuegians 122

Gadamer, Hans Georg 103
Galapagos islands 120, 124, 126

Gallipoli 51, 52
Gama, Vasco da 10, 25–27, 55, 115, 116, 245
Gandhi, Mahatma 325
Genesis 53
George III (King of England) 213
Germany/Germans 34, 69, 90, 96, 267, 319
Gilbert, Sir Humphrey 16, 17, 19
Gilmore, Dame Mary 58
"Glorious Pacific Way, The" 301
Gloss, Molly 165
Go Down Moses 39, 44
"God Save the King" 325
Goethe, Johann Wolfgang von 164
Golden Gate Park 354
Goldsmith, Oliver (English and Canadian) 81
Gordimer, Nadine 111
"Gospel of Saint John" 53
"Gospel of Saint Matthew" 66
"Grace" 199
Grace, Patricia 235
Granada 15
Grapes of Wrath, The 46
Great Khan, the 12
Greece xiii, 203, 227
Green, H. Gordon 211
Greenblatt, Stephen 122
Greenland 192
Greicus, Mike 312
Grenville, Richard 19
Griffiths, Gareth 9
Grove, Frederick Philip 87, 88
Guam 116

Hakluyt, Richard 15, 16, 18, 19, 20, 21, 23, 27, 28, 35 see also The Principal Navigations, Voyages . . .
Halbert, Thomas 238
Halifax 87
Hall, Rodney 70, 151
Ham 26
Hardy, Thomas 108, 109

Harland's Half Acre 70, 273, 276
Harlow, Robert 217, 227
Harte, Bret 133
Harvard Medical School 48
Hau'ofa, Epeli 299–302
Hawaii 46
Hawthorne, Nathaniel 36, 37, 45, 90
Head, Bessie 106, 111
Heaney, Seamus 197
Heart of Darkness 98
Hegel xii
"Height of the Land, The" 81
Helena, Montana 181
Hellenic States xiii
Hell's Gate 267
Henry VII (King of England) 19
Henry the Navigator (Portuguese Prince) 10, 26
Herbert, Xavier 65, 70, 185, 272, 305
"Highway, The" 196
Himalayas 139
His Natural Life 59
Hispaniola 11
History of Australia, A 52
Hobart 269
Hodgins, Jack 217, 220, 224, 227, 229, 231
Holland 20, 319
Holy City 3
Holy Land 10
Homer xiii 37
Hong Kong 334
Hook's Mountain 145
Huckleberry Finn 56
Hudson, W.H. 185
Hudson's Bay 81
Hudson's Bay Company 77, 187, 209
Hughes, Billy (Prime Minister of Australia) 52
Hugo, Victor 108
Hulme, Keri 235, 258

I Heard the Owl Call My Name 185, 192
Iberian peninsula 15
Idriess, Ion 258
Ihaemara, Witi 235–241, 244, 258, 259, 283
Ihalmiut 189–192
Iliad, the 245
Imaginary Life, An 70
Inca empire 3, 25, 27
India/Indians 3, 11, 25, 26, 28, 29, 93, 94, 115, 224, 319, 324, 325
Indian Wars 77
Indians *see* India/Indians
Indies *see* West Indies
Indonesia 319, 328
Indus Valley 26
Innocent Cities 217, 224, 226
Inquisition (Spanish) 15
Instant in the Wind, An 101
Invention of the World, The 217, 220, 226
Ireland 195, 274
Ireland, David 74
Irving, Washington 36
Isabella *see* Ferdinand and Isabella
Islam 15
Israelites 204
Italy 3, 20, 33
Ithaca 245
It's Raining in Mango 276–280

Jacobite rebellion 37
Japan/Japanese 12, 46, 69 319, 346–349
Jerusalem 10, 26
Jews 15, 112
"Joe Wilson Stories" 62
Johnson, Colin (Mudrooroo Narogin) *see* Narogin, Mudrooroo
Johnson, E. Pauline 199
Jose, F. Sionil 329, 330–341
Joyce, James 4, 229
Just Relations 70, 151

Kaffirs 96, 111
Kafka, Franz 74
Kasaipwalova, John 312
Keats, John 79, 90
Kelley, Celsus 118
Kensington 67, 68
Kerouac, Jack 47, 74
Kesey, Ken 47, 151, 161, 164, 168, 231
Kindness Cup, A 276, 277
King Lear 188, 191, 220
King of the Congo 25
King, Thomas 193
Kingsley, Henry 55, 185
Kingston, Maxine Hong 74, 350–354
Kipling, Rudyard 93
Klein, Melanie 90
Klinck, Carl F. 80, 81
Koch, Christopher 164, 264, 266, 270, 271, 273
Kogawa, Joy 346–349
Korea 154, 199

"Labrie's Wife" 83
Lacan vii
Ladies' Home Journal 58
Lake Nipigon 83
Lake Superior 81
Landtakers, The 272
Lane, Master Ralfe 18, 19, 20
Lane, William 58
Last Exit to Brooklyn 74
Latin America 27, 28, 31, 74, 139, 182
Laurentian Shield 78
"Laurentian Shield" 85
Lawson, Henry 57, 61, 62, 64, 133
Lawson, Louisa 58
Leacock, Stephen 83, 83, 86
Leaves of the Banyan Tree 293
Lee Lok Liang 342
Lerner, Andrea 196
Levi-Strauss, C. 91

Leys, Simon (Pierre Ryckmans) 7, 8
Life Rarely Tells 69
Lim, Catherine 342
Lima 212
Lindsay, Jack 67
London 67, 98, 99
London, Jack 133
London Missionary Society 310
Long Live Sandawara 256, 258, 260
Loss of El Dorado, The 28
Louisiana 77, 161
Lovecraft, H.P. 90
Lusiads, The 3, 10, 25, 115
Luther, Martin 15

Macarthur, John, 55
McDonald's restaurant 248
Maclean, Norman 141, 148
MacLennan, Hugh 84, 86, 87, 187
McQueen, James 145, 148, 164
Magellan, Ferdinand 116, 117
Maiba: A Papuan Novel 313
Mair, Charles 79
Malaysia 319
Malouf, David 70, 73, 273, 274
Mammon 119
"Man Who Wore Glasses, The" 111
Manchuria 139
Mandela, Nelson 4, 5, 6, 8, 113
Manhattan 74
Manhattan 335
Manila 329, 330, 334, 338
Manitoba 88
Mann, Thomas 164
Manteo (American Indian Chief) 20
Maoists 7
Marianas Islands 116
Maritime Provinces 75
Marks, Andrew 344
Marlatt, Daphne 215, 217, 228, 229, 231

Marshall, Alan 73
Marx, Leo 28
Marxism vii
Mass 330, 335, 338
Master of Ballantrae, The 128
Master of the Mill, The 88
Mathews, Ray 343
Matriarch, The 235–241, 244
Matshoba, Mtutuzeli 107, 111
Matthews, Brian 58
Maugham, Somerset 93
Maui 291
Mediterranean, the 20, 26
Melanesia 302
Melville, Herman 36, 124–134, 244, 245, 248, 249
Mendana, Alvaro de 117
Merry-Go-Round in the Sea, The 68, 69
Middle East 139
Million, Dian 196, 197
Milton, John 5, 3, 104, 127
Missing Heir, The 66
Mississippi 42, 77
Mitchell, Major Thomas 58
Moby Dick 124, 125, 127, 244, 248
Monkey 353
Montana 165, 167, 170, 172, 177, 178, 181
Montreal 77
Moorhouse, Frank 73
Moors 3, 10
Moreton Bay 272
Moses 204, 205, 273
Mount Vaea 128
Mowatt, Farley 187–193, 197
"Mrs. Maclaggan's Billy" 133
Muir, John 185
Munch, Edvard 292
Munilla, Fray Martin de 117, 118, 119 *see also* Kelley, Celsus
Murdoch, Keith 52
Murray, Les A. 184
Murray River 139

My Brilliant Career 97
My Brother, My Executioner 337

Nagasaki 349
Naipaul, V.S. 17, 28
Nandan, Satendra 324–328
Nantucket 124
Narayan, R.K. 94
Narogin, Mudrooroo (Colin
    Johnson) 256, 258, 259, 260, 261,
    262, 284
Native peoples of Africa 5, 6, 24,
    26, 96, 108 America (includes
    Canada and Latin America) 12,
    25, 26, 27, 36, 37, 42, 44, 46, 51,
    112, 117, 169, 181–209, 209–234
    Australia 9, 51, 61, 70, 112, 123,
    184, 185, 195, 246, 254–280, 319
    New Zealand 51, 73, 122, 235–
    252 Pacific Islands 119, 120, 193,
    195, 283–317
Nazis 34, 89, 90
New Bedford 124
New England 24, 28, 54, 73, 75,
    124, 181
New France 75
New Guinea *see* Papua New
    Guinea
New Hebrides *see* Vanuatu
New Orleans 36, 335
New South Wales 58, 253
New Spain 15, 28
New York 4, 124
New Zealand 51, 73, 93, 122, 140,
    195, 235–252, 253, 283, 291, 299,
    301
Newfoundland 16
Nietzsche, Friedrich vii
Noonuccal, Oodgeroo (Kath
    Walker) 256
Nootka Sound 213
North America *see also* names of
    states 31, 31, 37–45, 91, 319, 343
North Queensland 277
North West Company 77

Northern Territory 272

Oakland 353
Obasan 346, 351
O'Brien, Tim 354
"Obstinacy of Mrs. Tattan" 134
Occam's Razor viii
Odysseus 4, 127, 204, 245, 273
Odyssey, The 37, 245, 327
Oedipus 155
Oklahoma 139
"Old-Time Episode in Tasmania,
    An" 60
On the Highest Hill 211
On the Road 74
Ontario 75, 78
Oregon 151, 154, 160, 197
Orlando Furioso 15
Orwell, George 7
Otaheitans 122
Over Prairie Trails 88
Ovid 70
Oyster Bay 261

Pacific Ocean 119
Pacific (region) *see also* names of
    countries 3, 29, 46, 74, 115–137,
    140, 169, 183, 184, 195, 215, 253,
    283–317, 319–355
Pale Rider 56
Papacy 25, 27
Papeete 130
Papua New Guinea 299, 302, 304–
    209, 309–317
"Paradise Lost" 54
Parthia 26
Patagonia 116
Paul, Saint 27
Pearl Harbor 69
Peckham, Sir George 19, 24, 25
Pemisan (American Indian Chief)
    20
Penton, Brian 272, 273
People Make You Cry 341
People of the Deer 187

Peru 130
Peter, Saint 27
Philippines, the 116, 319, 328–341
Phillip, Governor Arthur 51, 256
Phillip, Saint 27
Phillips, A.A. (Arthur) 57
Pilgrim Fathers, the 28, 35, 169, 198
"Pilgrimage to the Isle of Makana, A" 112
Pillai, Roger 320
Pinto and Sons 48, 163
Pizarro, Francisco 14
Plantagenets 33
Po-on 339, 340
Poe, Edgar Allan 90
Polo, Marco 26
Polynesia 302, 312
Poor Fellow My Country 65
Port Moresby 310
Port Phillip 261
Porter, Hal 67, 68
Portrait of an Artist 229
Portugal/Portuguese 3, 25, 26, 93, 319
Portuguese Empire 3, 15, 16, 26, 245
Pouliuli 291
Prague 90
Prairies, the 75
Pratt, Edwin John 84, 85, 86
Prester John 3, 10
Pretenders, The 330, 331, 333
Prichard, Katharine Susannah 64, 65, 185
"Prince Warung" *see* William Astley
Principal Navigations, Voyages, Traffiques & Discoveries the English nation made by sea or overland to the remote and farthest distant quarters of the earth at anytime within the compass of these 1600 years, The 18
Prospero 220

Puget Sound 209
Puritans 36
Pybus, Cassandra 261, 262

Quebec 75, 79
Queensland 276, 277, 305
Quiros, Pedro Fernandez de 117, 118, 285

Rabelais 223
Rakshasas (demons) 327
Raleigh, Sir Walter 16, 17, 19, 22, 23
Rama 327
Ramayana 324, 326
Rao, Raja 94
Reivers, The 39
Reynolds, Henry 163
Rhys, Jean 98
Richardson, Henry Handel 64, 181, 271, 272, 273
Ricoeur, Paul 87
Ride With Me, Mariah Montana 172, 173, 176, 178
River Runs Through It, A, and Other Stories 141
Roanoke 17, 21, 46
Roberts, Charles 80
Robinson, William Augustus 260, 261, 262
Robson, Lloyd 59
Rocky Mountains 78
Rolls, Eric 163, 183
Roman Empire xiii 3, 99, 100
Rome xiii 3, 26, 33, 70, 203, 245
Ross, Sinclair 87
Rousseau, Jean Jacques 66, 73, 90
Royal Canadian Mounted Police 77, 347
Russia 9, 18, 20, 209, 211
Ryckmans, Pierre *see* Leys, Simon

Sahara 26
St. John's, Newfoundland 16

St. Lawrence River 88
Samoa 127, 132, 290, 291, 299
San Francisco 48, 74, 224, 354
Sartre, Jean Paul 164
Satan 16
"Sauna" 321
Saunana, John 302, 304
Scann 217
Scarlet Letter, The 37
Schreiner, Olive 95, 98
Schweitzer, Albert 186
Scotland/Scots 37, 54, 142, 165,
    170, 172, 173, 174, 181, 195, 227,
    238, 274
Scott, Duncan 75, 81, 83
Scott, F.R. 85–87
Scott, Sir Walter 108
Sears, Vicki L. 199
Selby, Hubert 74
Settlers of the Marsh 88
Seven Rivers of Canada, The 84
"Seventh and Other Days, The"
    301
"Shadows of the Dead" 133
Shakespeare, William 164, 188, 191
Shearston, Trevor 304–309, 310
Shelley, Percy Bysshe 79
Shoemaker, Adam 258, 261
Siberia 209
Silko, Leslie Marmon 198, 200,
    257, 259
Singapore 341–343
Sitting Bull (American Indian
    Chief) 347
Skvorecky, Josef 74, 75, 89, 90
Smith River Valley 165, 167
Snyder, Gary 47
Soaba, Russell 312, 313
Solomon Islands 302, 304
Sometimes a Great Notion 151, 231
Song of Roland 15
Sons for the Return Home 291
Sound and the Fury, The 38, 39
South Africa 5, 6, 100, 104, 111, 112
South African Emergency of 1985,
    103

South America 139
South Ocean 267
South Seas 115, 285
Soweto 107
Soyinka, Wole 107, 113
Spain 3, 11, 13, 15, 16, 17, 20–28,
    31, 116, 211, 319, 328
Spanish Armada 18
Spanish Empire 3, 14, 116, 117,
    118, 119
Spenser, Edmund 269
Spice Islands 116
*Spider Woman's Daughters:
    Traditional Tales and Contempo-
    rary Writing by Native American
    Women* 194
"Spit Delaney's Island" 217
"Squeaker's Mate" 63
Stagecoach 210
Stalin, Joseph 89
Stanbury, David 120, 121
States of Emergency 101
Statue of Liberty 6
Steinbeck, John 46
Stevens, Jimmy 284
Stevenson, Robert Louis 127, 128,
    131, 132, 133, 294
Steveston 215, 228
Sticks that Kill 304
Story of a Man 107
Story of an African Farm, The 95
Stow, Randolph 68, 69, 164
Strait of Georgia 231
*Strange Case of Doctor Jekyll and
    Mr. Hyde, The* 128
Subramani 321–324
"Summer" 79
Sunshine Sketches of a Little Town
    84
Supreme Court of the United
    States 113
Suva 321, 325
Swansea 269
Sydney 67, 123, 132, 270
Sydney Cove 51, 253

Sylvestre, Guy 211
Symmes Hole 244–251

Tahiti 120, 127, 130, 213, 245
Tali 313
Tan, Amy 354
"Tasma" *see* Jessie Couvreur
Tasmania 61, 145, 259, 260, 261,
    262, 264, 266, 267, 270
Te Kooti 237
Tennant, Kylie 65, 66, 73
Terra Australis *see* Australia
Thames River 98, 101
Things Fall Apart 108, 110
*This House of Sky: Landscapes of a
    Western Mind* 165, 167
Thomas, Audrey 227
Thomas, Saint 27
Thoreau, Henry David 73, 79
Thrace 70
Tiananmen Square 6, 7
Tiffin, Helen 9
Time of the Peacock 343
"To an Old Barn" 80
Tonga 299
Toronto 90
"Towards the Last Spike" 85
Tower of London 16
Treasure Island 128
Treaty of Paris 77
Tree 329, 330, 331, 332
Tree of Man, The 65
Trieste 211
Tripmaster Monkey: His Fake Book
    353–354
Trojan War xiii
Tropical Gothic 329
Troy 204
Truganini (Trucaninni,
    Trugernanna) 61, 260–261
Tudors 33
Turkey 20, 24
Turner, Frederick 163, 182
Tutuola, Amos 107

"Twain, Mark" (Samuel Clemens)
    56, 90
Typee 249

Umba, Benjamin 312
United States of America *see also*
    North America, names of states
    xiii, xv, 4, 19, 32, 34, 35, 38, 41,
    46, 51, 54, 59, 70, 73, 75, 77, 79,
    80, 88, 124, 140, 151–162, 165,
    173, 183, 184, 210, 211, 253, 319,
    350–354
University of Papua New Guinea
    302
University of the South Pacific 299

Vailima 127
Van Diemen's Land 47, 263
Van Diemen's Land Company
    262, 264, 267
Vancouver, Canada 209, 215, 224
Vancouver City Archives 231
Vancouver, George 211, 229
Vancouver Island 221, 224
Vanuatu 117, 284
Venice 20, 24, 236
Venus 119
Verdi, Guiseppe 236
Victoria, Australia 55, 139, 224
Victoria, B.C. 224, 225
Vietnam 46
Virgil xiii, 11, 15, 26, 112, 198, 204,
    262, 263
Virginia 17, 18, 19, 24
Voyage of Madoc 19

Wakefield, Edward Gibbon 250
Wales 195
Walk on the Wild Side, A 335
Walker, Kath *see* Noonuccal,
    Oodgeroo
Wallis, Samuel 120
Walters, Anna Lee 199
Wanderer, The 81

War of Independence (U.S.) 77, 78
Ward, Russell 58
"Warriors, The" 199
Watcher on the Cast-Iron Balcony 67
Watson, Don 163
Watters, Reginald E. 80, 81
Wedde, Ian 244–251, 283, 285
Weir of Hermistoun 128
Welch, James 200
Wellington 241, 248
Wendt, Albert 290, 291–298, 299, 302
West Indies 93
Western Australia 69, 123, 213
White, Patrick 65, 66, 70, 262, 266
Wi Pere 238
Wide Sargasso Sea 98
Wiebe, Rudy 210
Wieland, James 33
Wild Cat Falling 256
Wilde, W.H. 58
Wilson, Ethel 210, 211
"Wind and a Boy, A" 106

Winter Brothers: A Season at the Edge of America 167
Winter in the Blood 200, 256
Woman Warrior 350
Woodcock, George 84
Wooreddy 259–261
Wordsworth, William 73, 79
Working Bullocks 64
"World as Object, The" 345
Wounded Sea, The 324, 327
Wright, Judith 70
"'Write, Right, Rite'; or How Catherine Lim Tries to Offer Only the Best on the Altar of Good Singapore Writing" 342
Wyatt, David 47, 48

Xu Dun, 7

Yale (University) 151
"Yellow Woman" 198

Zulu 112

DATE DUE